Marmalade Boy

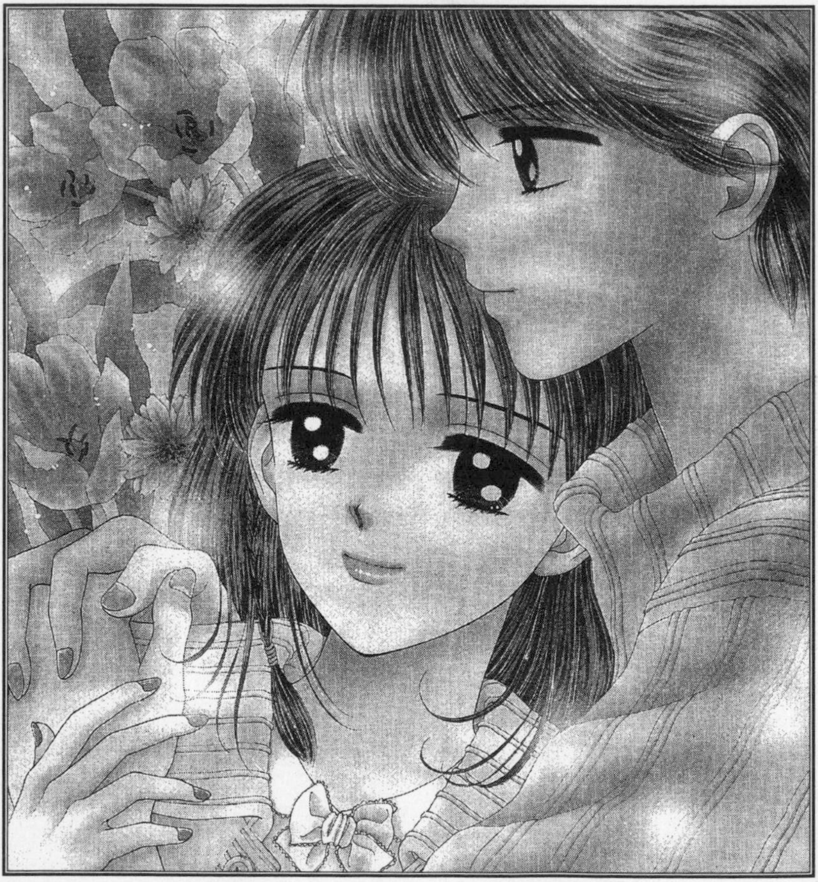

ALSO AVAILABLE FROM TOKYOPOP®

MANGA

*INDICATES TITLE IS IN THE RIGHT-TO-LEFT FORMAT

ACTION

ANGELIC LAYER*
CLAMP SCHOOL DETECTIVES* (April 2003)
DIGIMON (March 2003)
DUKLYON: CLAMP SCHOOL DEFENDERS* (September 2003)
GATEKEEPERS* (March 2003)
GTO*
HARLEM BEAT
INITIAL D*
ISLAND
JING: KING OF BANDITS* (June 2003)
JULINE
LUPIN III*
MONSTERS, INC.
PRIEST
RAVE*
REAL BOUT HIGH SCHOOL*
REBOUND* (April 2003)
SAMURAI DEEPER KYO* (June 2003)
SCRYED* (March 2003)
SHAOLIN SISTERS* (February 2003)
THE SKULL MAN*

FANTASY

CHRONICLES OF THE CURSED SWORD (July 2003)
DEMON DIARY (May 2003)
DRAGON HUNTER (June 2003)
DRAGON KNIGHTS*
KING OF HELL (June 2003)
PLANET LADDER*
RAGNAROK
REBIRTH (March 2003)
SHIRAHIME: TALES OF THE SNOW PRINCESS* (December 2003)
SORCERER HUNTERS
WISH*

ROMANCE

HAPPY MANIA* (April 2003)
I.N.V.U. (February 2003)
LOVE HINA*
KARE KANO*
KODOCHA*
MAN OF MANY FACES* (May 2003)
MARMALADE BOY*
MARS*
PARADISE KISS*
PEACH GIRL
UNDER A GLASS MOON (June 2003)

SCIENCE FICTION

CHOBITS*
CLOVER
COWBOY BEBOP*
COWBOY BEBOP: SHOOTING STAR* (June 2003)
G-GUNDAM*
GUNDAM WING
GUNDAM WING: ENDLESS WALTZ*
GUNDAM: THE LAST OUTPOST*
PARASYTE
REALITY CHECK (March 2003)

MAGICAL GIRLS

CARDCAPTOR SAKURA
CARDCAPTOR SAKURA: MASTER OF THE CLOW*
CORRECTOR YUI
MAGIC KNIGHT RAYEARTH* (August 2003)
MIRACLE GIRLS
SAILOR MOON
SAINT TAIL
TOKYO MEW MEW* (April 2003)

CINE-MANGA™

AKIRA*
CARDCAPTORS
KIM POSSIBLE (March 2003)
LIZZIE McGUIRE (March 2003)
POWER RANGERS (May 2003)
SPY KIDS 2 (March 2003)

ANIME GUIDES

GUNDAM TECHNICAL MANUALS
COWBOY BEBOP
SAILOR MOON SCOUT GUIDES

NOVELS

SAILOR MOON
SUSHI SQUAD (April 2003)

ART BOOKS

CARDCAPTOR SAKURA*
MAGIC KNIGHT RAYEARTH*

TOKYOPOP KIDS

STRAY SHEEP (September 2003)

Marmalade Boy

Vol. 5

By

Wataru Yoshizumi

Los Angeles • Tokyo

Story and Art – Wataru Yoshizumi

Translator – Takae Brewer
English Adaptation – Deb Baer
Retouch and Lettering – Monalisa de Asis
Cover Layout and Graphic Designer – Anna Kernbaum

Senior Editor – Julie Taylor
Production Managers – Jennifer Miller and Jennifer Wagner
Art Director – Matthew Alford
VP of Production & Manufacturing – Ron Klamert
President & C.O.O. – John Parker
Publisher – Stuart Levy

Email: editor@tokyopop.com
Come visit us online at www.TOKYOPOP.com

A  MANGA
TOKYOPOP® is an imprint of Mixx Entertainment, Inc.
5900 Wilshire Blvd. Ste 2000, Los Angeles, CA 90036

"MARMALADE BOY"
© 1992 by WATARU YOSHIZUMI.
All rights reserved. First published in Japan in 1992 by SHUEISHA Inc., Tokyo.
English language translation rights in the United States of America and Canada
arranged by SHUEISHA Inc. through Cloverway, Inc.

English text © 2003 by Mixx Entertainment, Inc.
TOKYOPOP® is a registered trademark and the
Robofish logo is a trademark of Mixx Entertainment, Inc.

ISBN: 1-59182-071-5

First TOKYOPOP® printing: February 2003

10 9 8 7 6 5 4 3 2 1

Printed in the USA

Main Characters

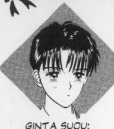

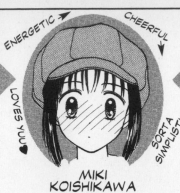

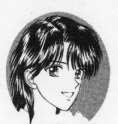

GINTA SUOU: MIKI'S CLASS-MATE. PROPOSED HIS LOVE TO MIKI...
ENERGETIC
CHEERFUL
LOVES YUU♥
SORTA SIMPLISTIC
MIKI KOISHIKAWA
MEIKO AKIZUKI: MIKI'S BEST FRIEND
ARIMI SUZUKI: YUU'S FORMER GIRLFRIEND. SHE STILL LOVES YUU.
LIVES WITH MIKI
HE LOOKS GOOD, BUT...
WHAT IS THE RELATIONSHIP WITH MIKI!?
A LITTLE MEAN
YUU MATSUURA
SATOSHI MIWA: STUDENT COUNCIL LEADER. STEPBROTHER OF YUU!?

THE STORY SO FAR...

DURING BREAKFAST ONE DAY, MIKI'S PARENTS BREAK IT TO HER THAT THEY'RE GETTING DIVORCED AND SWAPPING SPOUSES WITH ANOTHER COUPLE! NOW MIKI HAS FOUR PARENTS AND A NEW STEPBROTHER, YUU, WHO KEEPS TEASING HER. YUU'S SWEET ON THE OUTSIDE, BUT HE'S GOT A BITTER STREAK - HE'S A MARMALADE BOY! AS MIKI GETS TO KNOW YUU, SHE DEVELOPS A CRUSH ON HIM.

THINGS GET COMPLICATED WHEN MIKI'S OLD CRUSH, THE TENNIS CHAMP, GINTA, CONFESSES HIS LOVE FOR HER. AND THINGS GET EVEN MORE CONFUSING WHEN YUU'S EX-GIRLFRIEND, ARMINI, TRANSFERS TO MIKI'S SCHOOL AND TRIES TO WIN YUU BACK. DRAMA-RAMA!

WITH MAJOR CRUSHES ON BOTH GINTA AND YUU, MIKI FINDS HERSELF WAGING AN INNER BATTLE SHE KNOWS SHE CAN NEVER TRULY WIN. JUST WHEN MIKI'S WORLD CAN'T GET ANY MORE CONFUSING, HER BEST FRIEND CONFESSES SHE'S BEEN HAVING AN AFFAIR WITH NACHAN, THEIR TEACHER, AND NEEDS MIKI'S HELP—PRONTO!

THEN ALL HELL BREAKS LOOSE WHEN A CUTE DUDE NAMED MIWA ENTERS THE PICTURE AND DEVELOPS AN UNUSUAL OBSESSION WITH YUU. WHEN RUMORS SPREAD THAT MIWA AND YUU ARE HAVING AN AFFAIR. MIKI AND MEIKO INVESTIGATE AND DISCOVER THAT MIWA'S DAD MIGHT BE YUU'S REAL DAD, TOO! BUT WHEN MIWA'S DAD IS FINALLY CONFRONTED, HE DENIES THAT HE IS YUU'S FATHER. WHAT WILL HAPPEN NEXT?!

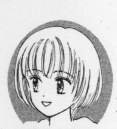

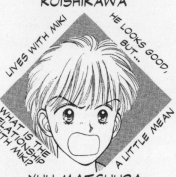

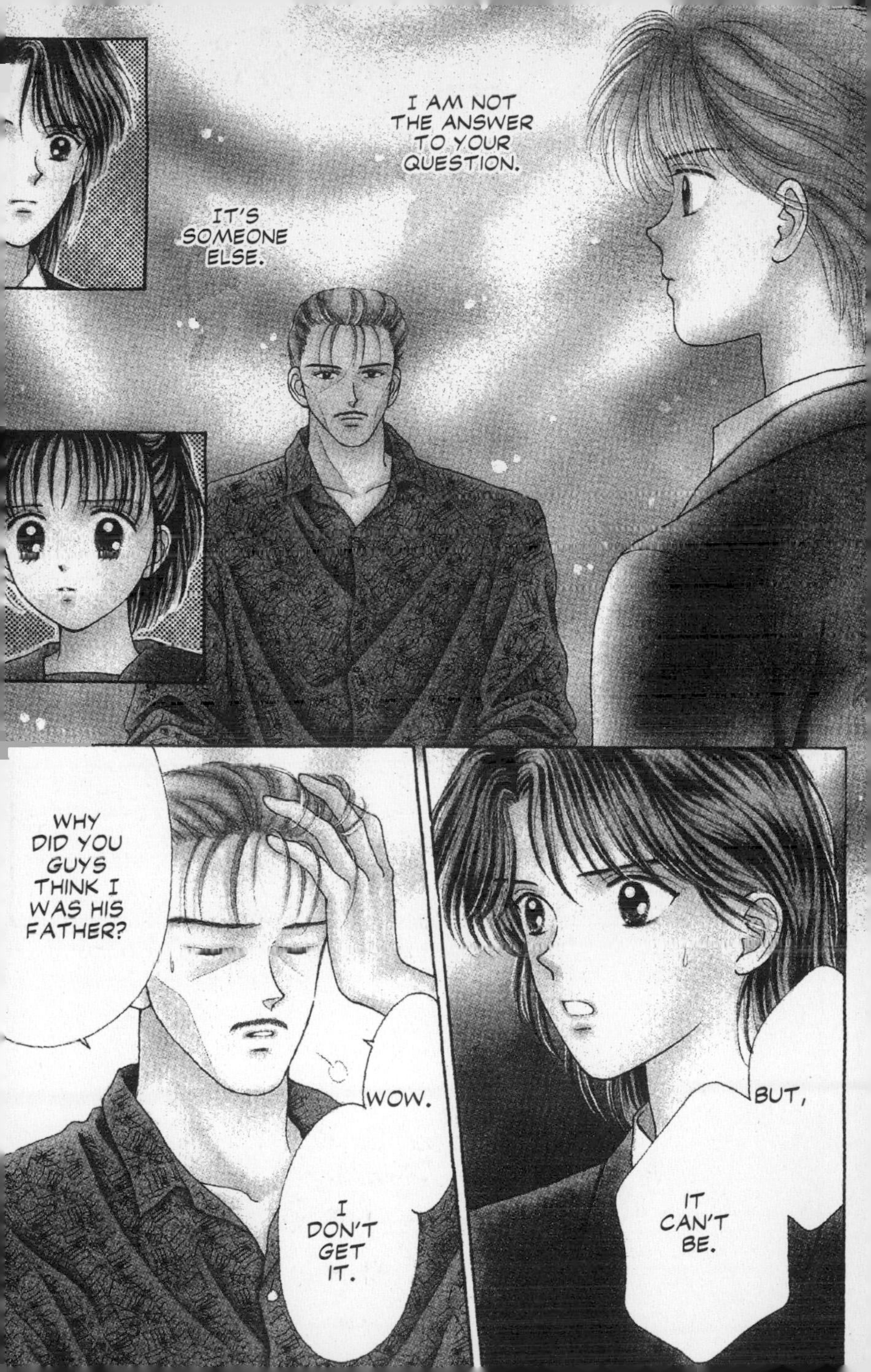
I AM NOT THE ANSWER TO YOUR QUESTION.
IT'S SOMEONE ELSE.
BUT,
IT CAN'T BE.
WHY DID YOU GUYS THINK I WAS HIS FATHER?
WOW.
I DON'T GET IT.

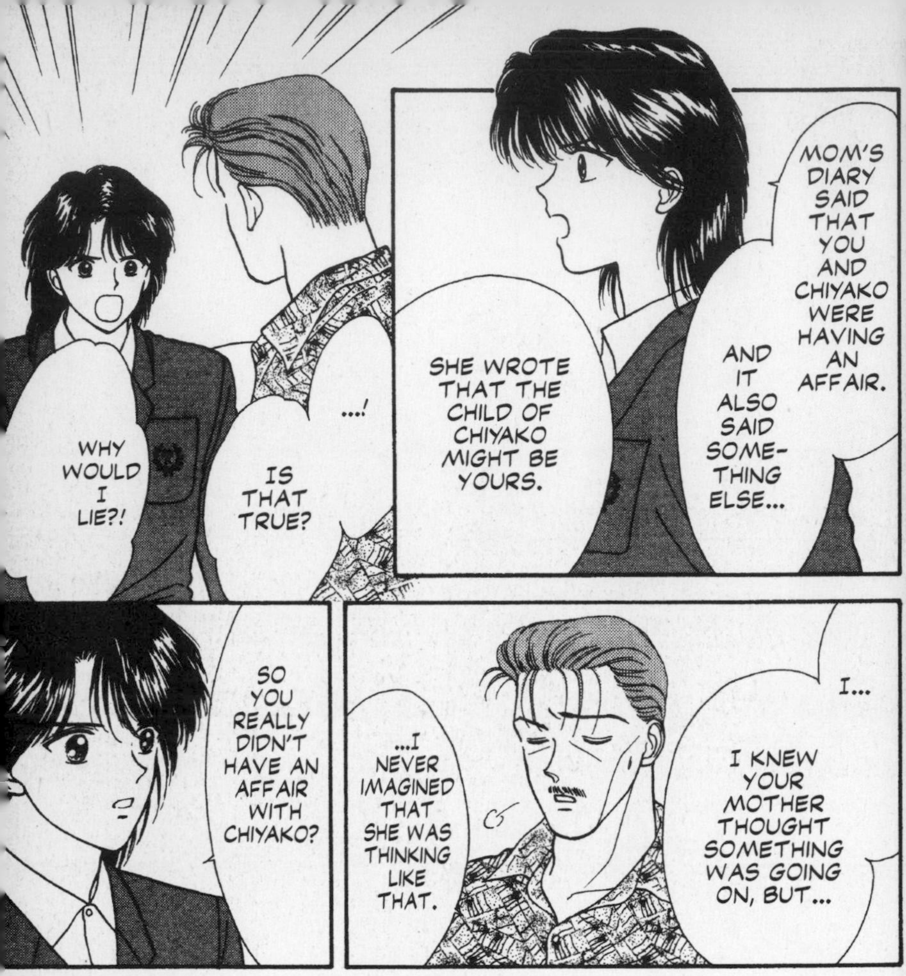
MOM'S DIARY SAID THAT YOU AND CHIYAKO WERE HAVING AN AFFAIR.
AND IT ALSO SAID SOMETHING ELSE...
SHE WROTE THAT THE CHILD OF CHIYAKO MIGHT BE YOURS.
...!
IS THAT TRUE?
WHY WOULD I LIE?!
I...
I KNEW YOUR MOTHER THOUGHT SOMETHING WAS GOING ON, BUT...
...I NEVER IMAGINED THAT SHE WAS THINKING LIKE THAT.
SO YOU REALLY DIDN'T HAVE AN AFFAIR WITH CHIYAKO?

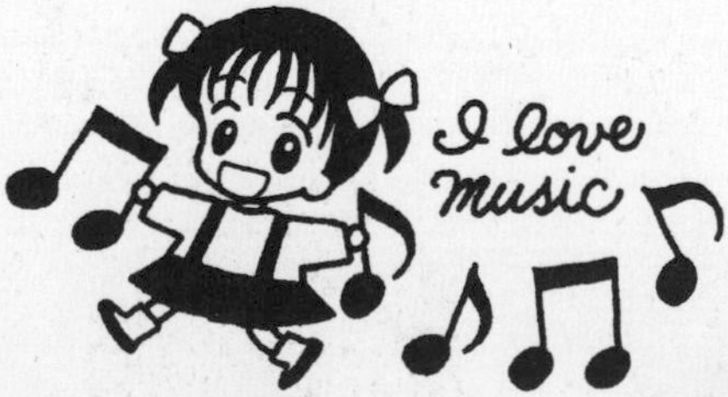
I love music

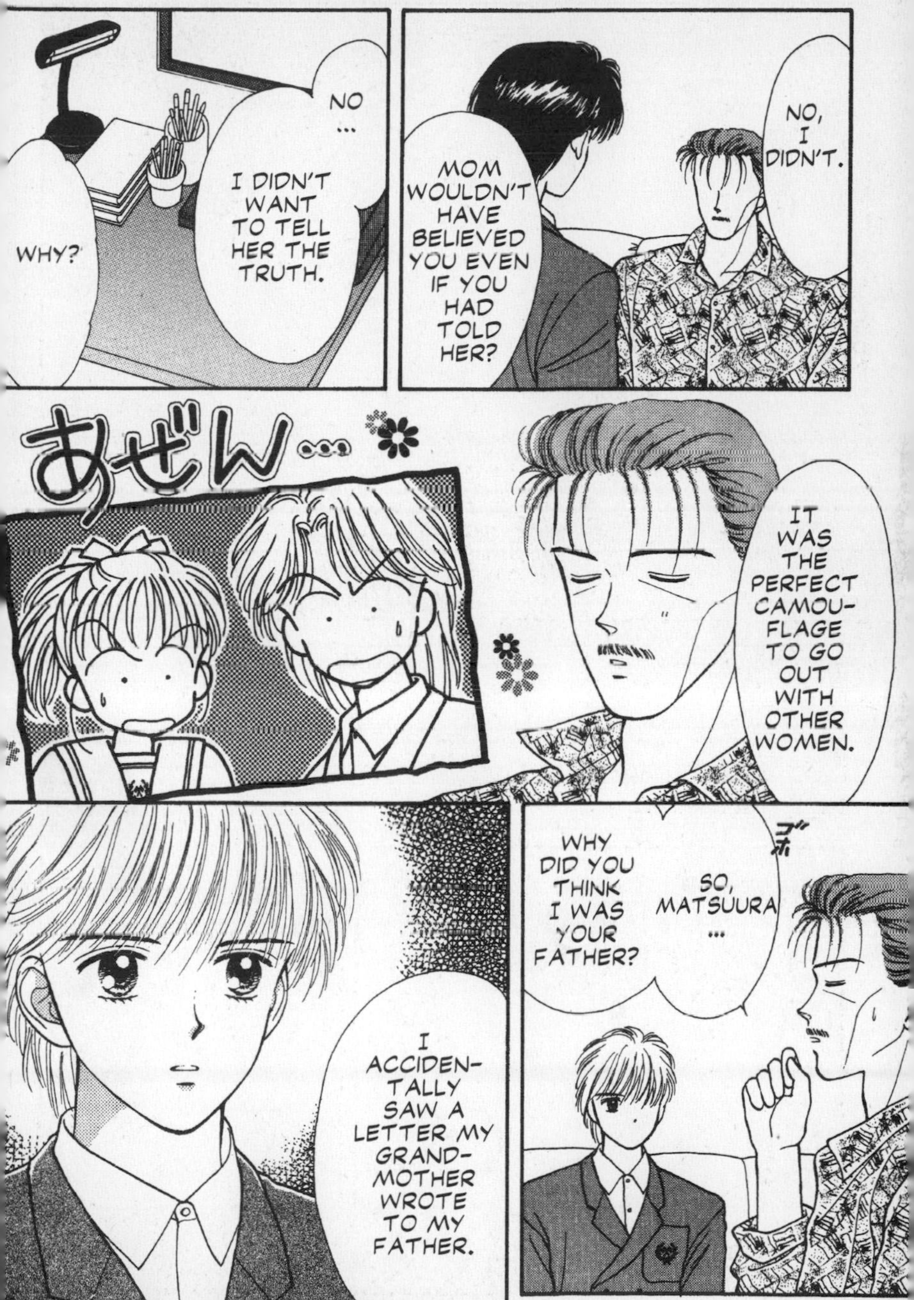
NO, I DIDN'T.
MOM WOULDN'T HAVE BELIEVED YOU EVEN IF YOU HAD TOLD HER?
NO ...
I DIDN'T WANT TO TELL HER THE TRUTH.
WHY?
IT WAS THE PERFECT CAMOUFLAGE TO GO OUT WITH OTHER WOMEN.
あぜん…
ゴホ
SO, MATSUURA ...
WHY DID YOU THINK I WAS YOUR FATHER?
I ACCIDENTALLY SAW A LETTER MY GRANDMOTHER WROTE TO MY FATHER.

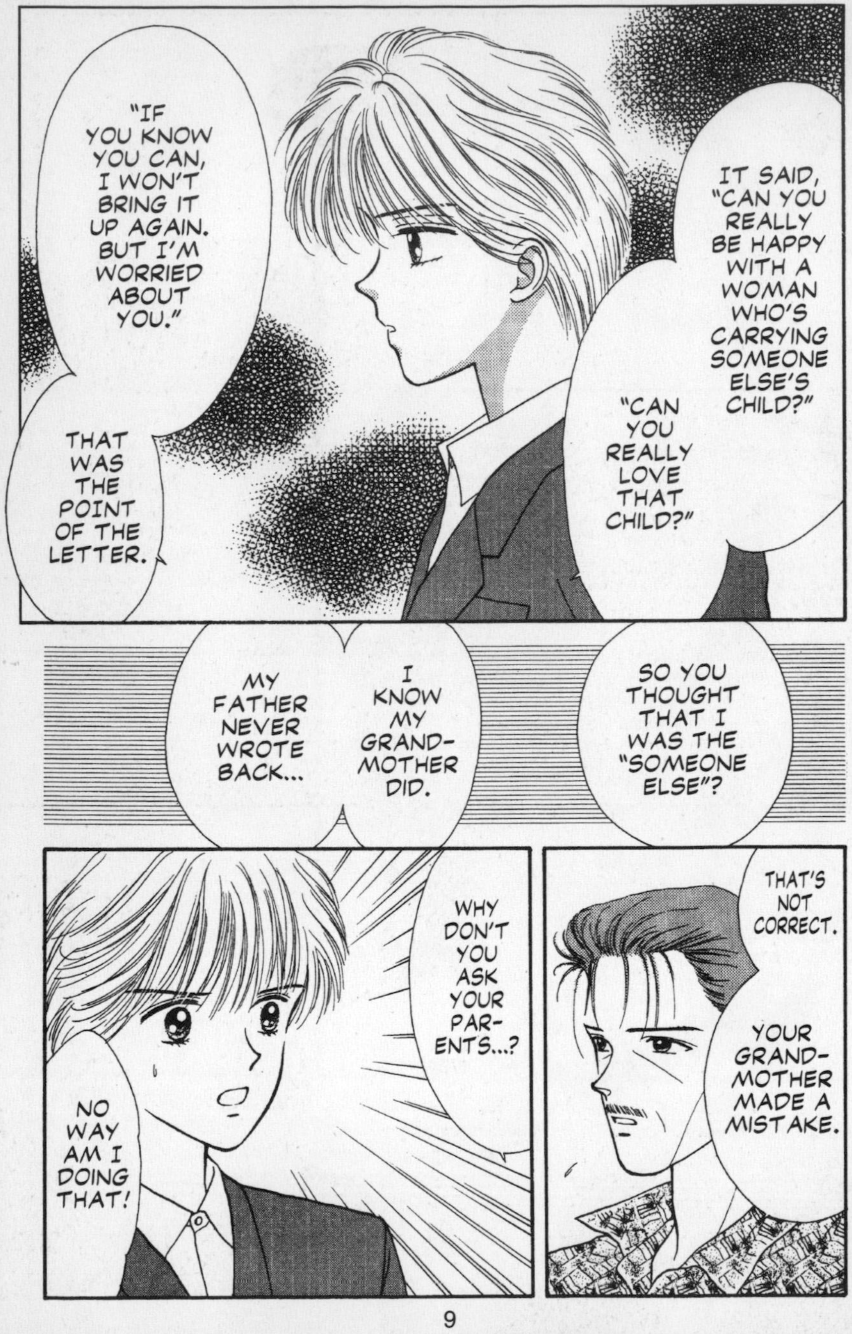
IT SAID, "CAN YOU REALLY BE HAPPY WITH A WOMAN WHO'S CARRYING SOMEONE ELSE'S CHILD?"
"CAN YOU REALLY LOVE THAT CHILD?"
"IF YOU KNOW YOU CAN, I WON'T BRING IT UP AGAIN. BUT I'M WORRIED ABOUT YOU."
THAT WAS THE POINT OF THE LETTER.
SO YOU THOUGHT THAT I WAS THE "SOMEONE ELSE"?
I KNOW MY GRAND-MOTHER DID.
MY FATHER NEVER WROTE BACK...
THAT'S NOT CORRECT.
YOUR GRAND-MOTHER MADE A MISTAKE.
WHY DON'T YOU ASK YOUR PAR-ENTS...?
NO WAY AM I DOING THAT!

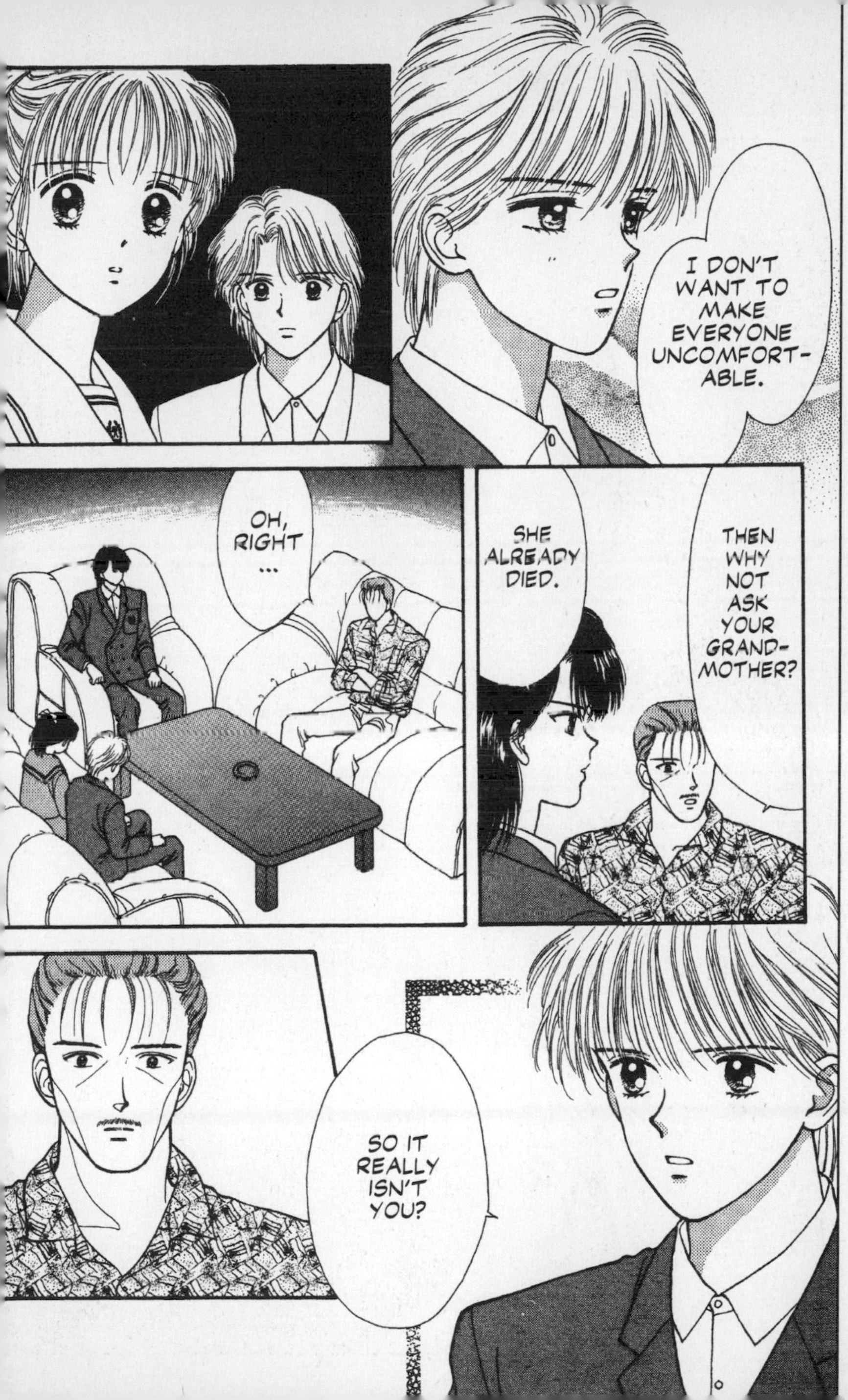
I DON'T WANT TO MAKE EVERYONE UNCOMFORT-ABLE.
THEN WHY NOT ASK YOUR GRAND-MOTHER?
SHE ALREADY DIED.
OH, RIGHT ...
SO IT REALLY ISN'T YOU?

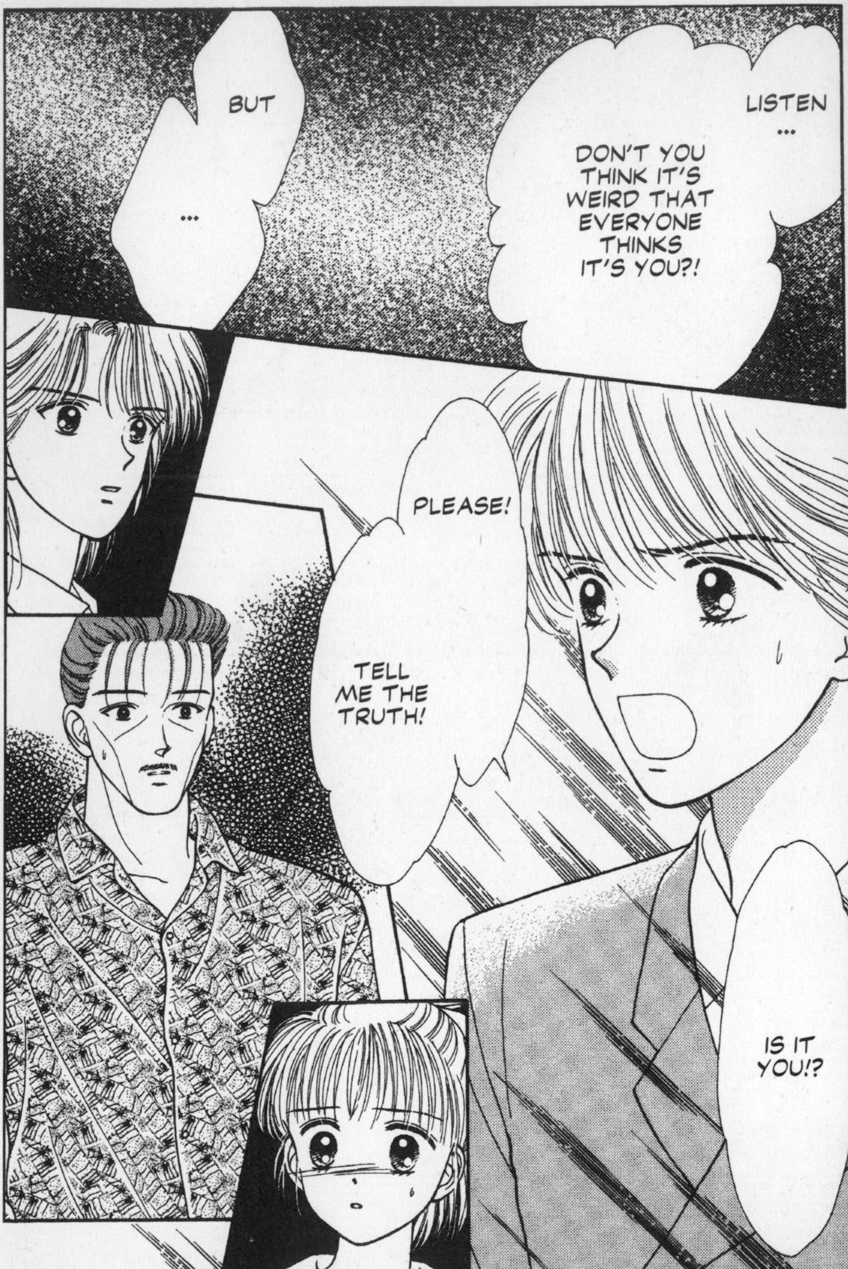
LISTEN ... DON'T YOU THINK IT'S WEIRD THAT EVERYONE THINKS IT'S YOU?!
BUT ...
PLEASE!
TELL ME THE TRUTH!
IS IT YOU!?

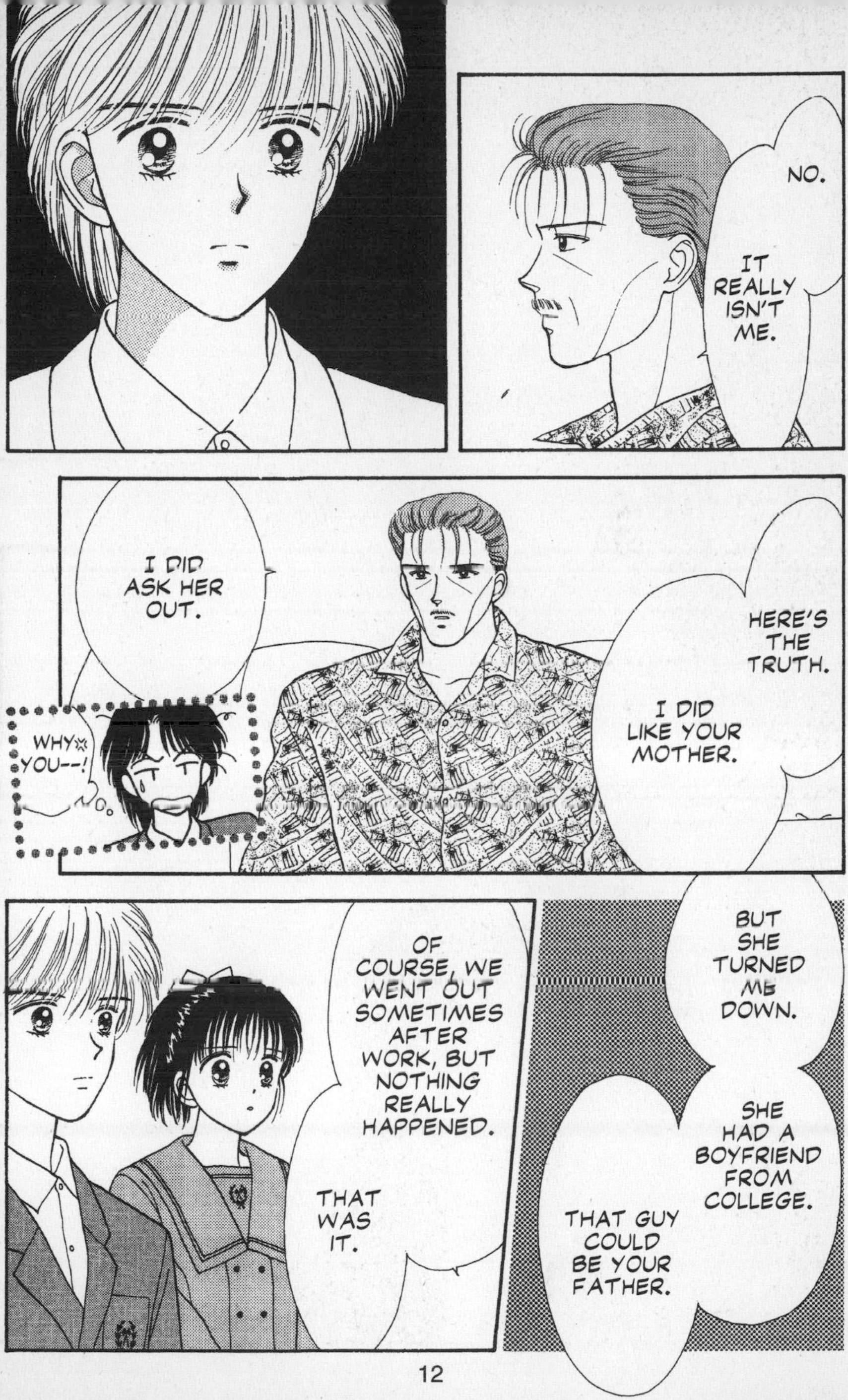

NO.
IT REALLY ISN'T ME.
HERE'S THE TRUTH.
I DID LIKE YOUR MOTHER.
I DID ASK HER OUT.
WHY☆ YOU--!
BUT SHE TURNED ME DOWN.
SHE HAD A BOYFRIEND FROM COLLEGE.
THAT GUY COULD BE YOUR FATHER.
OF COURSE, WE WENT OUT SOMETIMES AFTER WORK, BUT NOTHING REALLY HAPPENED.
THAT WAS IT.

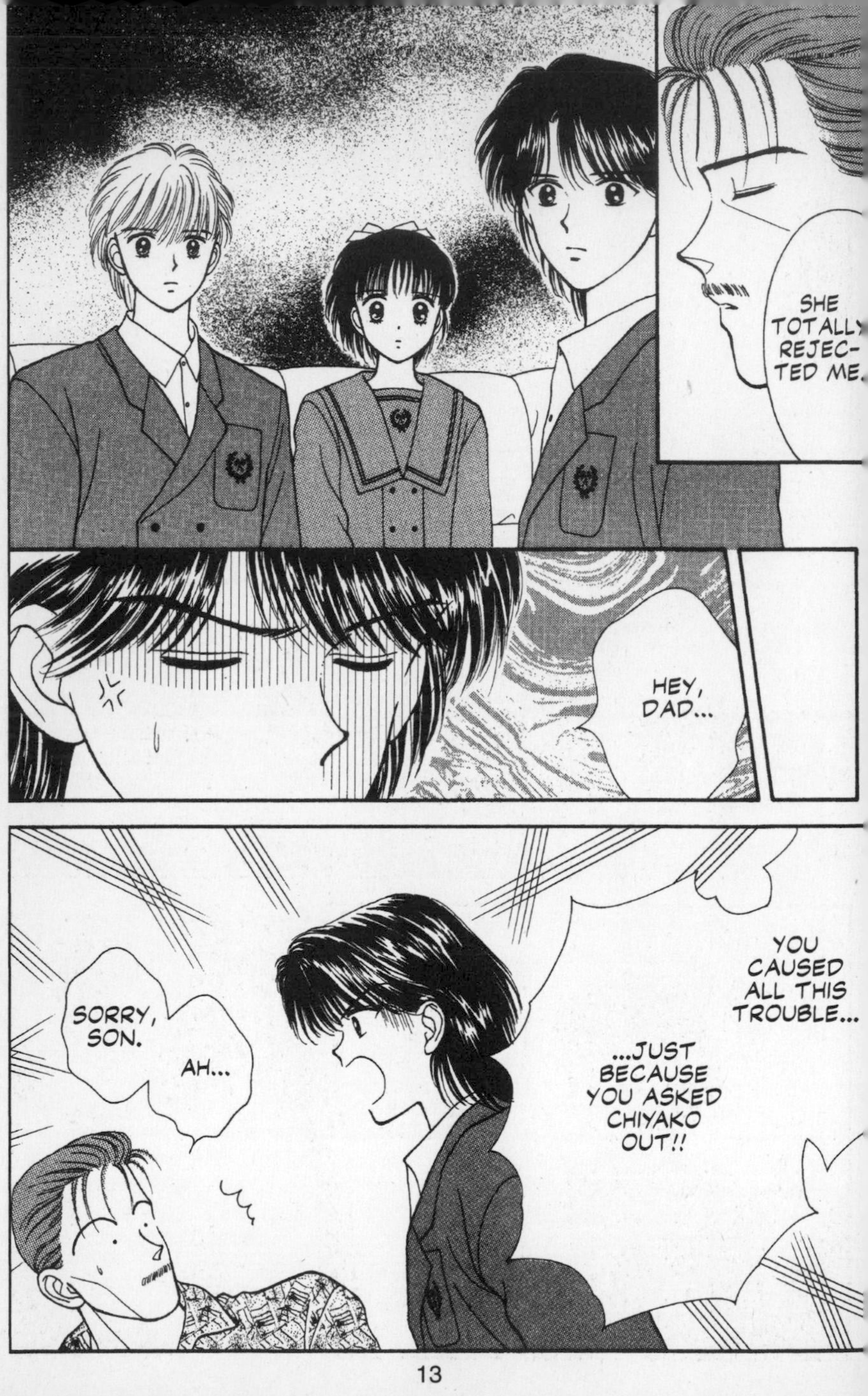
SHE TOTALLY REJECTED ME.
HEY, DAD...
YOU CAUSED ALL THIS TROUBLE...
...JUST BECAUSE YOU ASKED CHIYAKO OUT!!
SORRY, SON.
AH...

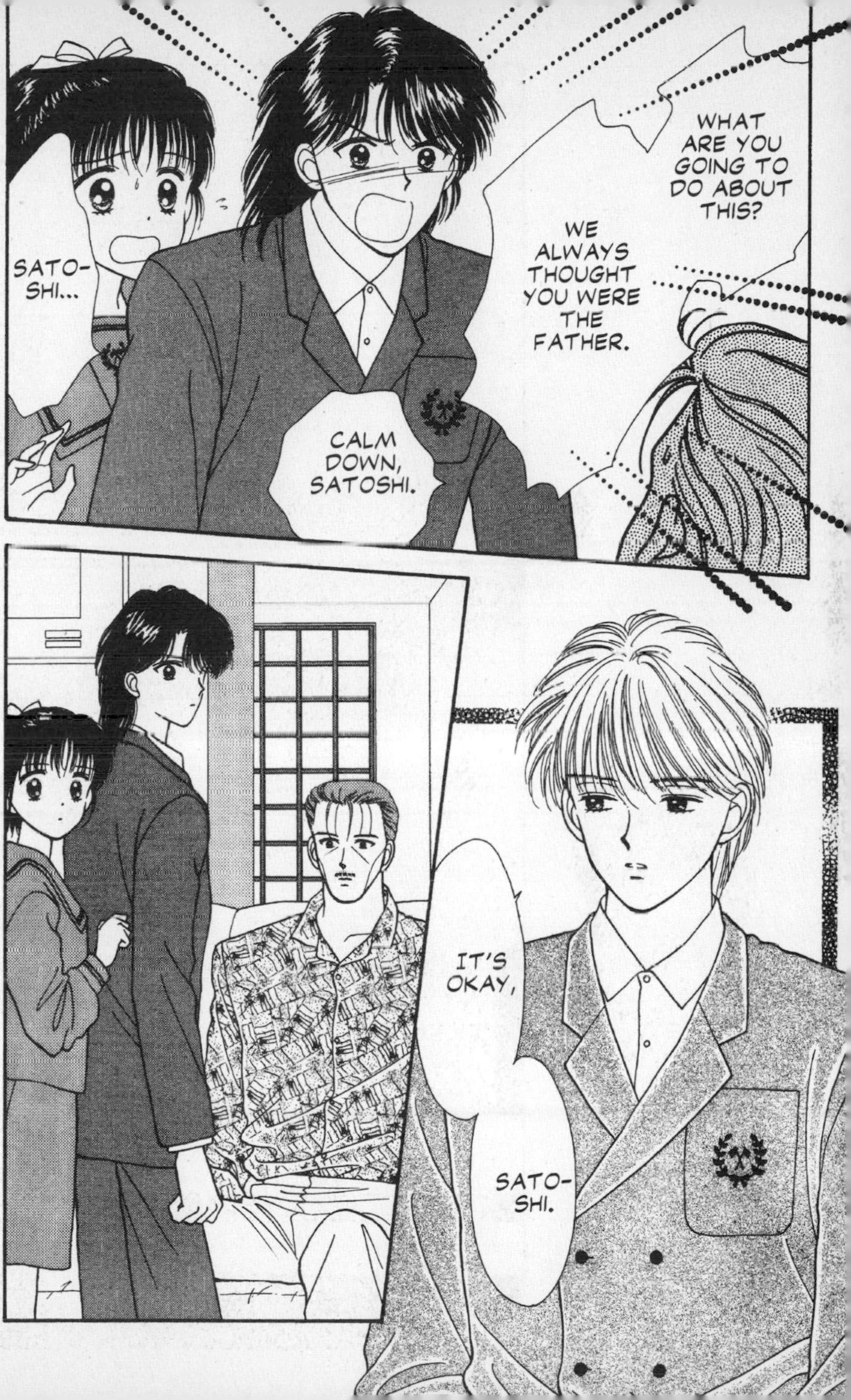
WHAT ARE YOU GOING TO DO ABOUT THIS?
WE ALWAYS THOUGHT YOU WERE THE FATHER.
SATO-SHI...
CALM DOWN, SATOSHI.
IT'S OKAY,
SATO-SHI.

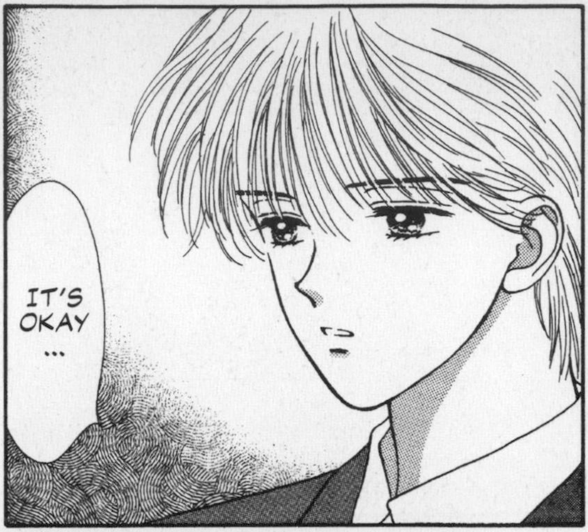
IT'S OKAY ...
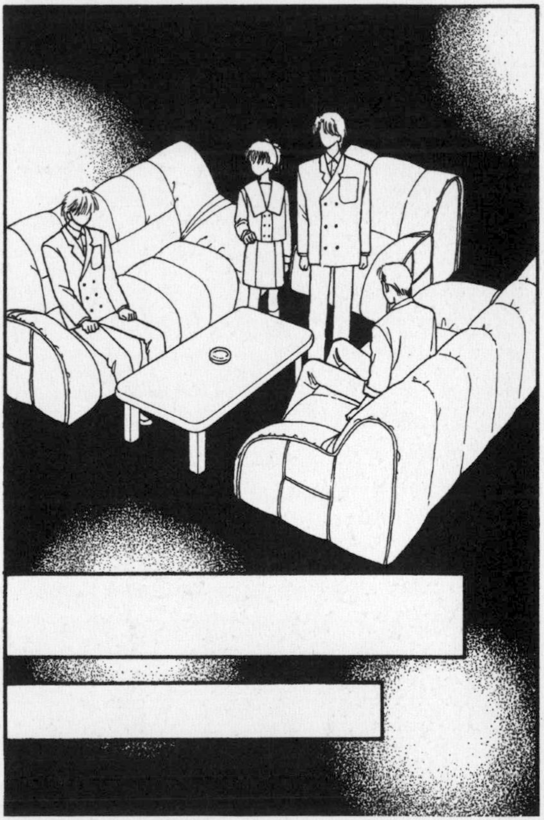
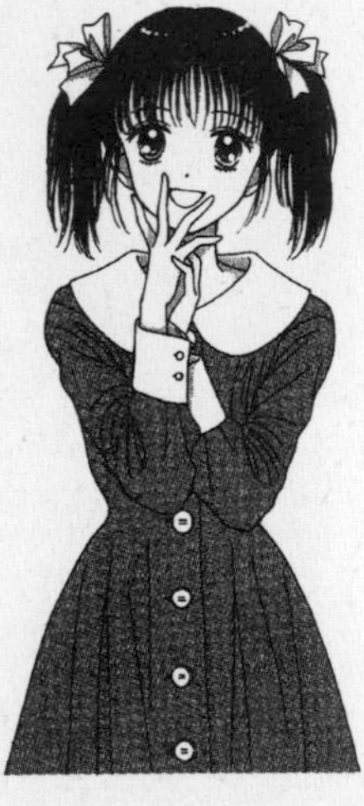

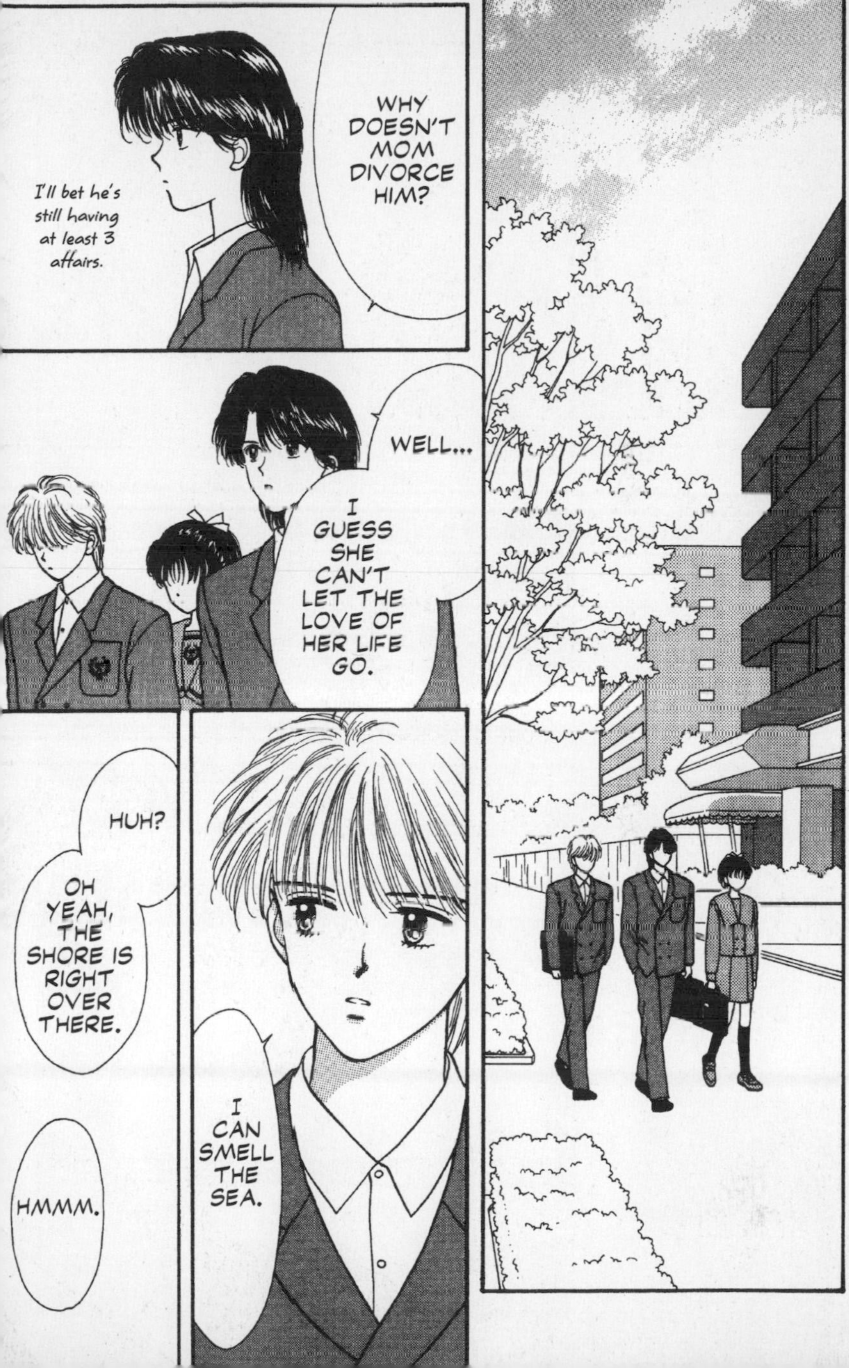
WHY DOESN'T MOM DIVORCE HIM?
I'll bet he's still having at least 3 affairs.
WELL...
I GUESS SHE CAN'T LET THE LOVE OF HER LIFE GO.
I CAN SMELL THE SEA.
HUH?
OH YEAH, THE SHORE IS RIGHT OVER THERE.
HMMM.

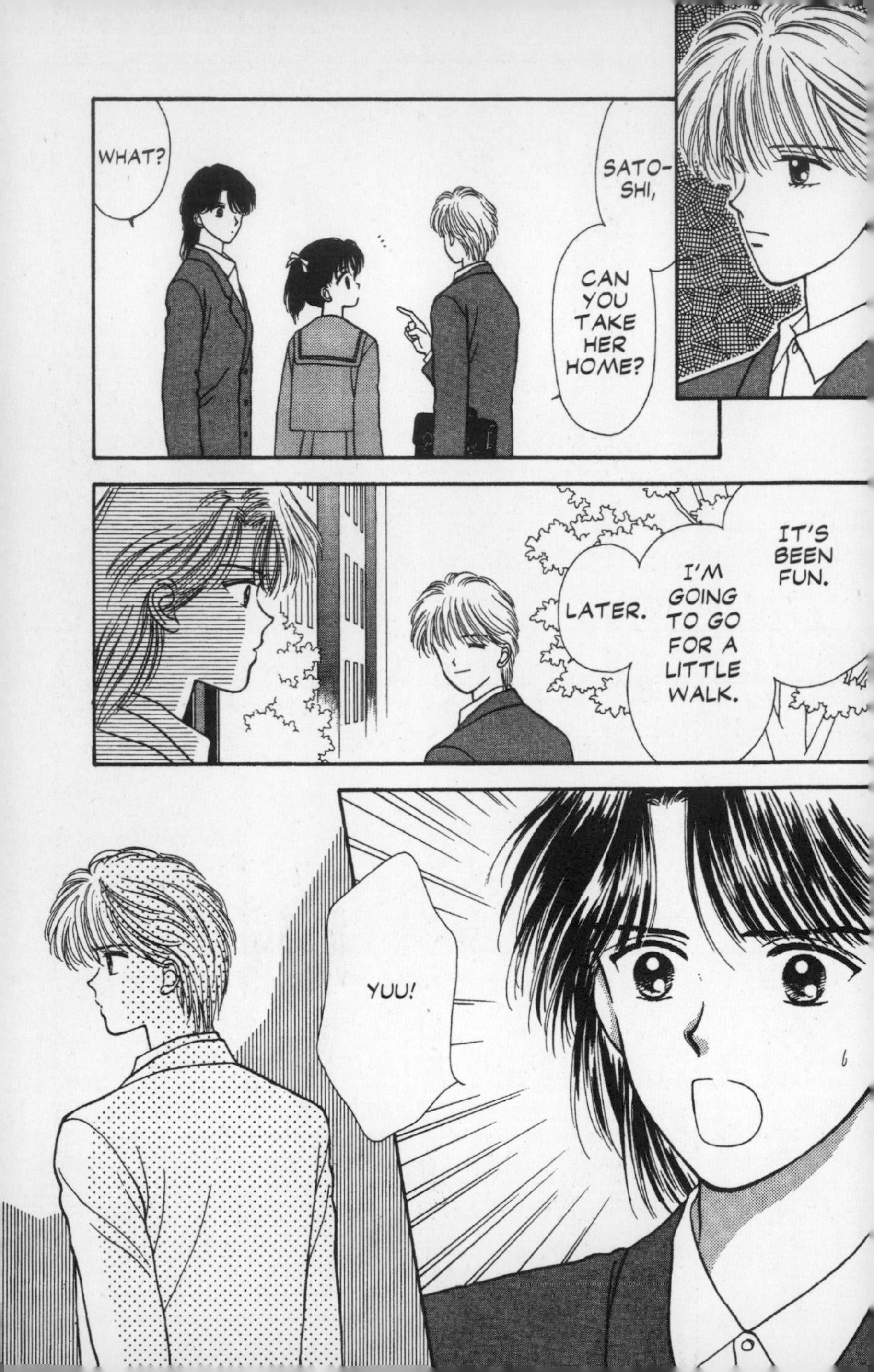
SATO-SHI,
CAN YOU TAKE HER HOME?
WHAT?
IT'S BEEN FUN.
I'M GOING TO GO FOR A LITTLE WALK.
LATER.
YUU!

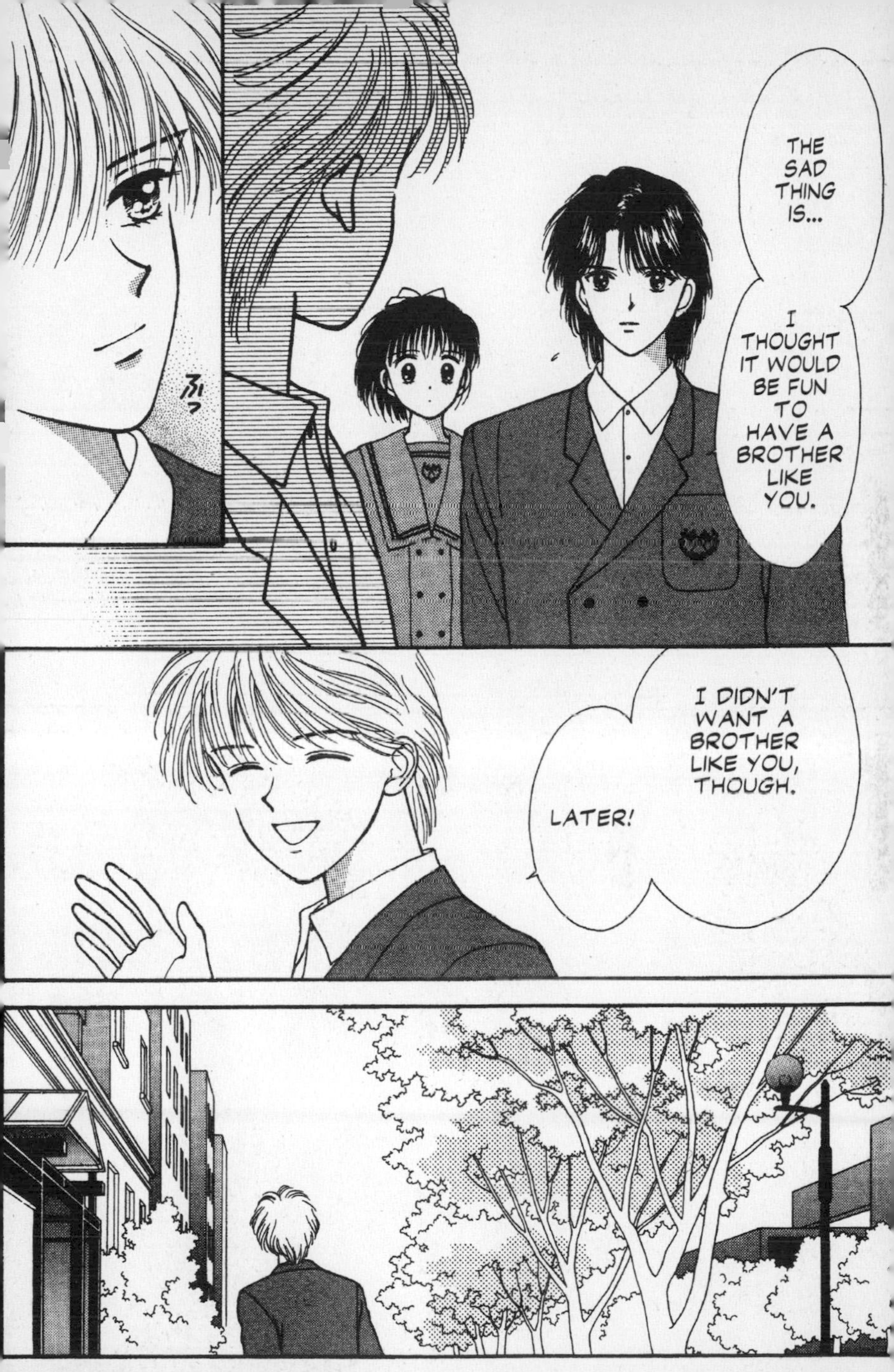
THE SAD THING IS...
I THOUGHT IT WOULD BE FUN TO HAVE A BROTHER LIKE YOU.
ふっ
I DIDN'T WANT A BROTHER LIKE YOU, THOUGH.
LATER!

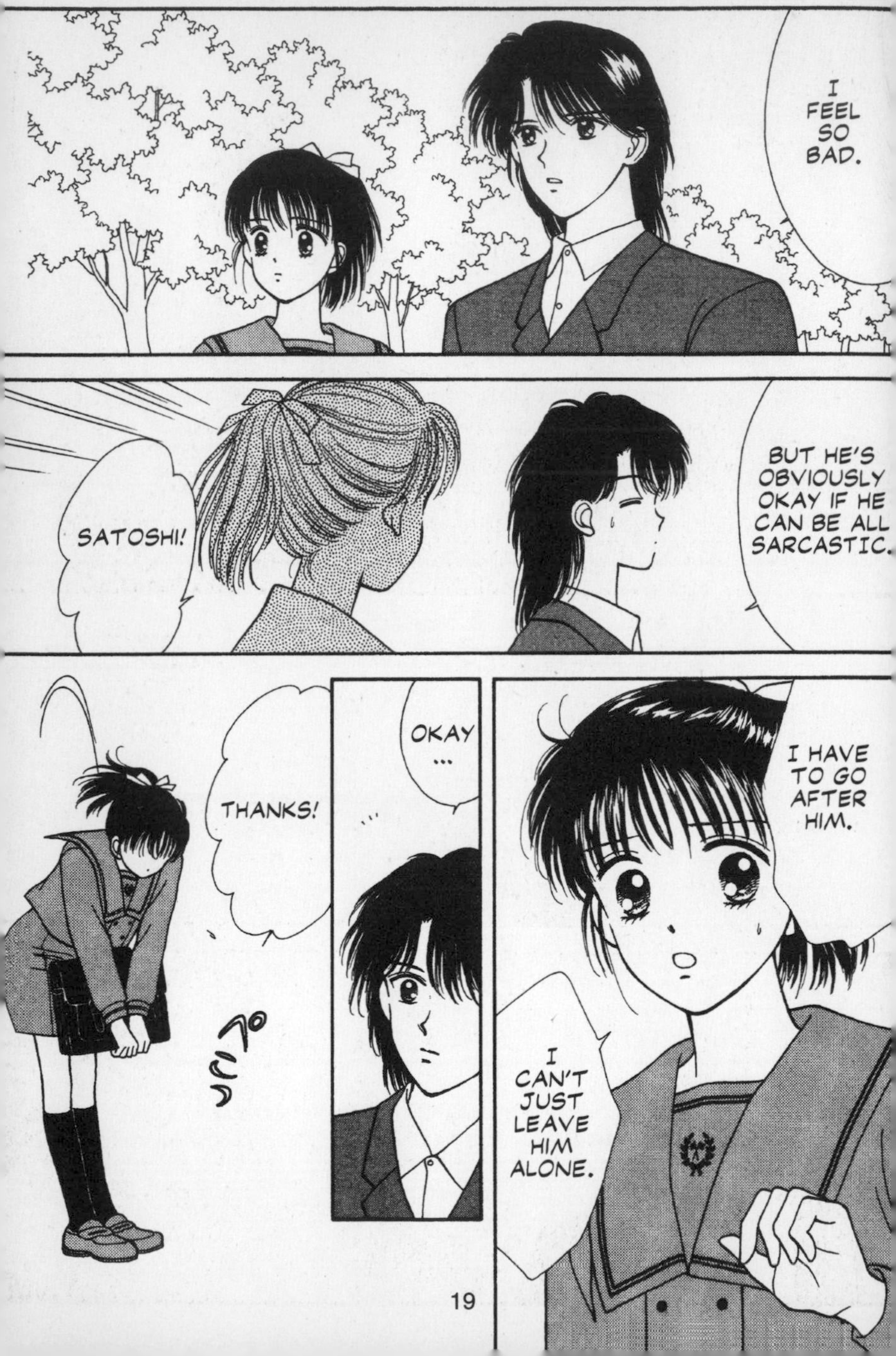
I FEEL SO BAD.
BUT HE'S OBVIOUSLY OKAY IF HE CAN BE ALL SARCASTIC.
SATOSHI!
I HAVE TO GO AFTER HIM.
I CAN'T JUST LEAVE HIM ALONE.
OKAY ...
...
THANKS!

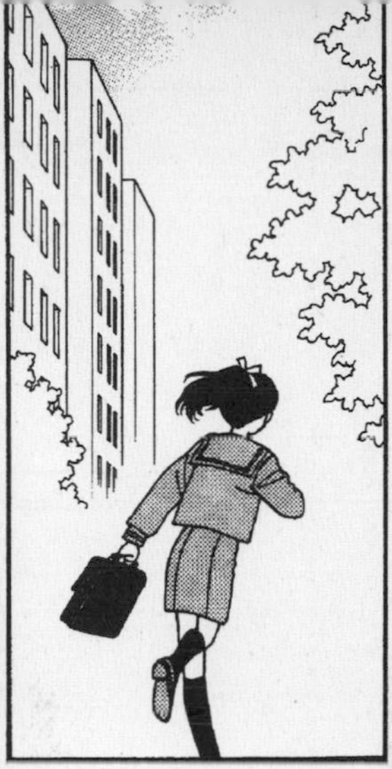

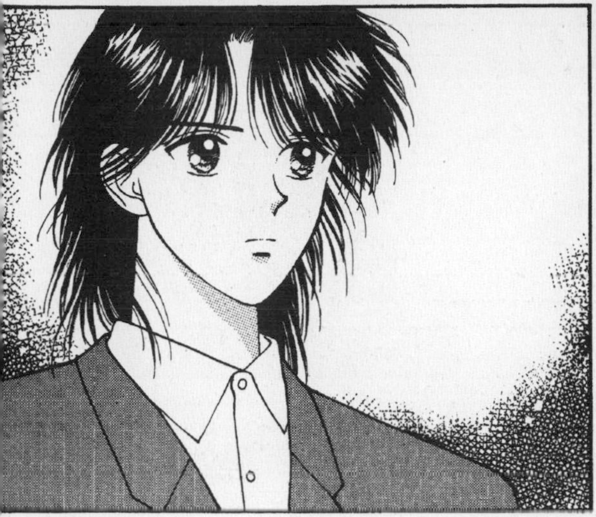

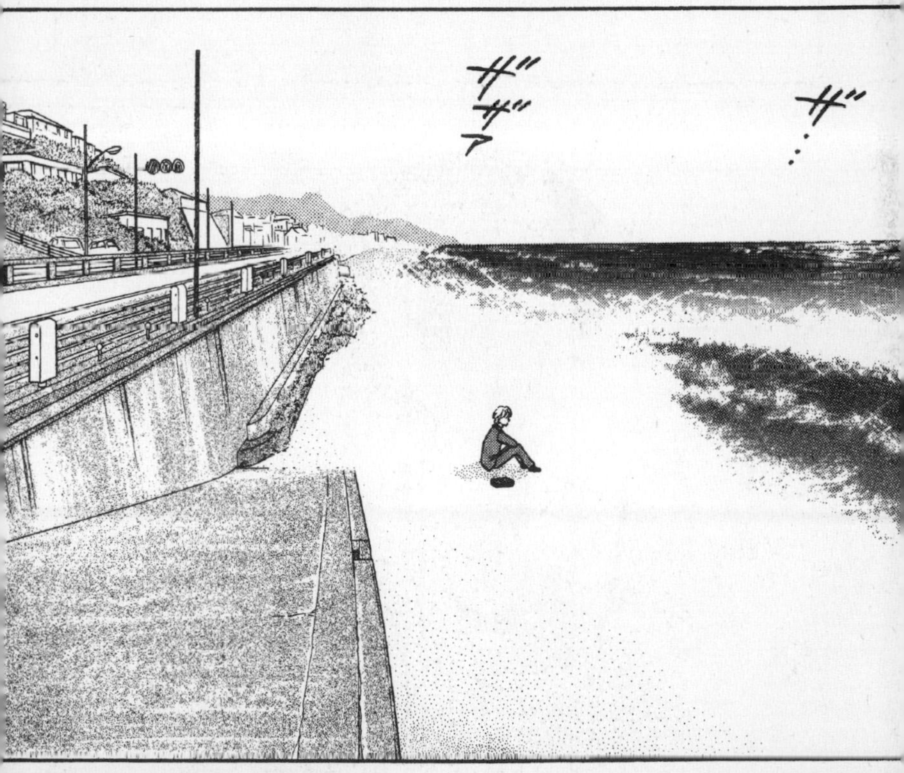
ザ…
ザザア

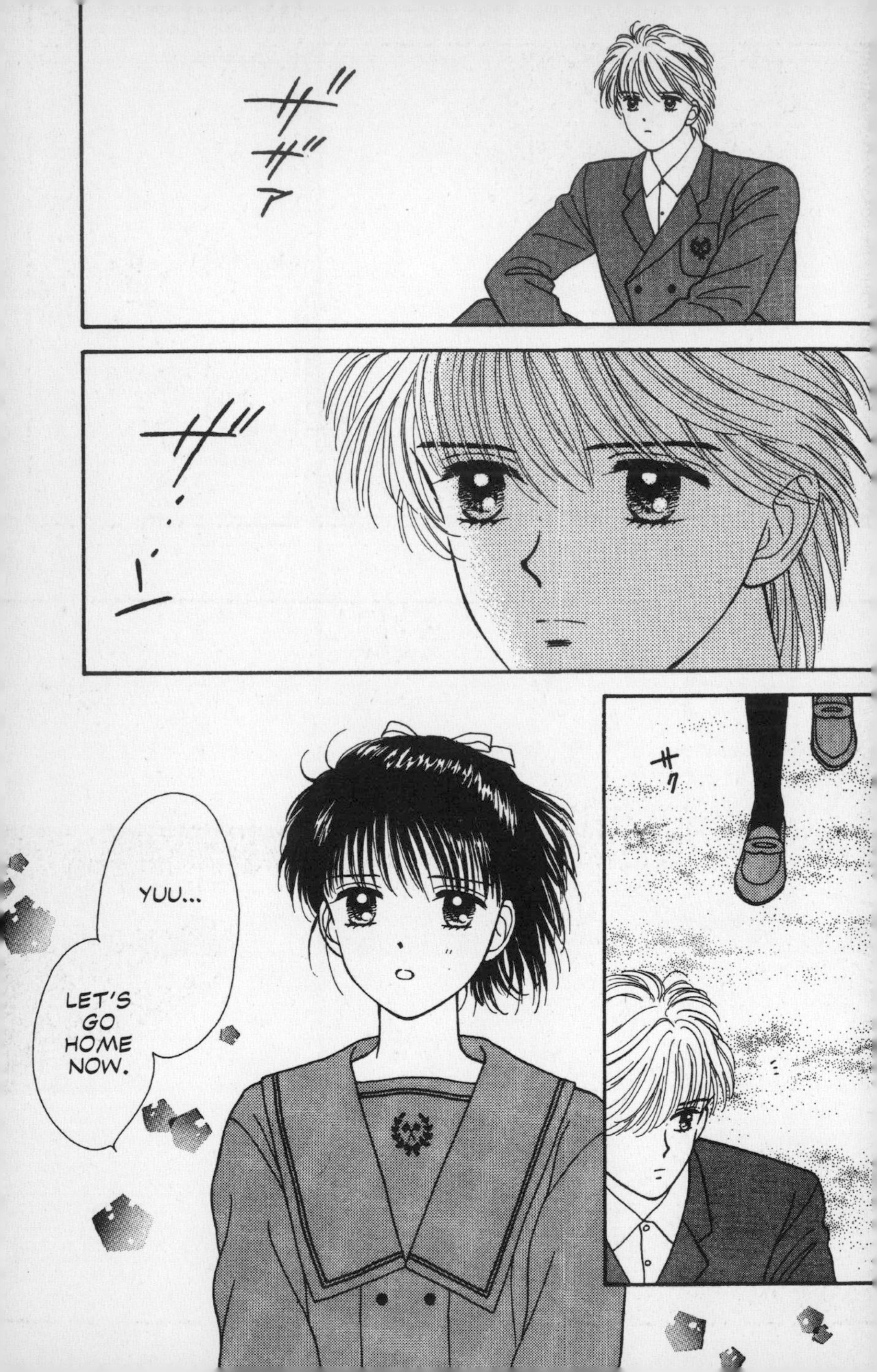
ザザア
ザ…
ザク
YUU...
LET'S GO HOME NOW.

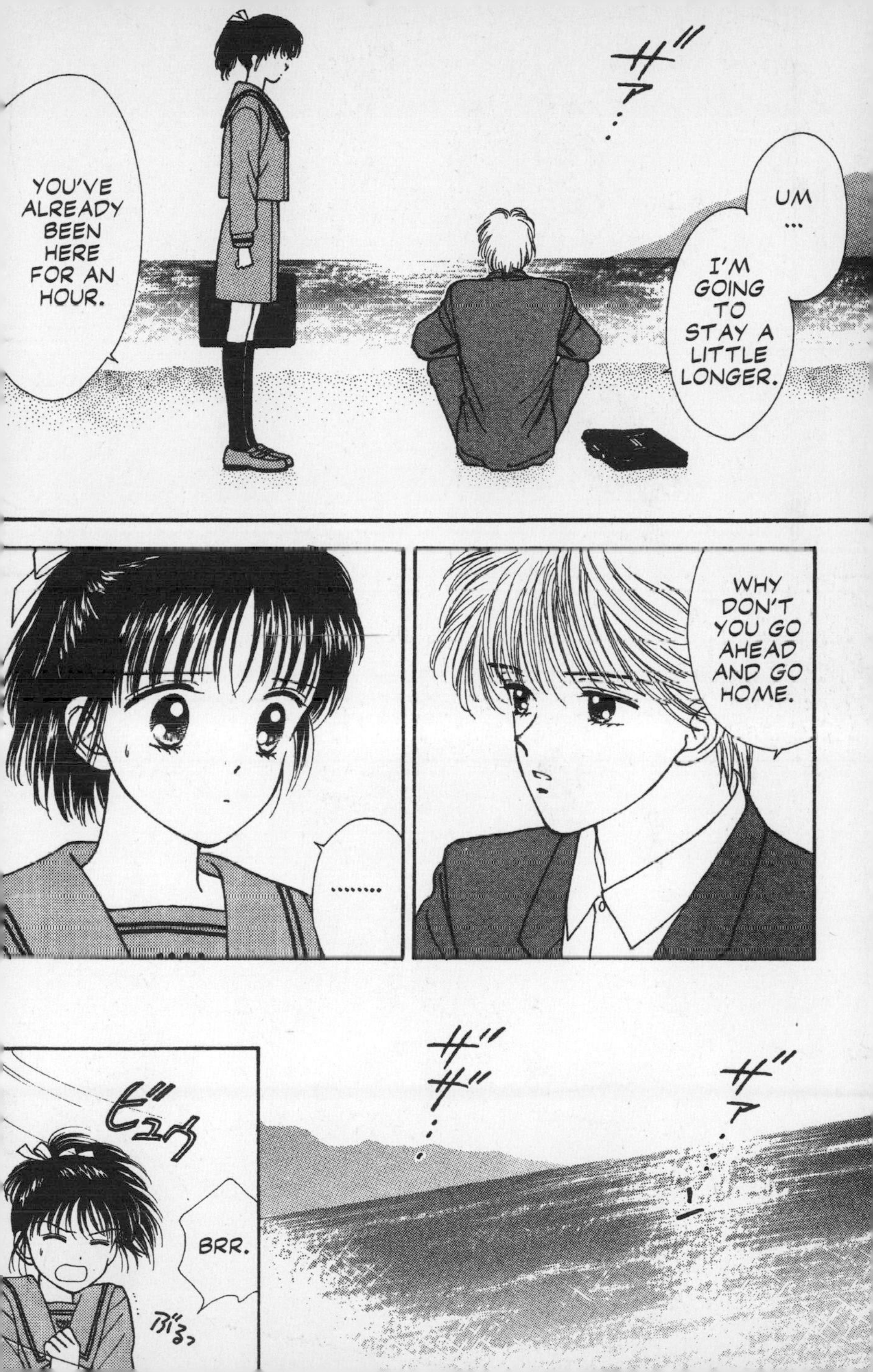
ザァ…
UM … I'M GOING TO STAY A LITTLE LONGER.
YOU'VE ALREADY BEEN HERE FOR AN HOUR.
WHY DON'T YOU GO AHEAD AND GO HOME.
....
ザァ…
ザザ…
ビュウ
BRR.
ぶるっ

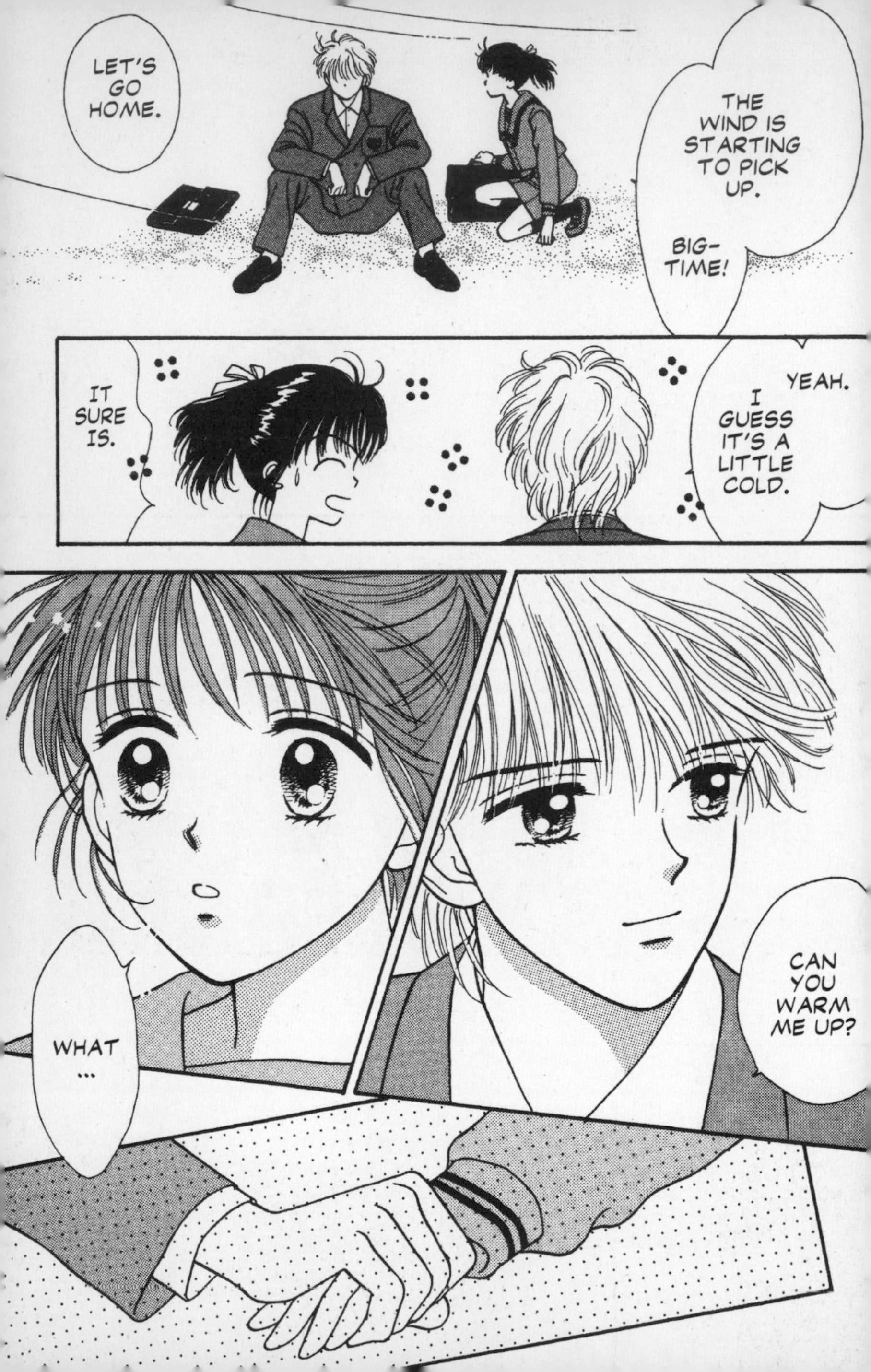
THE WIND IS STARTING TO PICK UP.
BIG-TIME!
LET'S GO HOME.
YEAH. I GUESS IT'S A LITTLE COLD.
IT SURE IS.
CAN YOU WARM ME UP?
WHAT ...

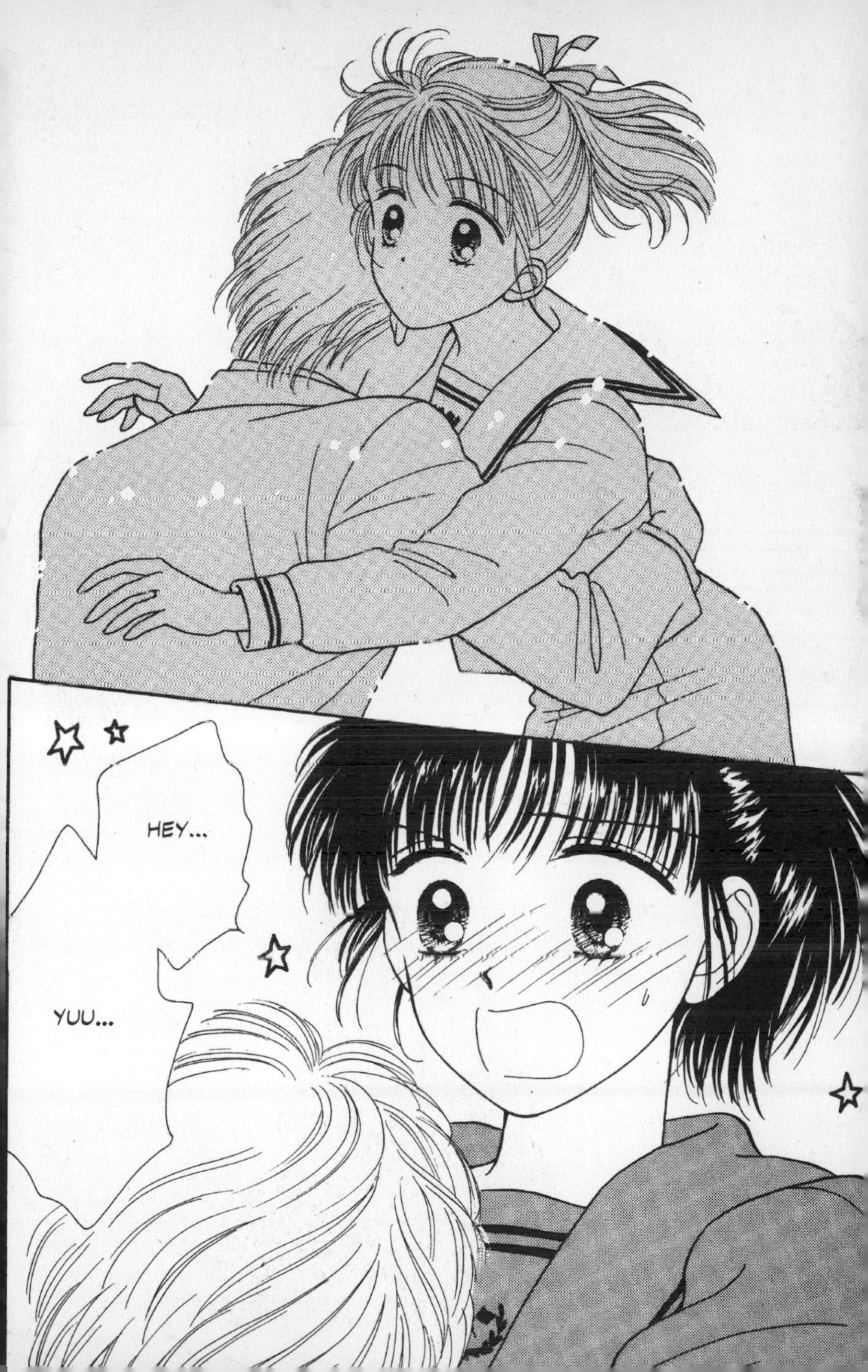
HEY...
YUU...

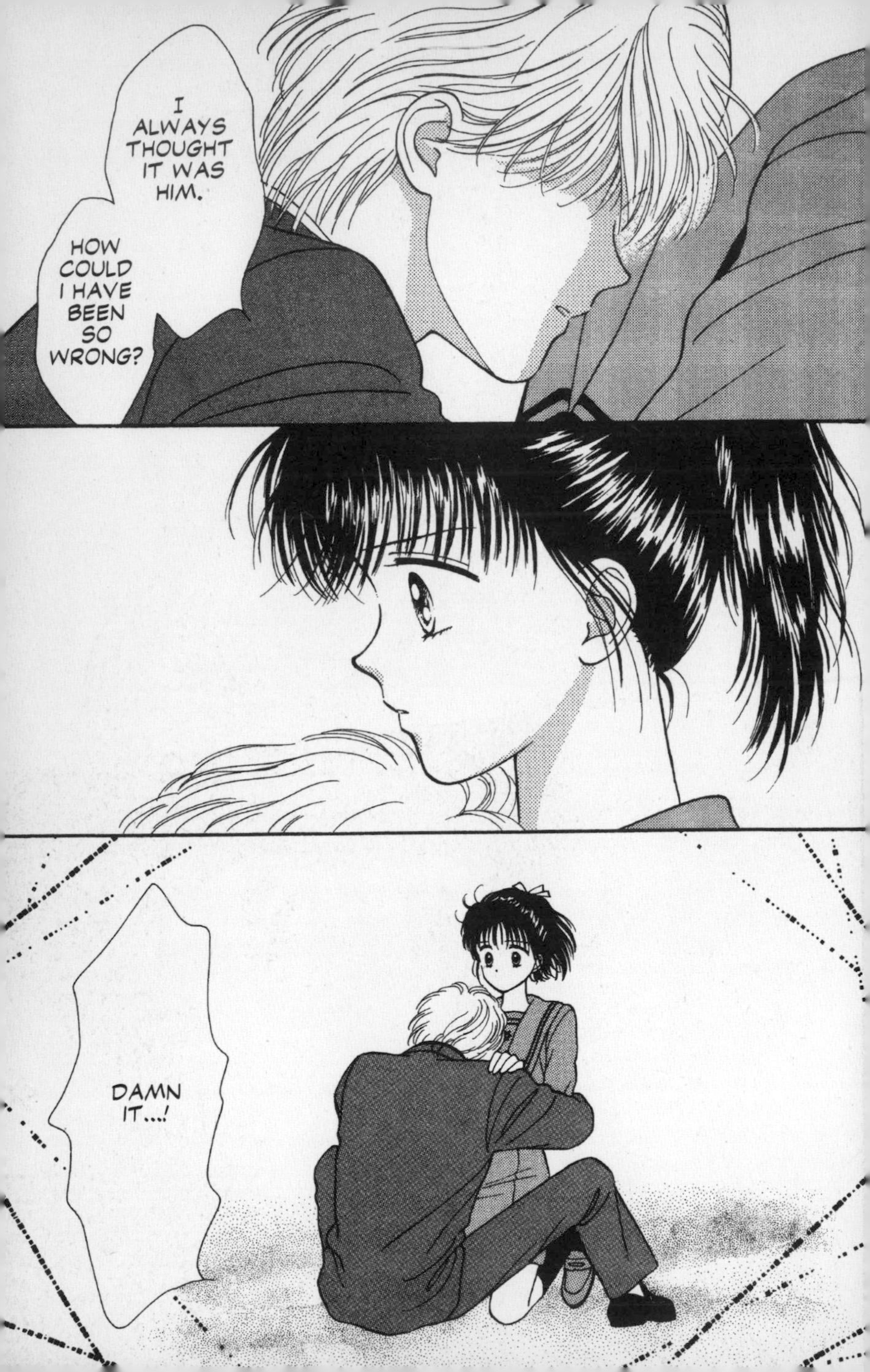
I ALWAYS THOUGHT IT WAS HIM.
HOW COULD I HAVE BEEN SO WRONG?
DAMN IT...!

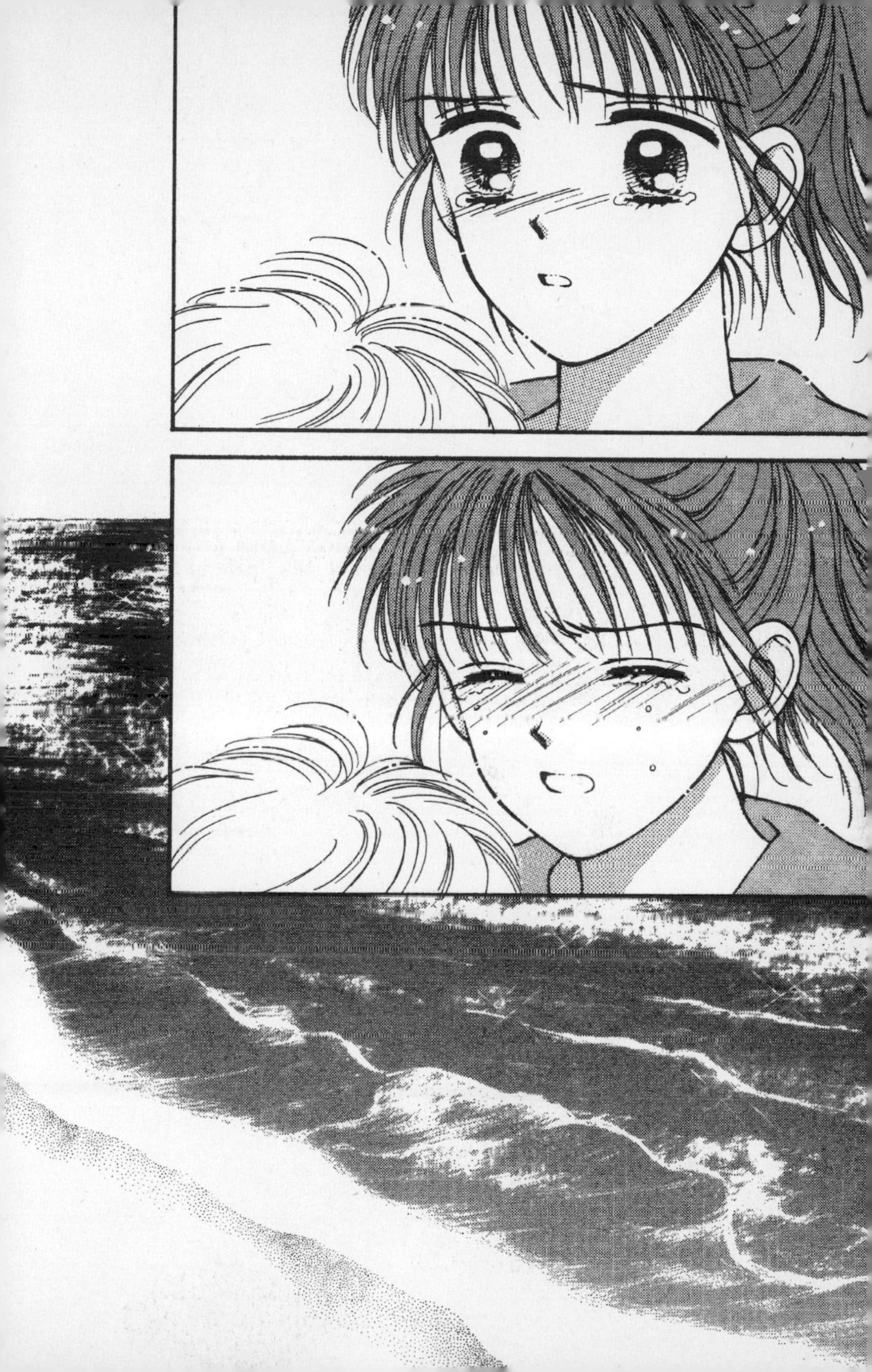

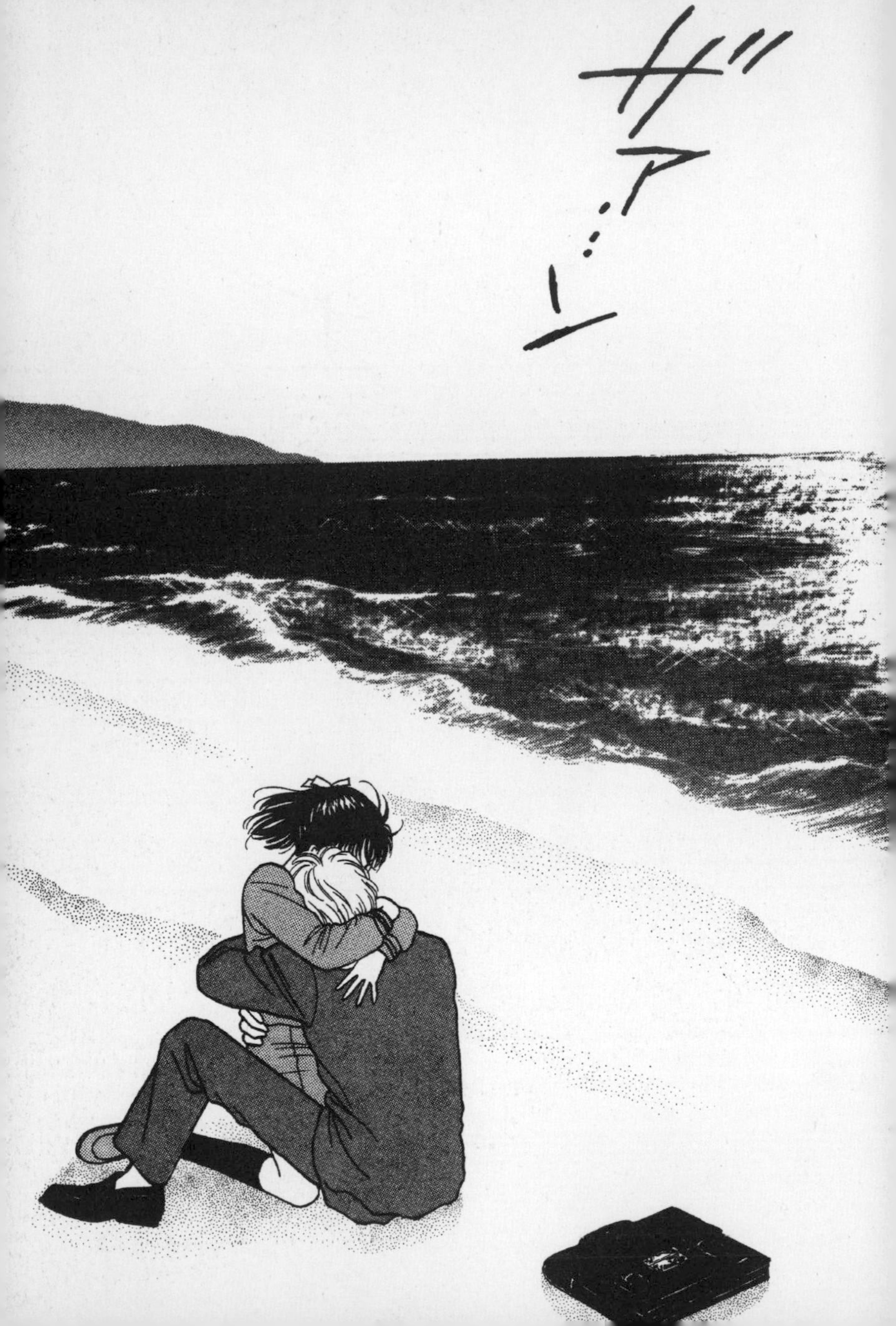
ザァ…ン

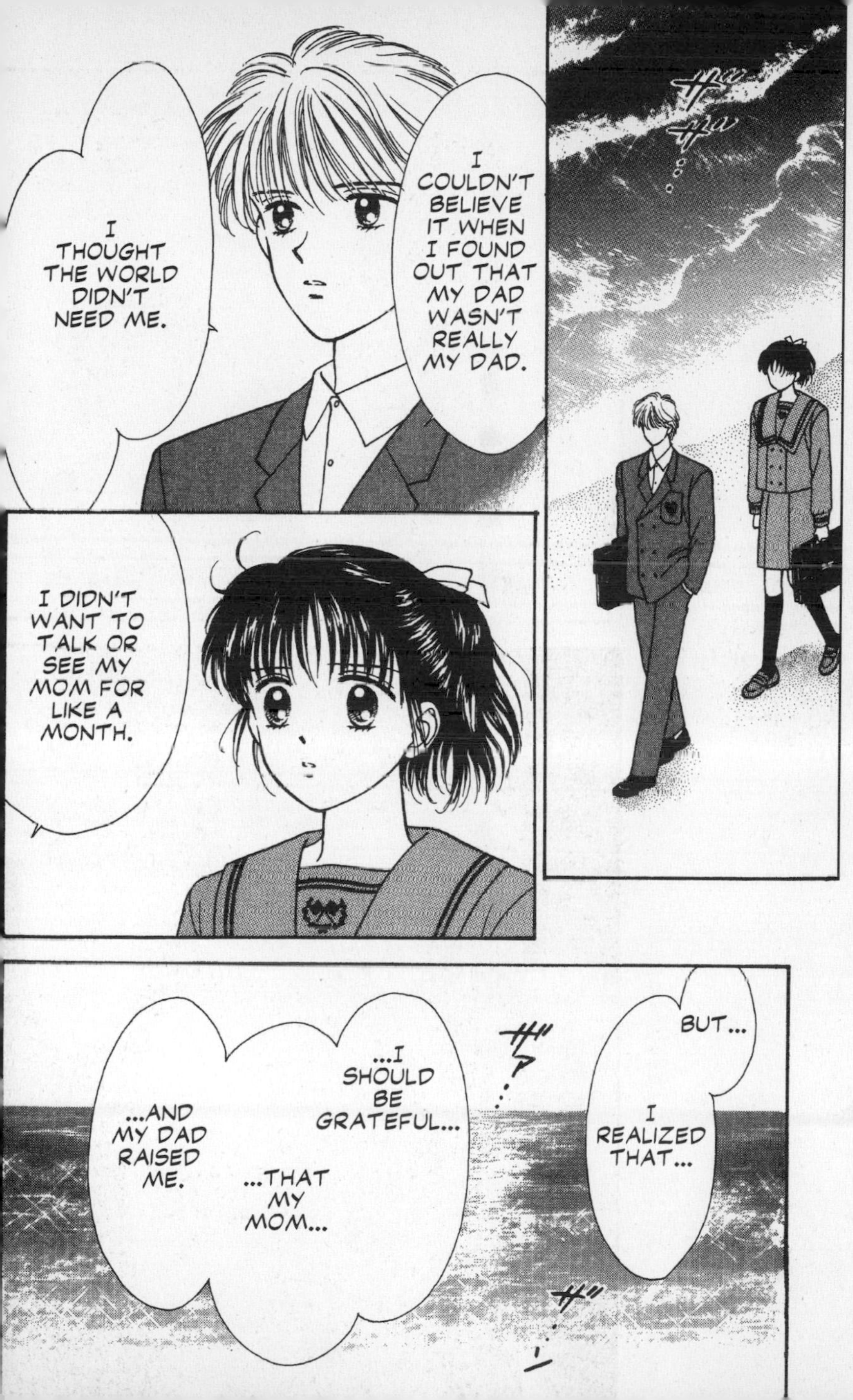
I COULDN'T BELIEVE IT WHEN I FOUND OUT THAT MY DAD WASN'T REALLY MY DAD.
I THOUGHT THE WORLD DIDN'T NEED ME.
I DIDN'T WANT TO TALK OR SEE MY MOM FOR LIKE A MONTH.
BUT...
I REALIZED THAT...
...I SHOULD BE GRATEFUL...
...THAT MY MOM...
...AND MY DAD RAISED ME.

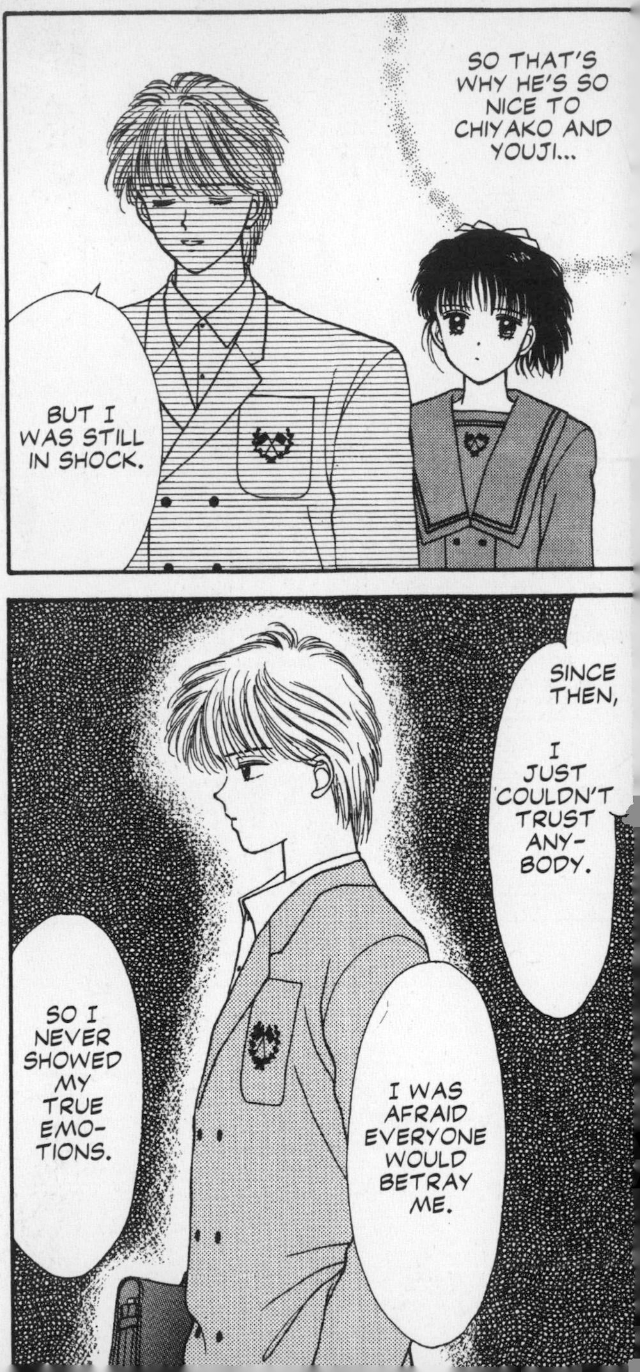
SO THAT'S WHY HE'S SO NICE TO CHIYAKO AND YOUJI...
BUT I WAS STILL IN SHOCK.
SINCE THEN,
I JUST COULDN'T TRUST ANY-BODY.
I WAS AFRAID EVERYONE WOULD BETRAY ME.
SO I NEVER SHOWED MY TRUE EMO-TIONS.
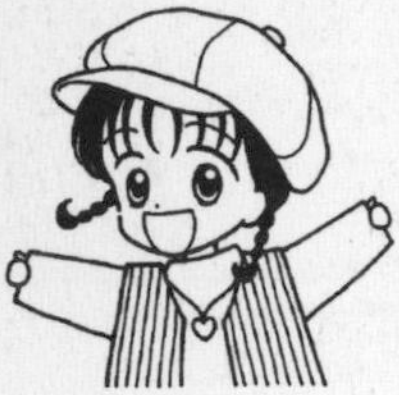

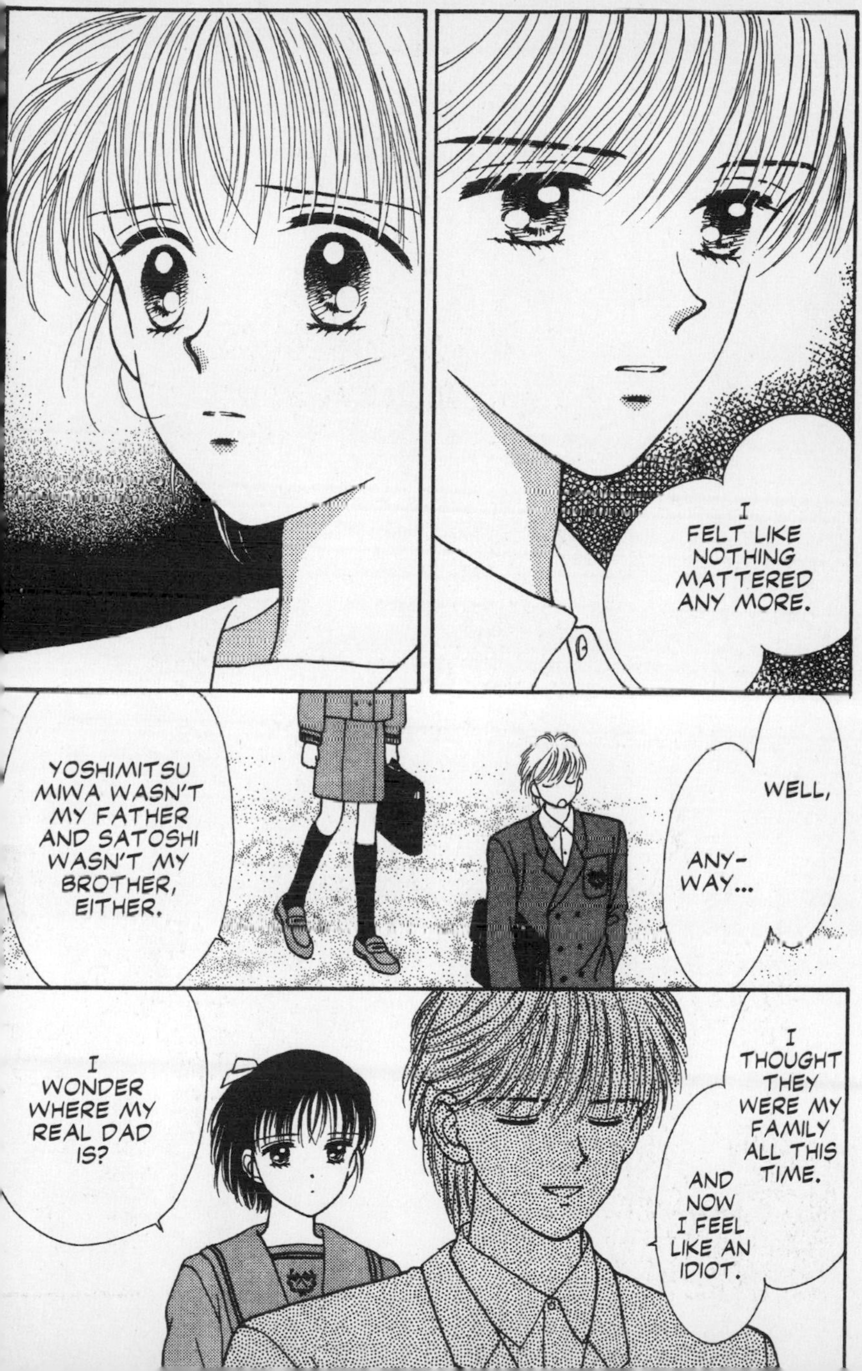
I FELT LIKE NOTHING MATTERED ANY MORE.
WELL,
ANY-WAY...
YOSHIMITSU MIWA WASN'T MY FATHER AND SATOSHI WASN'T MY BROTHER, EITHER.
I THOUGHT THEY WERE MY FAMILY ALL THIS TIME.
AND NOW I FEEL LIKE AN IDIOT.
I WONDER WHERE MY REAL DAD IS?

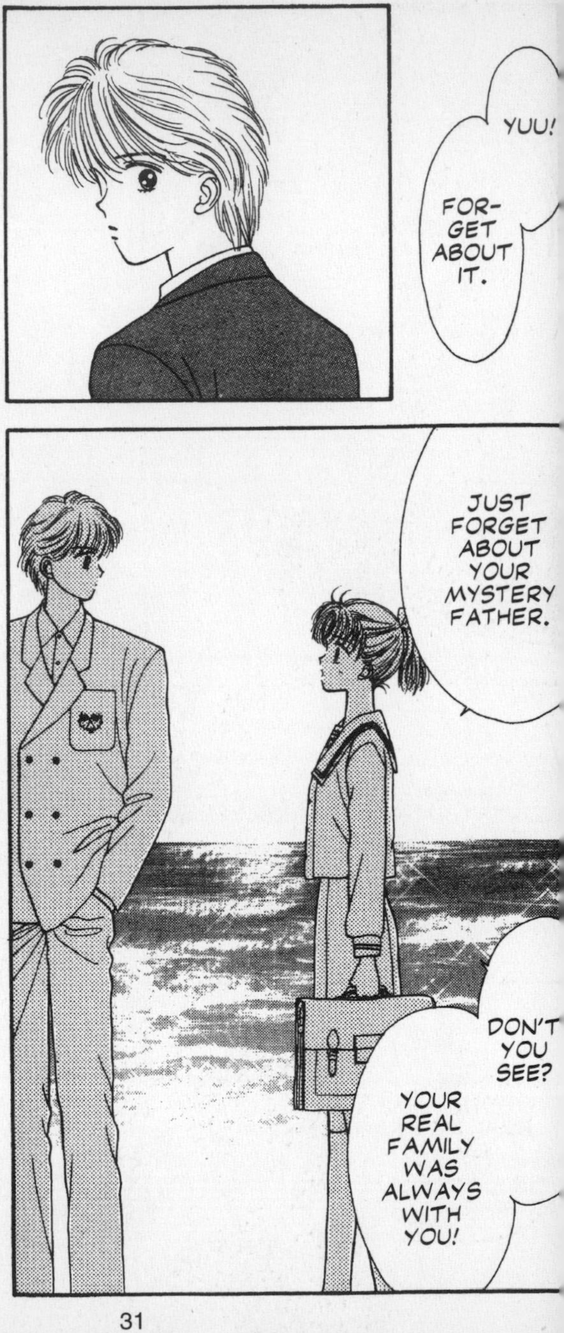
YUU!
FOR-GET ABOUT IT.
JUST FORGET ABOUT YOUR MYSTERY FATHER.
DON'T YOU SEE?
YOUR REAL FAMILY WAS ALWAYS WITH YOU!

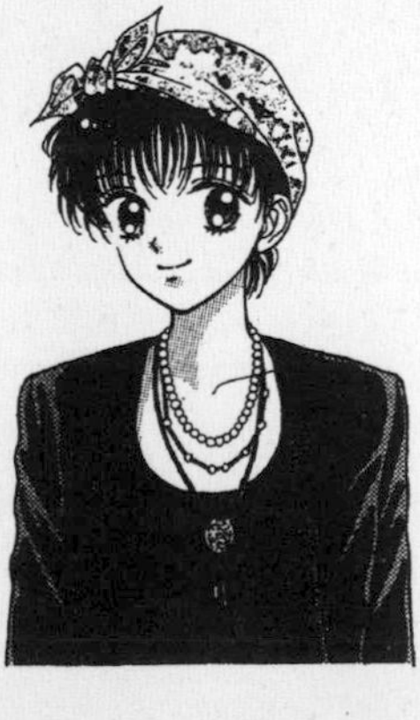

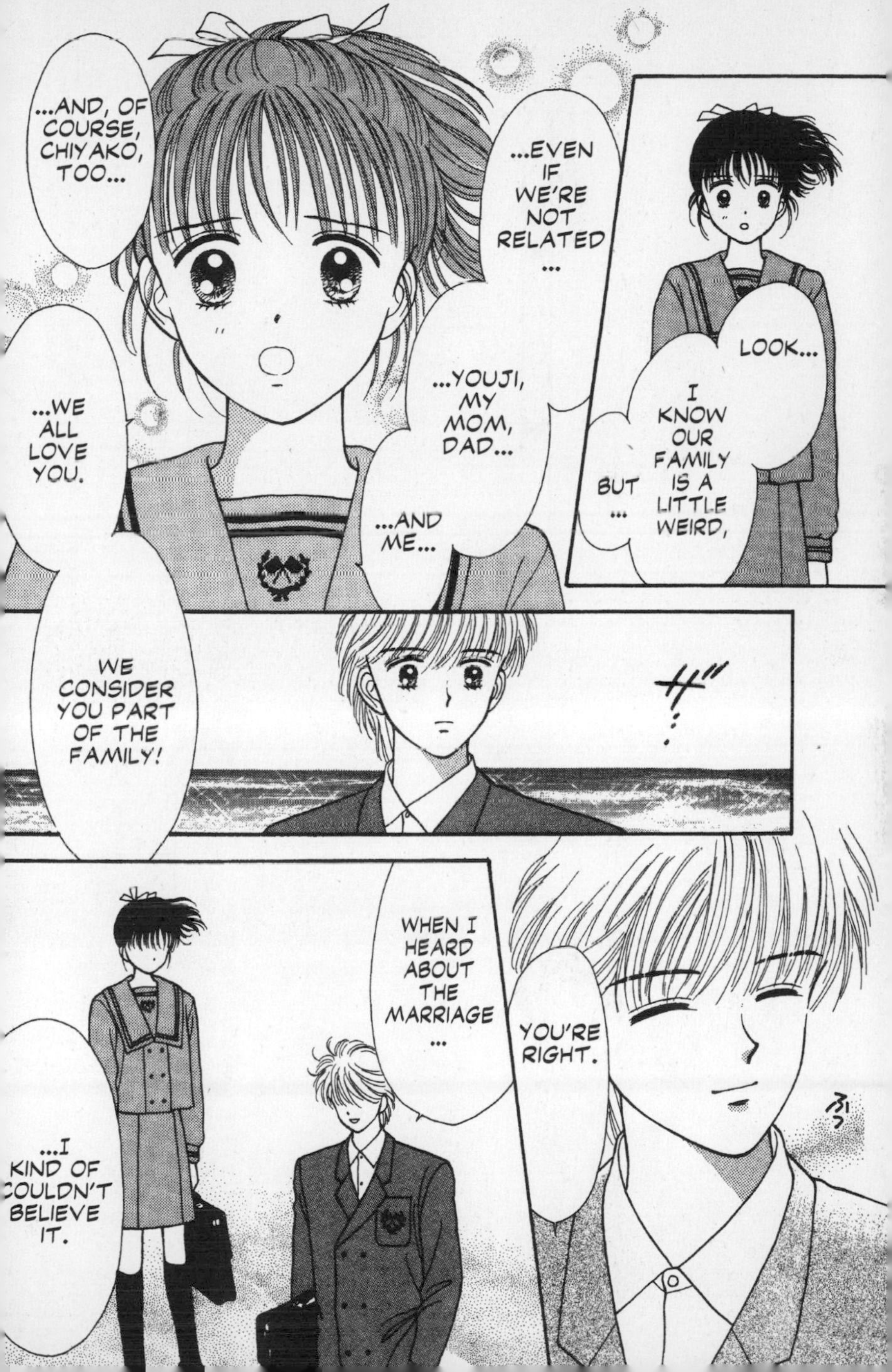
LOOK...
I KNOW OUR FAMILY IS A LITTLE WEIRD,
BUT ...
...EVEN IF WE'RE NOT RELATED ...
...YOUJI, MY MOM, DAD...
...AND ME...
...AND, OF COURSE, CHIYAKO, TOO...
...WE ALL LOVE YOU.
WE CONSIDER YOU PART OF THE FAMILY!
YOU'RE RIGHT.
ふっ
WHEN I HEARD ABOUT THE MARRIAGE ...
...I KIND OF COULDN'T BELIEVE IT.

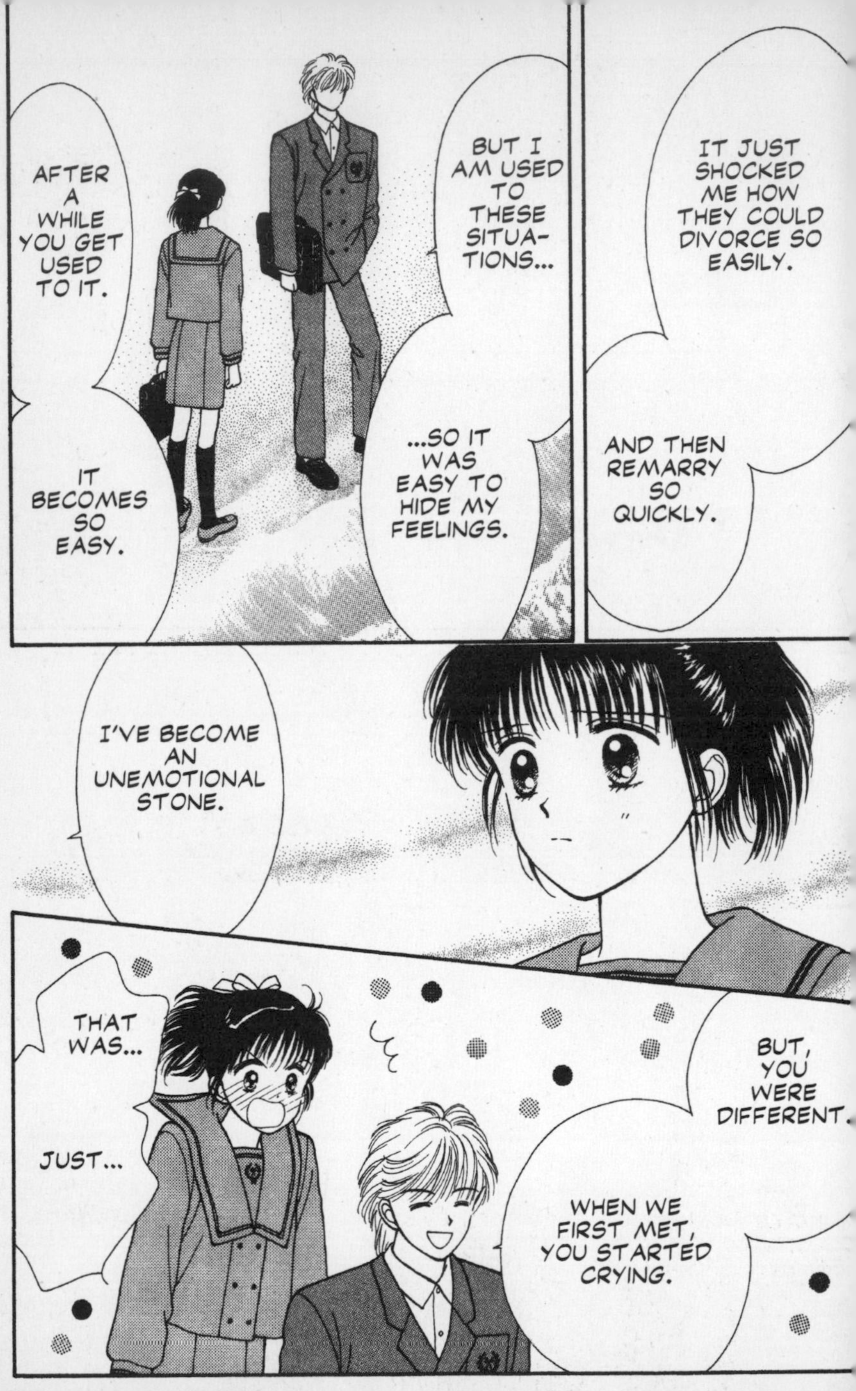
IT JUST SHOCKED ME HOW THEY COULD DIVORCE SO EASILY.
AND THEN REMARRY SO QUICKLY.
BUT I AM USED TO THESE SITUATIONS...
...SO IT WAS EASY TO HIDE MY FEELINGS.
AFTER A WHILE YOU GET USED TO IT.
IT BECOMES SO EASY.
I'VE BECOME AN UNEMOTIONAL STONE.
BUT, YOU WERE DIFFERENT.
WHEN WE FIRST MET, YOU STARTED CRYING.
THAT WAS...
JUST...

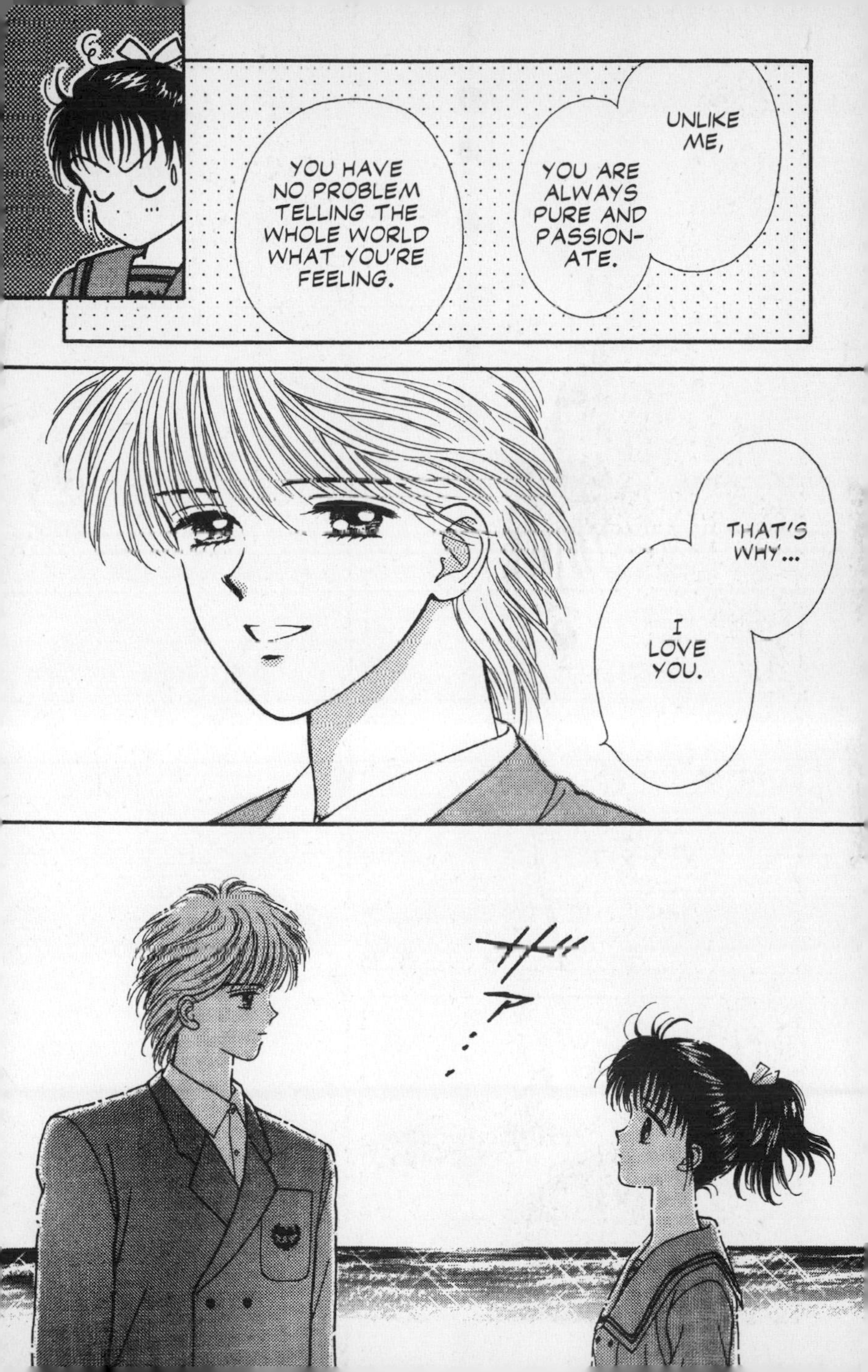
UNLIKE ME,
YOU ARE ALWAYS PURE AND PASSION-ATE.
YOU HAVE NO PROBLEM TELLING THE WHOLE WORLD WHAT YOU'RE FEELING.
THAT'S WHY...
I LOVE YOU.

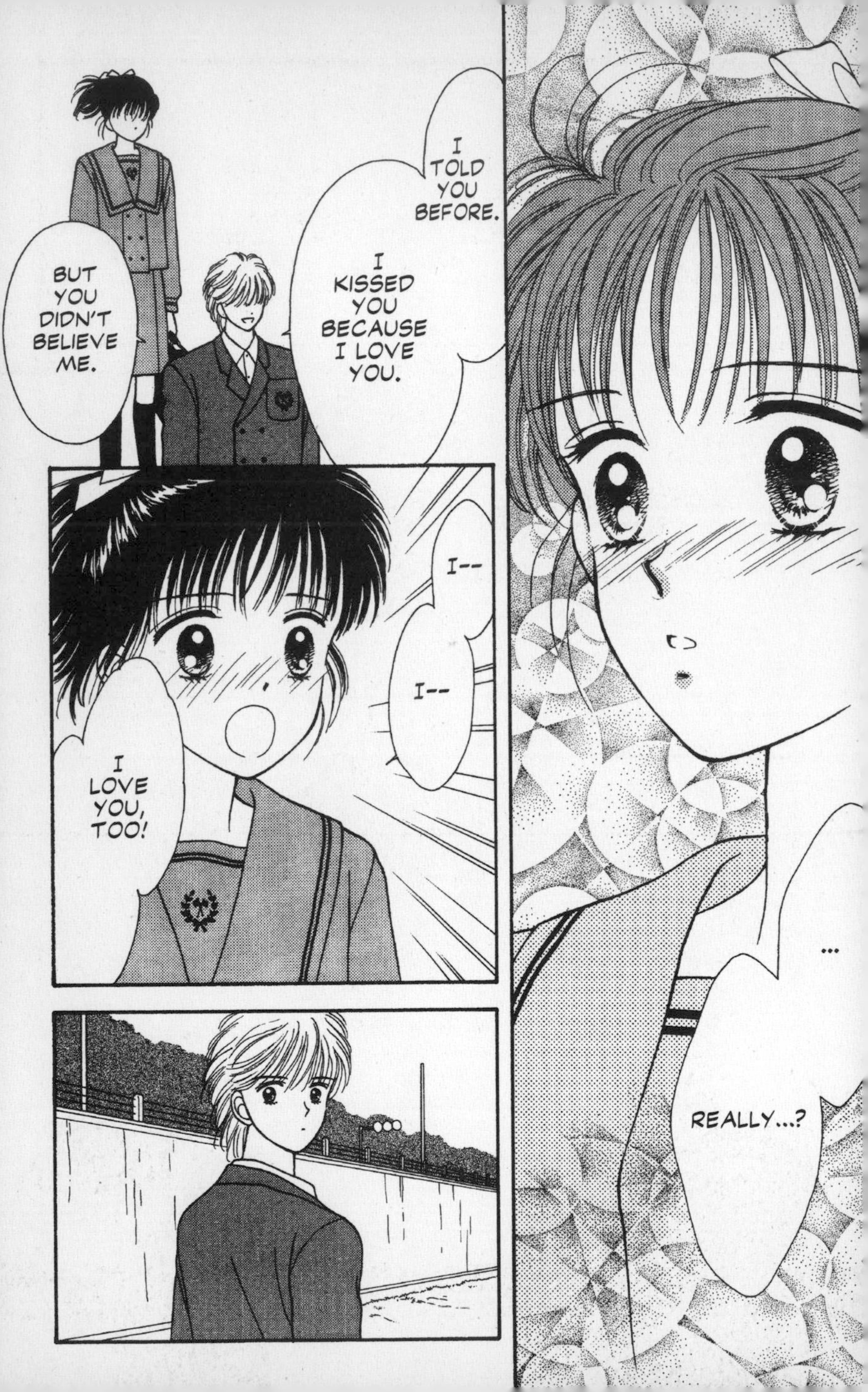
I TOLD YOU BEFORE.
I KISSED YOU BECAUSE I LOVE YOU.
BUT YOU DIDN'T BELIEVE ME.
I--
I--
I LOVE YOU, TOO!
...
REALLY...?

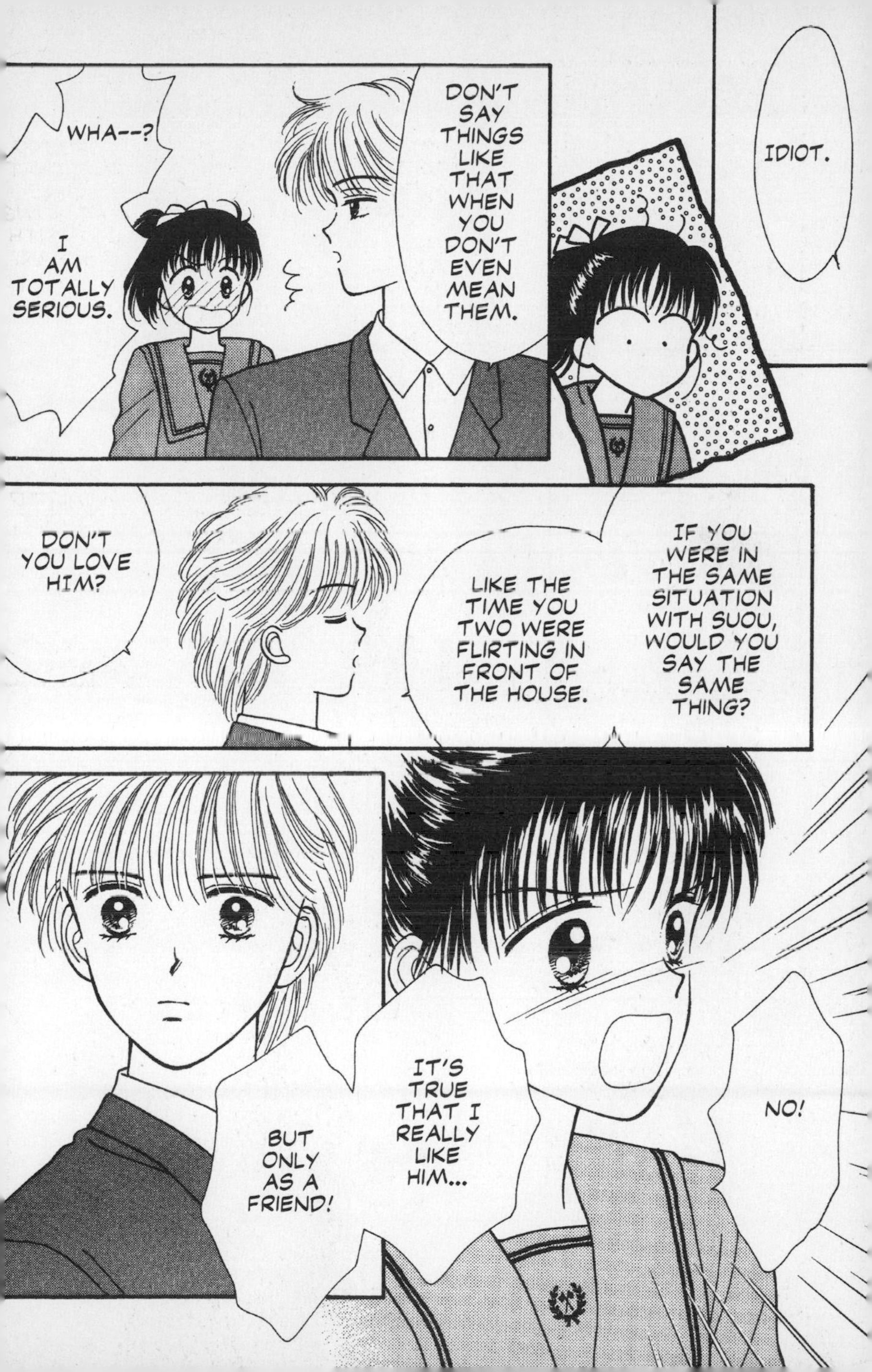
IDIOT.
DON'T SAY THINGS LIKE THAT WHEN YOU DON'T EVEN MEAN THEM.
WHA--?
I AM TOTALLY SERIOUS.
IF YOU WERE IN THE SAME SITUATION WITH SUOU, WOULD YOU SAY THE SAME THING?
LIKE THE TIME YOU TWO WERE FLIRTING IN FRONT OF THE HOUSE.
DON'T YOU LOVE HIM?
NO!
IT'S TRUE THAT I REALLY LIKE HIM...
BUT ONLY AS A FRIEND!

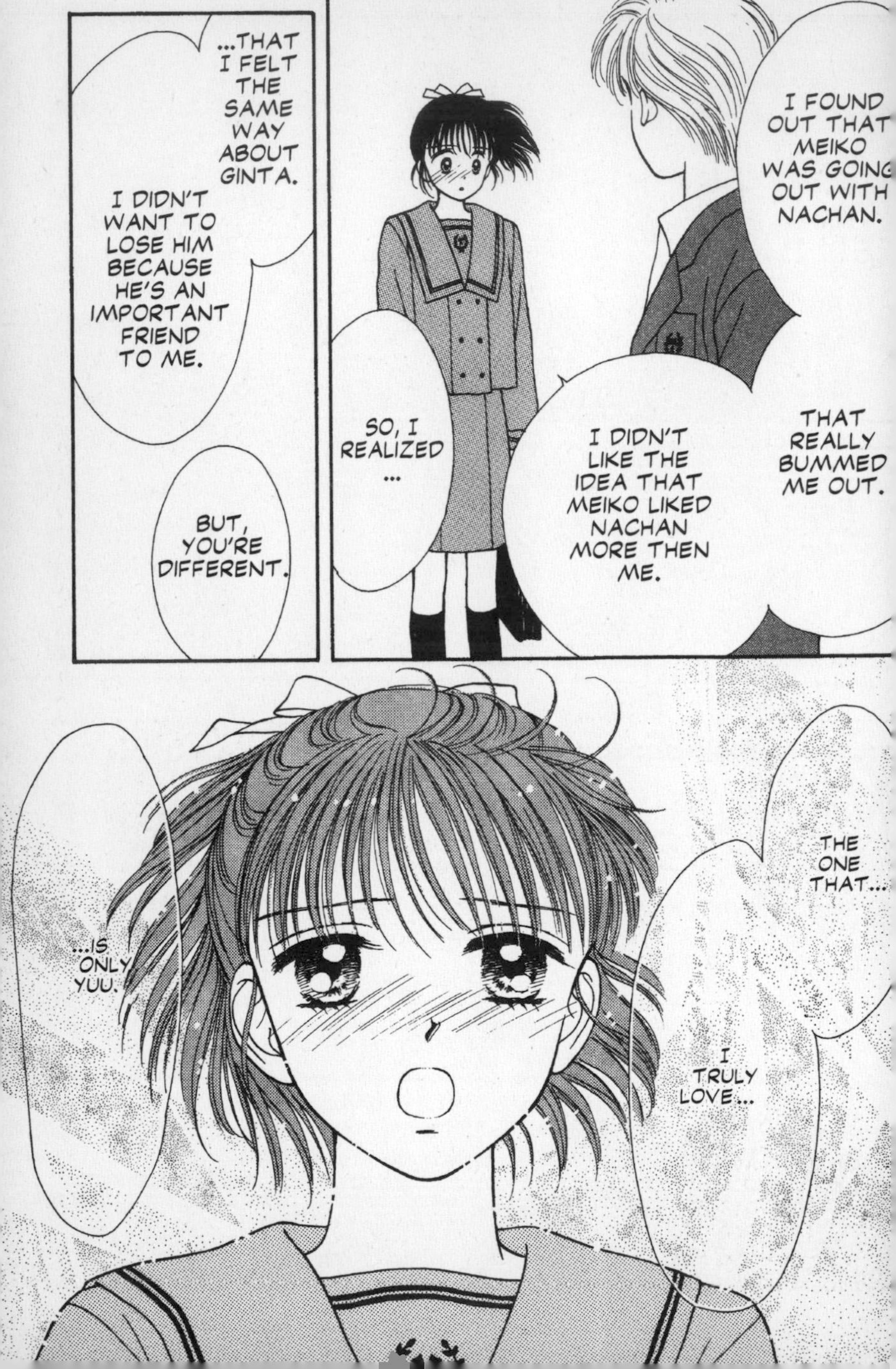
I FOUND OUT THAT MEIKO WAS GOING OUT WITH NACHAN.
THAT REALLY BUMMED ME OUT.
I DIDN'T LIKE THE IDEA THAT MEIKO LIKED NACHAN MORE THEN ME.
SO, I REALIZED ...
...THAT I FELT THE SAME WAY ABOUT GINTA.
I DIDN'T WANT TO LOSE HIM BECAUSE HE'S AN IMPORTANT FRIEND TO ME.
BUT, YOU'RE DIFFERENT.
THE ONE THAT...
I TRULY LOVE...
...IS ONLY YUU.

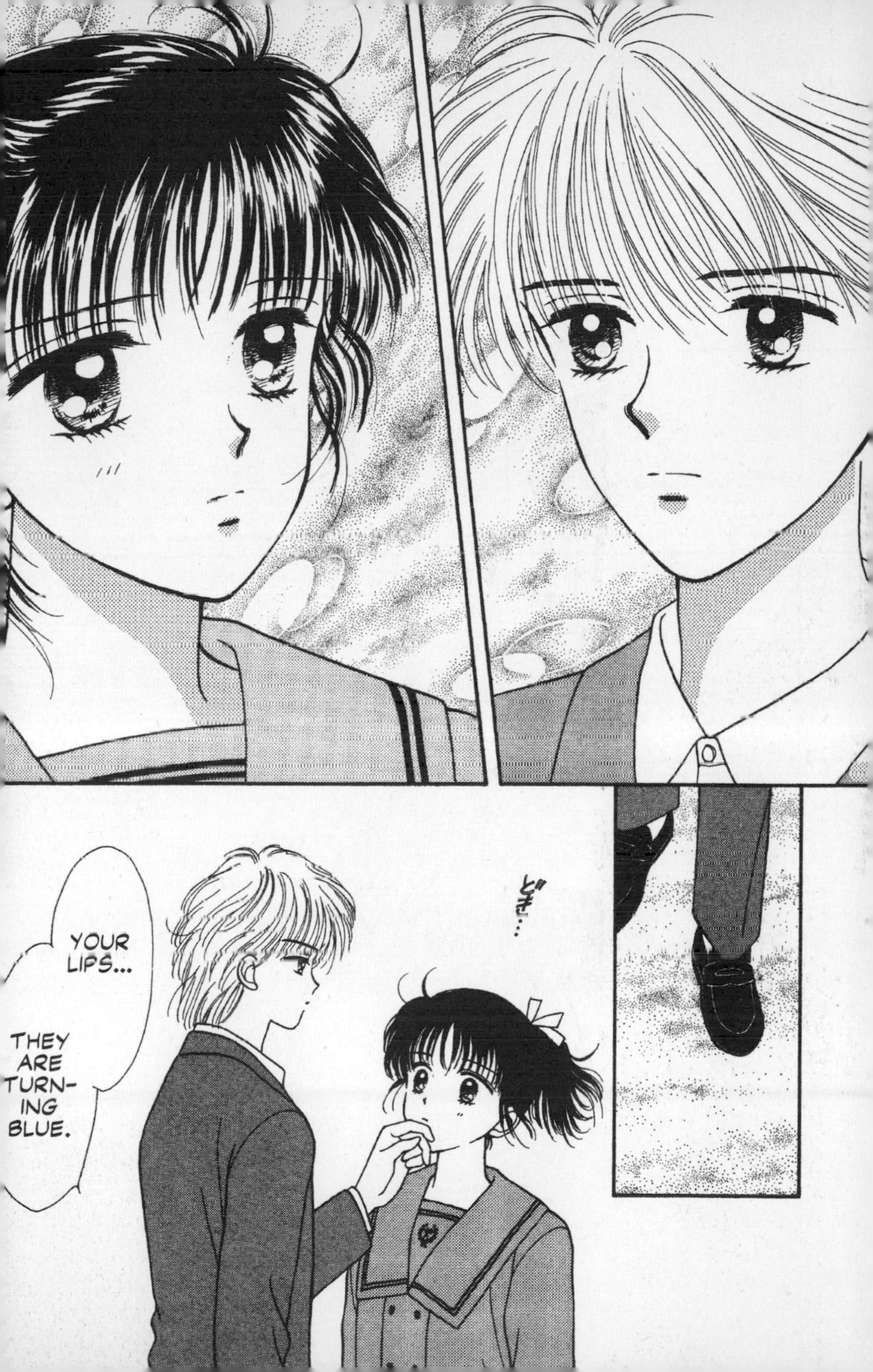
どき…
YOUR LIPS...
THEY ARE TURNING-ING BLUE.

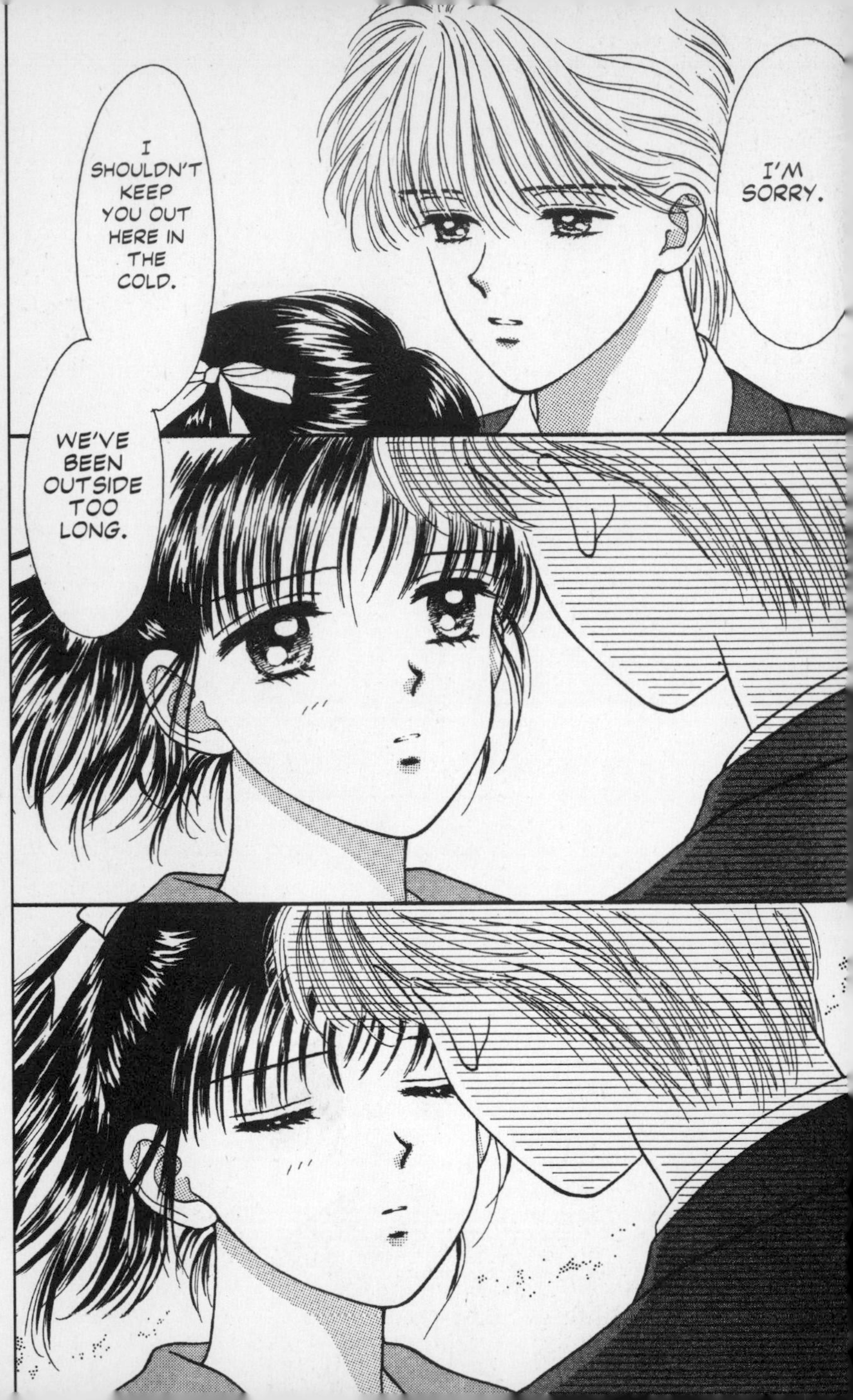
I'M SORRY.
I SHOULDN'T KEEP YOU OUT HERE IN THE COLD.
WE'VE BEEN OUTSIDE TOO LONG.

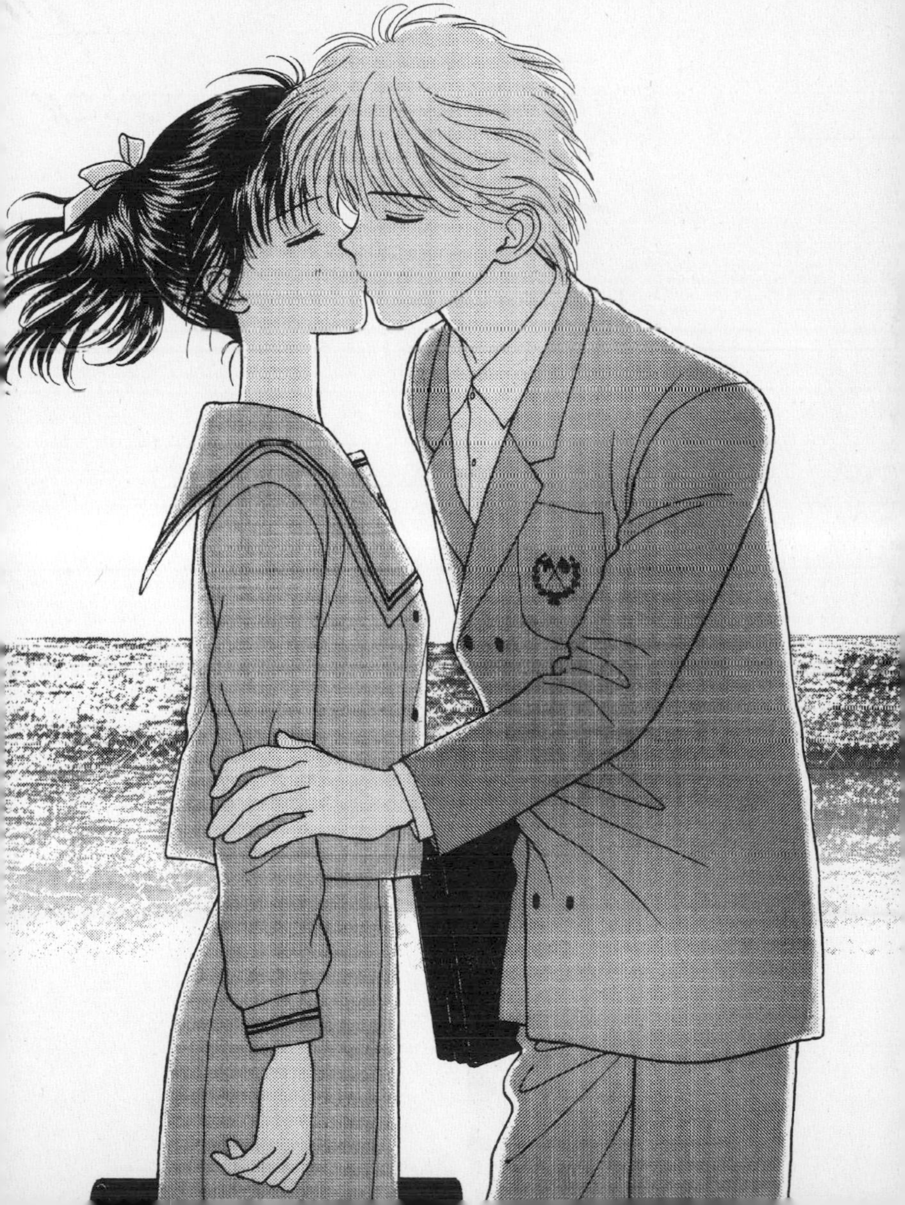

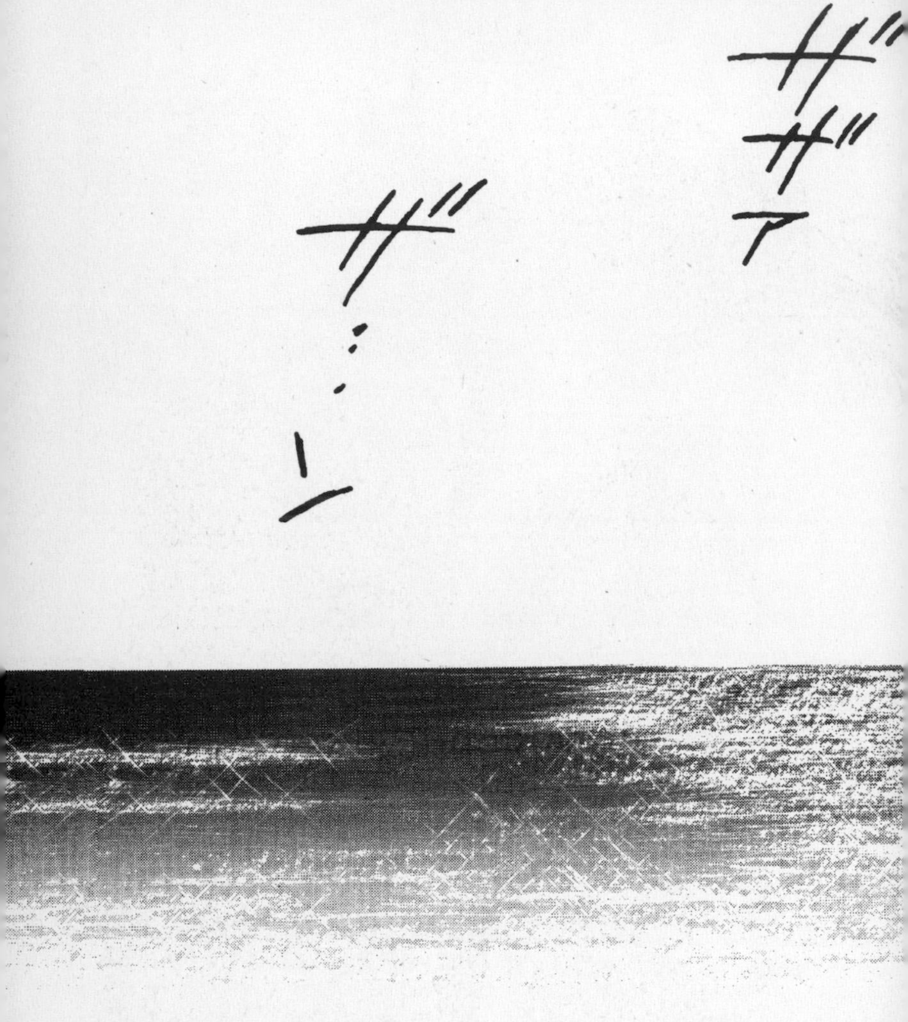
ザザァ
ザ…ー

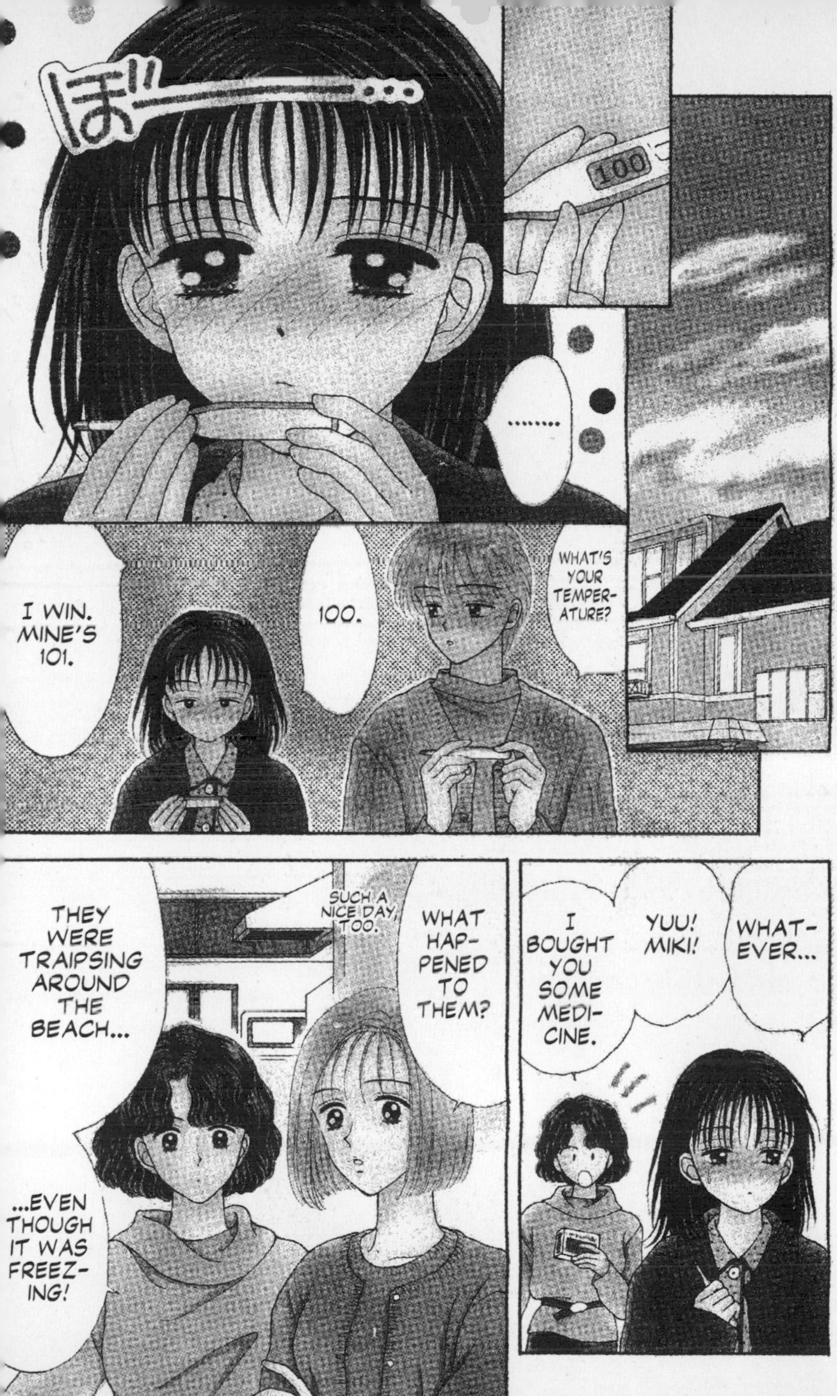
100
ぼー…
……
WHAT'S YOUR TEMPERATURE?
100.
I WIN. MINE'S 101.
WHAT-EVER...
YUU! MIKI!
I BOUGHT YOU SOME MEDICINE.
WHAT HAPPENED TO THEM?
SUCH A NICE DAY, TOO.
THEY WERE TRAIPSING AROUND THE BEACH...
...EVEN THOUGH IT WAS FREEZING!

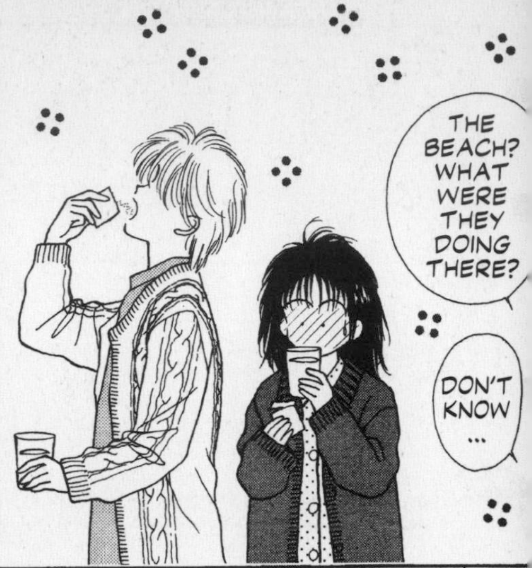
THE BEACH? WHAT WERE THEY DOING THERE?
DON'T KNOW ...
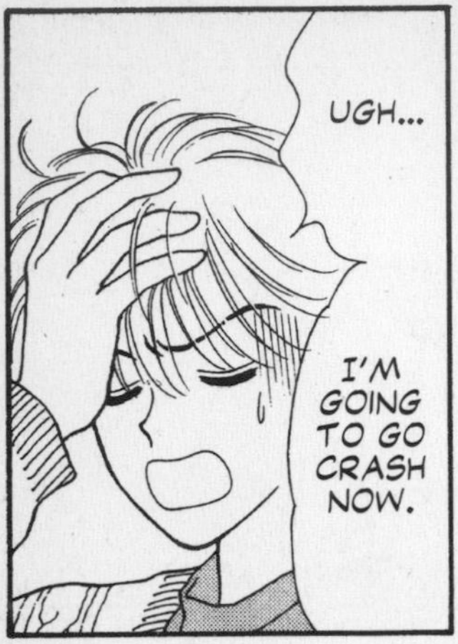
UGH...
I'M GOING TO GO CRASH NOW.
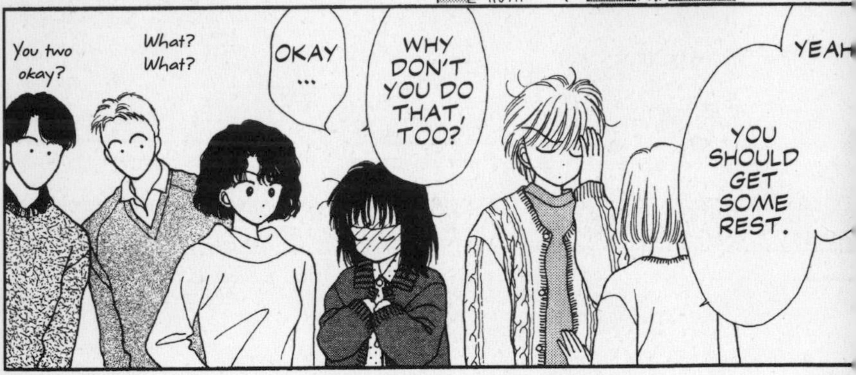
YEAH
YOU SHOULD GET SOME REST.
WHY DON'T YOU DO THAT, TOO?
OKAY ...
What? What?
You two okay?
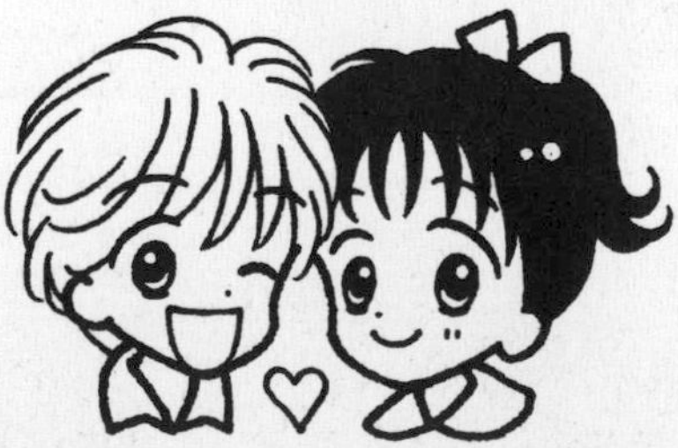

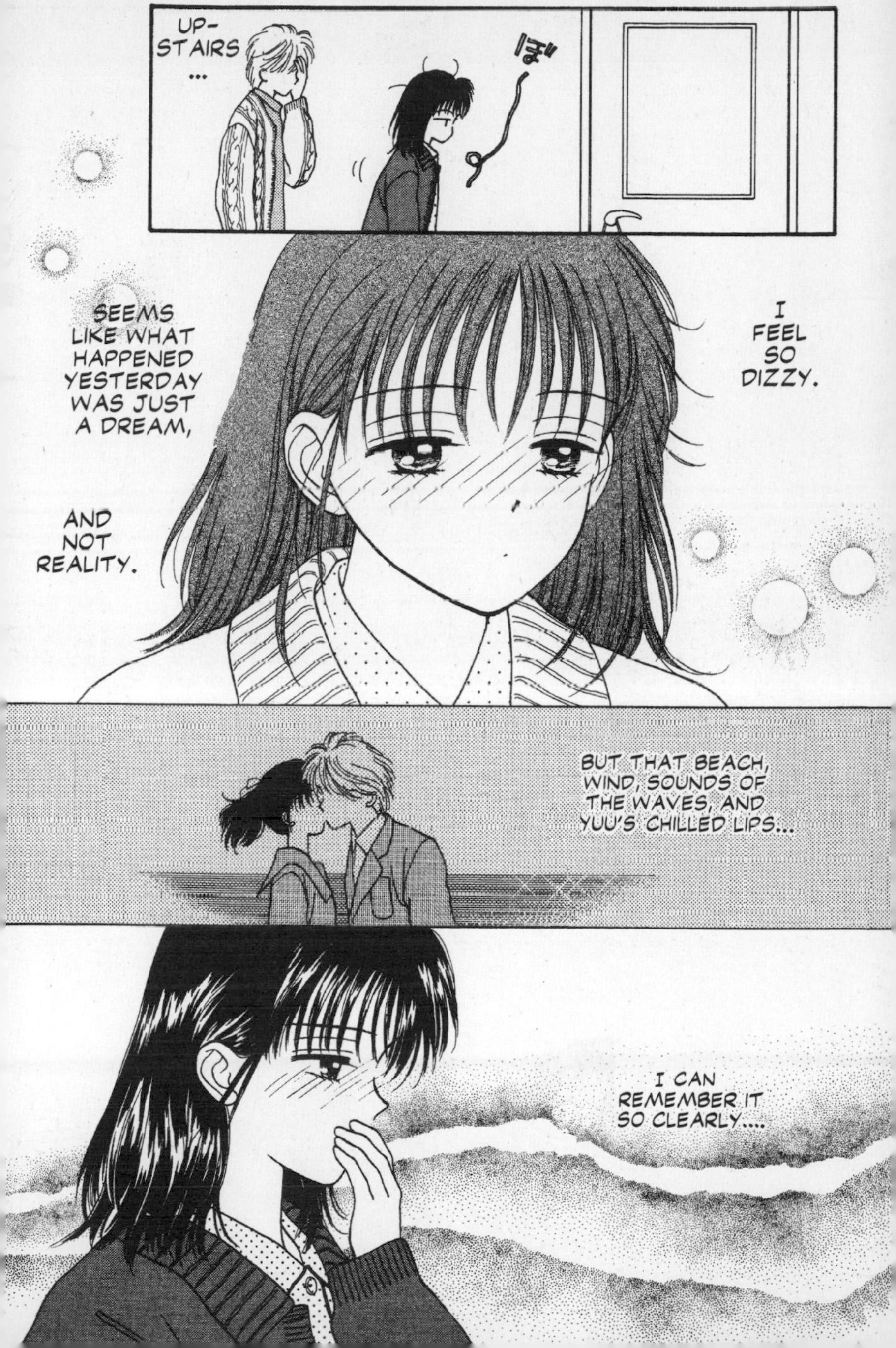
UP-STAIRS...
ぼ
I FEEL SO DIZZY.
SEEMS LIKE WHAT HAPPENED YESTERDAY WAS JUST A DREAM,
AND NOT REALITY.
BUT THAT BEACH, WIND, SOUNDS OF THE WAVES, AND YUU'S CHILLED LIPS...
I CAN REMEMBER IT SO CLEARLY....

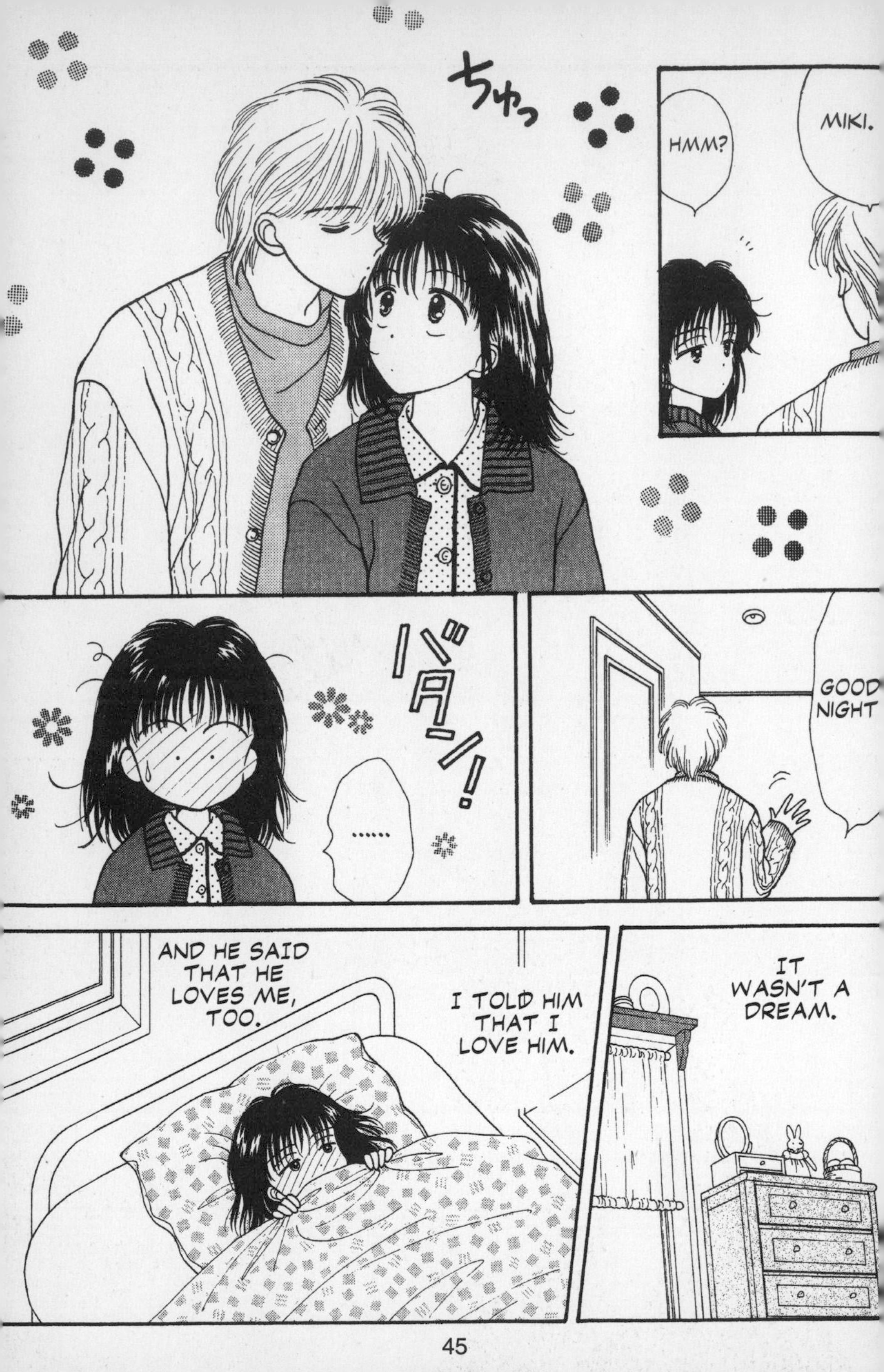
MIKI.
HMM?
ちゅっ
GOOD NIGHT
バタン!!
......
IT WASN'T A DREAM.
I TOLD HIM THAT I LOVE HIM.
AND HE SAID THAT HE LOVES ME, TOO.

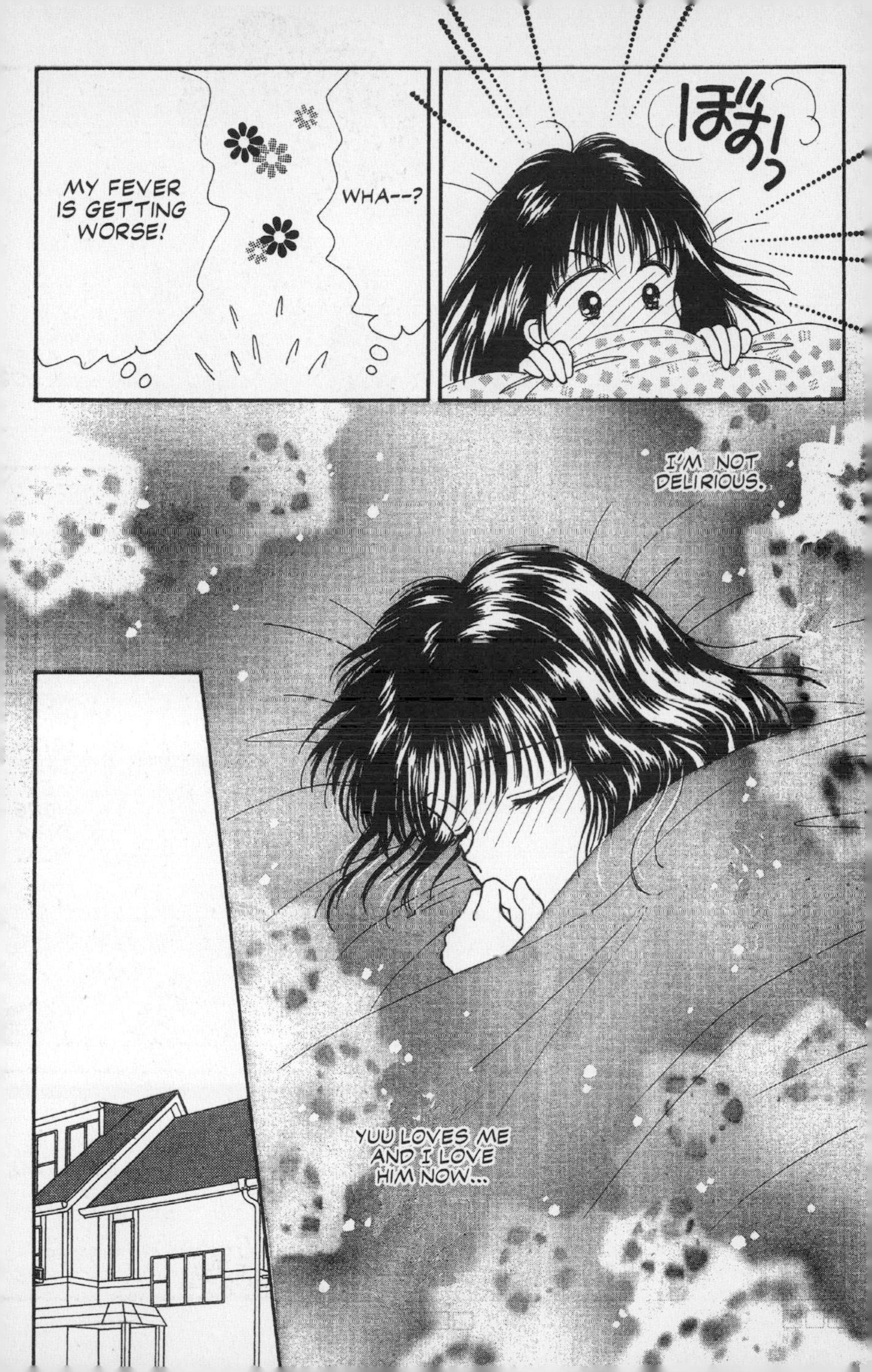
ぼおっ!
WHA--?
MY FEVER IS GETTING WORSE!
I'M NOT DELIRIOUS.
YUU LOVES ME AND I LOVE HIM NOW...

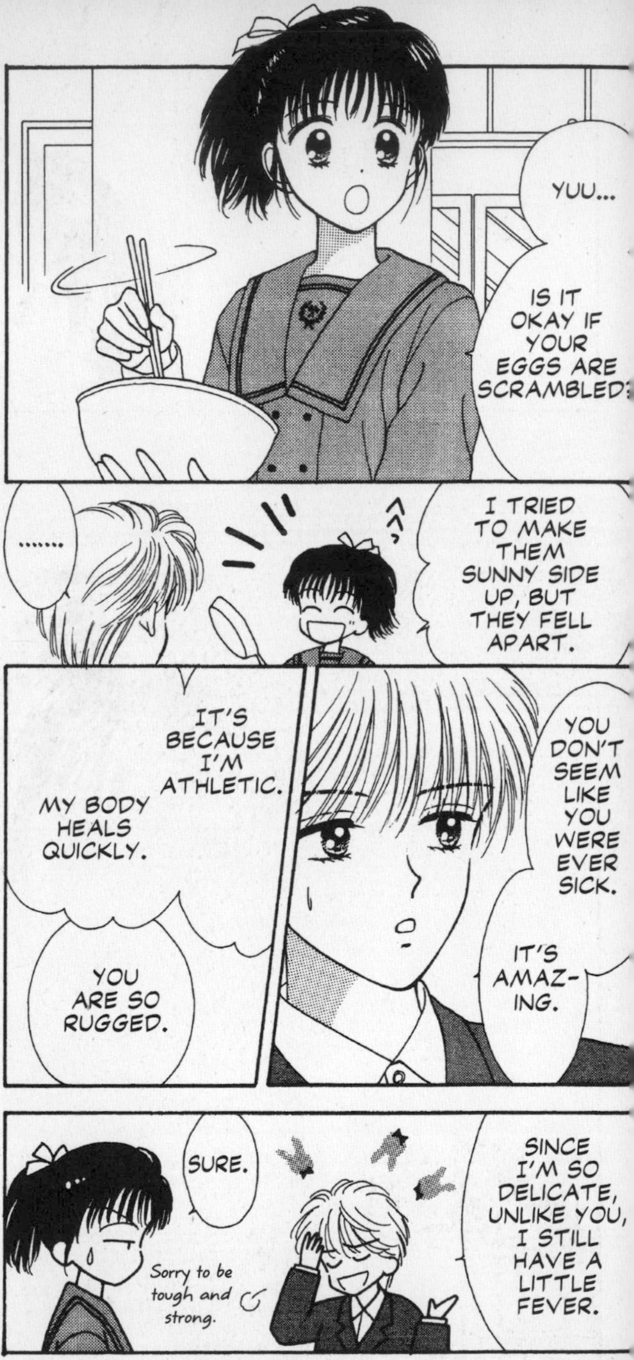
YUU...
IS IT OKAY IF YOUR EGGS ARE SCRAMBLED?
I TRIED TO MAKE THEM SUNNY SIDE UP, BUT THEY FELL APART.
....
YOU DON'T SEEM LIKE YOU WERE EVER SICK.
IT'S AMAZ-ING.
IT'S BECAUSE I'M ATHLETIC.
MY BODY HEALS QUICKLY.
YOU ARE SO RUGGED.
SINCE I'M SO DELICATE, UNLIKE YOU, I STILL HAVE A LITTLE FEVER.
SURE.
Sorry to be tough and strong.

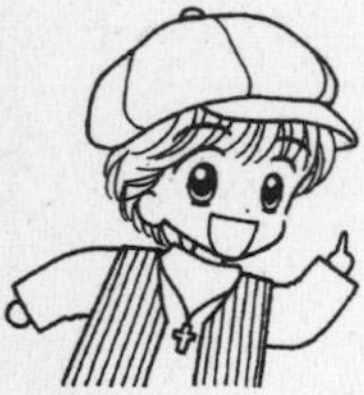

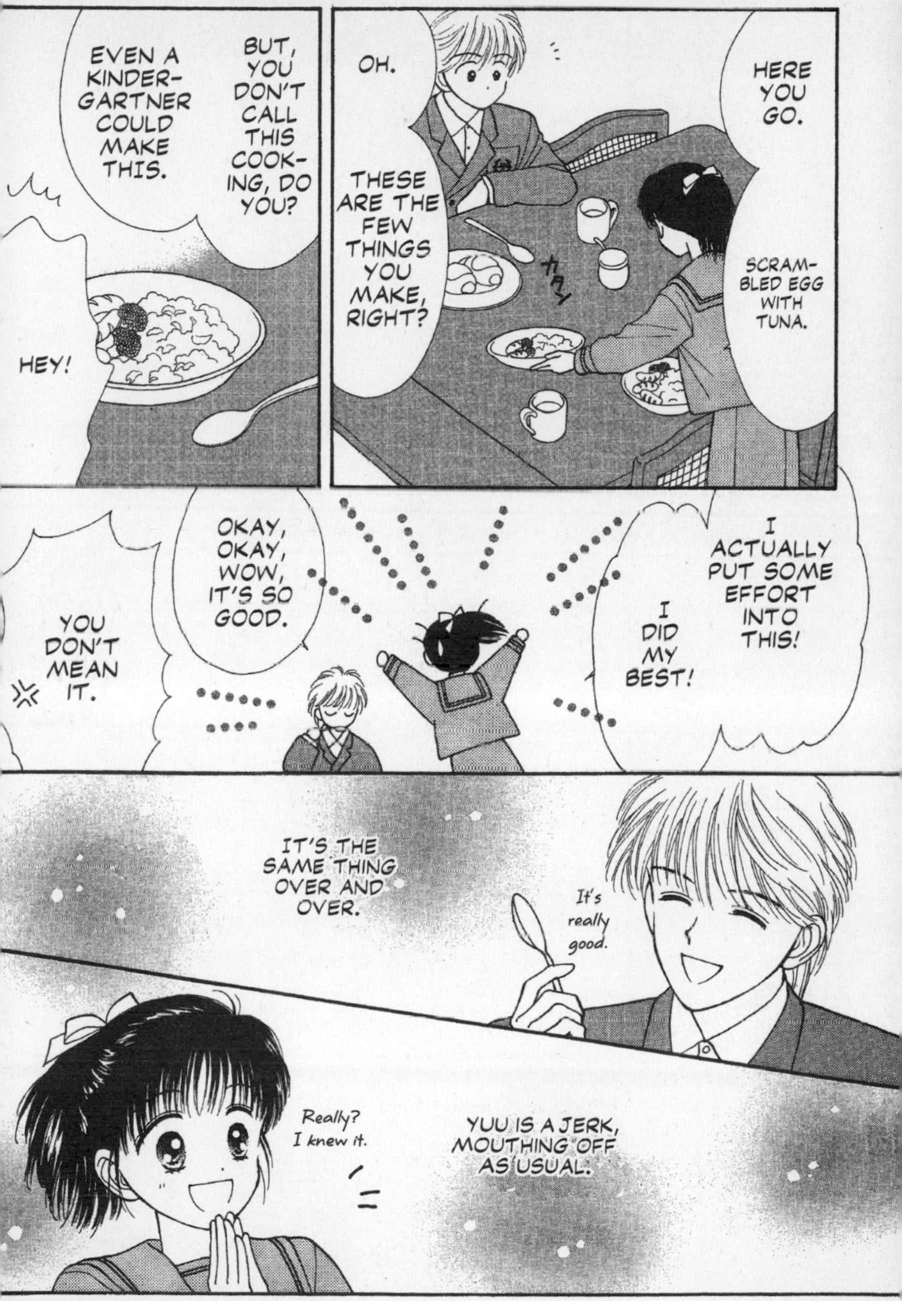
HERE YOU GO.
SCRAMBLED EGG WITH TUNA.
OH.
THESE ARE THE FEW THINGS YOU MAKE, RIGHT?
BUT, YOU DON'T CALL THIS COOKING, DO YOU?
EVEN A KINDERGARTNER COULD MAKE THIS.
HEY!
I ACTUALLY PUT SOME EFFORT INTO THIS!
I DID MY BEST!
OKAY, OKAY, WOW, IT'S SO GOOD.
YOU DON'T MEAN IT.
IT'S THE SAME THING OVER AND OVER.
It's really good.
Really? I knew it.
YUU IS A JERK, MOUTHING OFF AS USUAL.

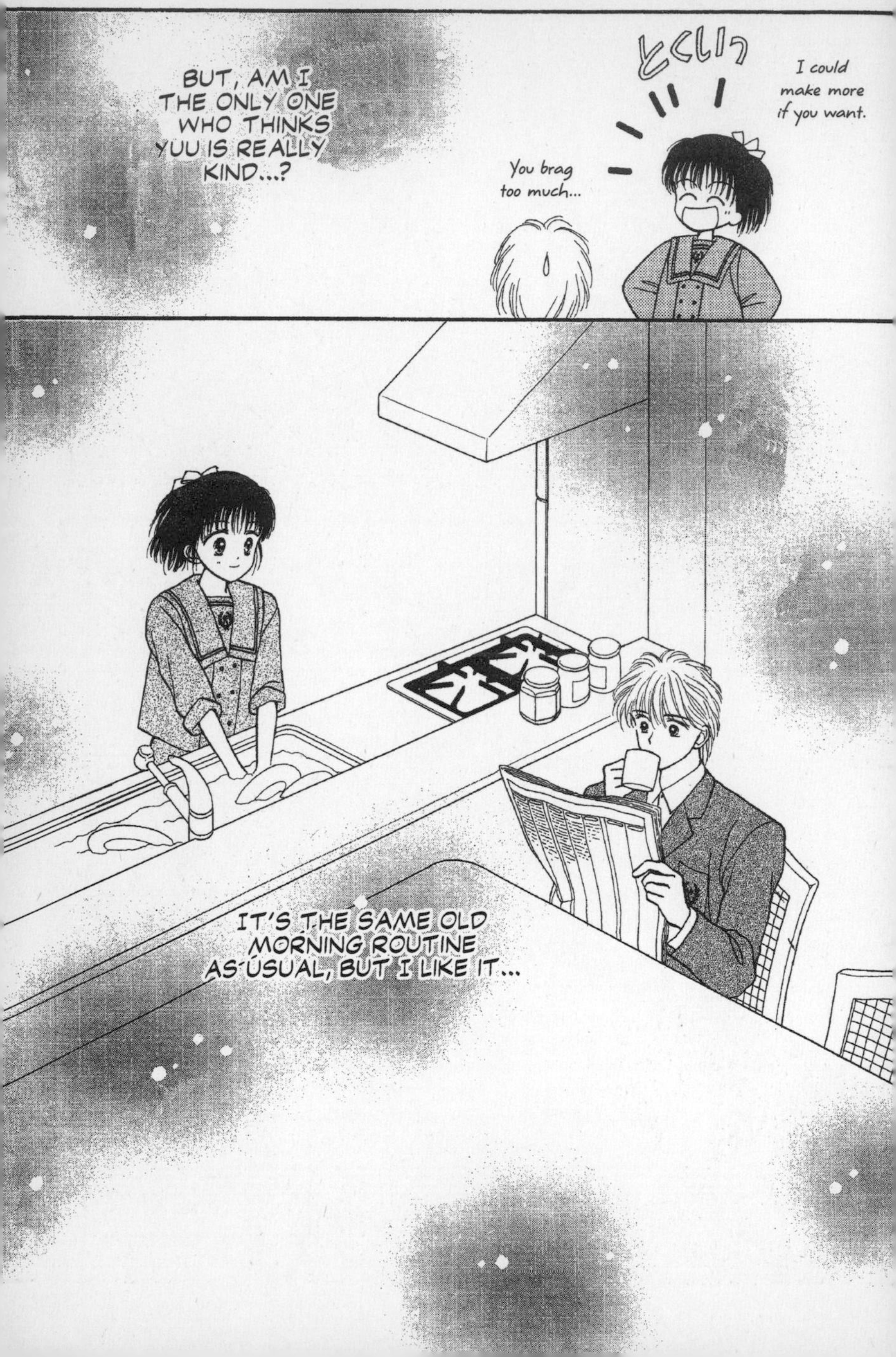
とくいっ
I could make more if you want.
You brag too much...
BUT, AM I THE ONLY ONE WHO THINKS YUU IS REALLY KIND...?
IT'S THE SAME OLD MORNING ROUTINE AS USUAL, BUT I LIKE IT...

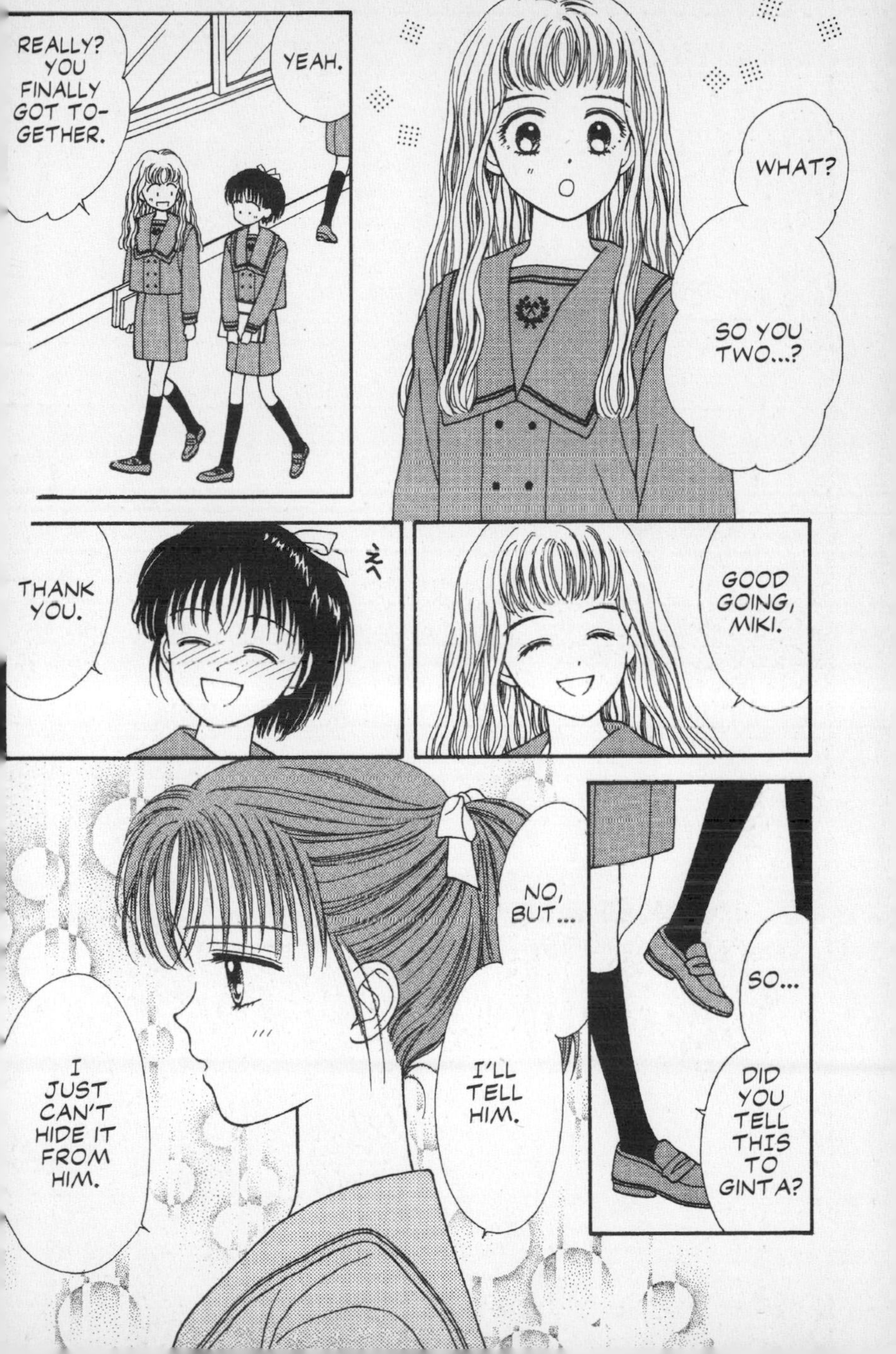
WHAT?
SO YOU TWO...?
REALLY? YOU FINALLY GOT TO-GETHER.
YEAH.
GOOD GOING, MIKI.
THANK YOU.
SO...
DID YOU TELL THIS TO GINTA?
NO, BUT...
I'LL TELL HIM.
I JUST CAN'T HIDE IT FROM HIM.

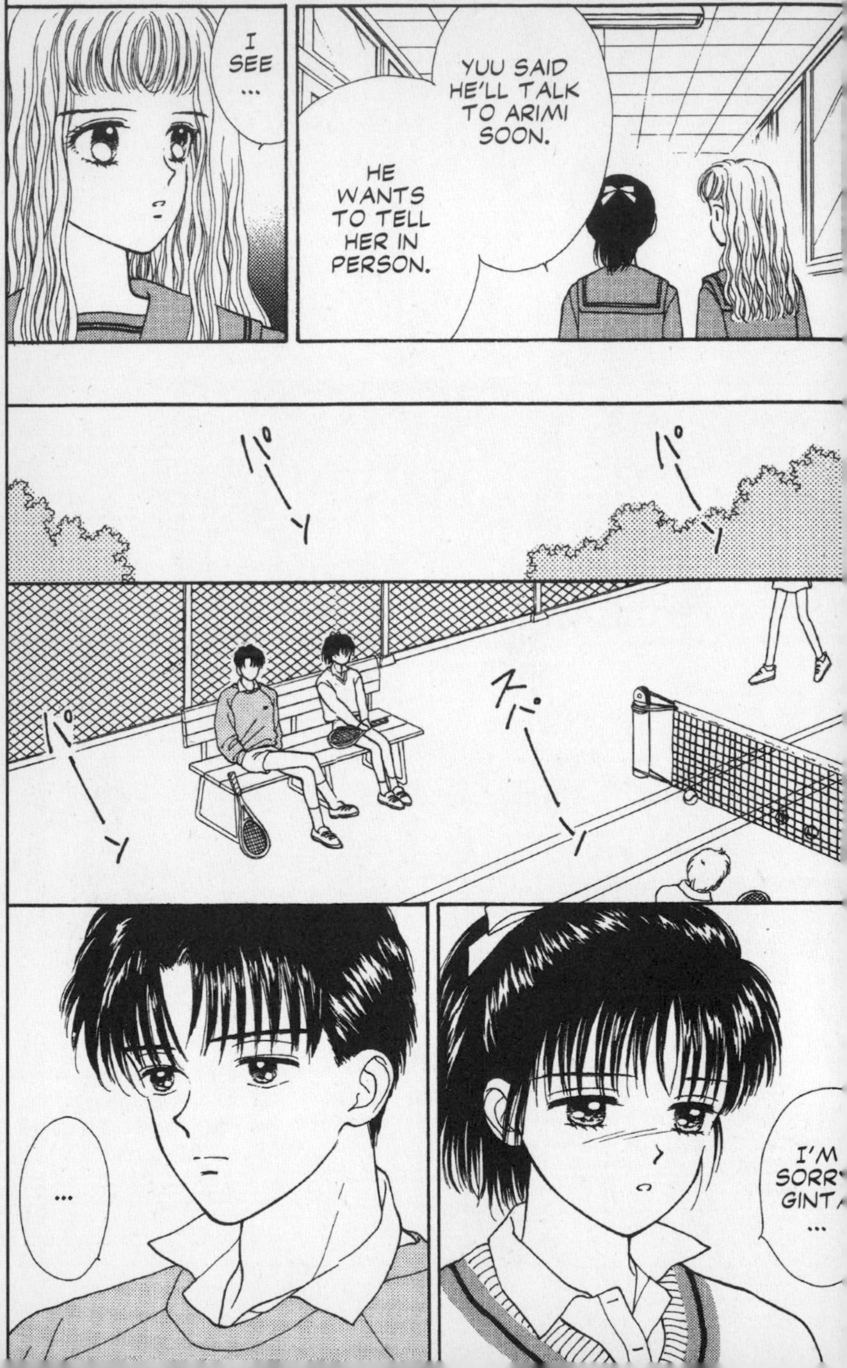
YUU SAID HE'LL TALK TO ARIMI SOON.
HE WANTS TO TELL HER IN PERSON.
I SEE ...
パーン
パーン
スパーン
パーン
I'M SORR GINT ...
...

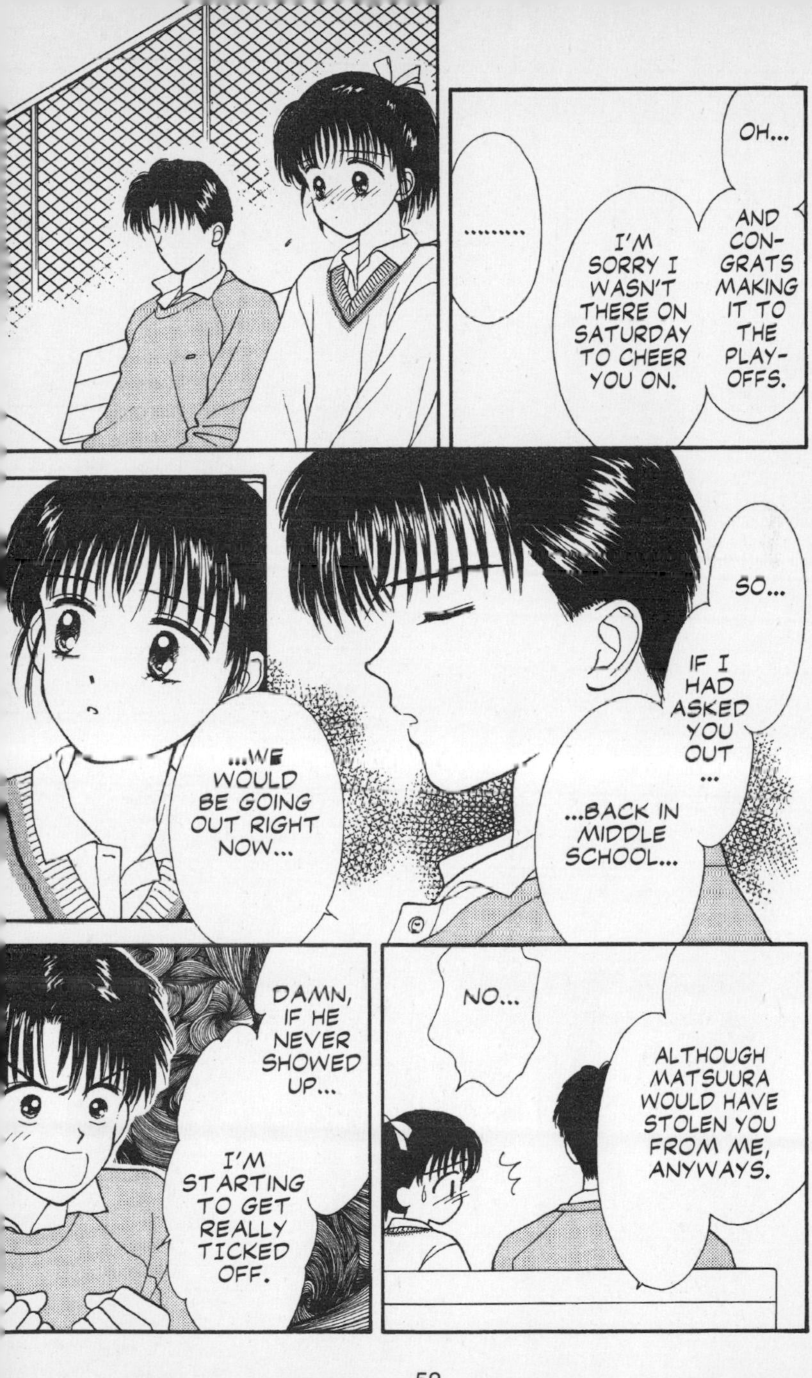
OH...
AND CON-GRATS MAKING IT TO THE PLAY-OFFS.
I'M SORRY I WASN'T THERE ON SATURDAY TO CHEER YOU ON.
....
SO...
IF I HAD ASKED YOU OUT ...
...BACK IN MIDDLE SCHOOL...
...WE WOULD BE GOING OUT RIGHT NOW...
NO...
ALTHOUGH MATSUURA WOULD HAVE STOLEN YOU FROM ME, ANYWAYS.
DAMN, IF HE NEVER SHOWED UP...
I'M STARTING TO GET REALLY TICKED OFF.

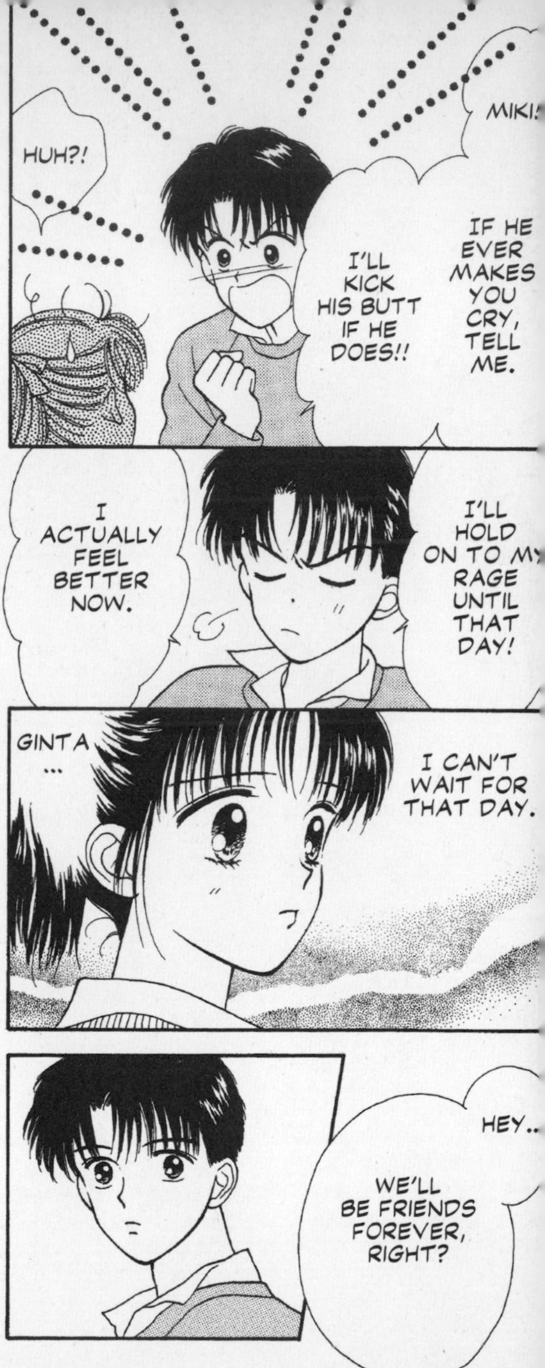
MIKI!
IF HE EVER MAKES YOU CRY, TELL ME.
I'LL KICK HIS BUTT IF HE DOES!!
HUH?!
I'LL HOLD ON TO MY RAGE UNTIL THAT DAY!
I ACTUALLY FEEL BETTER NOW.
I CAN'T WAIT FOR THAT DAY.
GINTA ...
HEY...
WE'LL BE FRIENDS FOREVER, RIGHT?

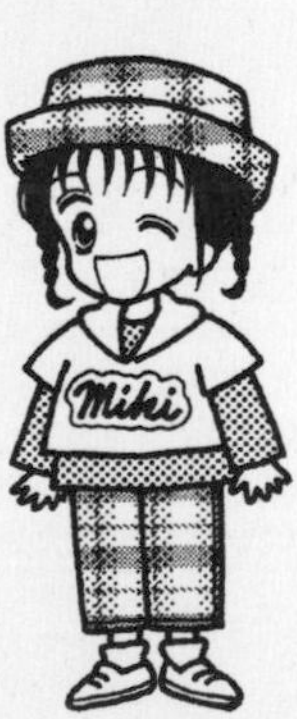
Miki

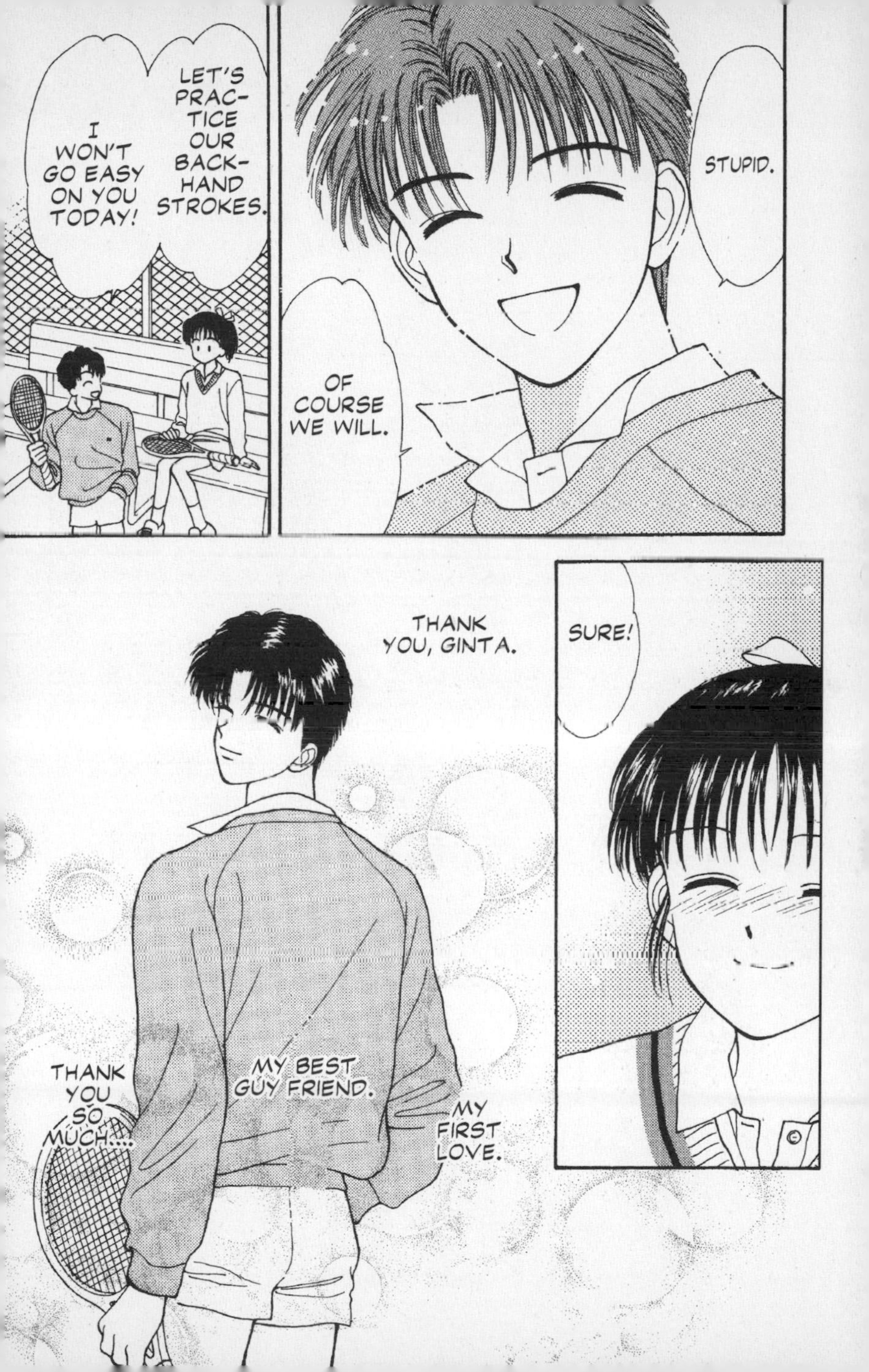
STUPID.
OF COURSE WE WILL.
LET'S PRACTICE OUR BACKHAND STROKES.
I WON'T GO EASY ON YOU TODAY!
SURE!
THANK YOU, GINTA.
MY FIRST LOVE.
MY BEST GUY FRIEND.
THANK YOU SO MUCH...

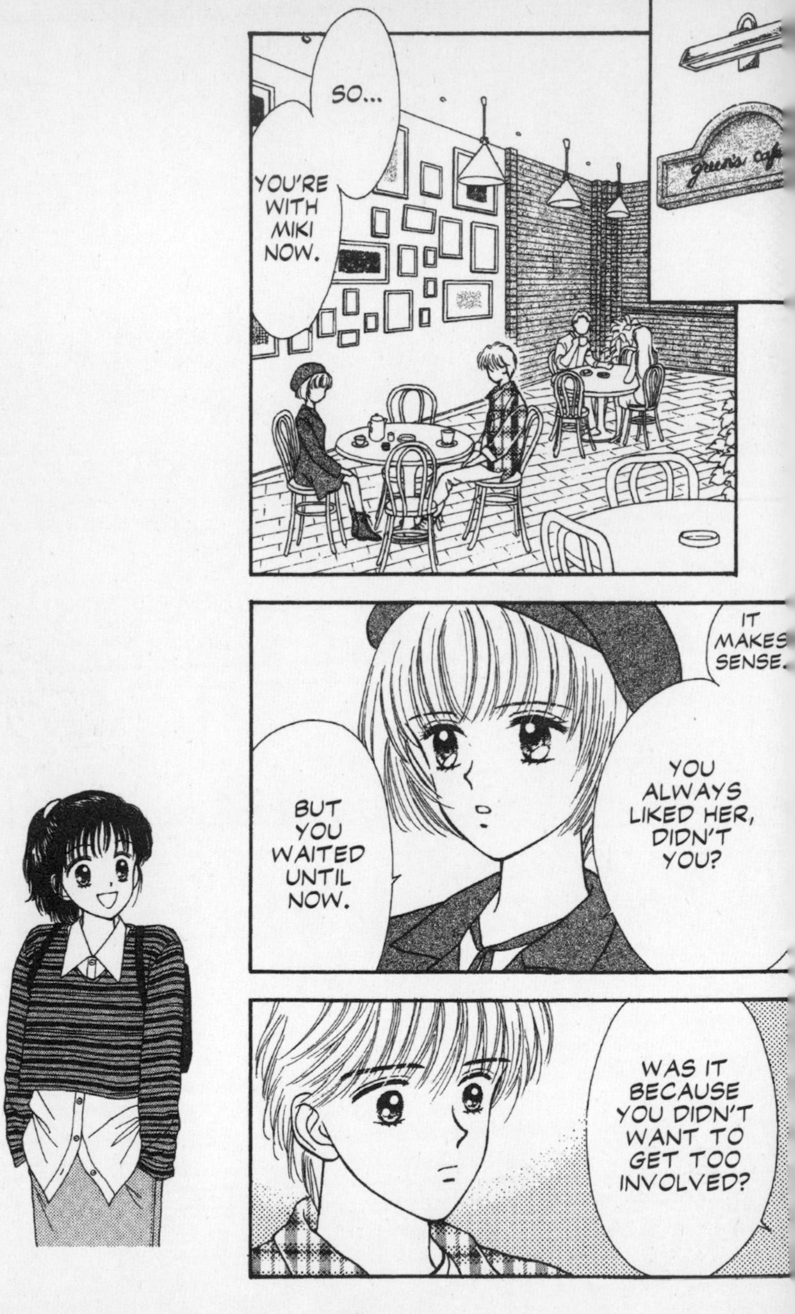
SO...
YOU'RE WITH MIKI NOW.
IT MAKES SENSE.
YOU ALWAYS LIKED HER, DIDN'T YOU?
BUT YOU WAITED UNTIL NOW.
WAS IT BECAUSE YOU DIDN'T WANT TO GET TOO INVOLVED?

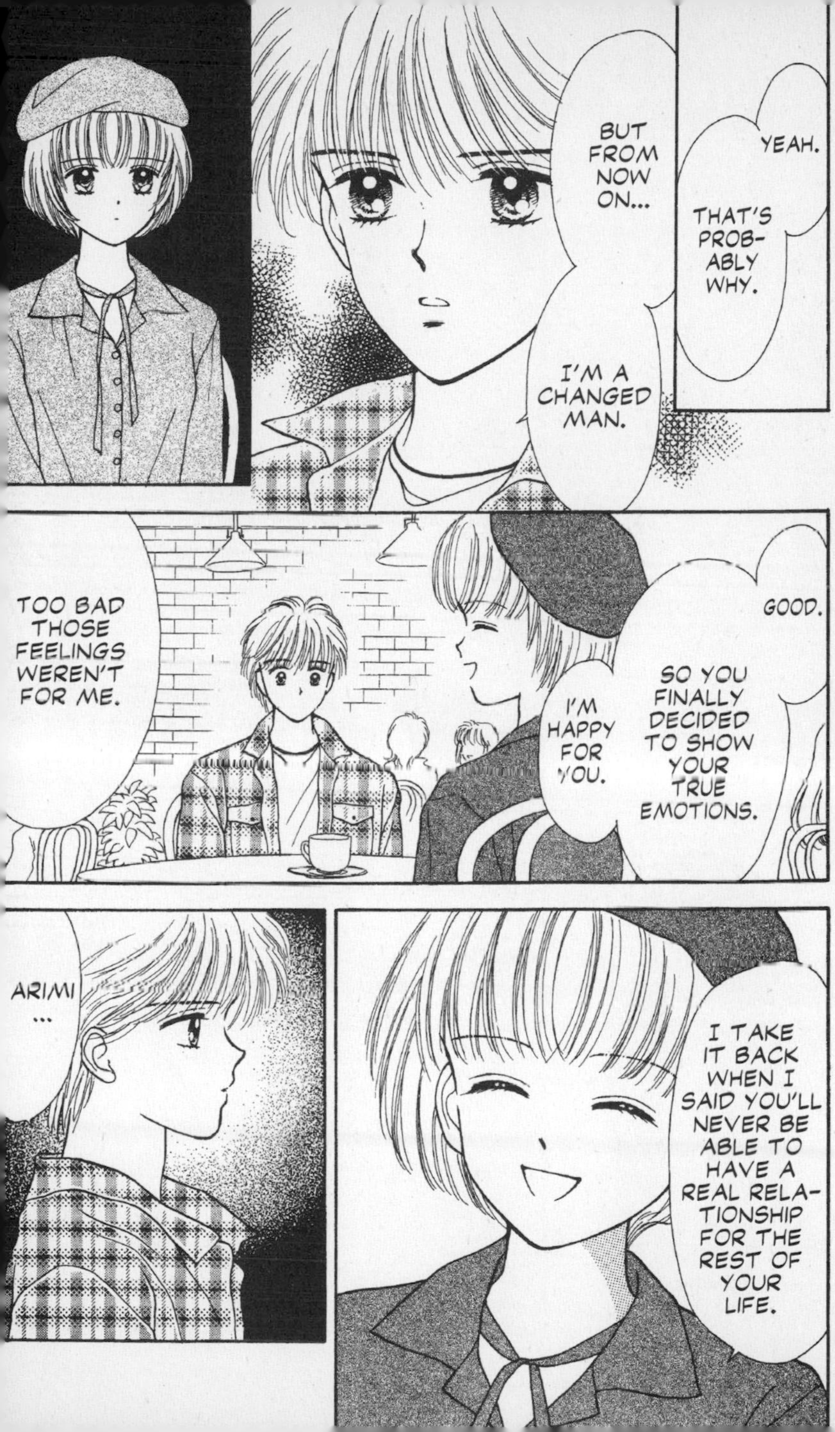
YEAH. THAT'S PROBABLY WHY.
BUT FROM NOW ON...
I'M A CHANGED MAN.
GOOD.
SO YOU FINALLY DECIDED TO SHOW YOUR TRUE EMOTIONS.
I'M HAPPY FOR YOU.
TOO BAD THOSE FEELINGS WEREN'T FOR ME.
I TAKE IT BACK WHEN I SAID YOU'LL NEVER BE ABLE TO HAVE A REAL RELATIONSHIP FOR THE REST OF YOUR LIFE.
ARIMI...

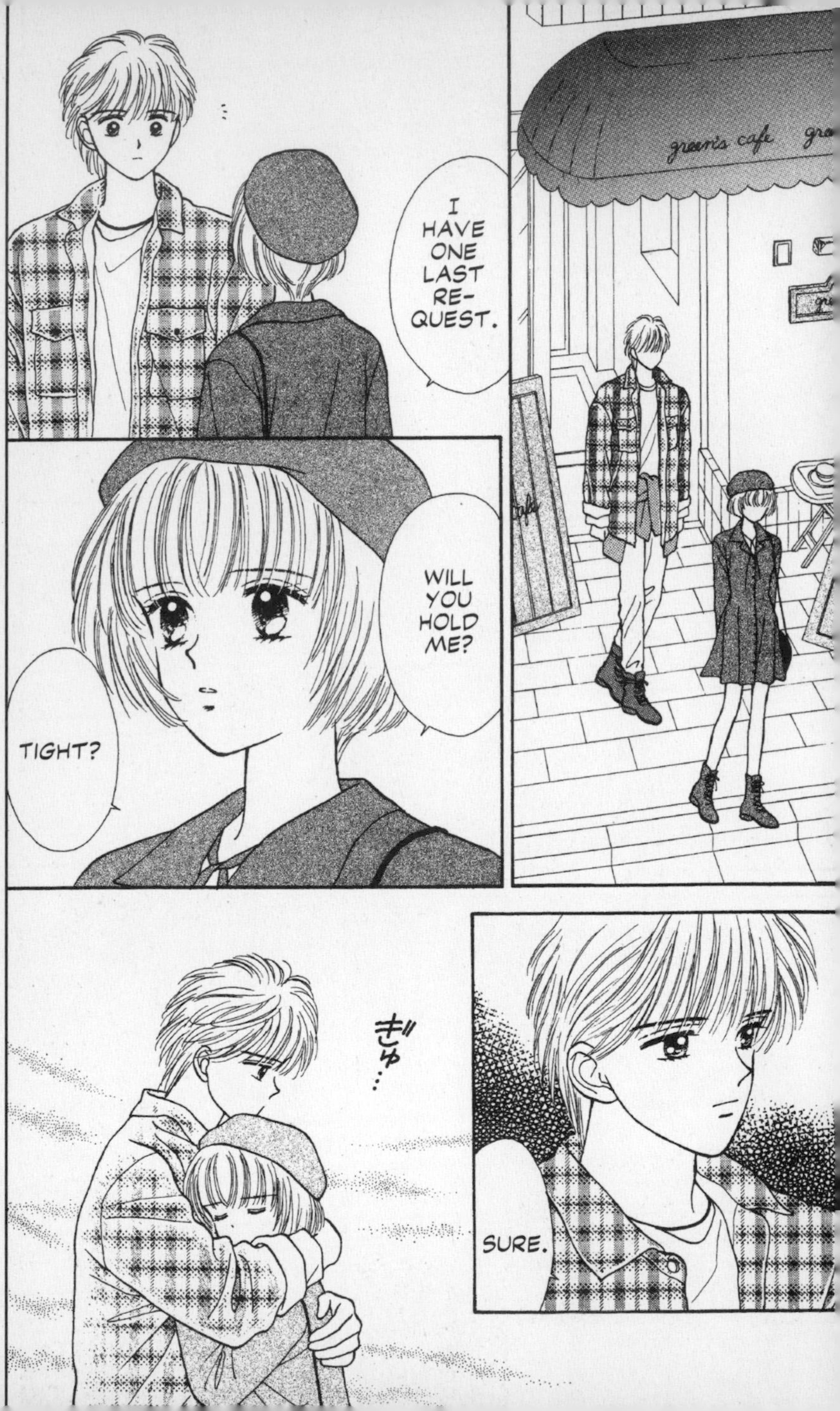
green's cafe
I HAVE ONE LAST RE-QUEST.
WILL YOU HOLD ME?
TIGHT?
SURE.
ぎゅ…

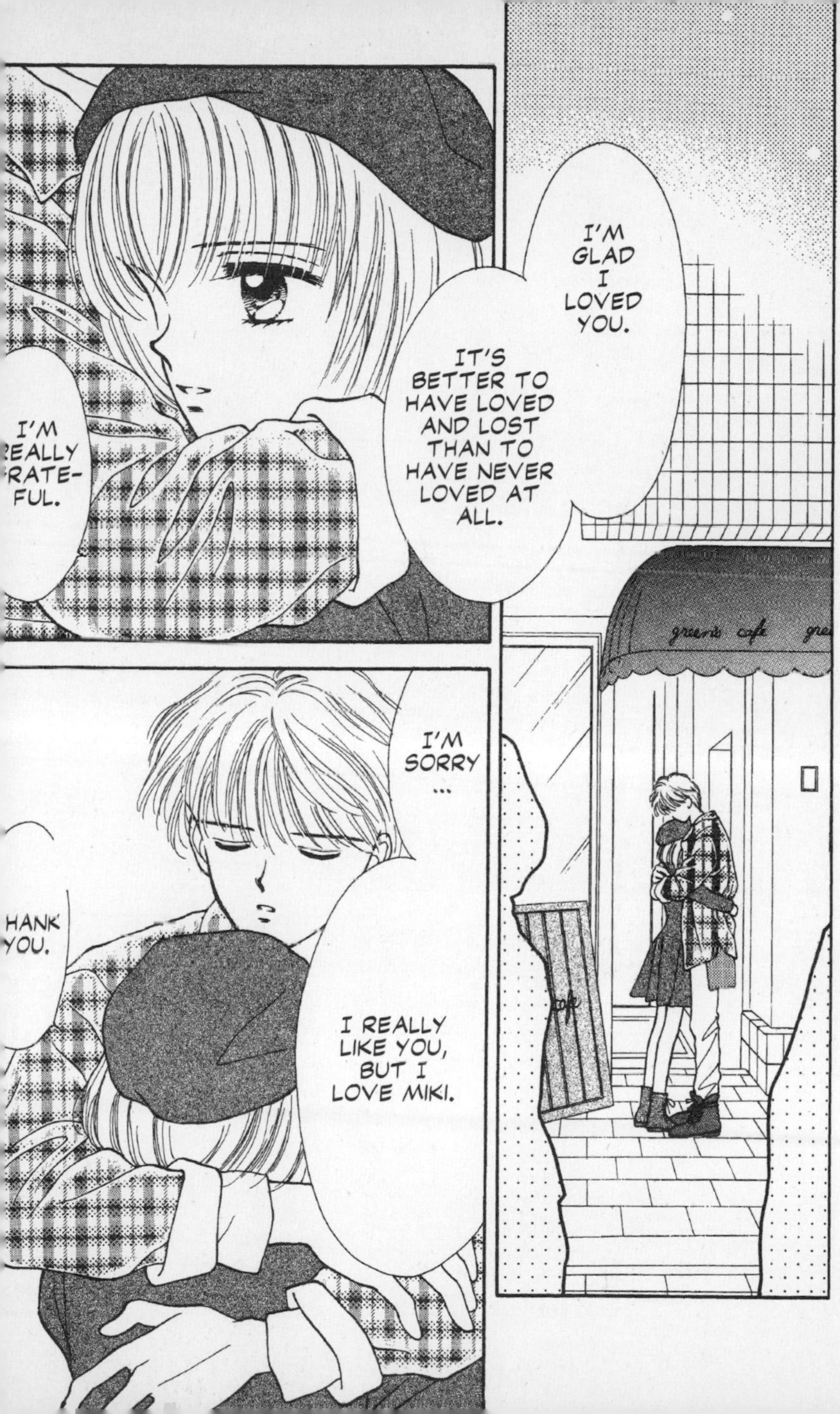
I'M GLAD I LOVED YOU.
IT'S BETTER TO HAVE LOVED AND LOST THAN TO HAVE NEVER LOVED AT ALL.
green's cafe
I'M EALLY RATE-FUL.
I'M SORRY ...
I REALLY LIKE YOU, BUT I LOVE MIKI.
HANK YOU.

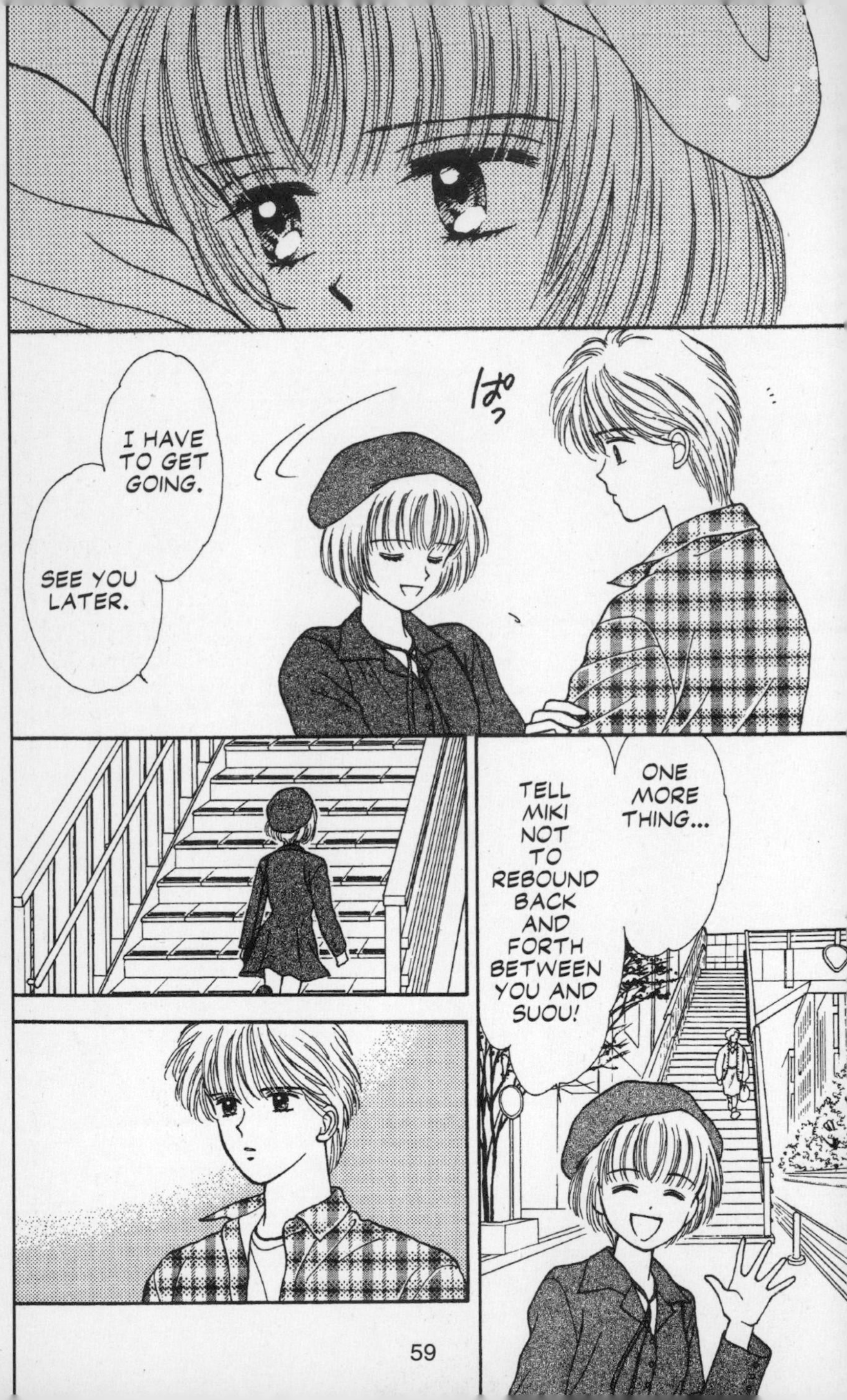
ぱっ
I HAVE TO GET GOING.
SEE YOU LATER.
ONE MORE THING...
TELL MIKI NOT TO REBOUND BACK AND FORTH BETWEEN YOU AND SUOU!

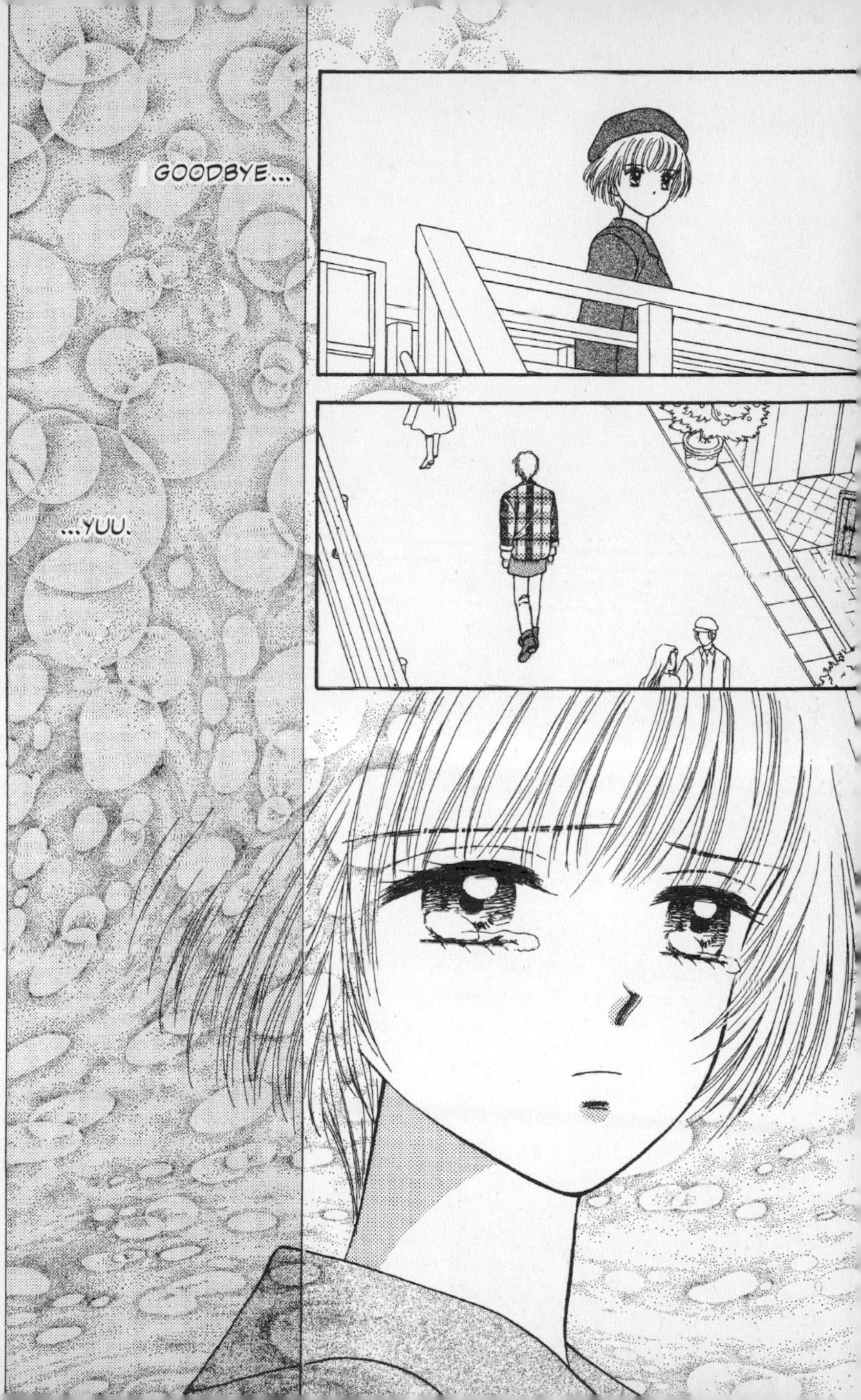
GOODBYE...
...YUU.

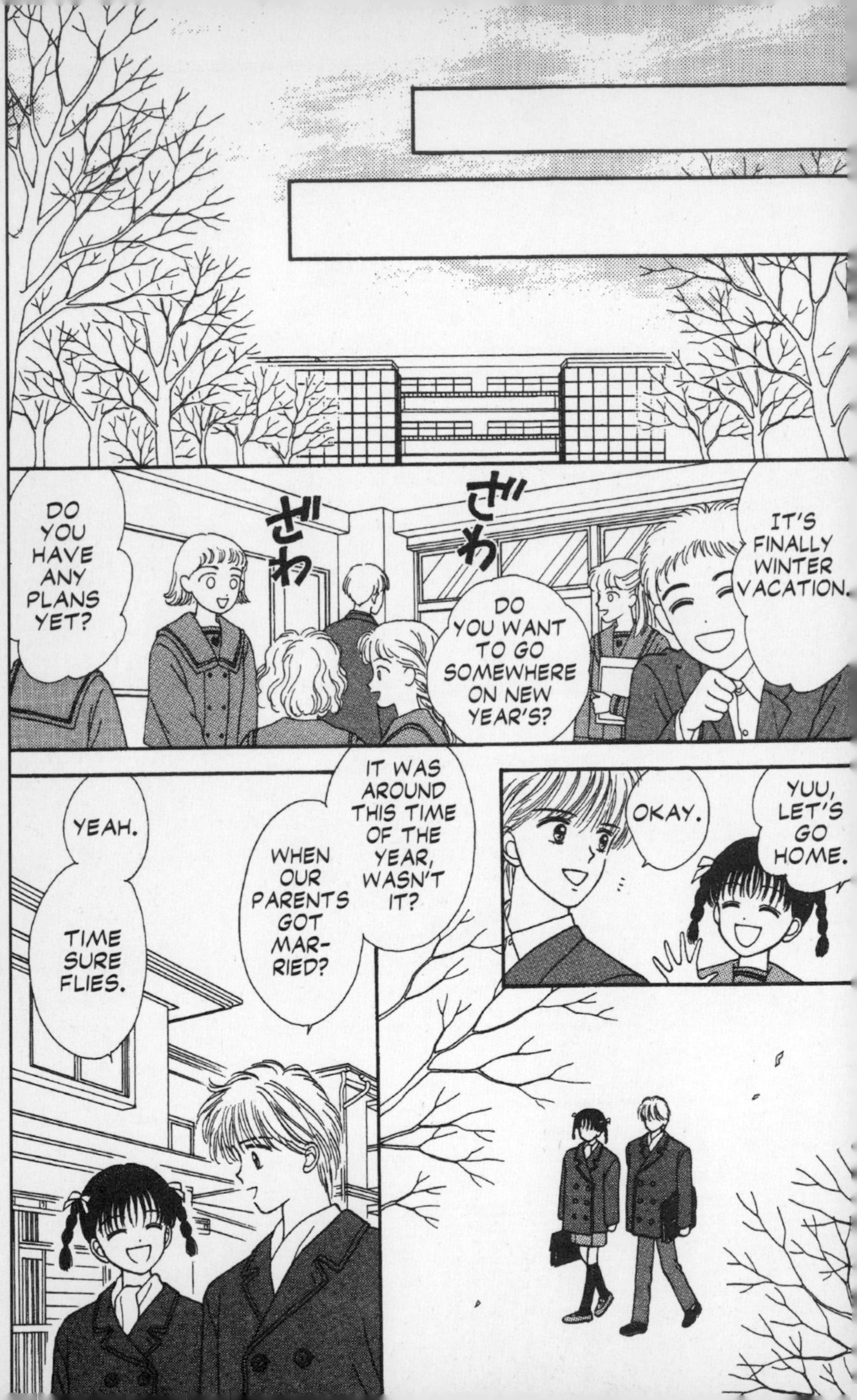
IT'S FINALLY WINTER VACATION.
DO YOU WANT TO GO SOMEWHERE ON NEW YEAR'S?
ざわ
ざわ
DO YOU HAVE ANY PLANS YET?
YUU, LET'S GO HOME.
OKAY.
IT WAS AROUND THIS TIME OF THE YEAR, WASN'T IT?
WHEN OUR PARENTS GOT MAR-RIED?
YEAH.
TIME SURE FLIES.

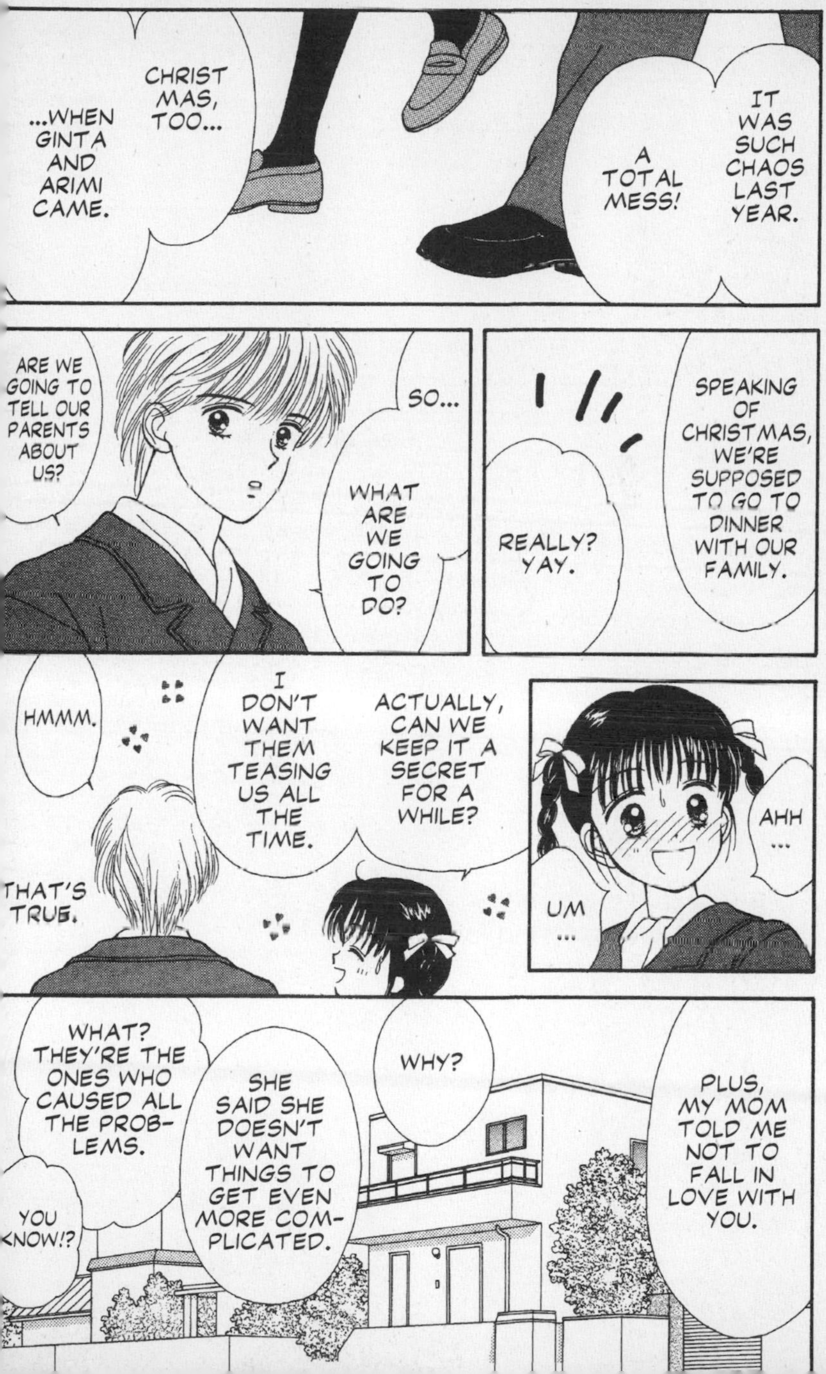
IT WAS SUCH CHAOS LAST YEAR.
A TOTAL MESS!
CHRISTMAS, TOO...
...WHEN GINTA AND ARIMI CAME.
SPEAKING OF CHRISTMAS, WE'RE SUPPOSED TO GO TO DINNER WITH OUR FAMILY.
REALLY? YAY.
SO...
WHAT ARE WE GOING TO DO?
ARE WE GOING TO TELL OUR PARENTS ABOUT US?
AHH ...
UM ...
ACTUALLY, CAN WE KEEP IT A SECRET FOR A WHILE?
I DON'T WANT THEM TEASING US ALL THE TIME.
HMMM.
THAT'S TRUE.
PLUS, MY MOM TOLD ME NOT TO FALL IN LOVE WITH YOU.
WHY?
SHE SAID SHE DOESN'T WANT THINGS TO GET EVEN MORE COMPLICATED.
WHAT? THEY'RE THE ONES WHO CAUSED ALL THE PROBLEMS.
YOU KNOW!?

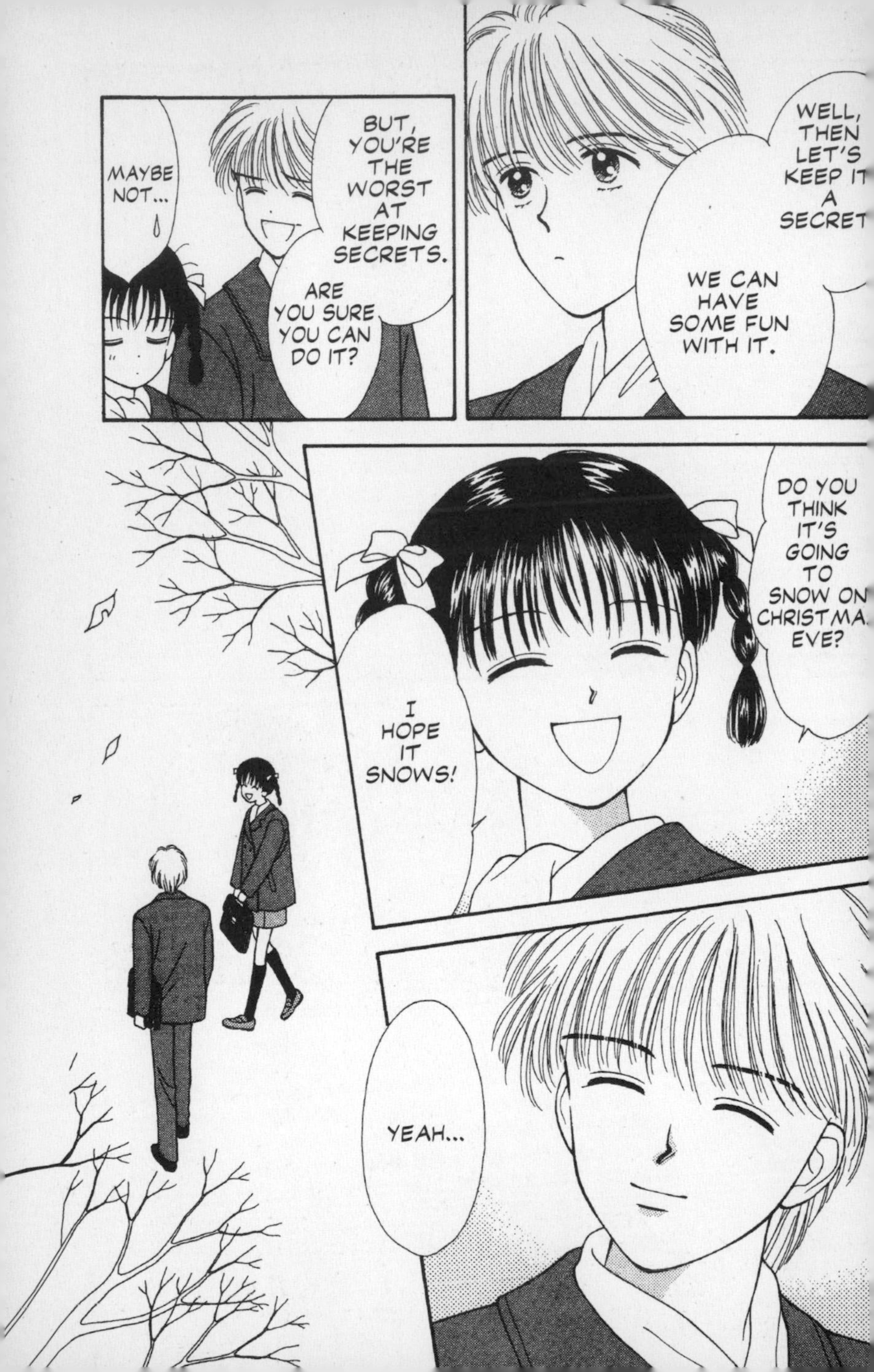
WELL, THEN LET'S KEEP IT A SECRET
WE CAN HAVE SOME FUN WITH IT.
BUT, YOU'RE THE WORST AT KEEPING SECRETS.
ARE YOU SURE YOU CAN DO IT?
MAYBE NOT...
DO YOU THINK IT'S GOING TO SNOW ON CHRISTMA EVE?
I HOPE IT SNOWS!
YEAH...

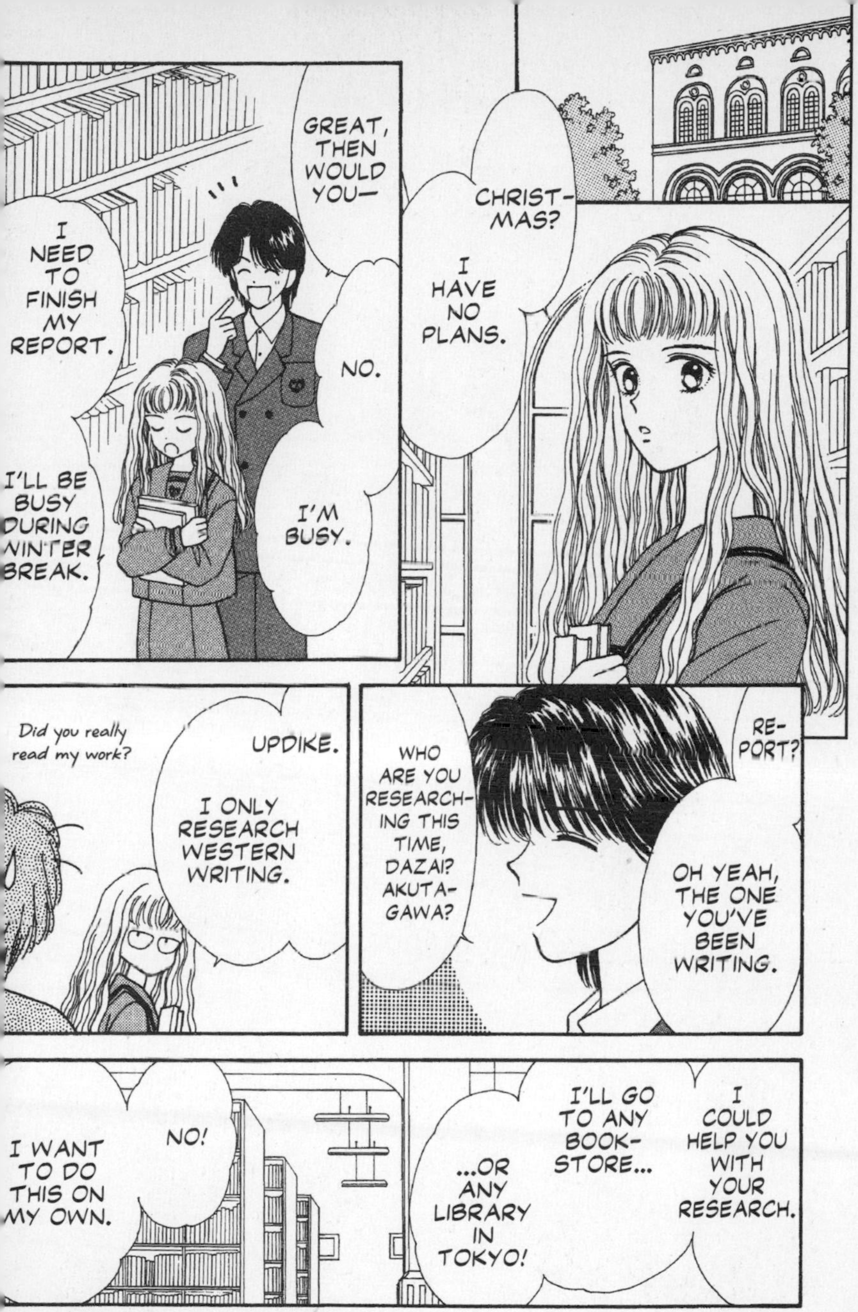
CHRIST-MAS?
I HAVE NO PLANS.
GREAT, THEN WOULD YOU—
NO.
I'M BUSY.
I NEED TO FINISH MY REPORT.
I'LL BE BUSY DURING WINTER BREAK.
RE-PORT?
OH YEAH, THE ONE YOU'VE BEEN WRITING.
WHO ARE YOU RESEARCHING THIS TIME, DAZAI? AKUTA-GAWA?
UPDIKE.
I ONLY RESEARCH WESTERN WRITING.
Did you really read my work?
I COULD HELP YOU WITH YOUR RESEARCH.
I'LL GO TO ANY BOOK-STORE...
...OR ANY LIBRARY IN TOKYO!
NO!
I WANT TO DO THIS ON MY OWN.

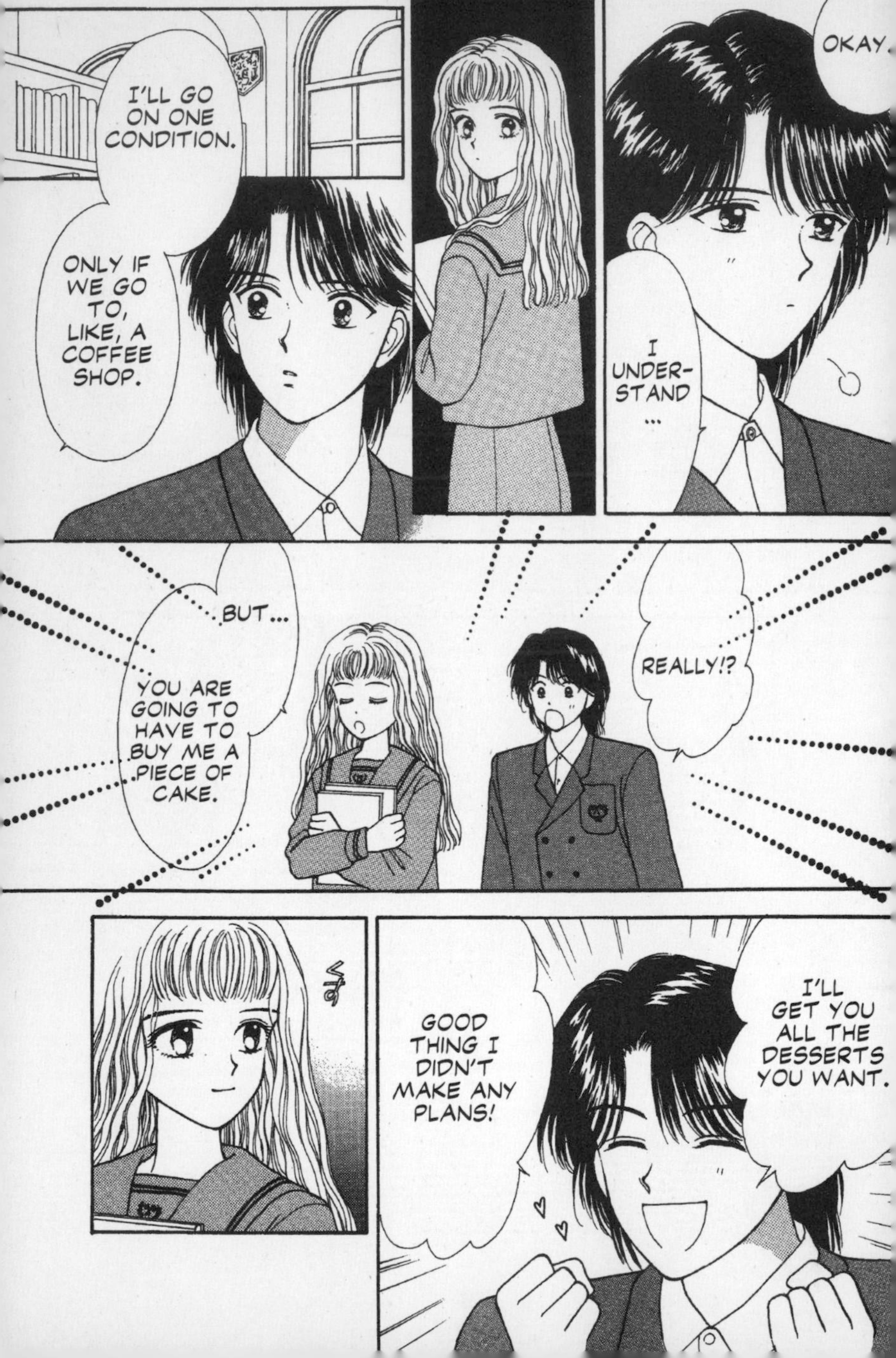
OKAY.
I UNDERSTAND ...
I'LL GO ON ONE CONDITION.
ONLY IF WE GO TO, LIKE, A COFFEE SHOP.
BUT...
YOU ARE GOING TO HAVE TO BUY ME A PIECE OF CAKE.
REALLY!?
I'LL GET YOU ALL THE DESSERTS YOU WANT.
GOOD THING I DIDN'T MAKE ANY PLANS!
くす

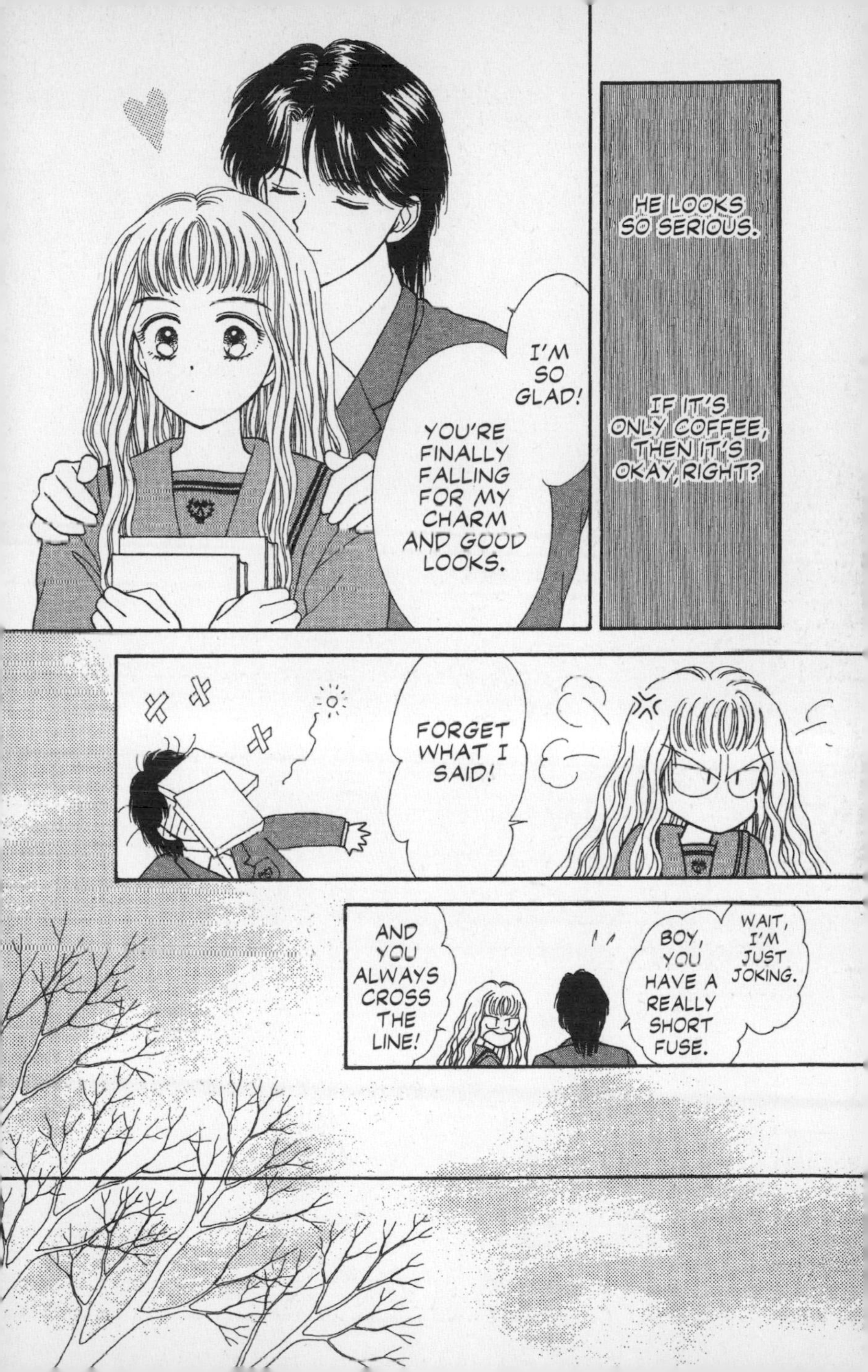
HE LOOKS SO SERIOUS.
IF IT'S ONLY COFFEE, THEN IT'S OKAY, RIGHT?
I'M SO GLAD!
YOU'RE FINALLY FALLING FOR MY CHARM AND GOOD LOOKS.
FORGET WHAT I SAID!
WAIT, I'M JUST JOKING.
BOY, YOU HAVE A REALLY SHORT FUSE.
AND YOU ALWAYS CROSS THE LINE!

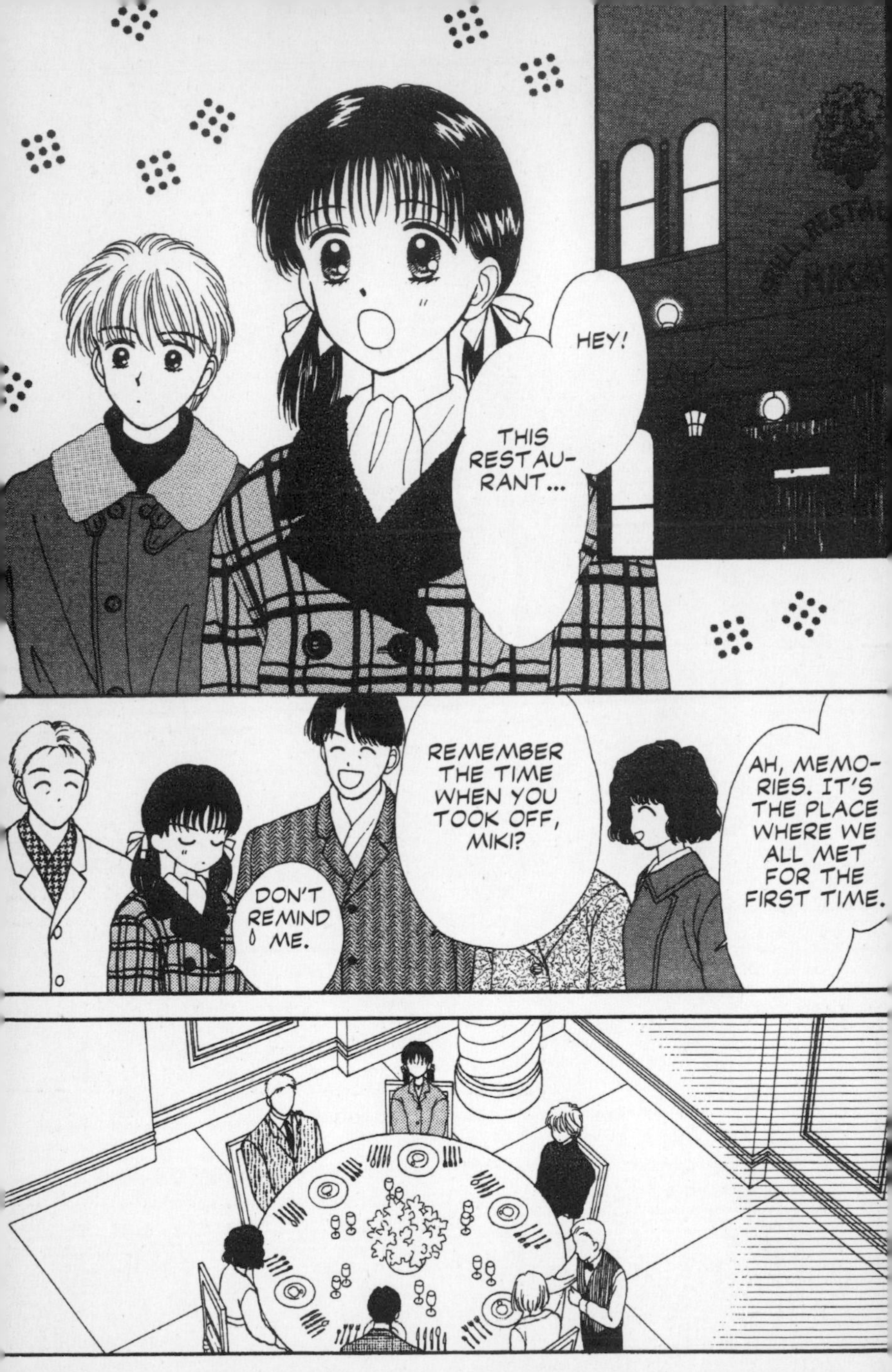
HEY!
THIS RESTAU-RANT...
AH, MEMO-RIES. IT'S THE PLACE WHERE WE ALL MET FOR THE FIRST TIME.
REMEMBER THE TIME WHEN YOU TOOK OFF, MIKI?
DON'T REMIND ME.

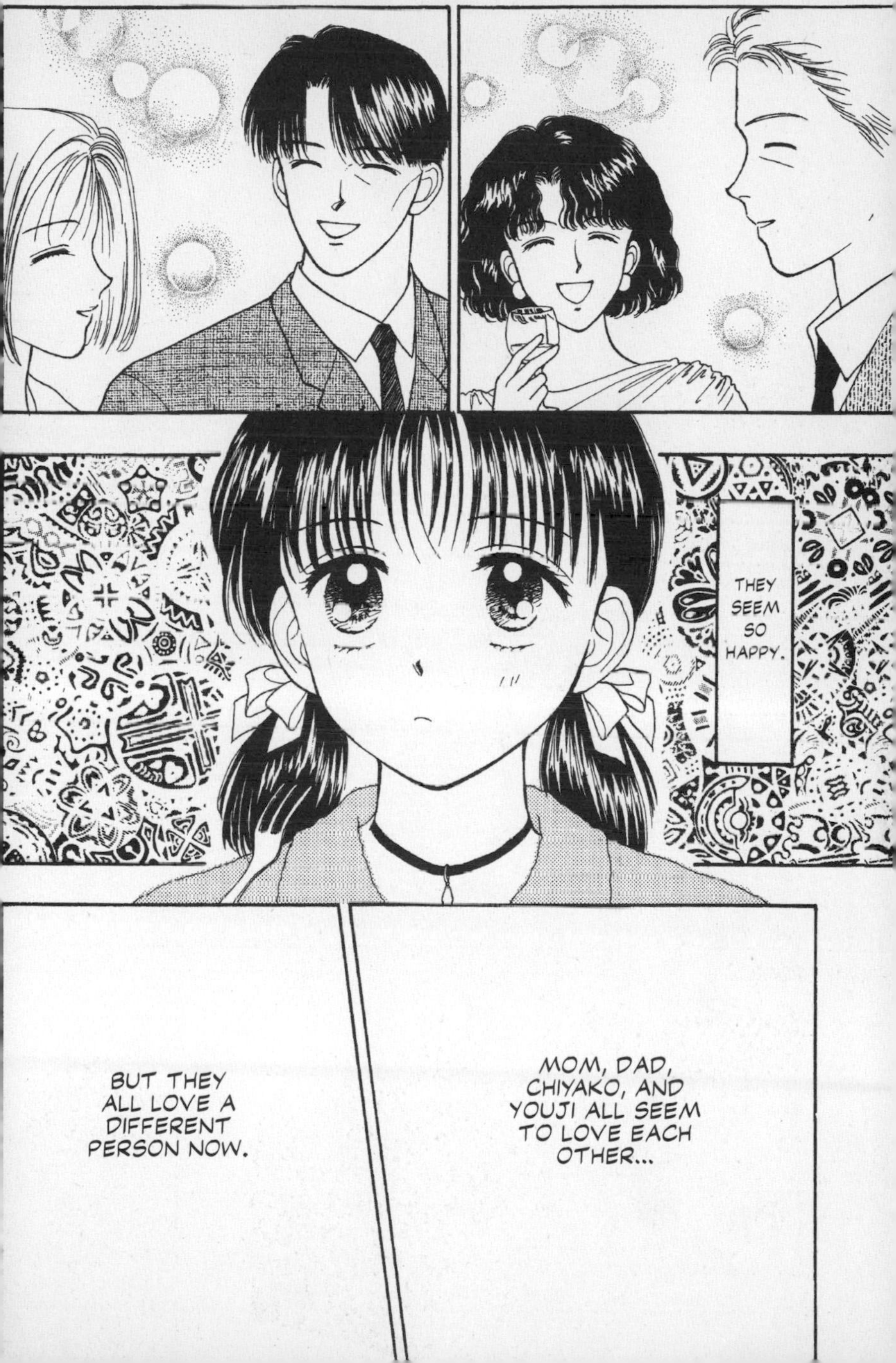
THEY SEEM SO HAPPY.
MOM, DAD, CHIYAKO, AND YOUJI ALL SEEM TO LOVE EACH OTHER...
BUT THEY ALL LOVE A DIFFERENT PERSON NOW.

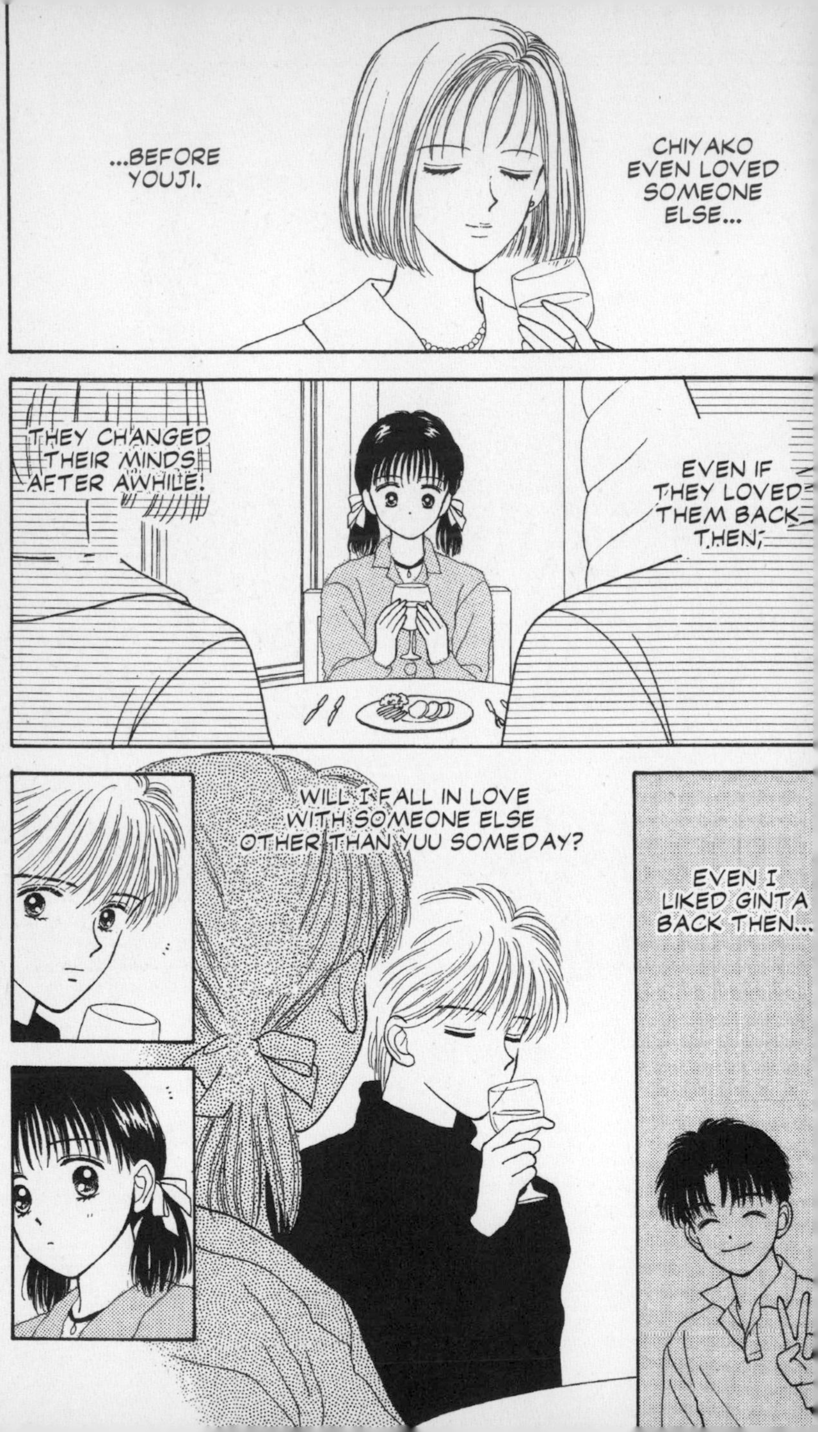
CHIYAKO EVEN LOVED SOMEONE ELSE...
...BEFORE YOUJI.
EVEN IF THEY LOVED THEM BACK THEN,
THEY CHANGED THEIR MINDS AFTER AWHILE!
EVEN I LIKED GINTA BACK THEN...
WILL I FALL IN LOVE WITH SOMEONE ELSE OTHER THAN YUU SOMEDAY?

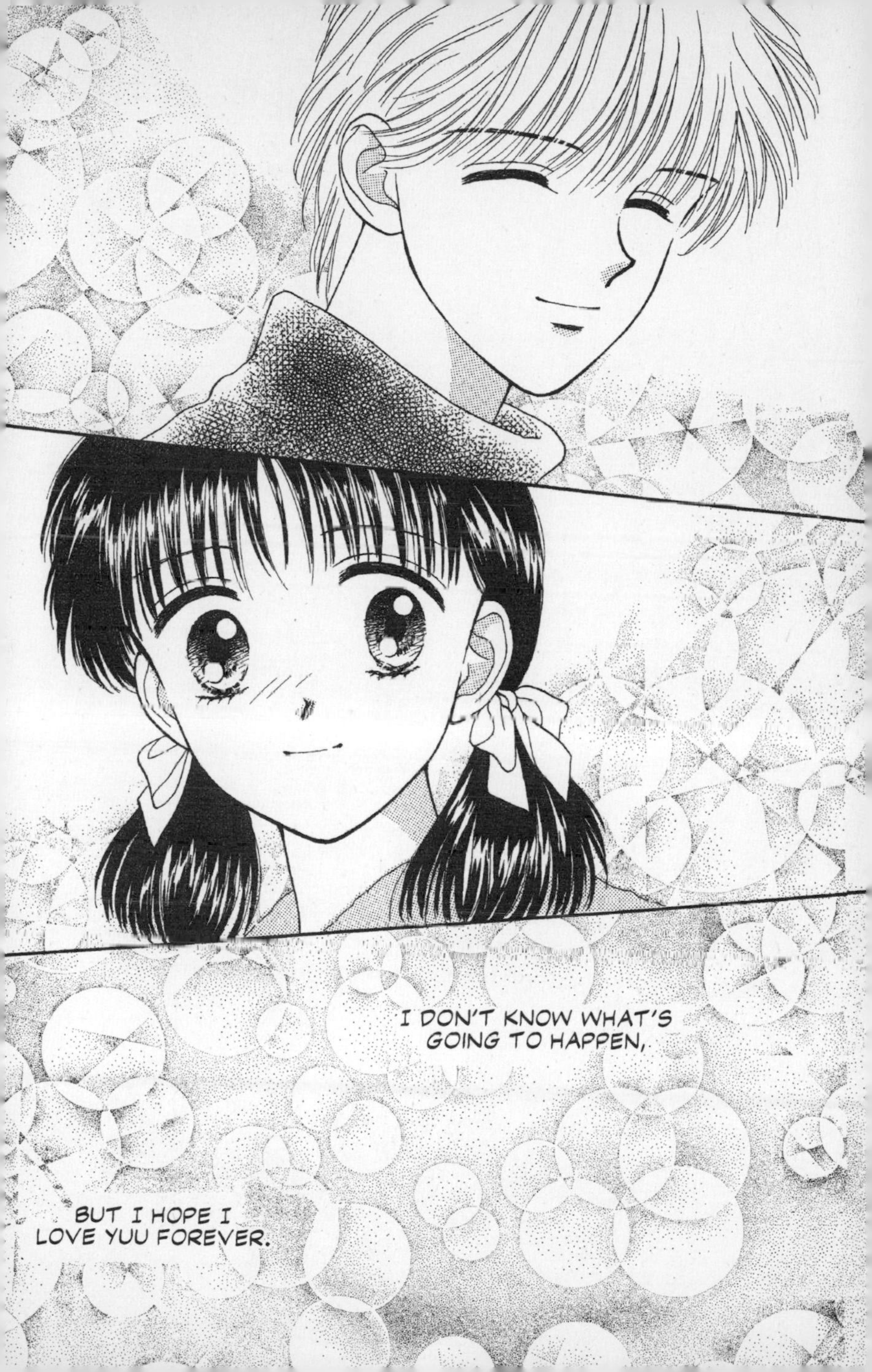
I DON'T KNOW WHAT'S GOING TO HAPPEN,
BUT I HOPE I LOVE YUU FOREVER.

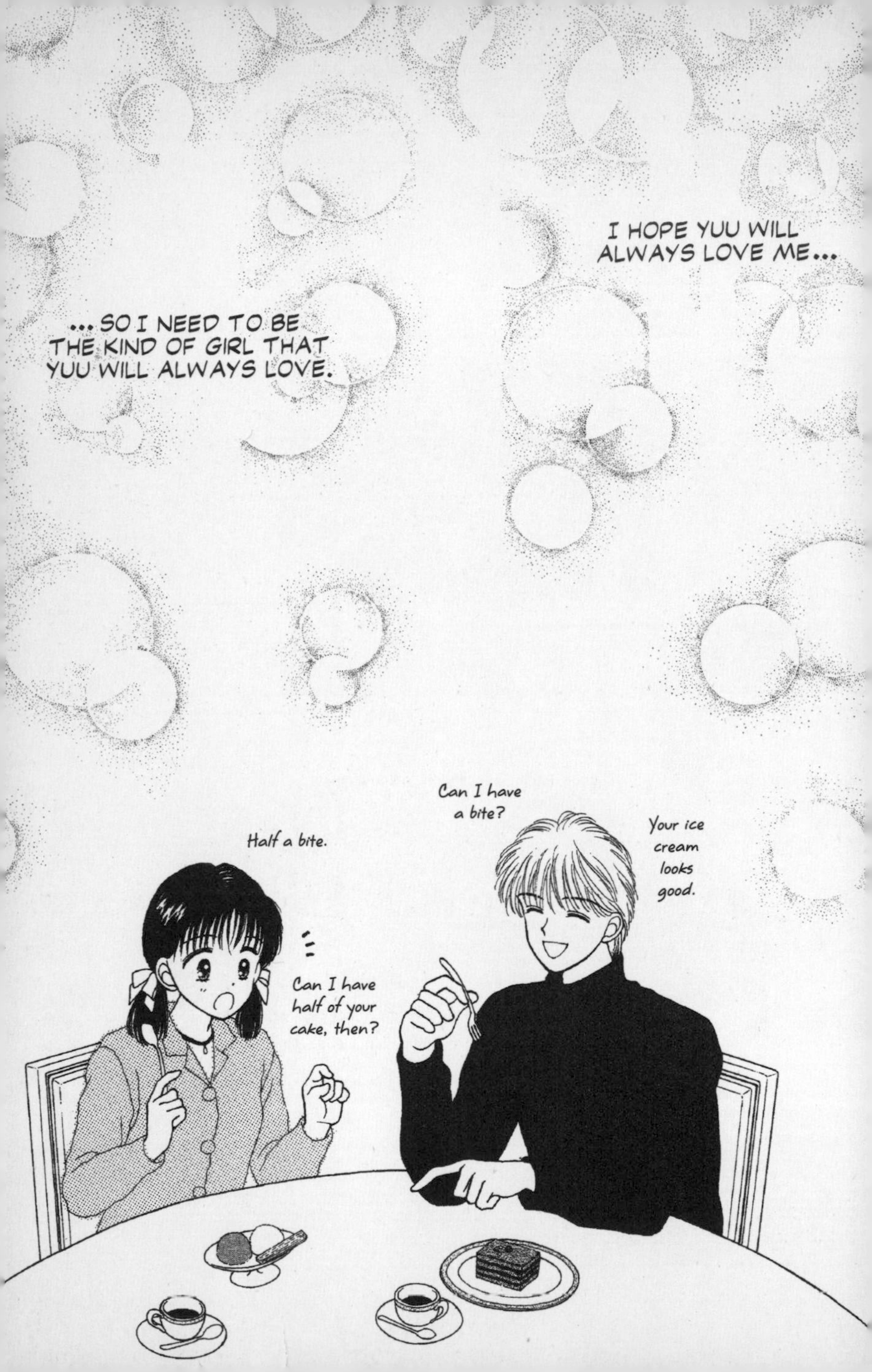
I HOPE YUU WILL ALWAYS LOVE ME...
...SO I NEED TO BE THE KIND OF GIRL THAT YUU WILL ALWAYS LOVE.
Your ice cream looks good.
Can I have a bite?
Half a bite.
Can I have half of your cake, then?

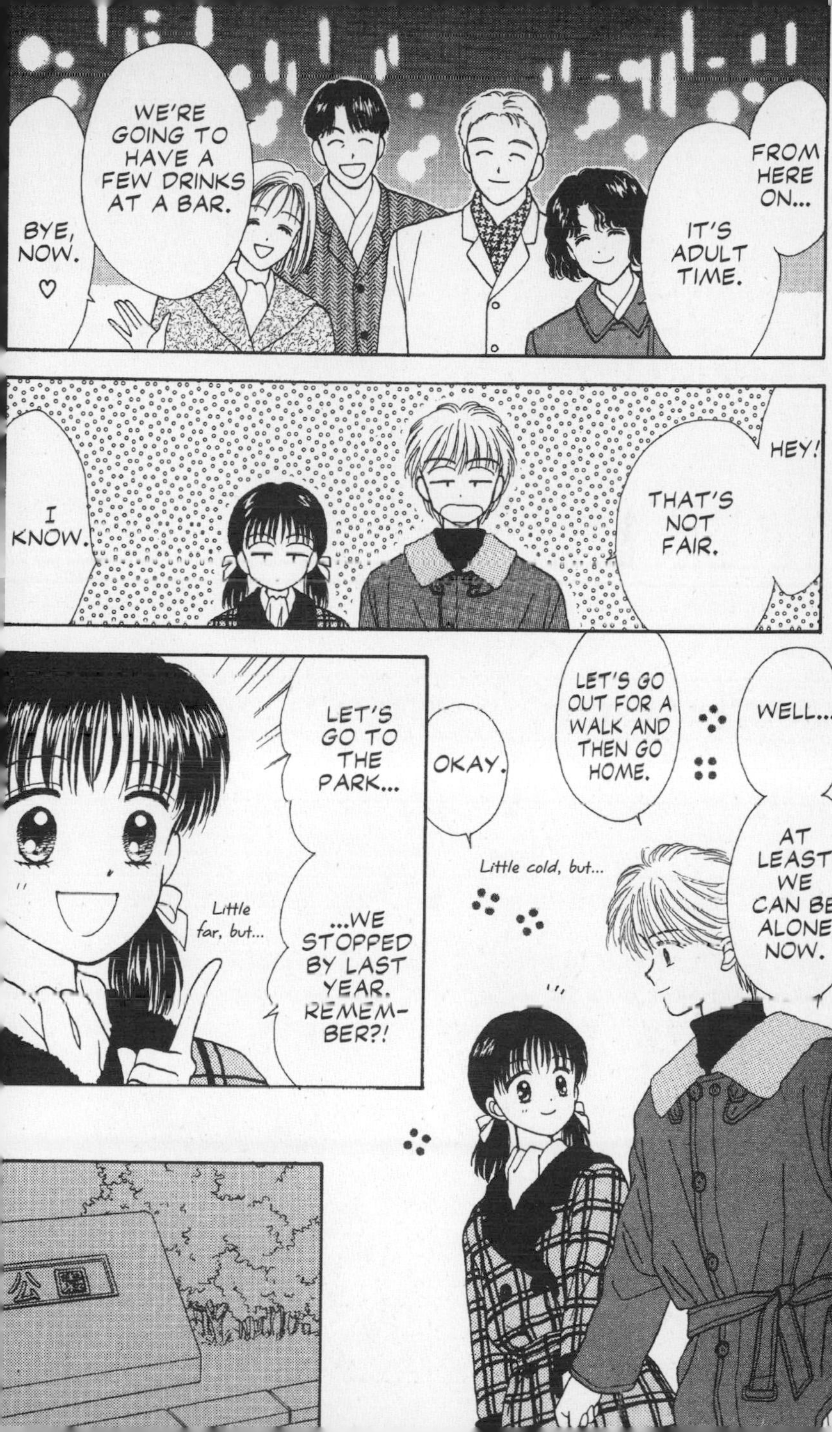
FROM HERE ON...
IT'S ADULT TIME.
WE'RE GOING TO HAVE A FEW DRINKS AT A BAR.
BYE, NOW. ♡
HEY!
THAT'S NOT FAIR.
I KNOW.
WELL...
AT LEAST WE CAN BE ALONE NOW.
LET'S GO OUT FOR A WALK AND THEN GO HOME.
OKAY.
Little cold, but...
LET'S GO TO THE PARK...
...WE STOPPED BY LAST YEAR. REMEMBER?!
Little far, but...
公園

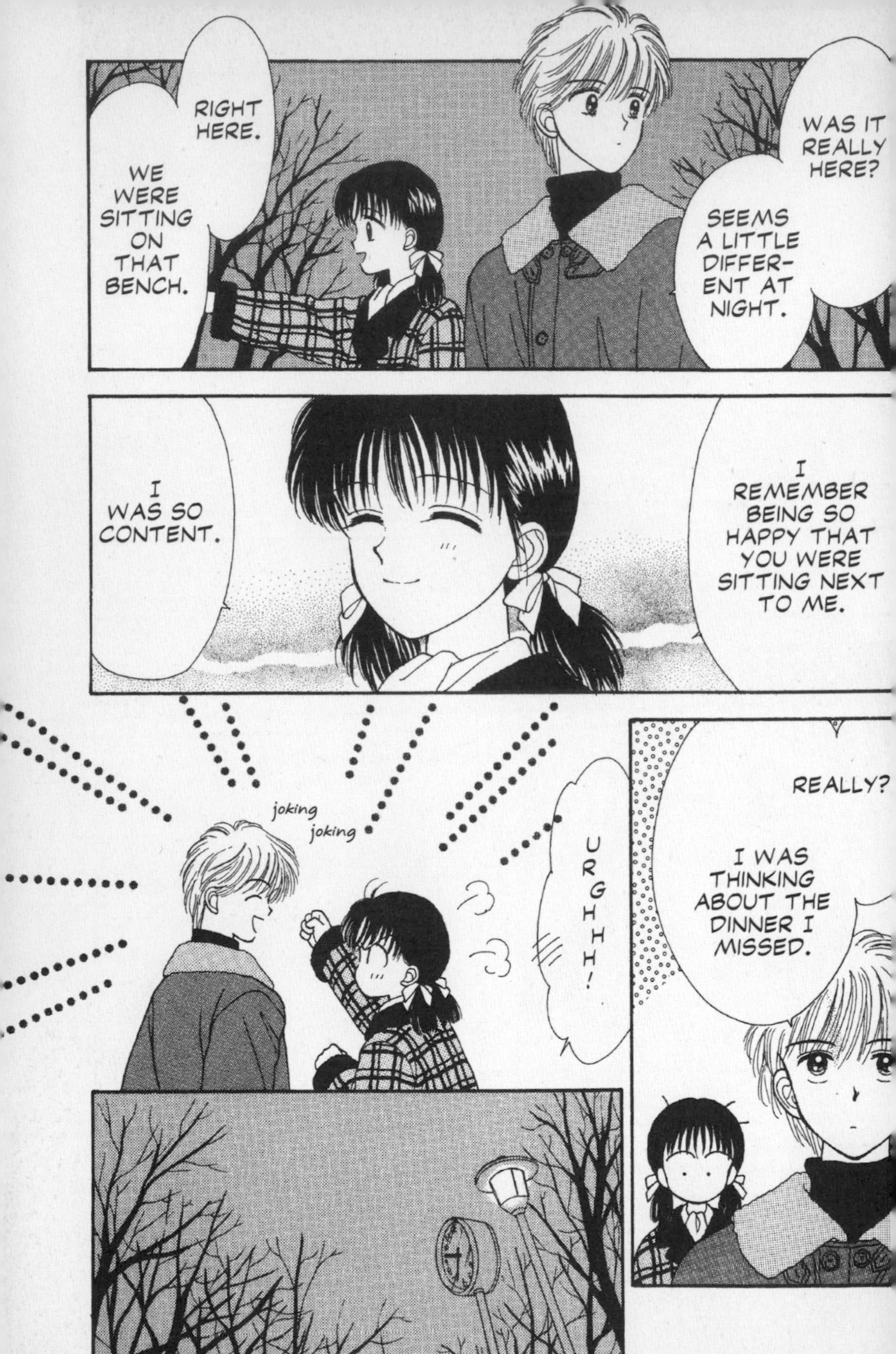
WAS IT REALLY HERE?
SEEMS A LITTLE DIFFER-ENT AT NIGHT.
RIGHT HERE.
WE WERE SITTING ON THAT BENCH.
I REMEMBER BEING SO HAPPY THAT YOU WERE SITTING NEXT TO ME.
I WAS SO CONTENT.
REALLY?
I WAS THINKING ABOUT THE DINNER I MISSED.
URGHH!
joking joking

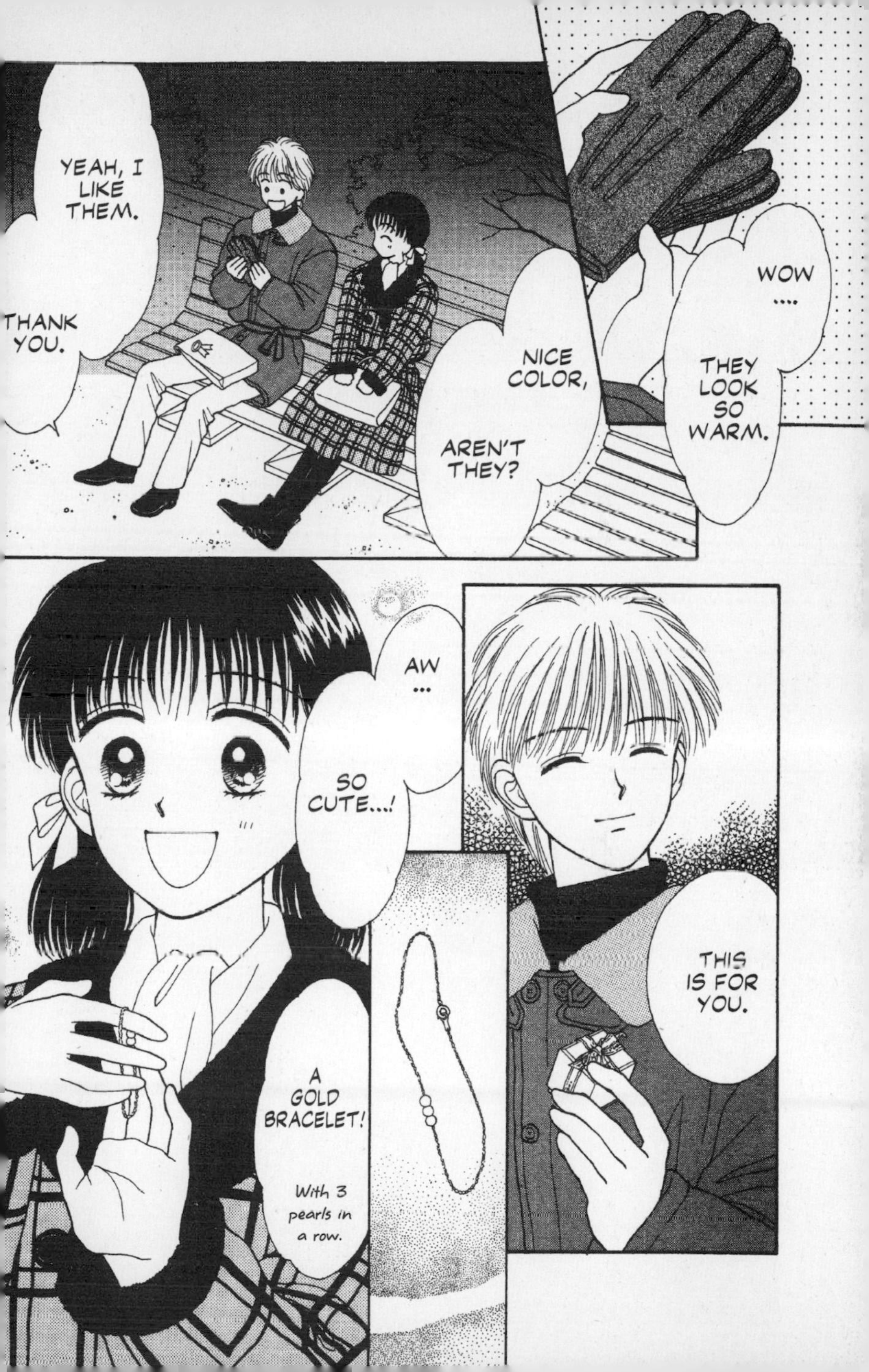
WOW ....
THEY LOOK SO WARM.
NICE COLOR,
AREN'T THEY?
YEAH, I LIKE THEM.
THANK YOU.
THIS IS FOR YOU.
AW ...
SO CUTE...!
A GOLD BRACELET!
With 3 pearls in a row.

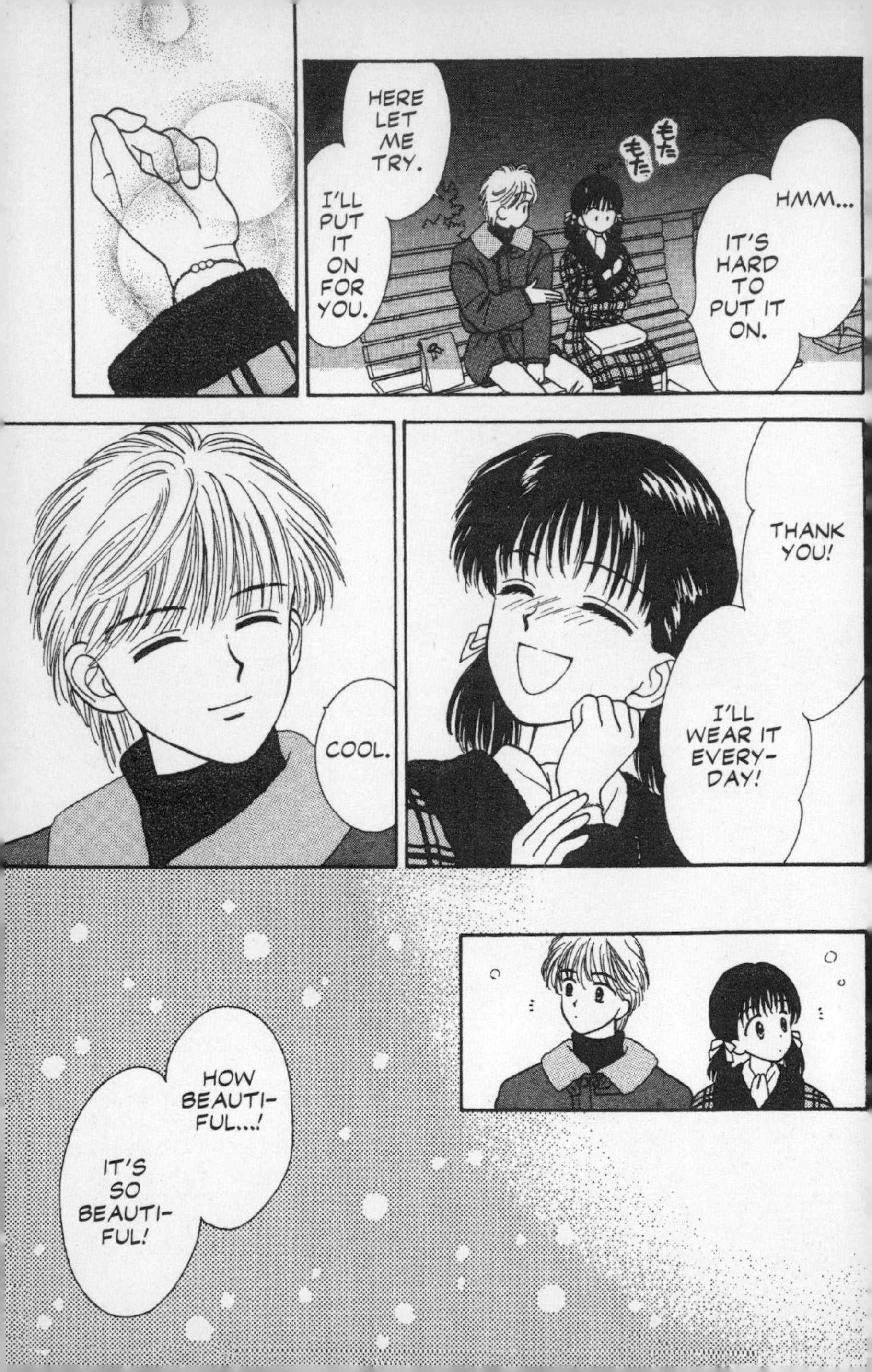
HMM... IT'S HARD TO PUT IT ON.
もたもた
HERE LET ME TRY. I'LL PUT IT ON FOR YOU.
THANK YOU! I'LL WEAR IT EVERY-DAY!
COOL.
HOW BEAUTI-FUL...! IT'S SO BEAUTI-FUL!

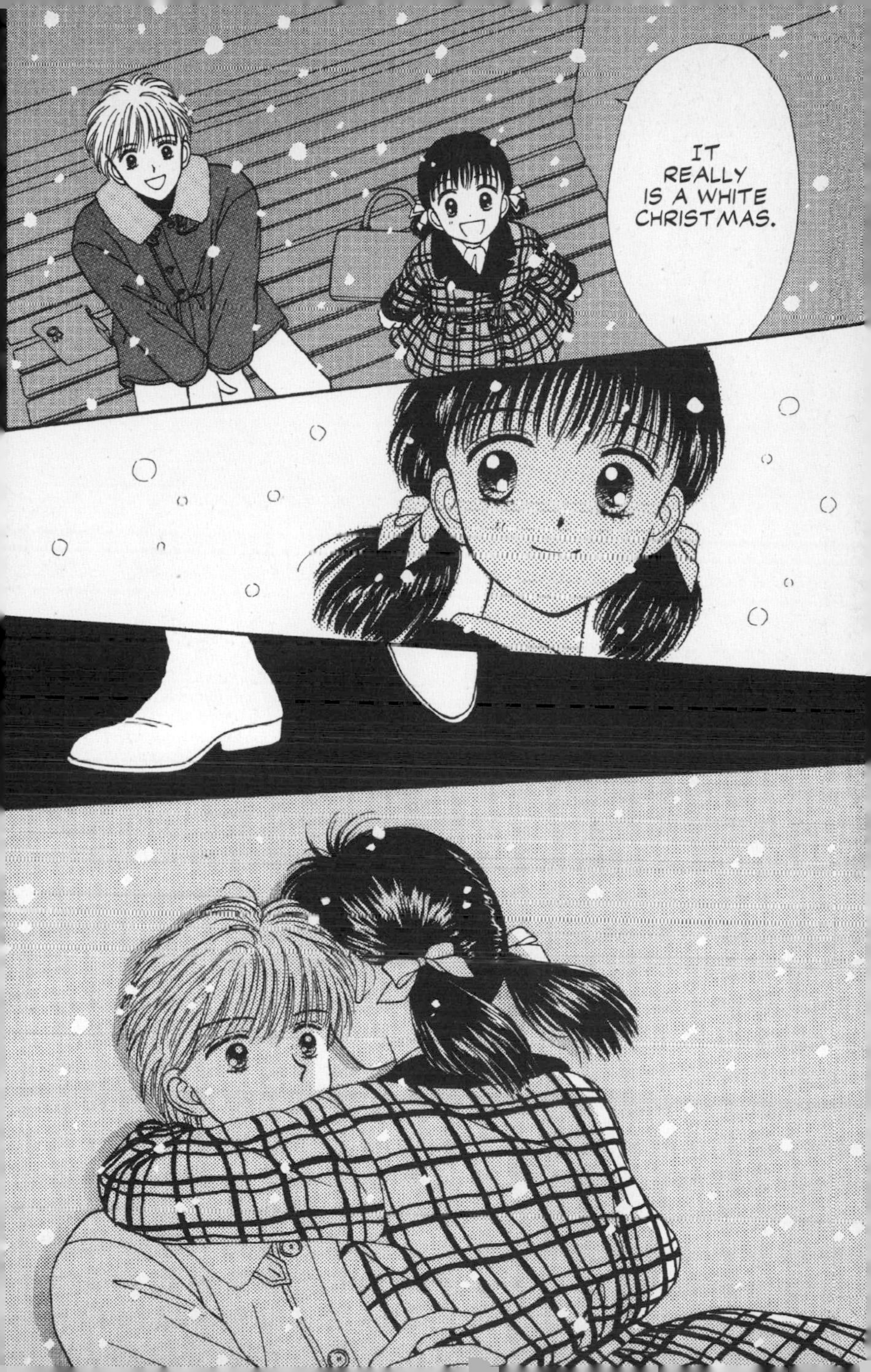
IT REALLY IS A WHITE CHRISTMAS.

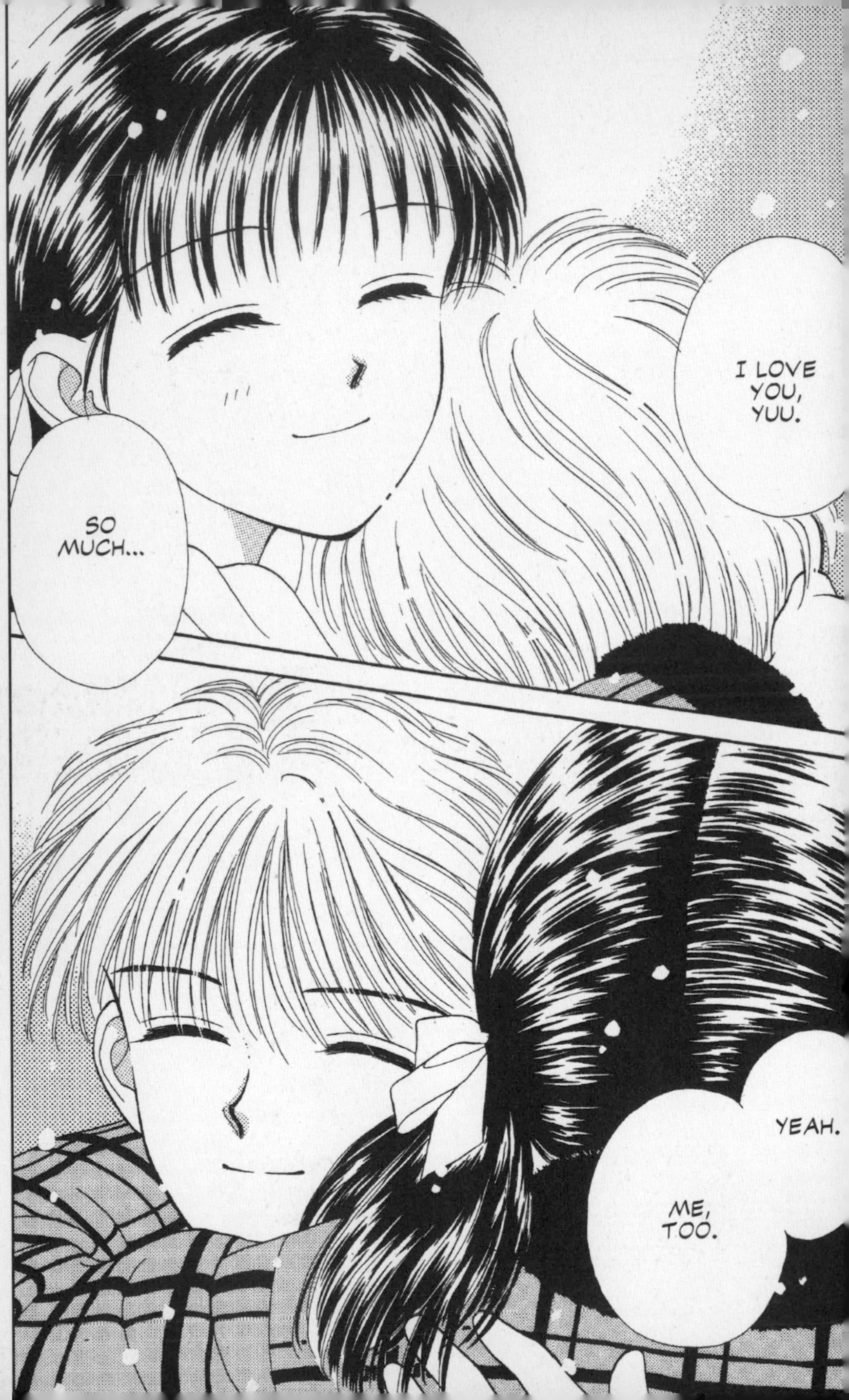
I LOVE YOU, YUU.
SO MUCH...
YEAH.
ME, TOO.

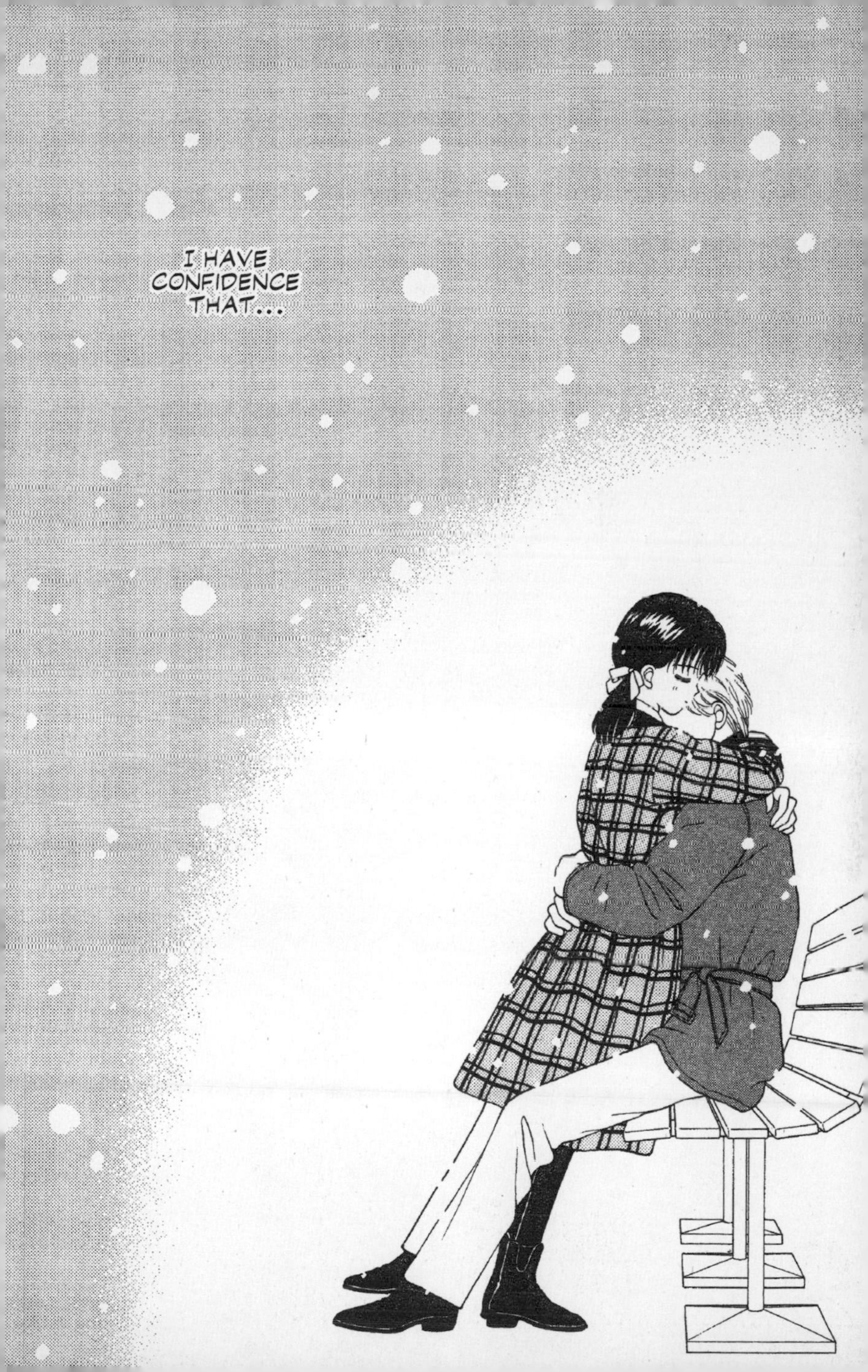
I HAVE CONFIDENCE THAT...

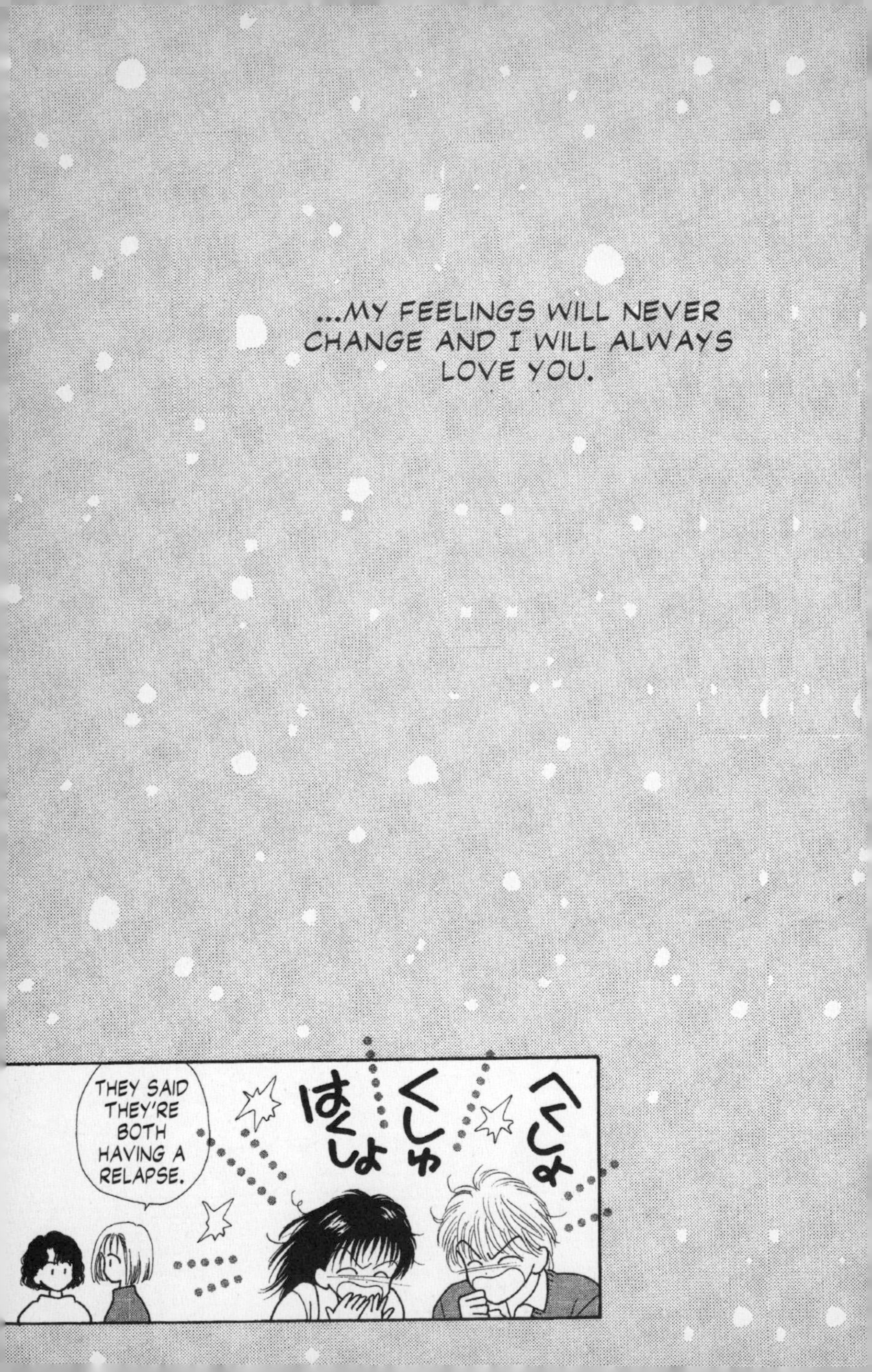
...MY FEELINGS WILL NEVER CHANGE AND I WILL ALWAYS LOVE YOU.
へくしょ
くしゅ
はくしょ
THEY SAID THEY'RE BOTH HAVING A RELAPSE.

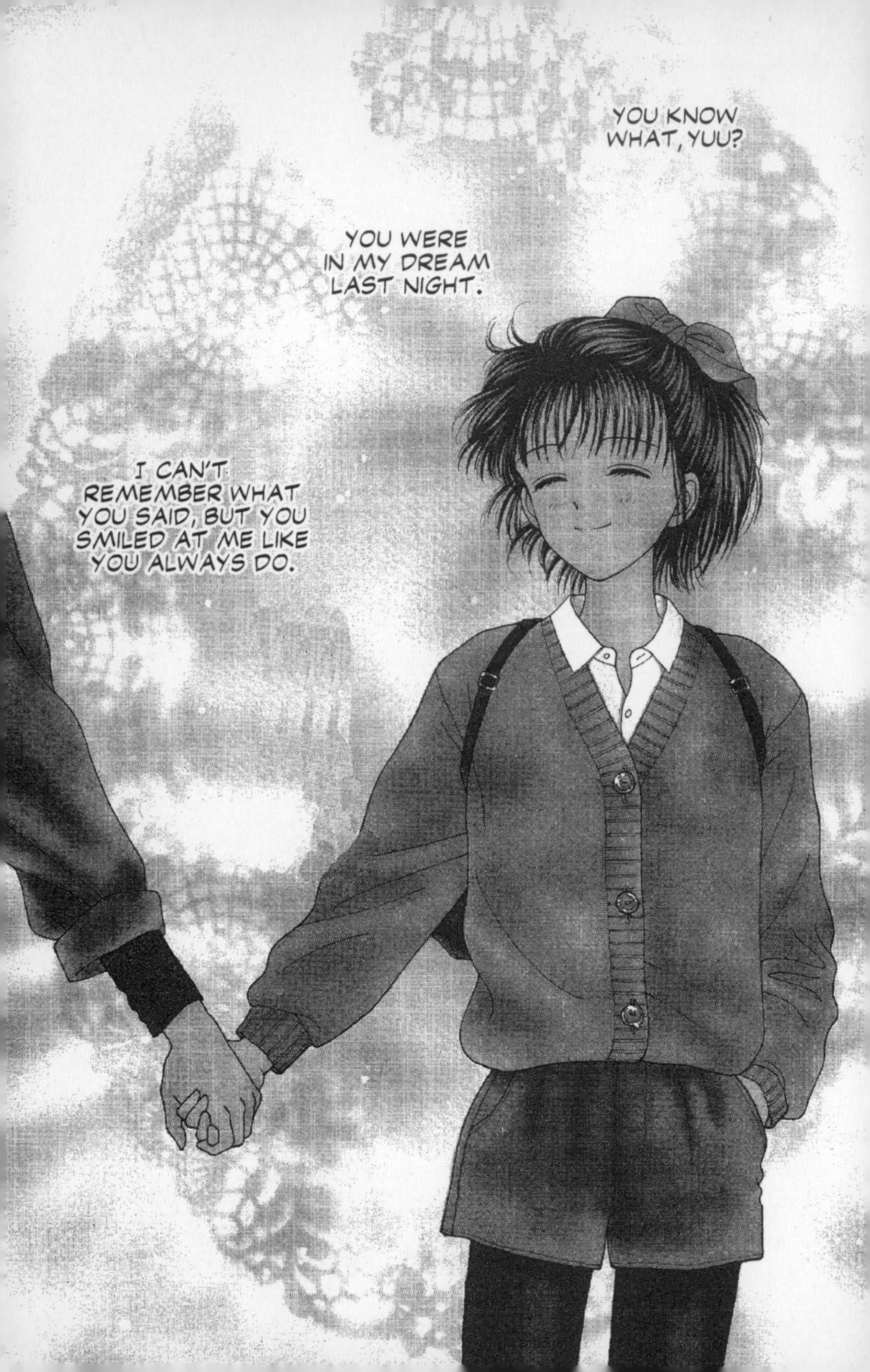
YOU KNOW WHAT, YUU?
YOU WERE IN MY DREAM LAST NIGHT.
I CAN'T REMEMBER WHAT YOU SAID, BUT YOU SMILED AT ME LIKE YOU ALWAYS DO.

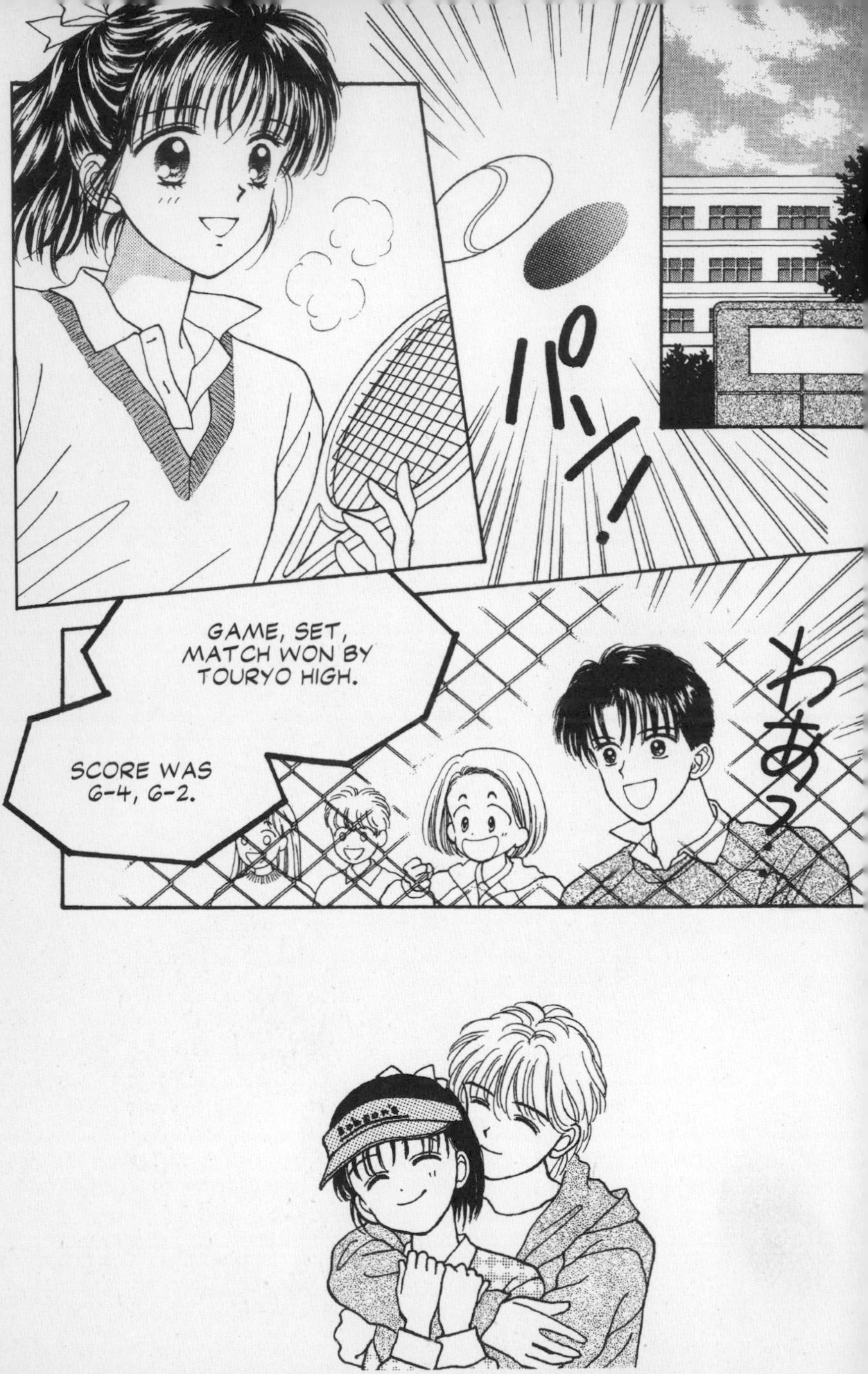
パン!!
GAME, SET, MATCH WON BY TOURYO HIGH.
SCORE WAS 6-4, 6-2.
わあっ

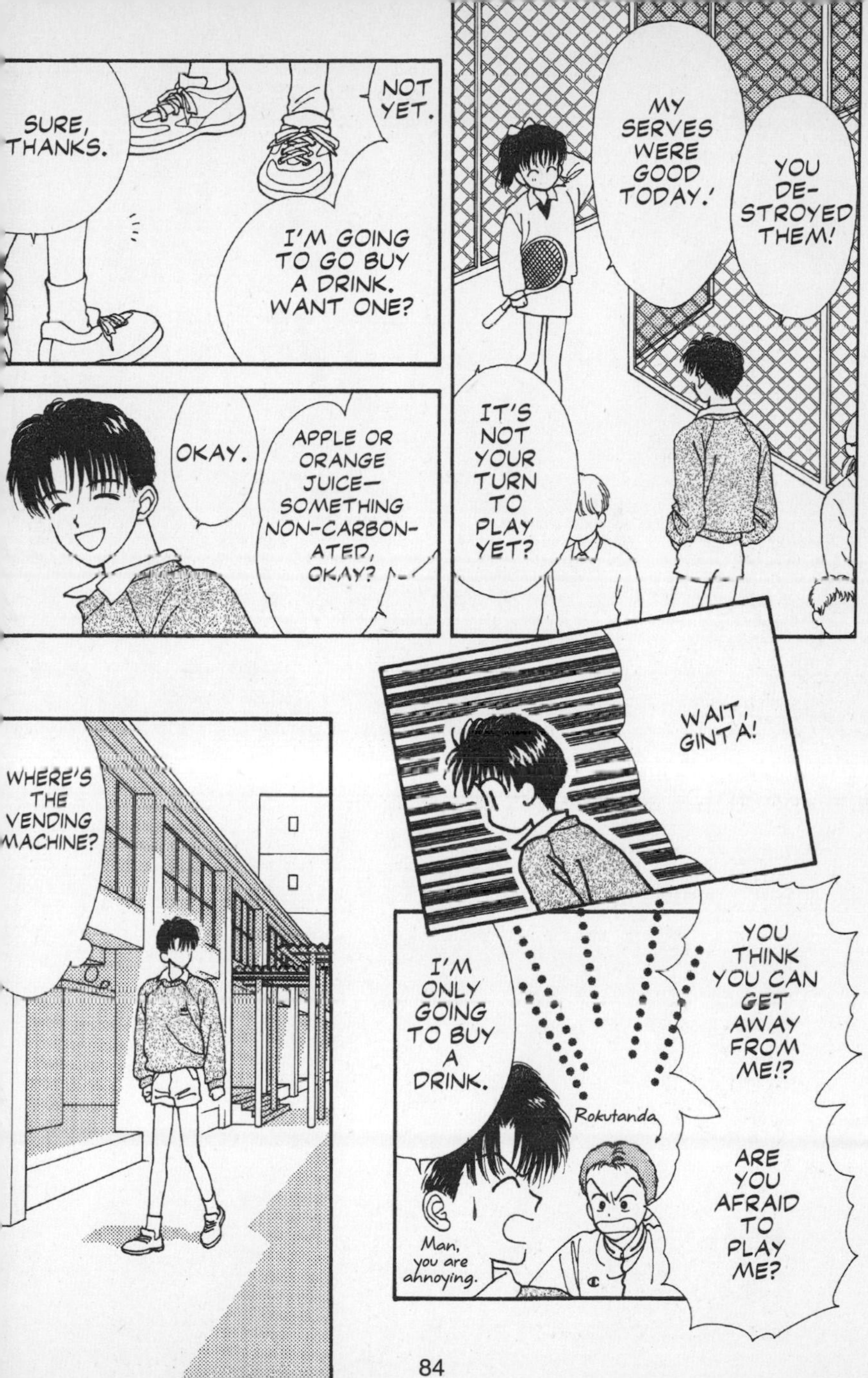
MY SERVES WERE GOOD TODAY.'
YOU DE-STROYED THEM!
IT'S NOT YOUR TURN TO PLAY YET?
NOT YET.
I'M GOING TO GO BUY A DRINK. WANT ONE?
SURE, THANKS.
APPLE OR ORANGE JUICE—SOMETHING NON-CARBON-ATED, OKAY?
OKAY.
WAIT, GINTA!
YOU THINK YOU CAN GET AWAY FROM ME!?
ARE YOU AFRAID TO PLAY ME?
I'M ONLY GOING TO BUY A DRINK.
Rokutanda
Man, you are annoying.
WHERE'S THE VENDING MACHINE?

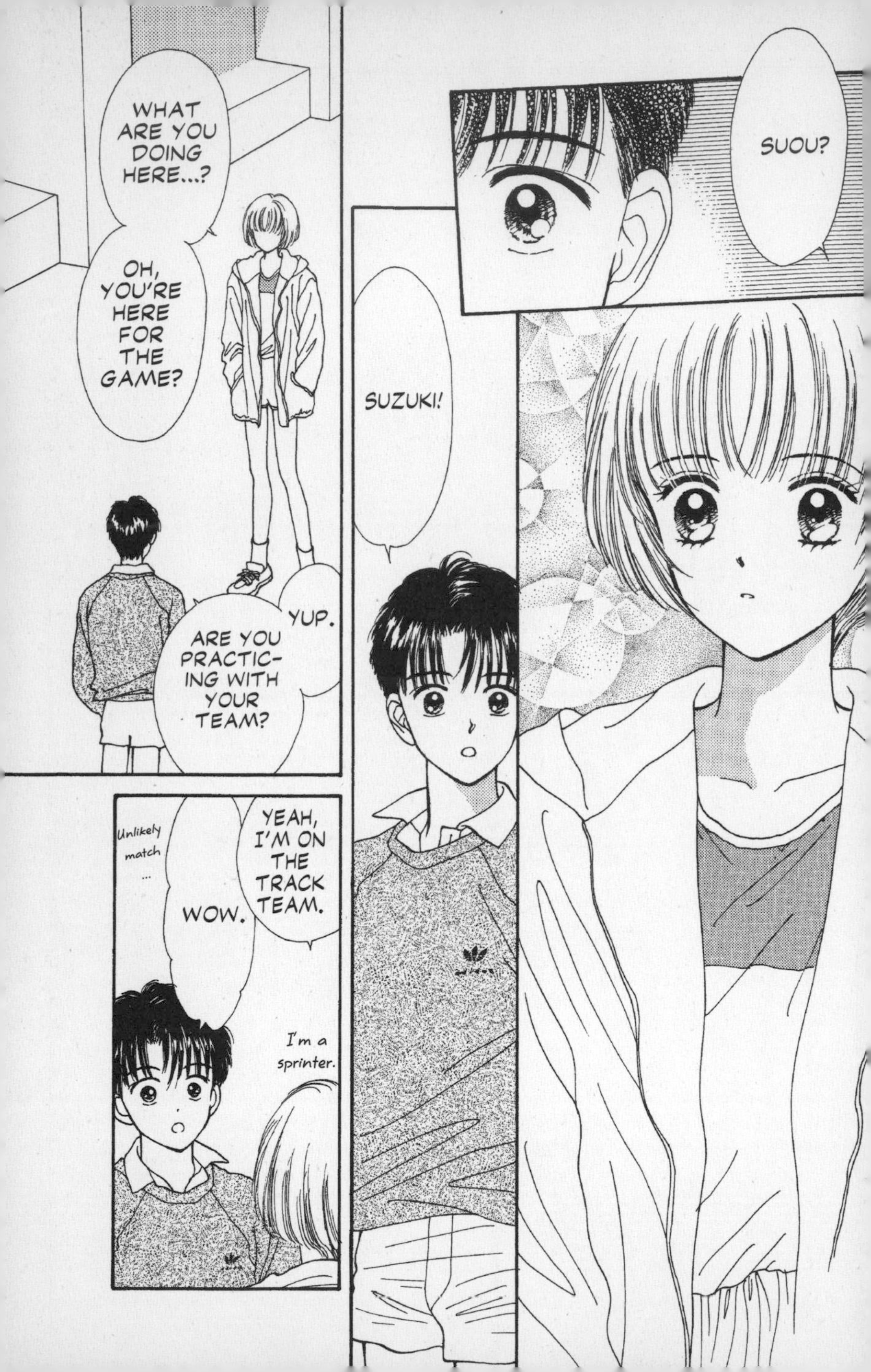
SUOU?
SUZUKI!
WHAT ARE YOU DOING HERE...?
OH, YOU'RE HERE FOR THE GAME?
YUP.
ARE YOU PRACTIC-ING WITH YOUR TEAM?
YEAH, I'M ON THE TRACK TEAM.
I'm a sprinter.
WOW.
Unlikely match ...

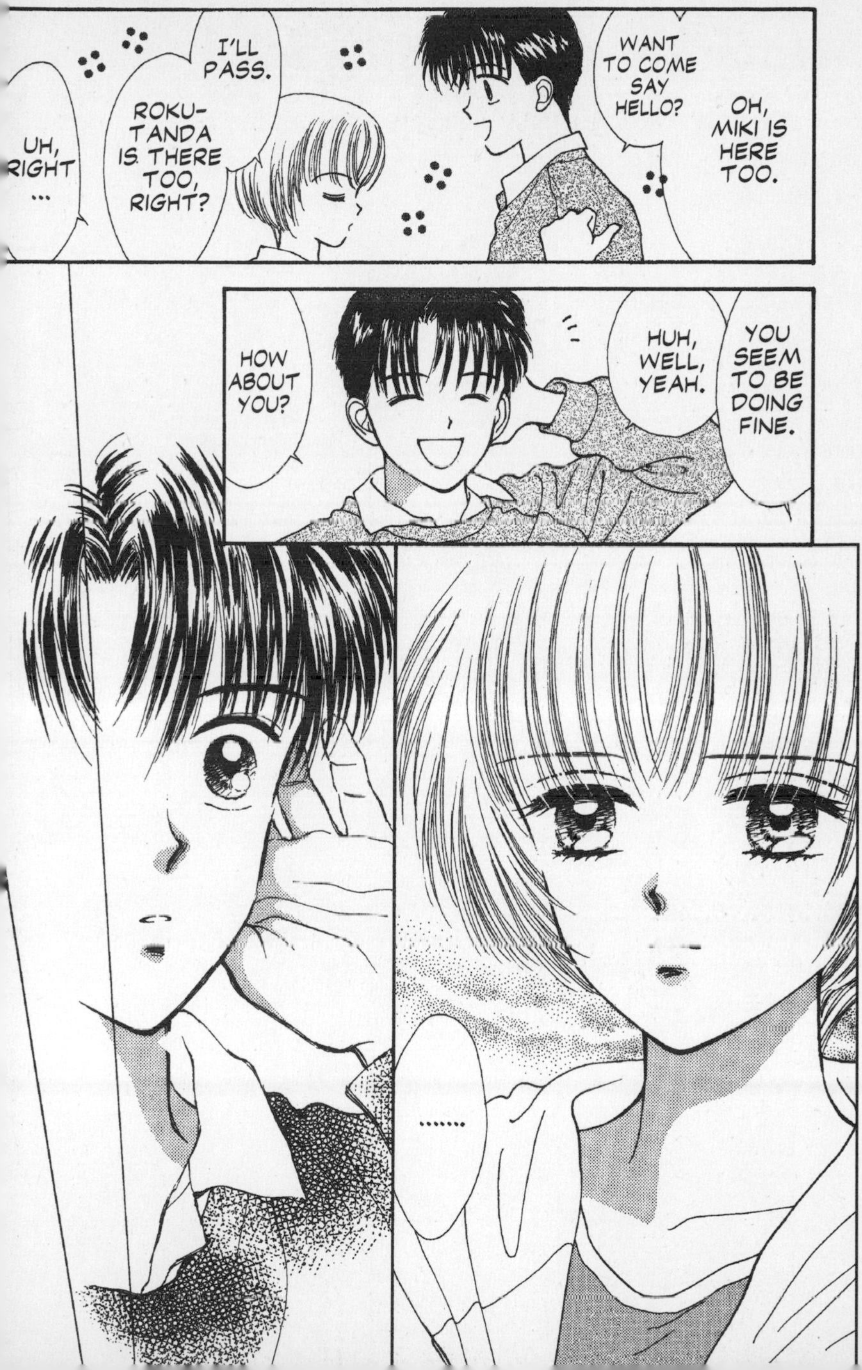

OH, MIKI IS HERE TOO.
WANT TO COME SAY HELLO?
I'LL PASS.
ROKU-TANDA IS THERE TOO, RIGHT?
UH, RIGHT ...
YOU SEEM TO BE DOING FINE.
HUH, WELL, YEAH.
HOW ABOUT YOU?
....

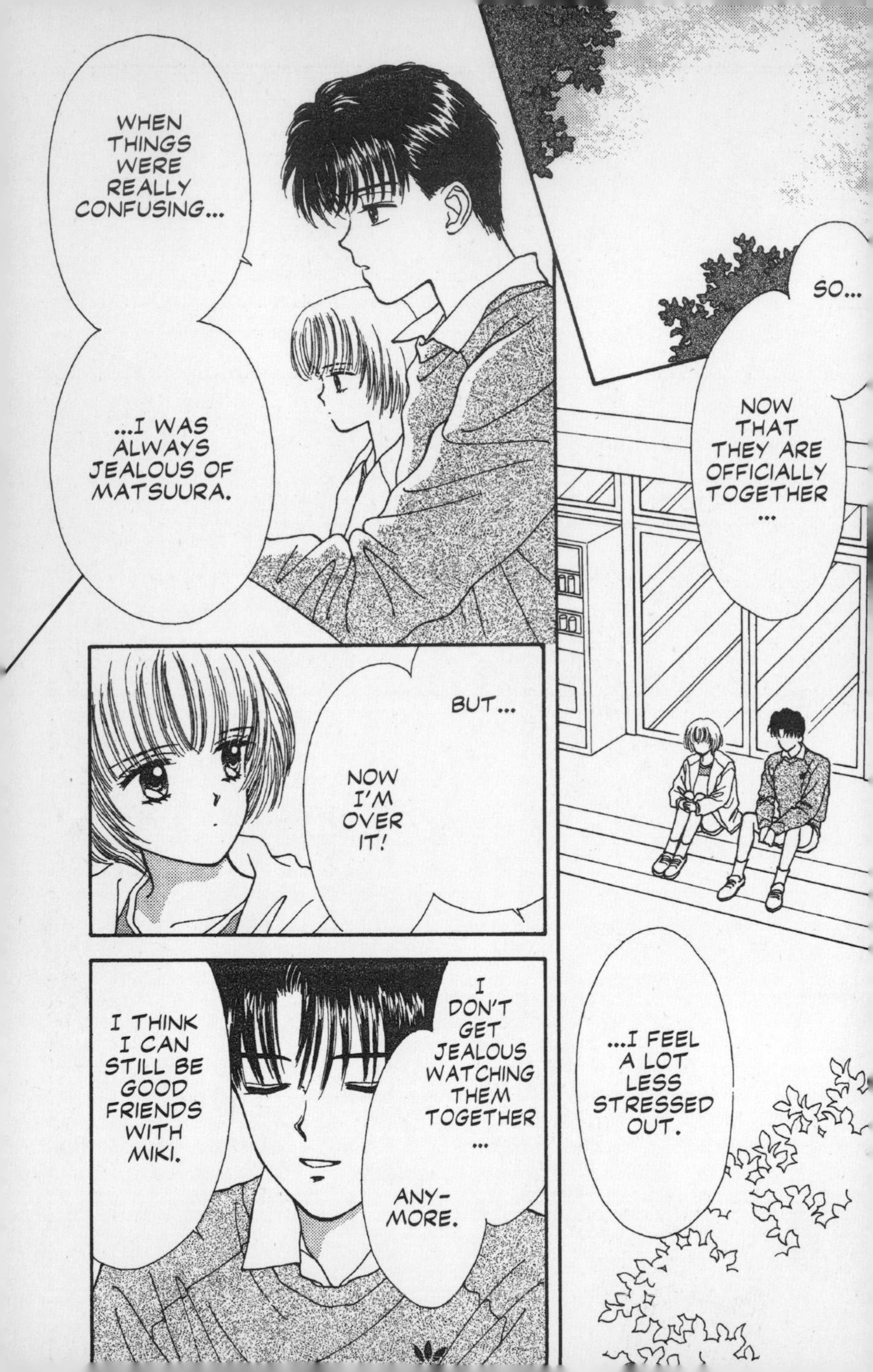
SO...
NOW THAT THEY ARE OFFICIALLY TOGETHER...
...I FEEL A LOT LESS STRESSED OUT.
WHEN THINGS WERE REALLY CONFUSING...
...I WAS ALWAYS JEALOUS OF MATSUURA.
BUT...
NOW I'M OVER IT!
I DON'T GET JEALOUS WATCHING THEM TOGETHER...
ANY-MORE.
I THINK I CAN STILL BE GOOD FRIENDS WITH MIKI.

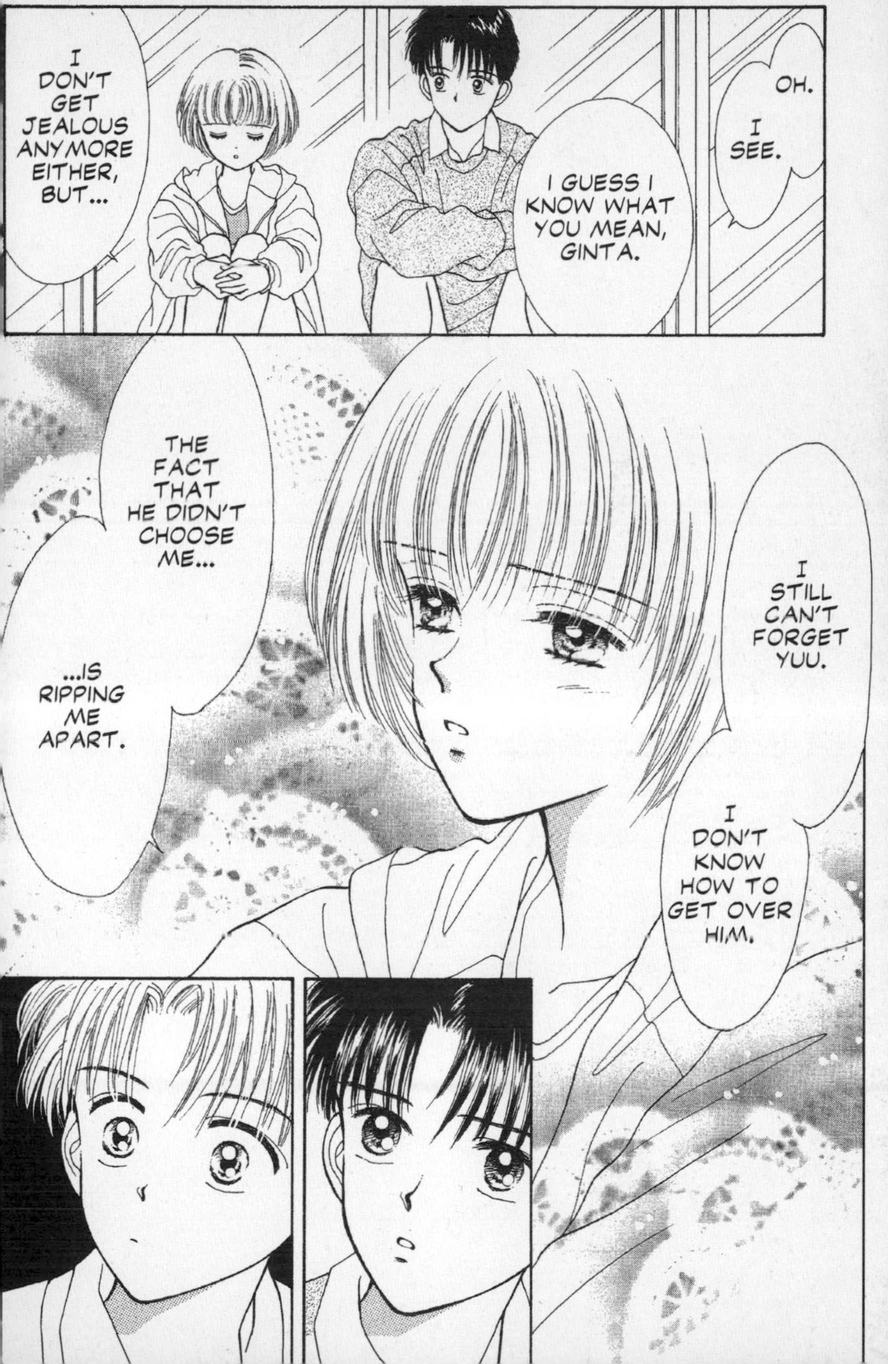
OH. I SEE.
I GUESS I KNOW WHAT YOU MEAN, GINTA.
I DON'T GET JEALOUS ANYMORE EITHER, BUT...
I STILL CAN'T FORGET YUU.
I DON'T KNOW HOW TO GET OVER HIM.
THE FACT THAT HE DIDN'T CHOOSE ME...
...IS RIPPING ME APART.

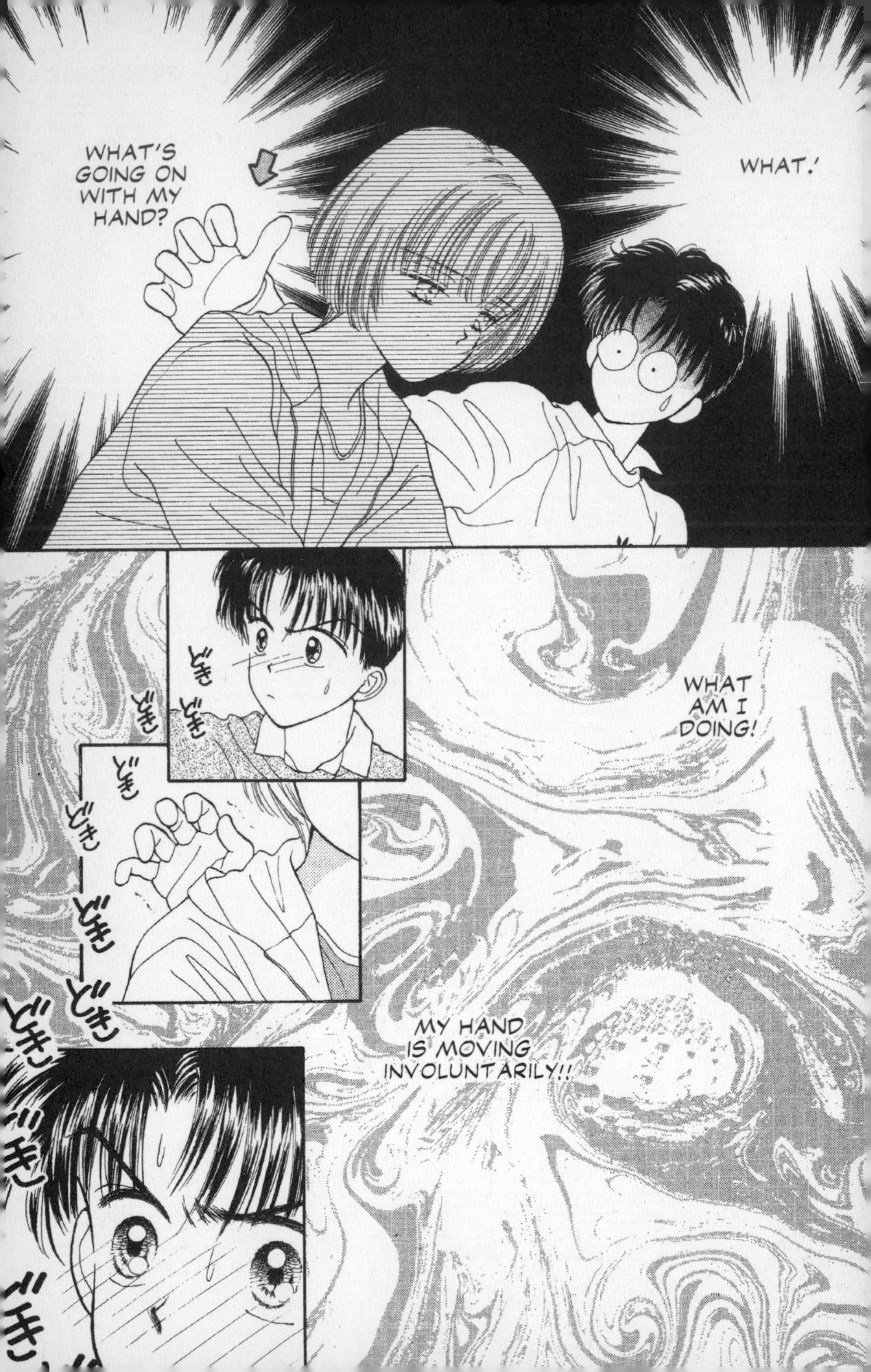
WHAT.'
WHAT'S GOING ON WITH MY HAND?
どき どき どき
WHAT AM I DOING!
どき どき どき どき
MY HAND IS MOVING INVOLUNTARILY!!

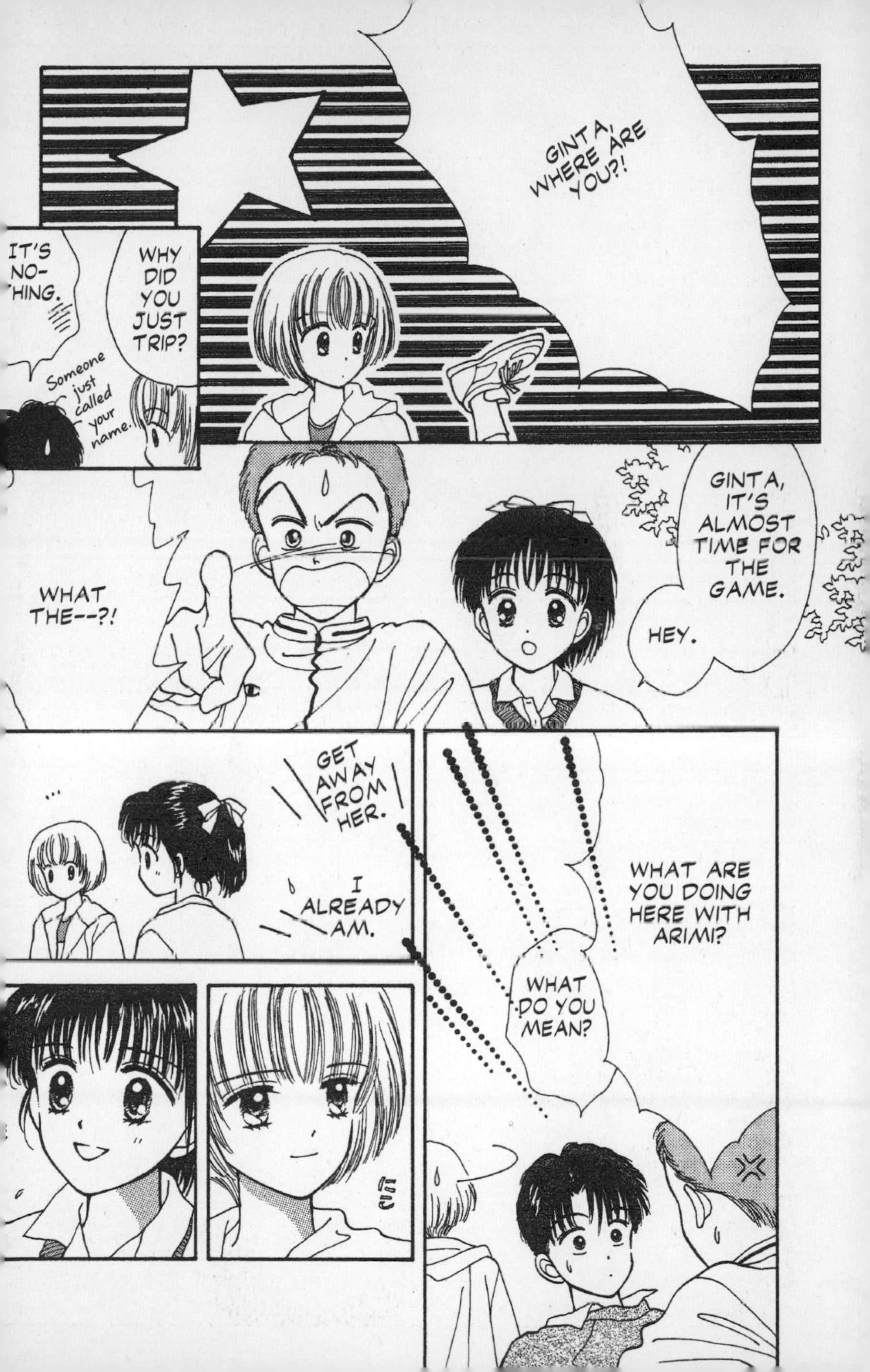
GINTA, WHERE ARE YOU?!
WHY DID YOU JUST TRIP?
IT'S NO-THING.
Someone just called your name.
GINTA, IT'S ALMOST TIME FOR THE GAME.
HEY.
WHAT THE--?!
WHAT ARE YOU DOING HERE WITH ARIMI?
WHAT DO YOU MEAN?
GET AWAY FROM HER.
I ALREADY AM.
...
にこ

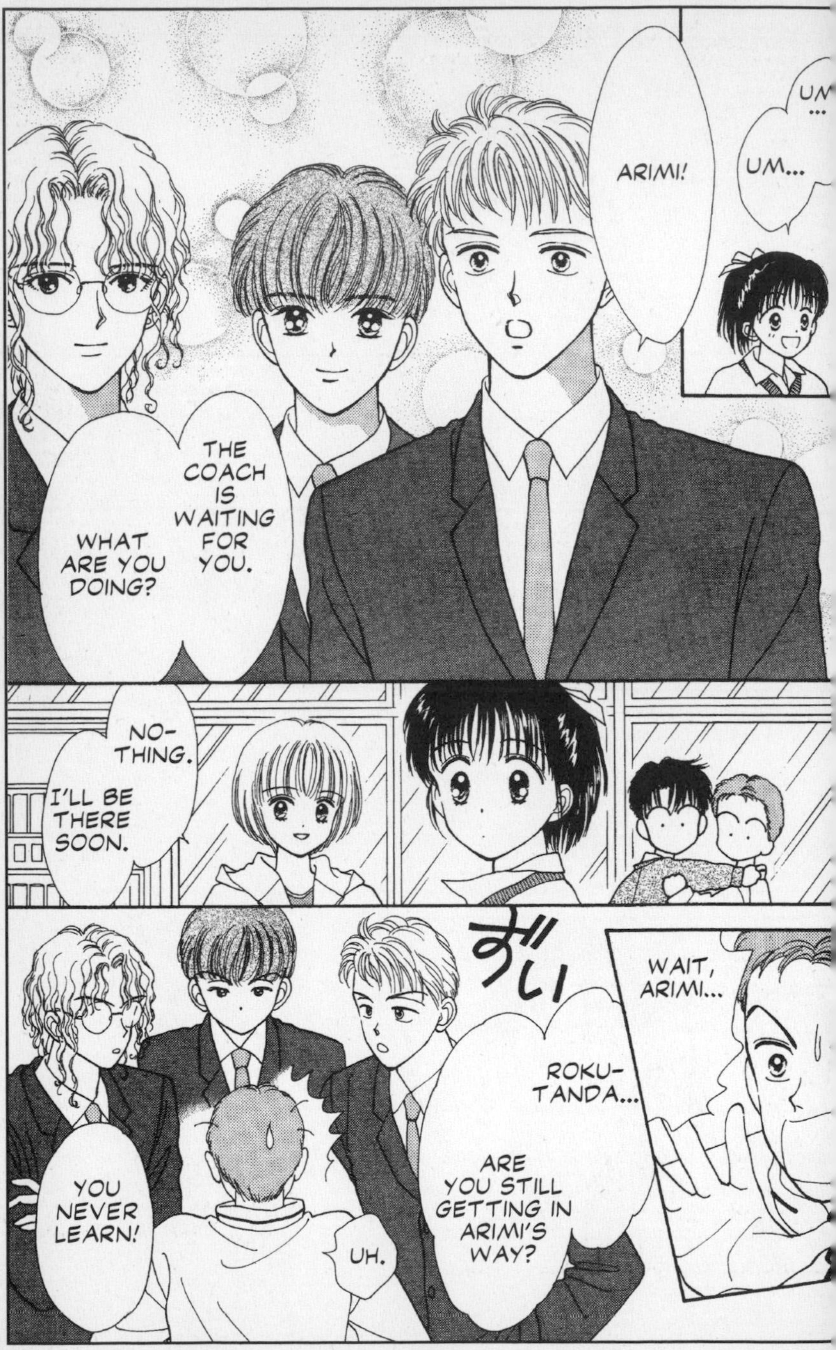
UM...
UM...
ARIMI!
THE COACH IS WAITING FOR YOU.
WHAT ARE YOU DOING?
NO-THING.
I'LL BE THERE SOON.
WAIT, ARIMI...
ずい
ROKU-TANDA...
ARE YOU STILL GETTING IN ARIMI'S WAY?
UH.
YOU NEVER LEARN!

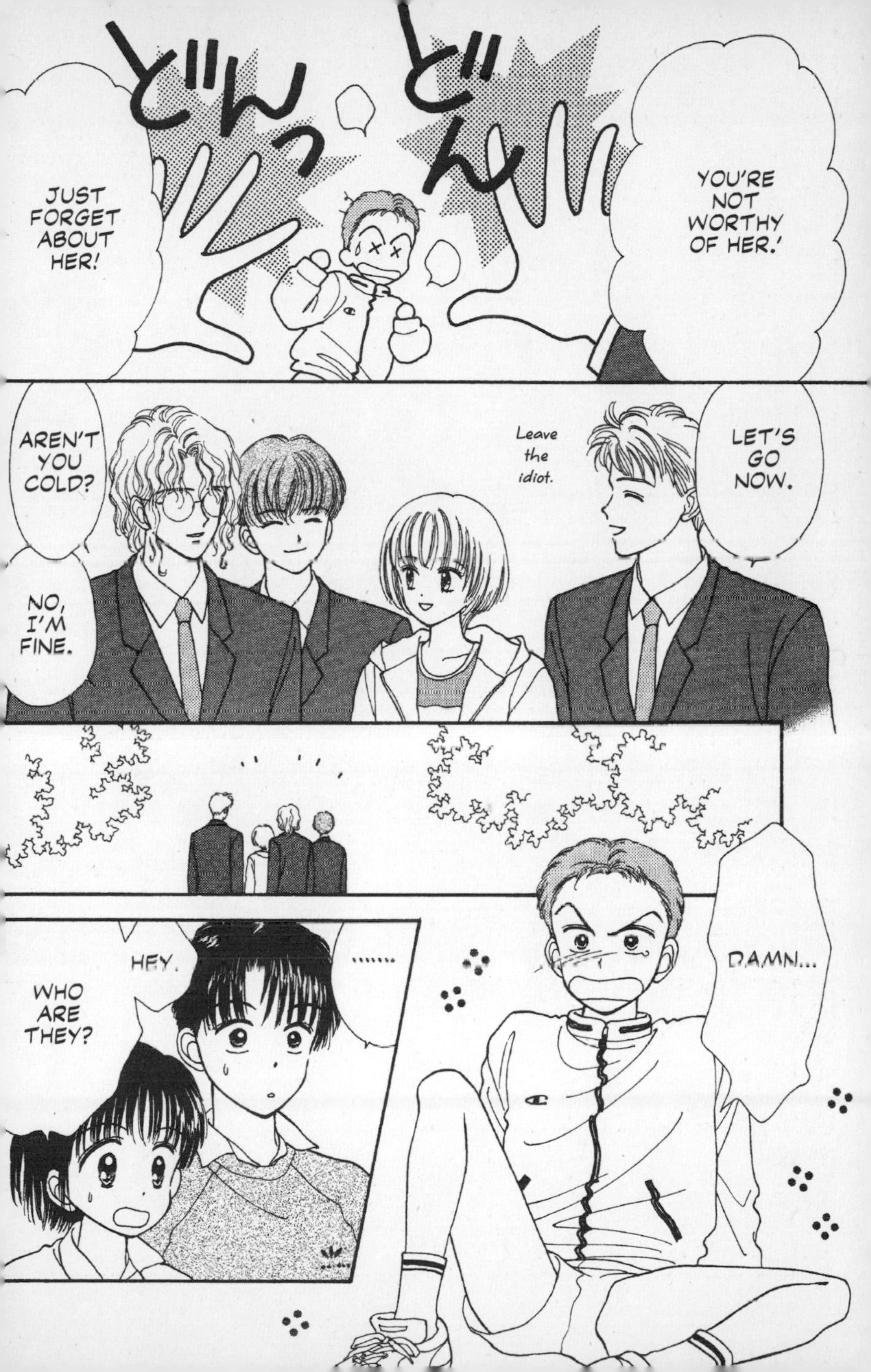
YOU'RE NOT WORTHY OF HER!
どん!!
どんっ
JUST FORGET ABOUT HER!
LET'S GO NOW.
Leave the idiot.
AREN'T YOU COLD?
NO, I'M FINE.
DAMN...
......
HEY.
WHO ARE THEY?

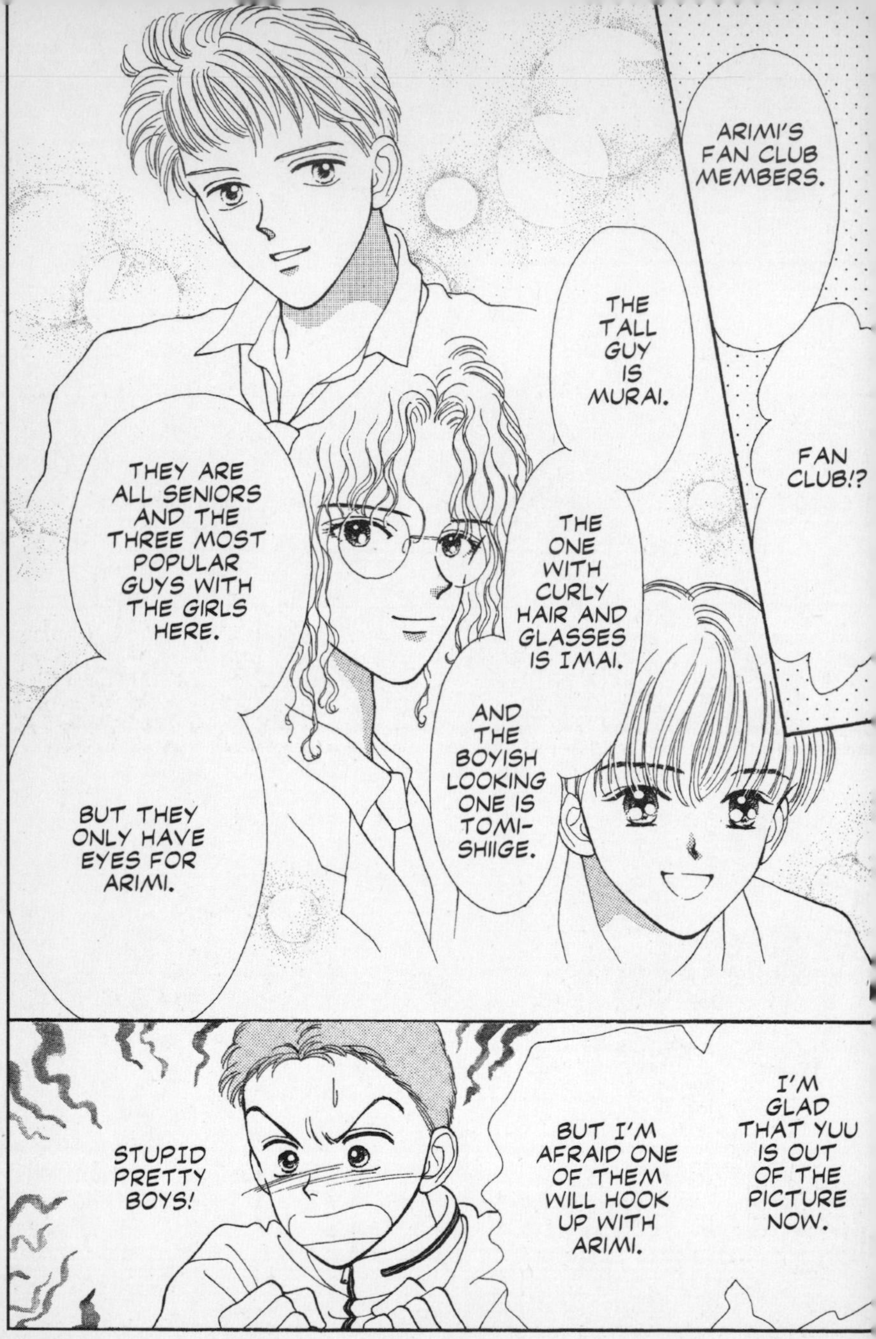
ARIMI'S FAN CLUB MEMBERS.
FAN CLUB!?
THE TALL GUY IS MURAI.
THE ONE WITH CURLY HAIR AND GLASSES IS IMAI.
AND THE BOYISH LOOKING ONE IS TOMI-SHIIGE.
THEY ARE ALL SENIORS AND THE THREE MOST POPULAR GUYS WITH THE GIRLS HERE.
BUT THEY ONLY HAVE EYES FOR ARIMI.
I'M GLAD THAT YUU IS OUT OF THE PICTURE NOW.
BUT I'M AFRAID ONE OF THEM WILL HOOK UP WITH ARIMI.
STUPID PRETTY BOYS!

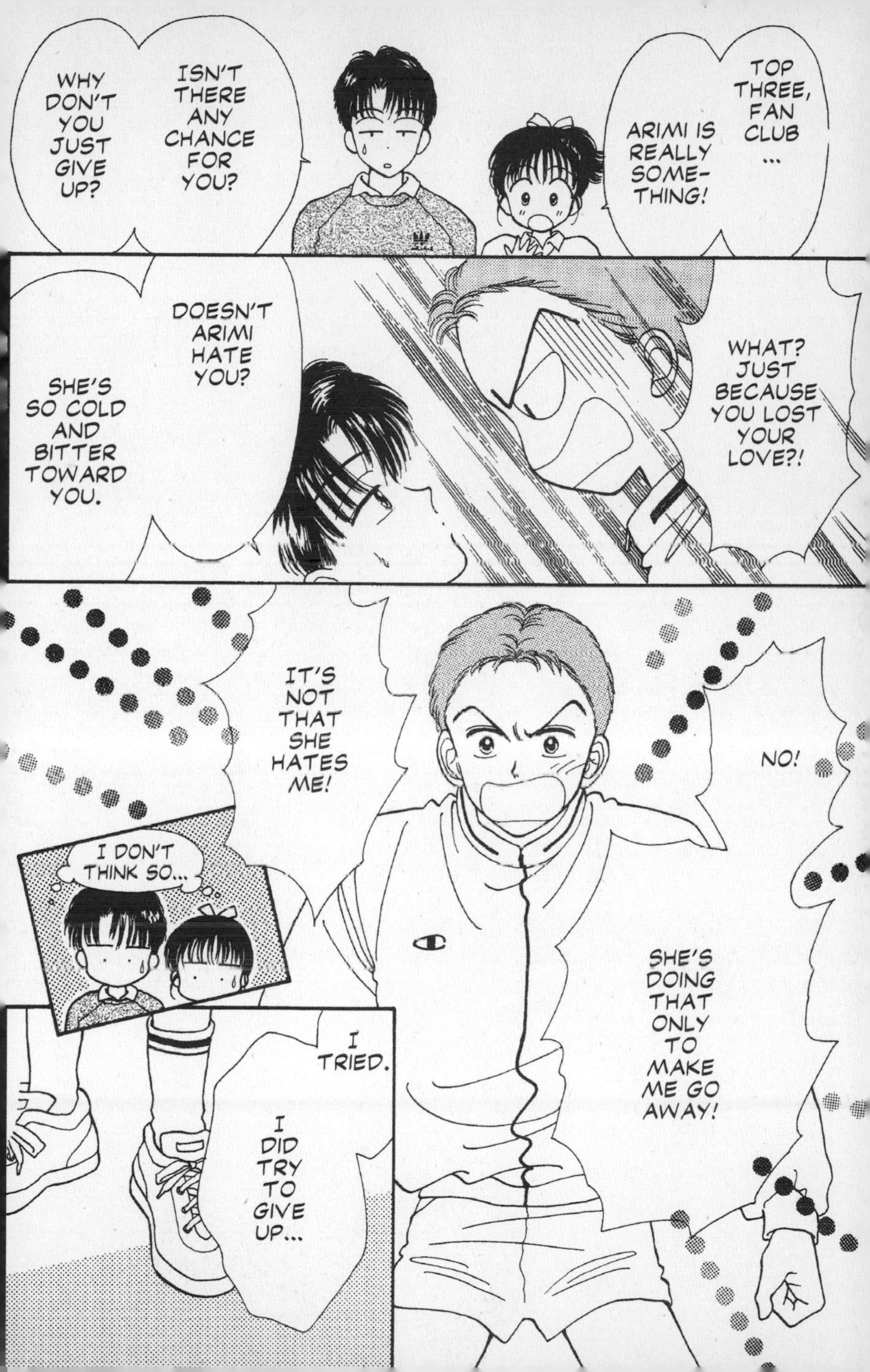
TOP THREE, FAN CLUB ...
ARIMI IS REALLY SOME-THING!
ISN'T THERE ANY CHANCE FOR YOU?
WHY DON'T YOU JUST GIVE UP?
WHAT? JUST BECAUSE YOU LOST YOUR LOVE?!
DOESN'T ARIMI HATE YOU?
SHE'S SO COLD AND BITTER TOWARD YOU.
NO!
IT'S NOT THAT SHE HATES ME!
SHE'S DOING THAT ONLY TO MAKE ME GO AWAY!
I DON'T THINK SO...
I TRIED.
I DID TRY TO GIVE UP...

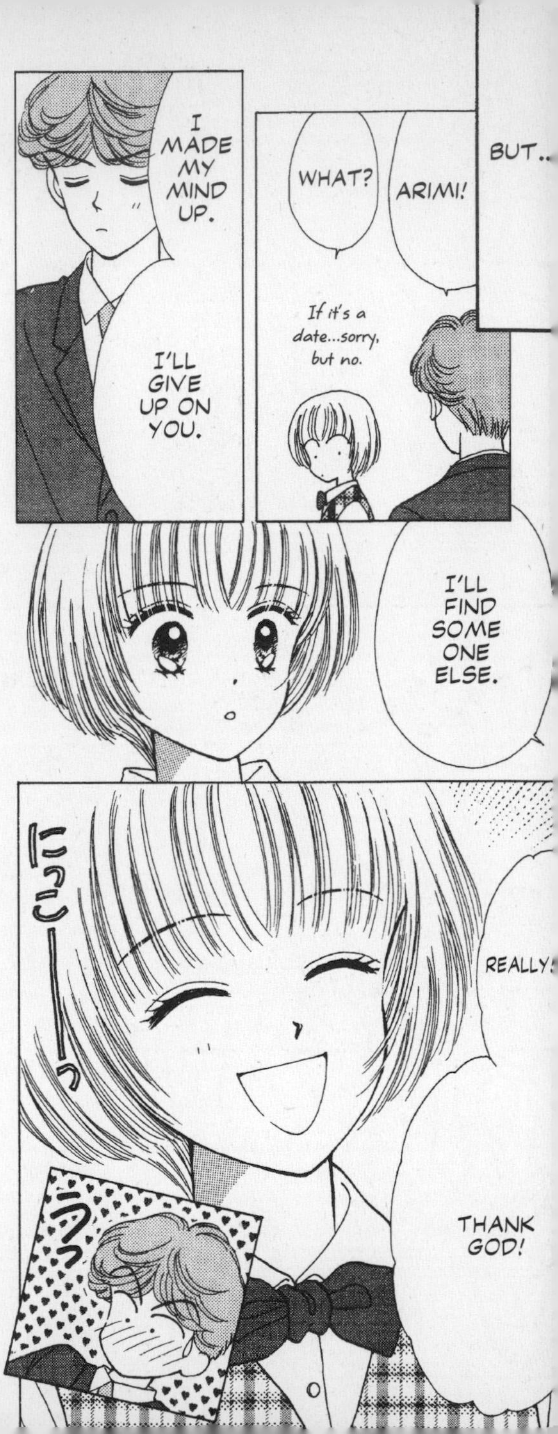
BUT..
ARIMI!
WHAT?
If it's a date...sorry, but no.
I MADE MY MIND UP.
I'LL GIVE UP ON YOU.
I'LL FIND SOME ONE ELSE.
REALLY!
THANK GOD!
にっこーっ
う

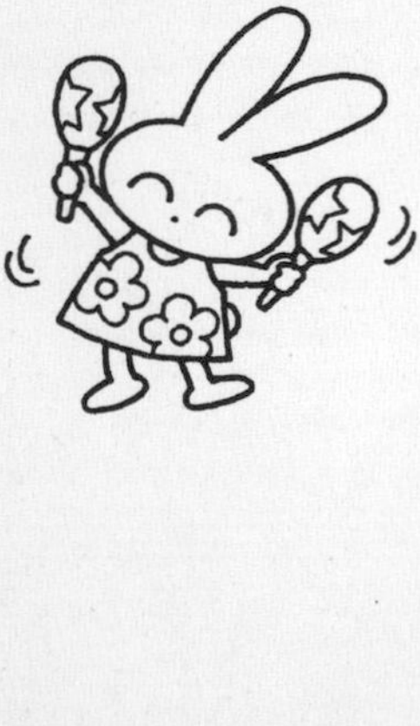

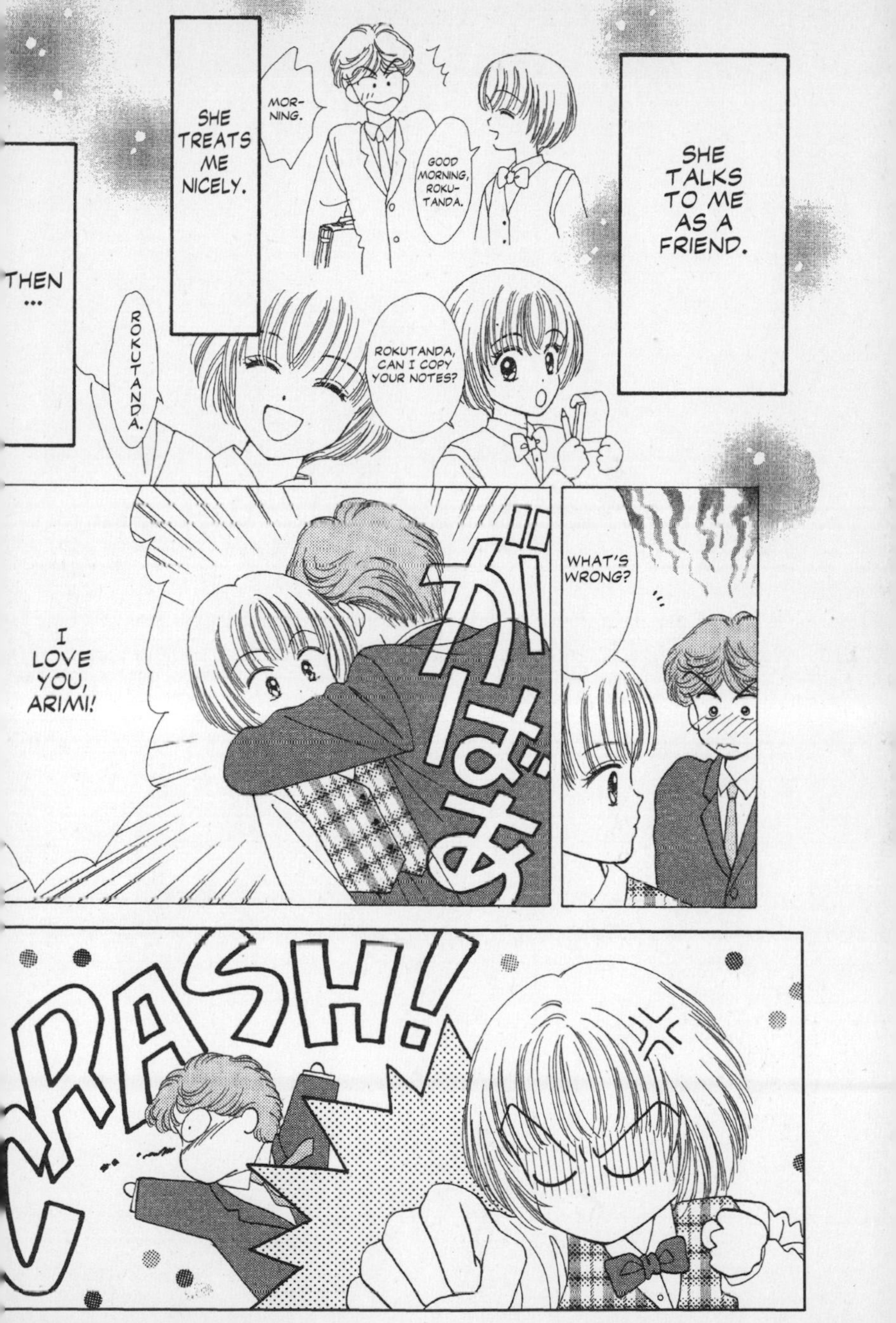
SHE TALKS TO ME AS A FRIEND.
GOOD MORNING, ROKUTANDA.
MORNING.
SHE TREATS ME NICELY.
ROKUTANDA, CAN I COPY YOUR NOTES?
ROKUTANDA.
THEN...
WHAT'S WRONG?
がばあ
I LOVE YOU, ARIMI!
CRASH!

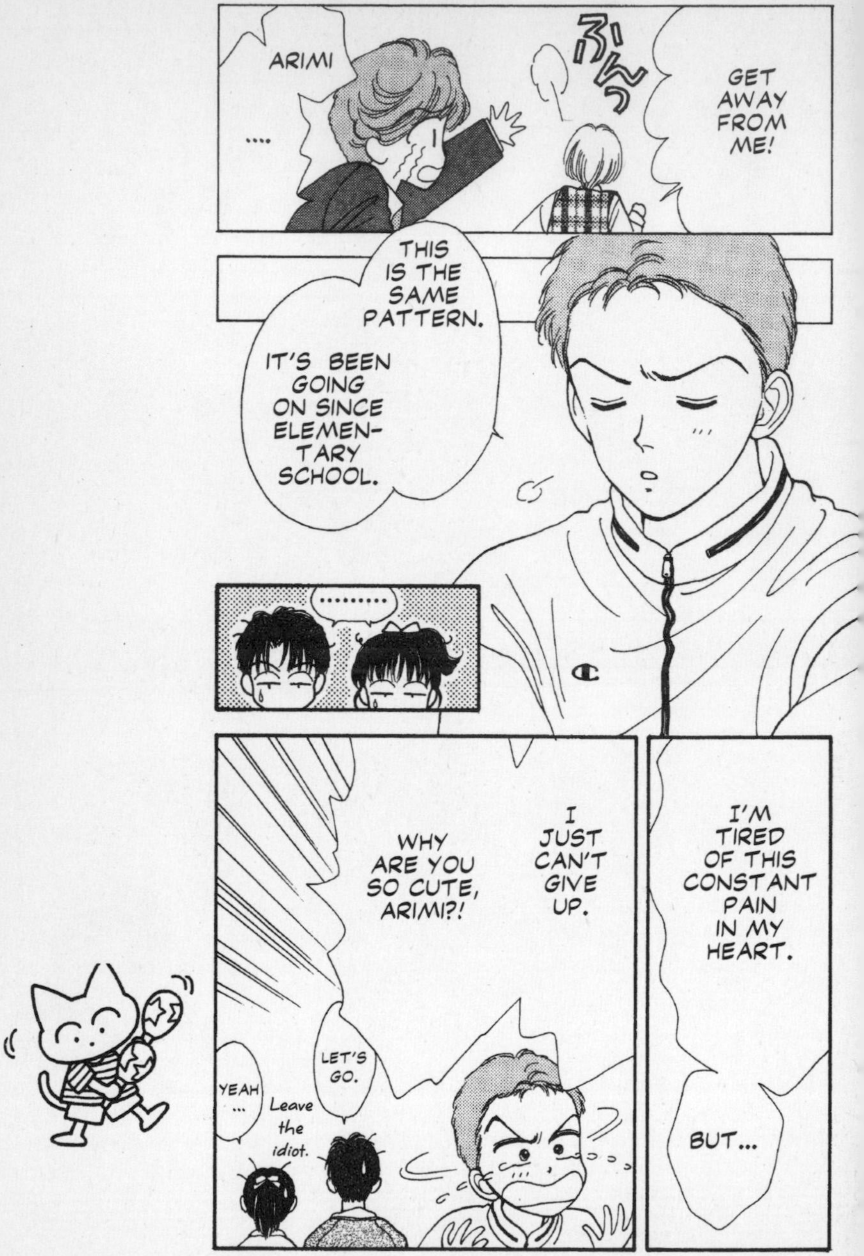

GET AWAY FROM ME!
ふんっ
ARIMI
....
...
THIS IS THE SAME PATTERN.
IT'S BEEN GOING ON SINCE ELEMENTARY SCHOOL.
....
I'M TIRED OF THIS CONSTANT PAIN IN MY HEART.
BUT...
I JUST CAN'T GIVE UP.
WHY ARE YOU SO CUTE, ARIMI?!
LET'S GO.
Leave the idiot.
YEAH ...

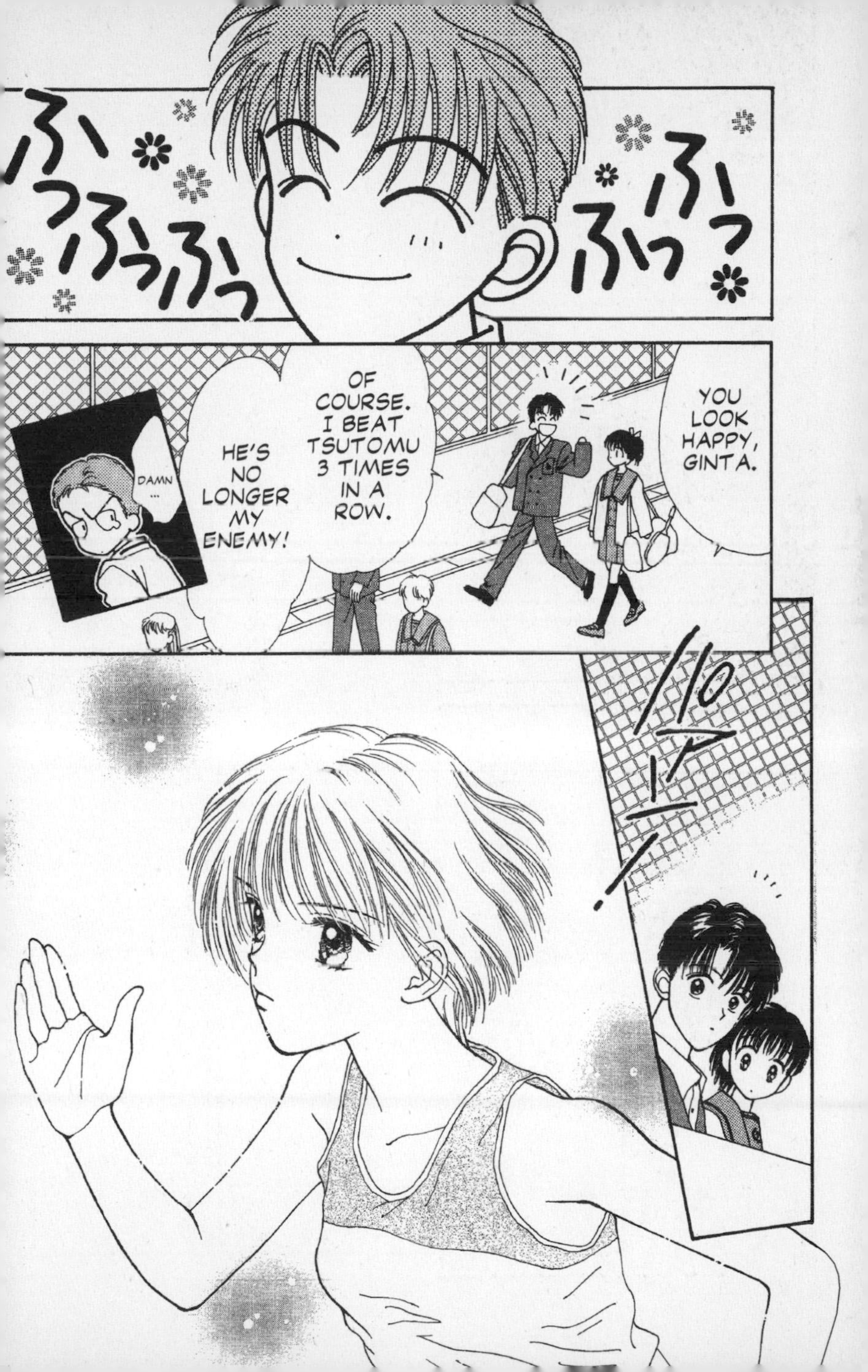
ふっふっ
ふっふっふっ
YOU LOOK HAPPY, GINTA.
OF COURSE. I BEAT TSUTOMU 3 TIMES IN A ROW.
HE'S NO LONGER MY ENEMY!
DAMN ...

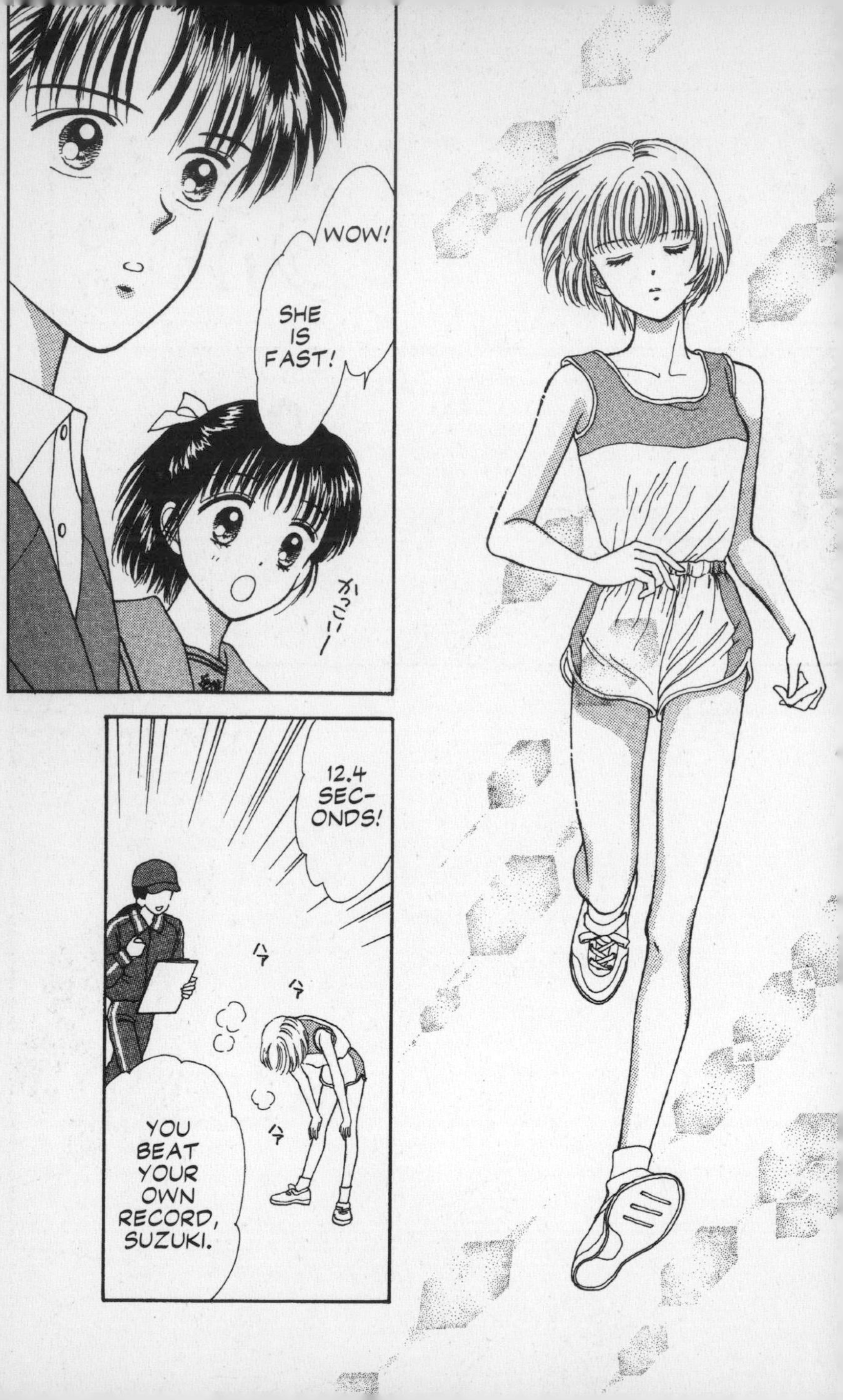
WOW!
SHE IS FAST!
12.4 SECONDS!
YOU BEAT YOUR OWN RECORD, SUZUKI.

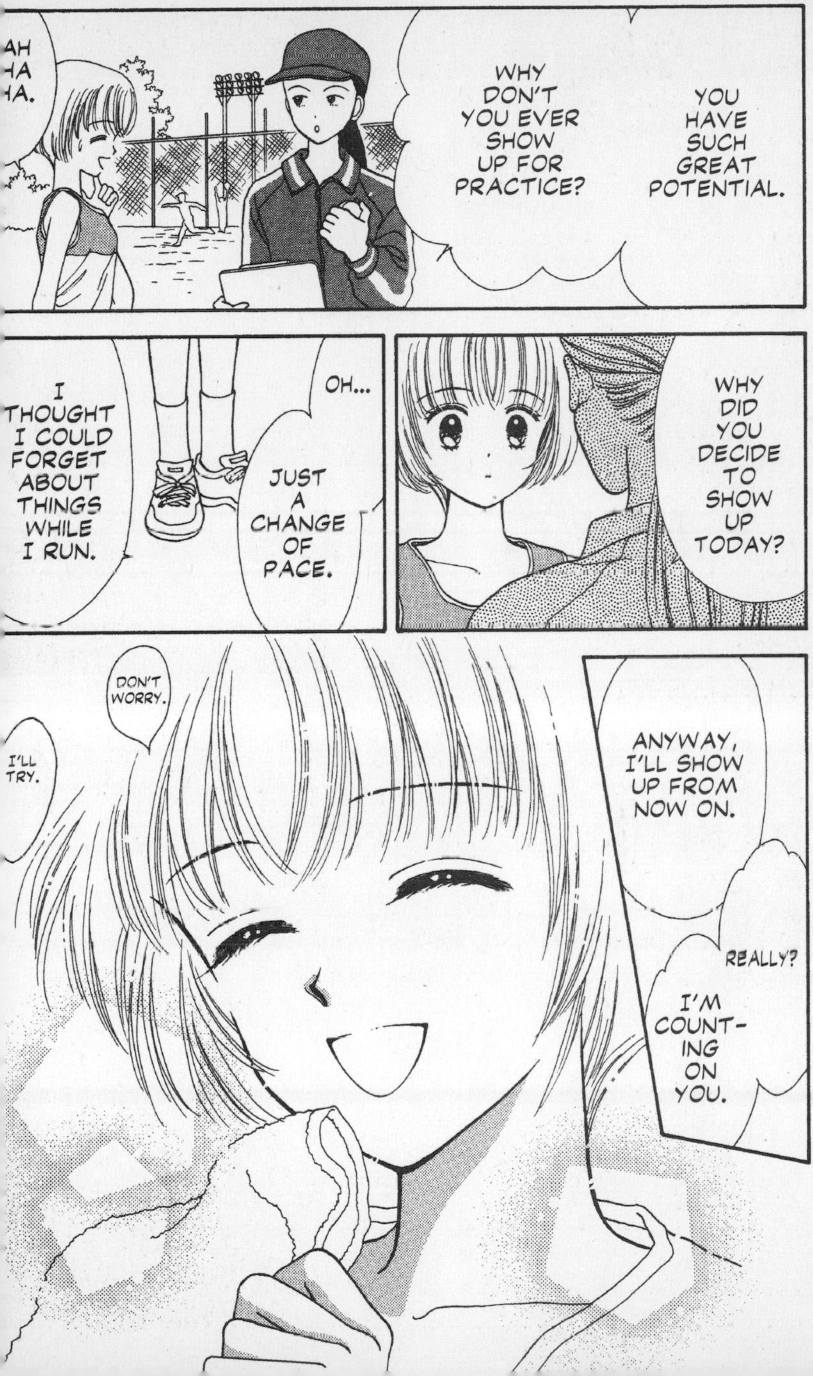
YOU HAVE SUCH GREAT POTENTIAL.
WHY DON'T YOU EVER SHOW UP FOR PRACTICE?
AH HA HA.
WHY DID YOU DECIDE TO SHOW UP TODAY?
OH...
JUST A CHANGE OF PACE.
I THOUGHT I COULD FORGET ABOUT THINGS WHILE I RUN.
ANYWAY, I'LL SHOW UP FROM NOW ON.
REALLY?
I'M COUNTING ON YOU.
DON'T WORRY.
I'LL TRY.

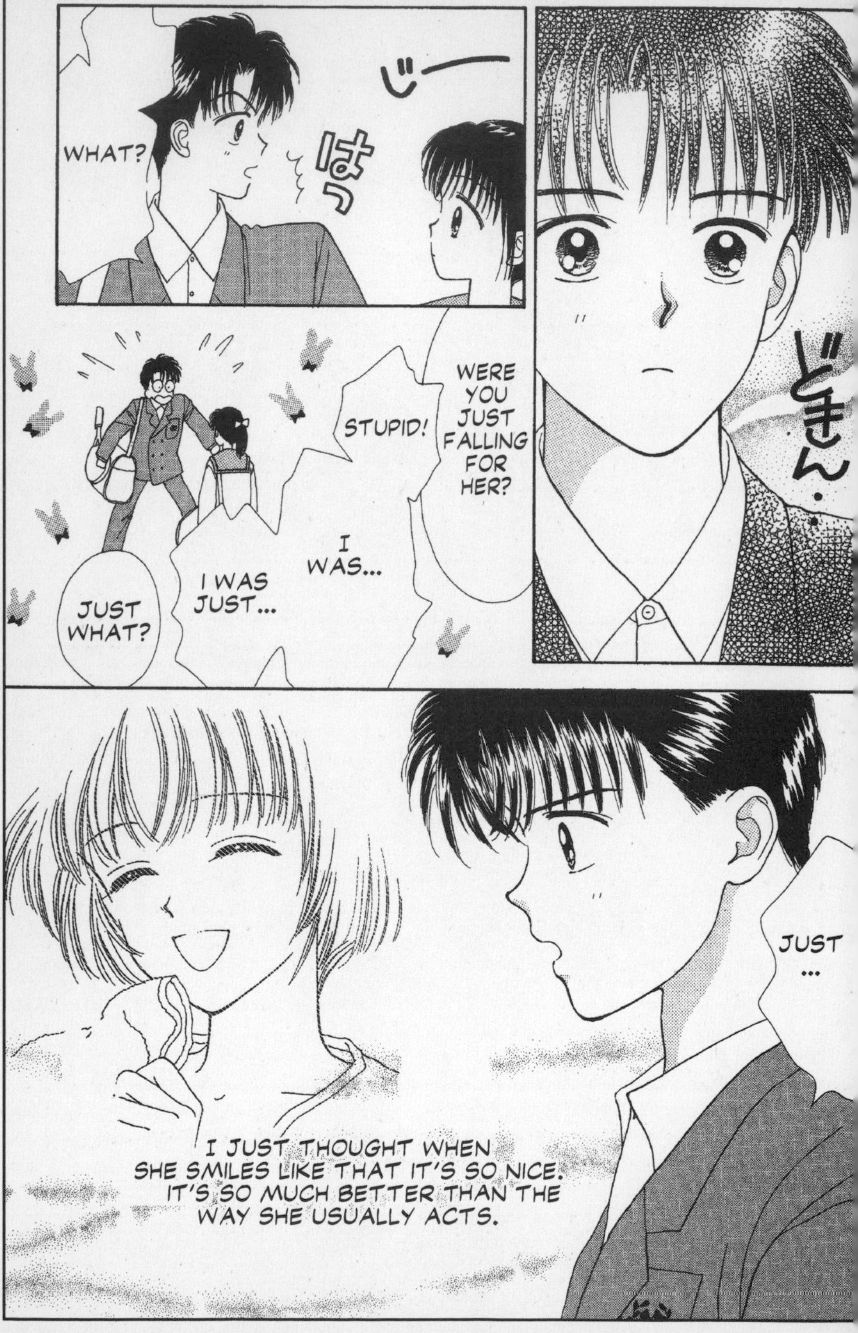
どきん・・
じー
はっ
WHAT?
WERE YOU JUST FALLING FOR HER?
STUPID!
I WAS...
I WAS JUST...
JUST WHAT?
JUST ...
I JUST THOUGHT WHEN SHE SMILES LIKE THAT IT'S SO NICE. IT'S SO MUCH BETTER THAN THE WAY SHE USUALLY ACTS.

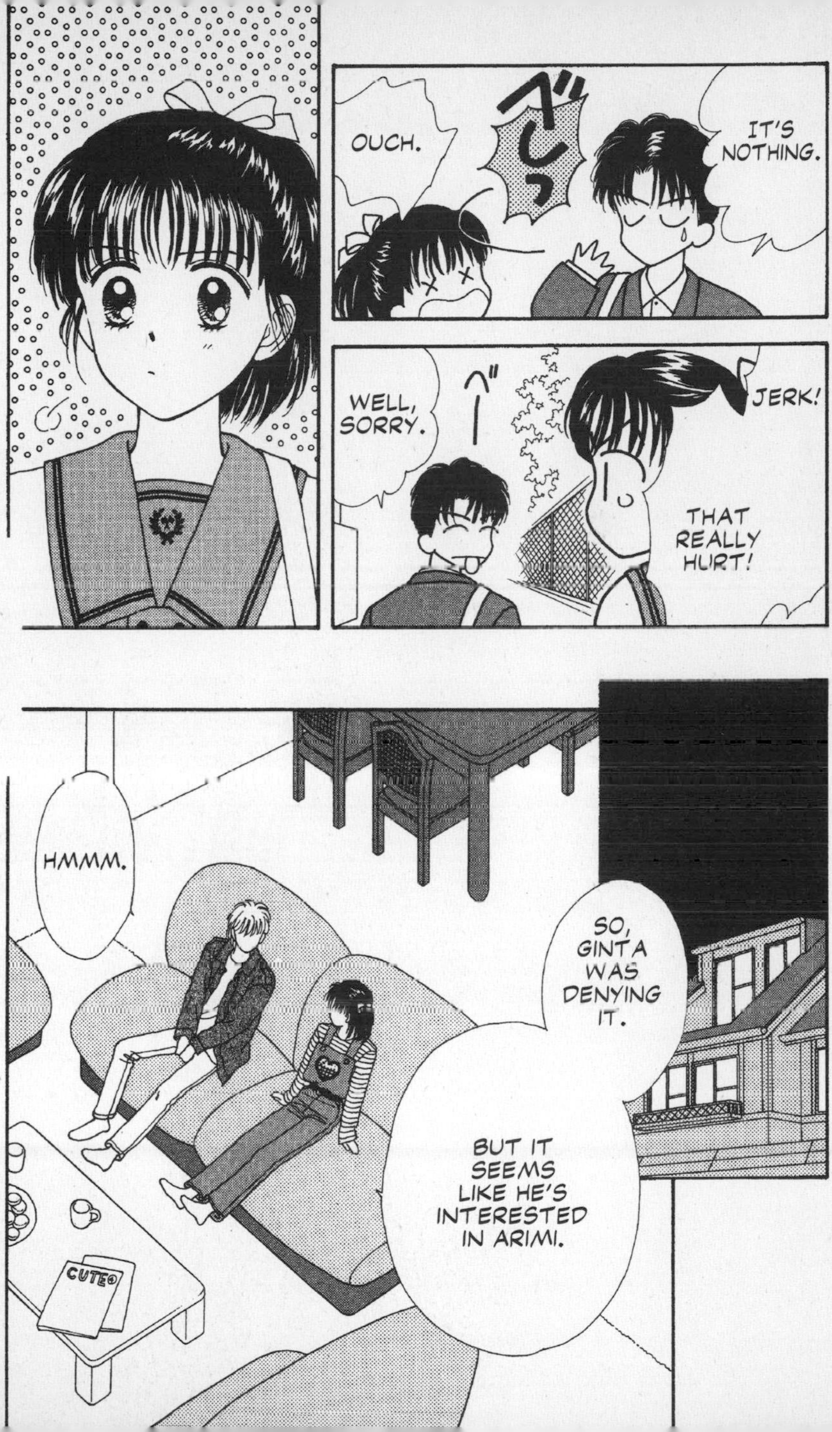
IT'S NOTHING.
べしっ
OUCH.
JERK!
THAT REALLY HURT!
べー
WELL, SORRY.
SO, GINTA WAS DENYING IT.
BUT IT SEEMS LIKE HE'S INTERESTED IN ARIMI.
HMMM.
CUTE

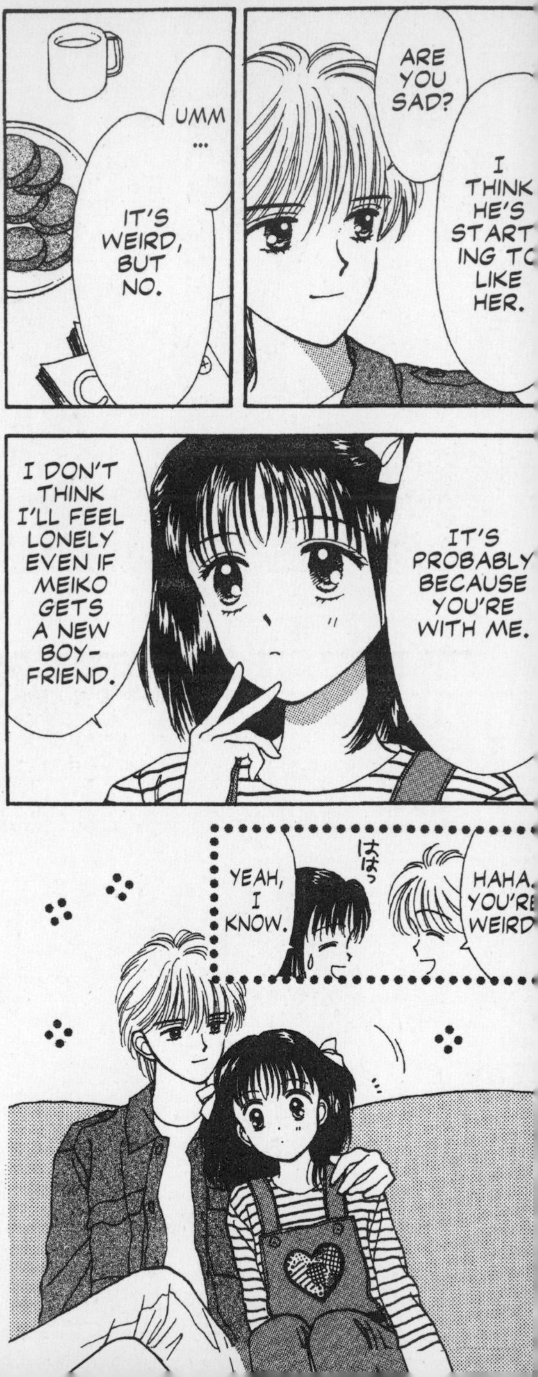
ARE YOU SAD?
I THINK HE'S STARTING TO LIKE HER.
UMM...
IT'S WEIRD, BUT NO.
I DON'T THINK I'LL FEEL LONELY EVEN IF MEIKO GETS A NEW BOY-FRIEND.
IT'S PROBABLY BECAUSE YOU'RE WITH ME.
HAHA. YOU'RE WEIRD
ははっ
YEAH, I KNOW.
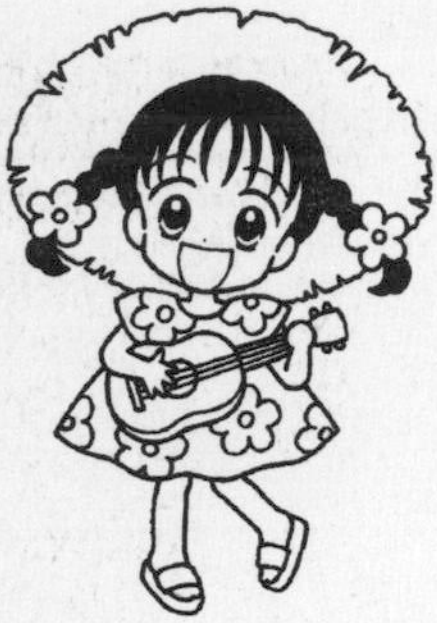

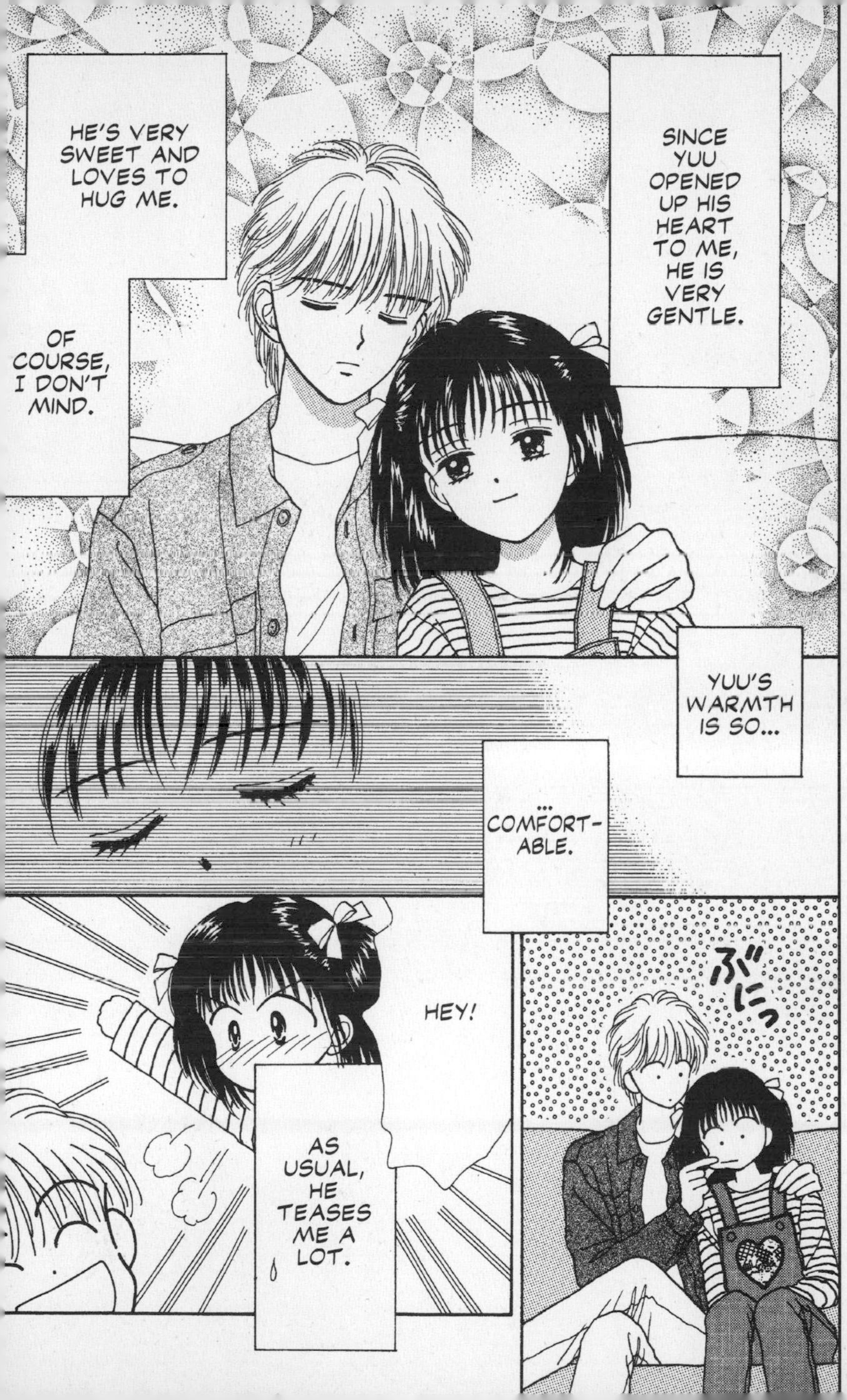
SINCE YUU OPENED UP HIS HEART TO ME, HE IS VERY GENTLE.
HE'S VERY SWEET AND LOVES TO HUG ME.
OF COURSE, I DON'T MIND.
YUU'S WARMTH IS SO...
... COMFORTABLE.
ぶにっ
HEY!
AS USUAL, HE TEASES ME A LOT.

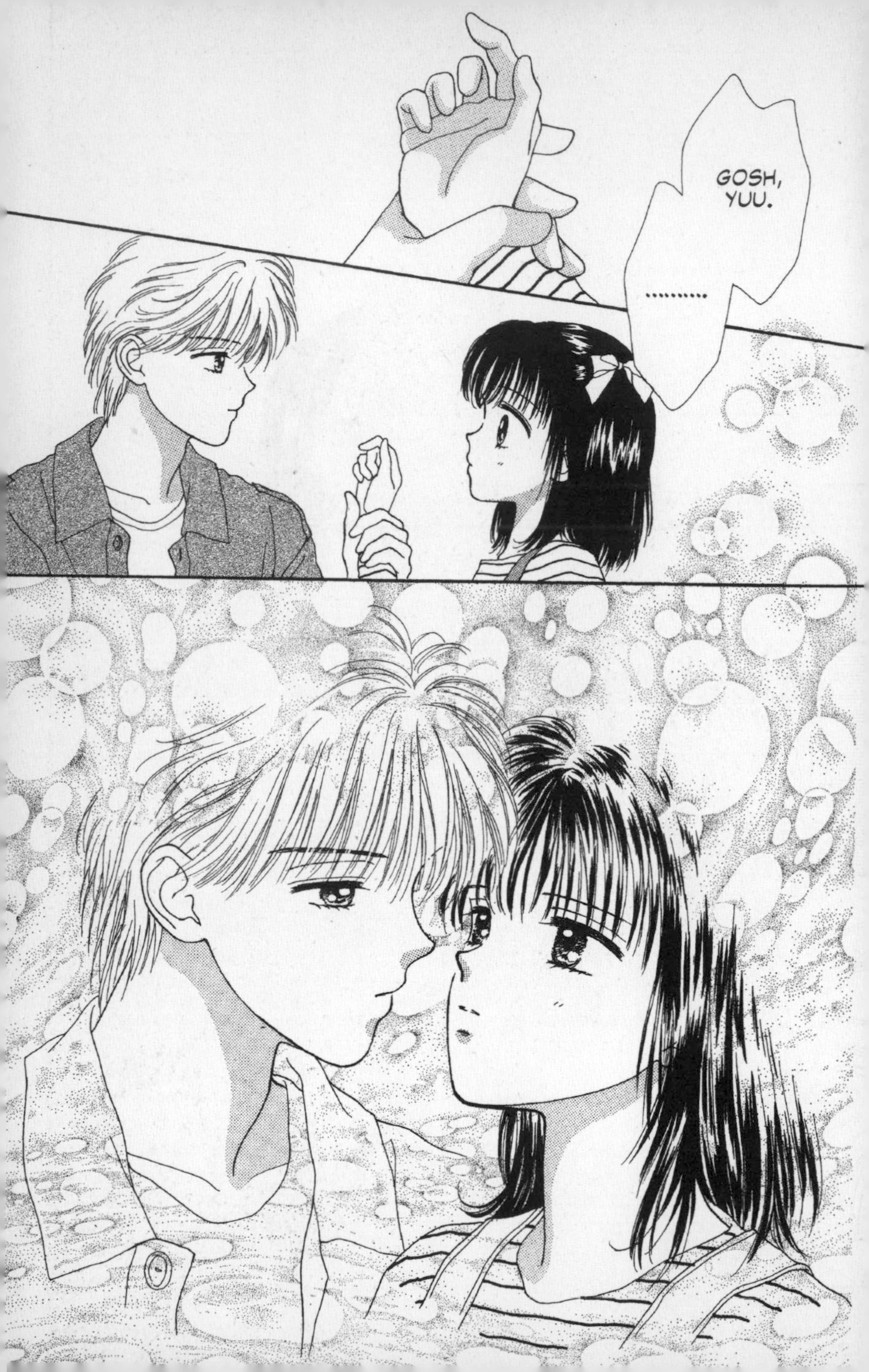
GOSH, YUU.
....

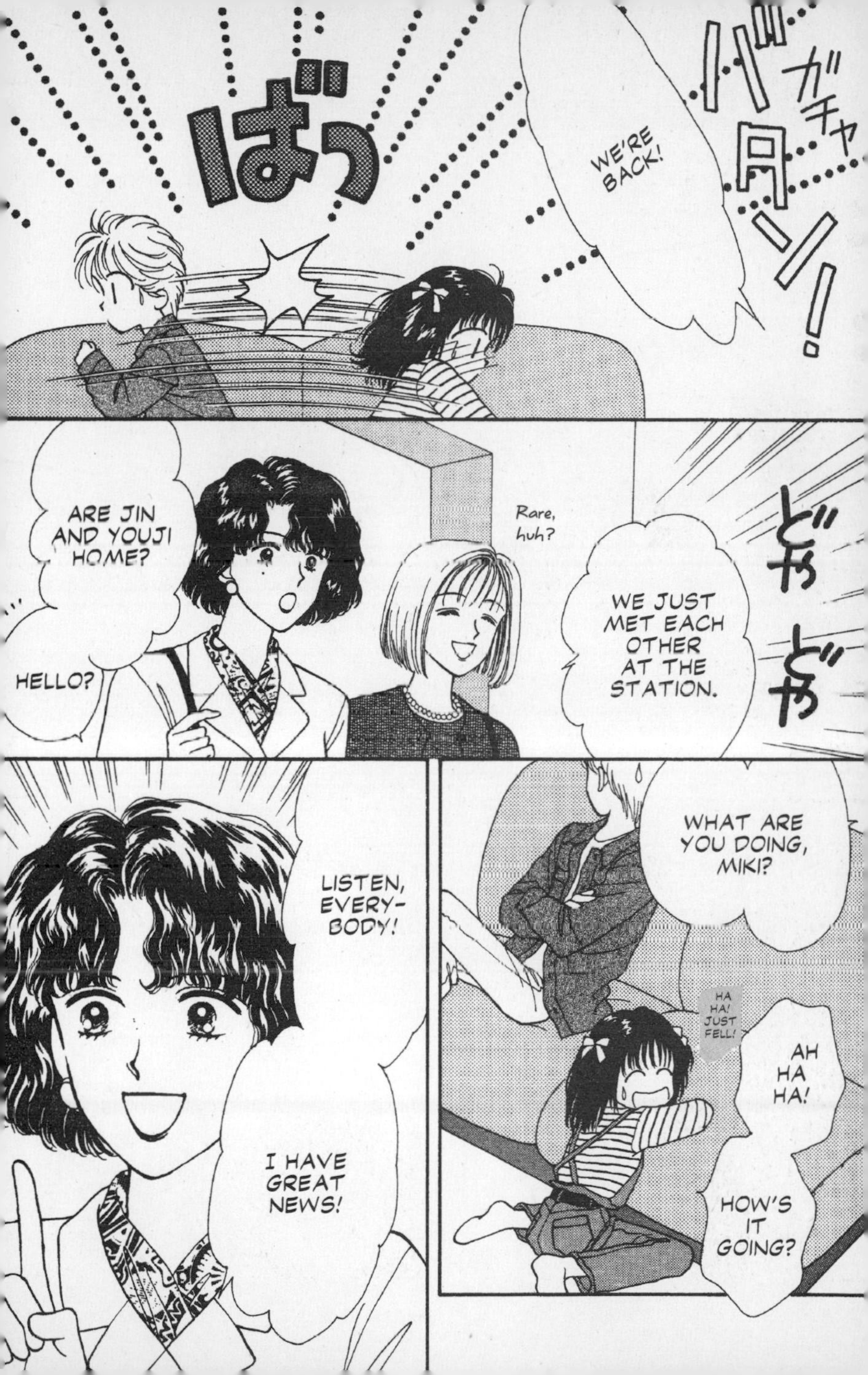
ガチャ
バタン!
WE'RE BACK!
ばっ
どやどや
WE JUST MET EACH OTHER AT THE STATION.
Rare, huh?
ARE JIN AND YOUJI HOME?
HELLO?
WHAT ARE YOU DOING, MIKI?
HA HA! JUST FELL!
AH HA HA!
HOW'S IT GOING?
LISTEN, EVERY-BODY!
I HAVE GREAT NEWS!

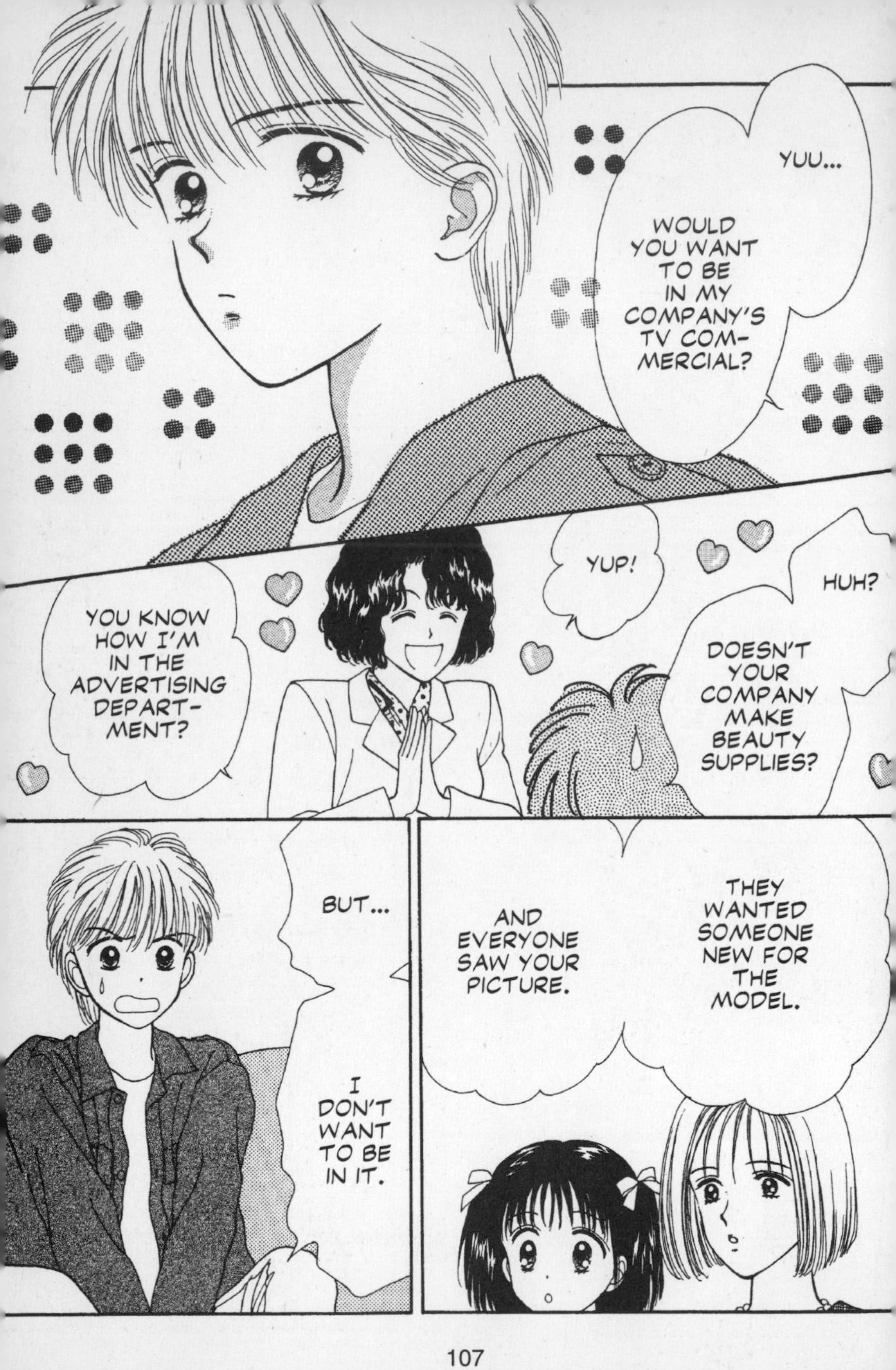
YUU...
WOULD YOU WANT TO BE IN MY COMPANY'S TV COM-MERCIAL?
HUH?
DOESN'T YOUR COMPANY MAKE BEAUTY SUPPLIES?
YUP!
YOU KNOW HOW I'M IN THE ADVERTISING DEPART-MENT?
THEY WANTED SOMEONE NEW FOR THE MODEL.
AND EVERYONE SAW YOUR PICTURE.
BUT...
I DON'T WANT TO BE IN IT.

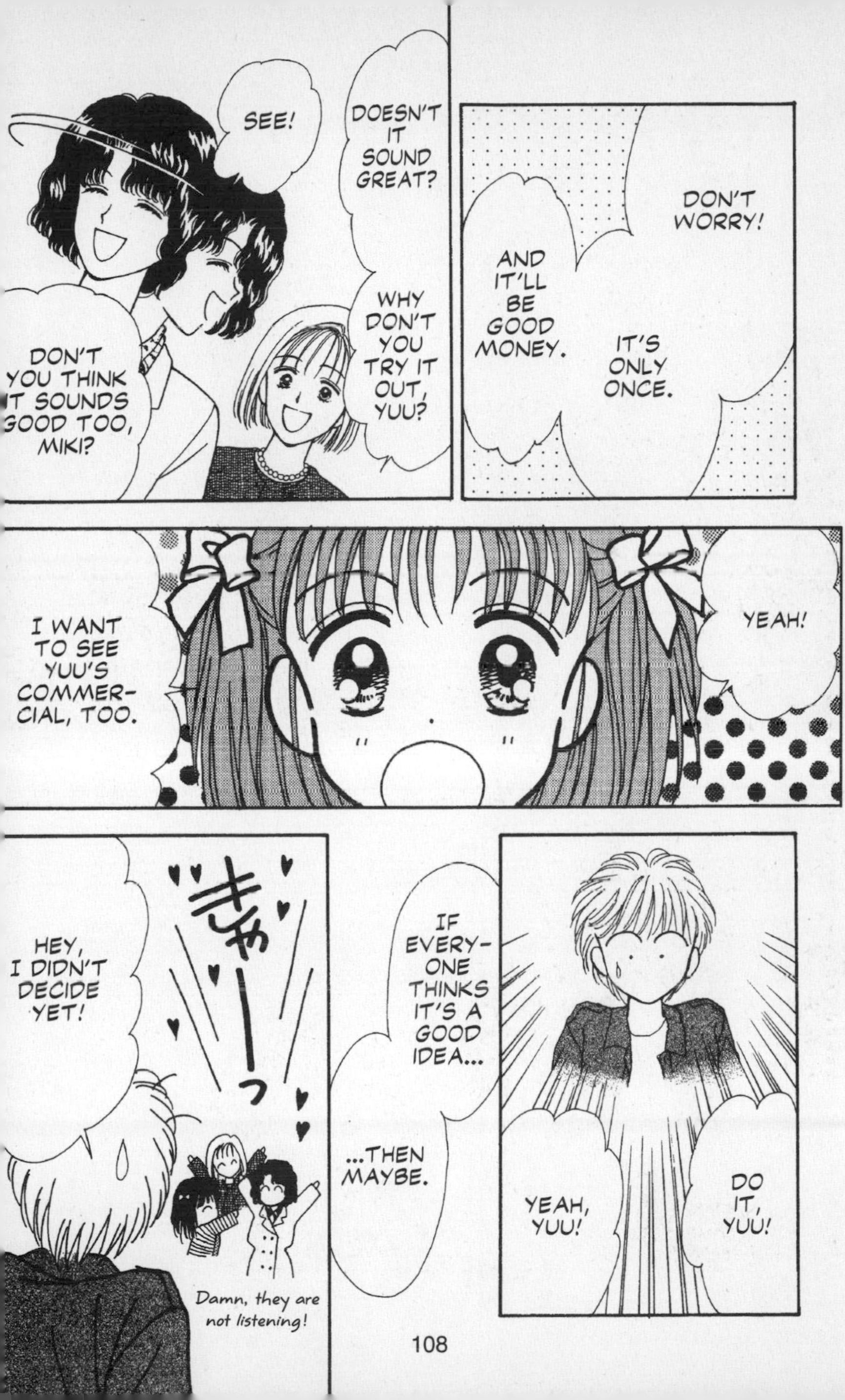
DON'T WORRY!
IT'S ONLY ONCE.
AND IT'LL BE GOOD MONEY.
DOESN'T IT SOUND GREAT?
SEE!
WHY DON'T YOU TRY IT OUT, YUU?
DON'T YOU THINK IT SOUNDS GOOD TOO, MIKI?
YEAH!
I WANT TO SEE YUU'S COMMERCIAL, TOO.
DO IT, YUU!
YEAH, YUU!
IF EVERY-ONE THINKS IT'S A GOOD IDEA...
...THEN MAYBE.
きゃーっ
HEY, I DIDN'T DECIDE YET!
Damn, they are not listening!

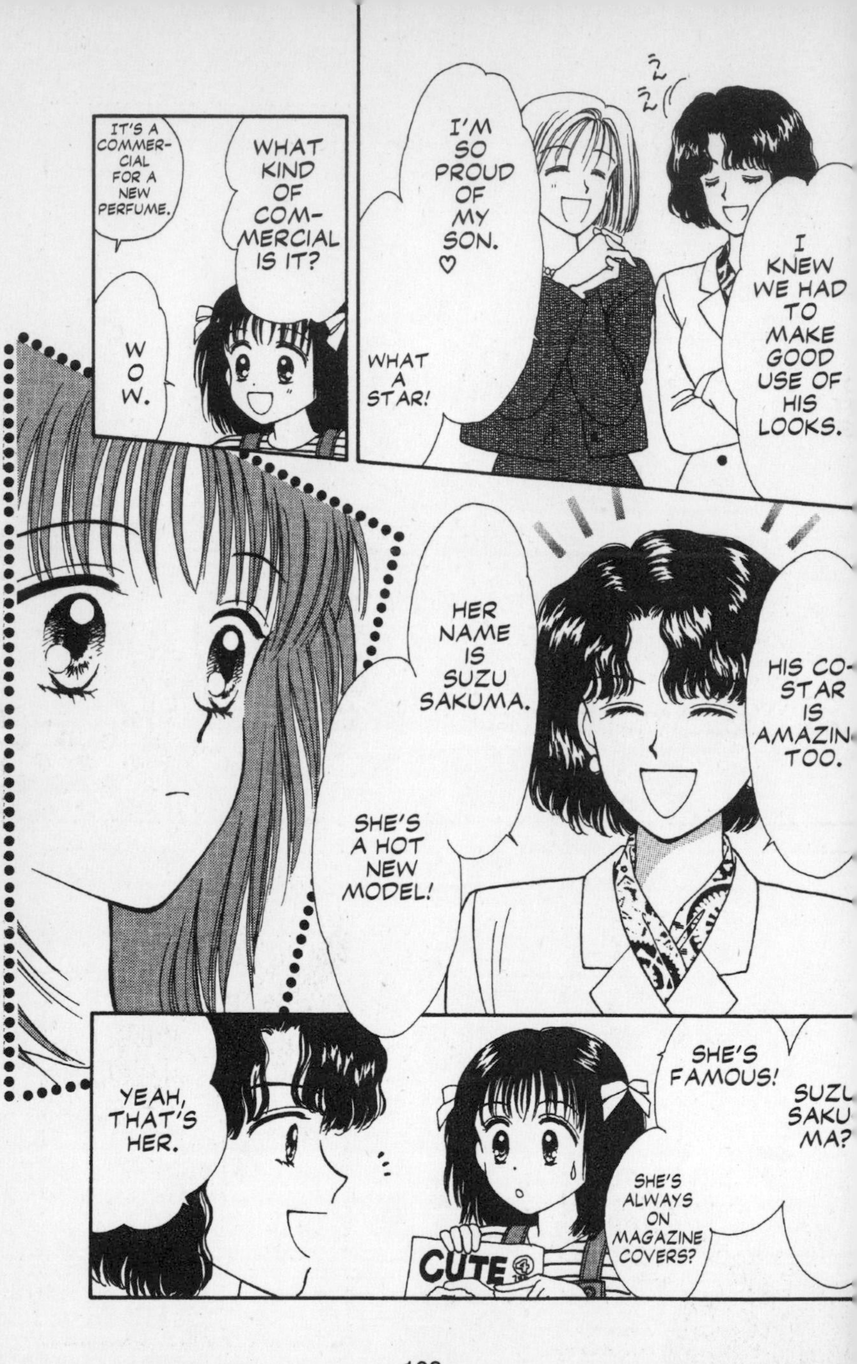
I KNEW WE HAD TO MAKE GOOD USE OF HIS LOOKS.
うん うん
I'M SO PROUD OF MY SON. ♡
WHAT A STAR!
WHAT KIND OF COMMERCIAL IS IT?
IT'S A COMMERCIAL FOR A NEW PERFUME.
WOW.
HIS CO-STAR IS AMAZIN TOO.
HER NAME IS SUZU SAKUMA.
SHE'S A HOT NEW MODEL!
SUZU SAKUMA?
SHE'S FAMOUS!
SHE'S ALWAYS ON MAGAZINE COVERS?
CUTE
YEAH, THAT'S HER.

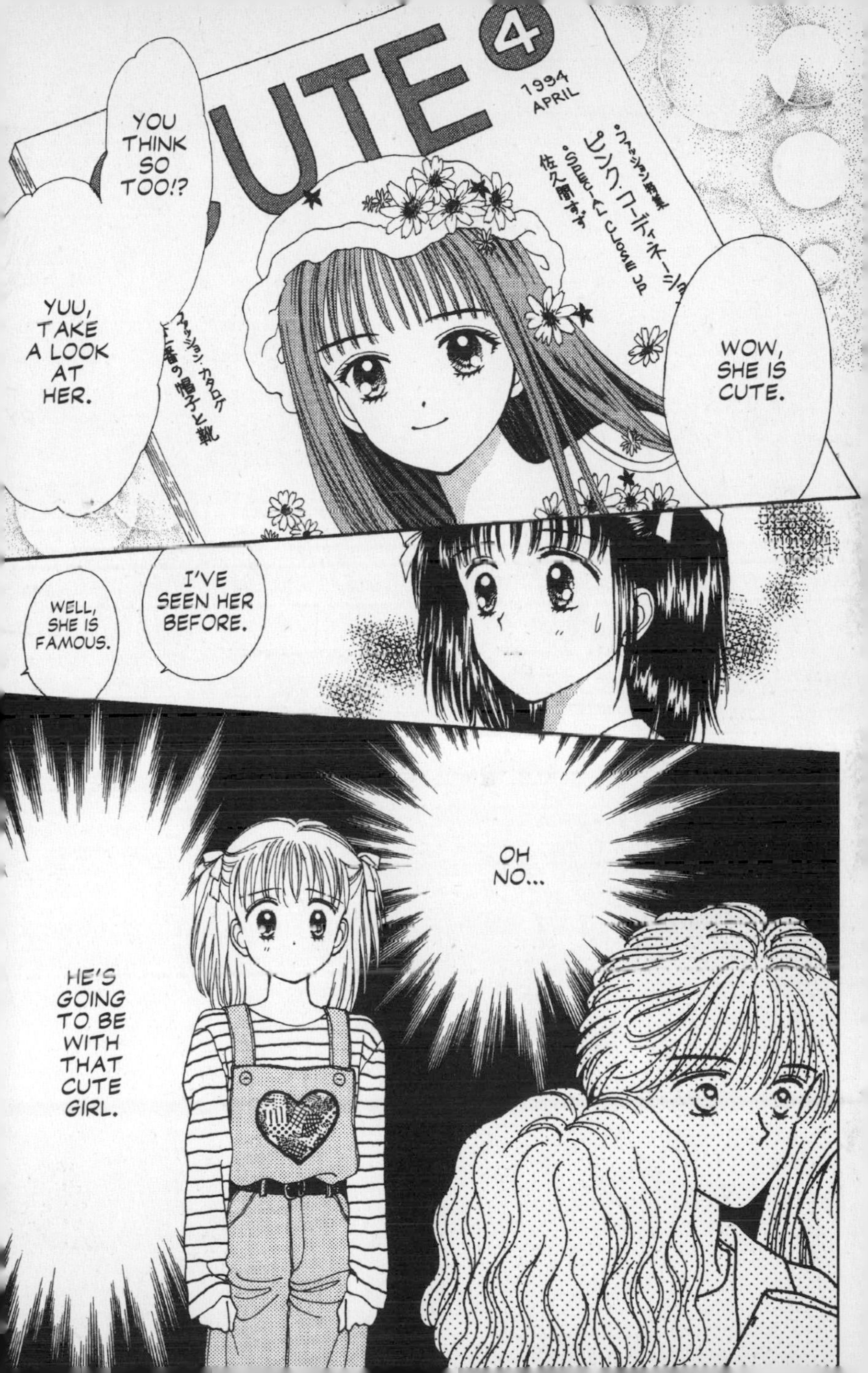
CUTE 4
1994 APRIL
ファッション特集 ピンク・コーディネーション
SPECIAL CLOSE UP 佐久間すず
ファッション・カタログ 一番の帽子と靴
WOW, SHE IS CUTE.
YOU THINK SO TOO!?
YUU, TAKE A LOOK AT HER.
I'VE SEEN HER BEFORE.
WELL, SHE IS FAMOUS.
OH NO...
HE'S GOING TO BE WITH THAT CUTE GIRL.

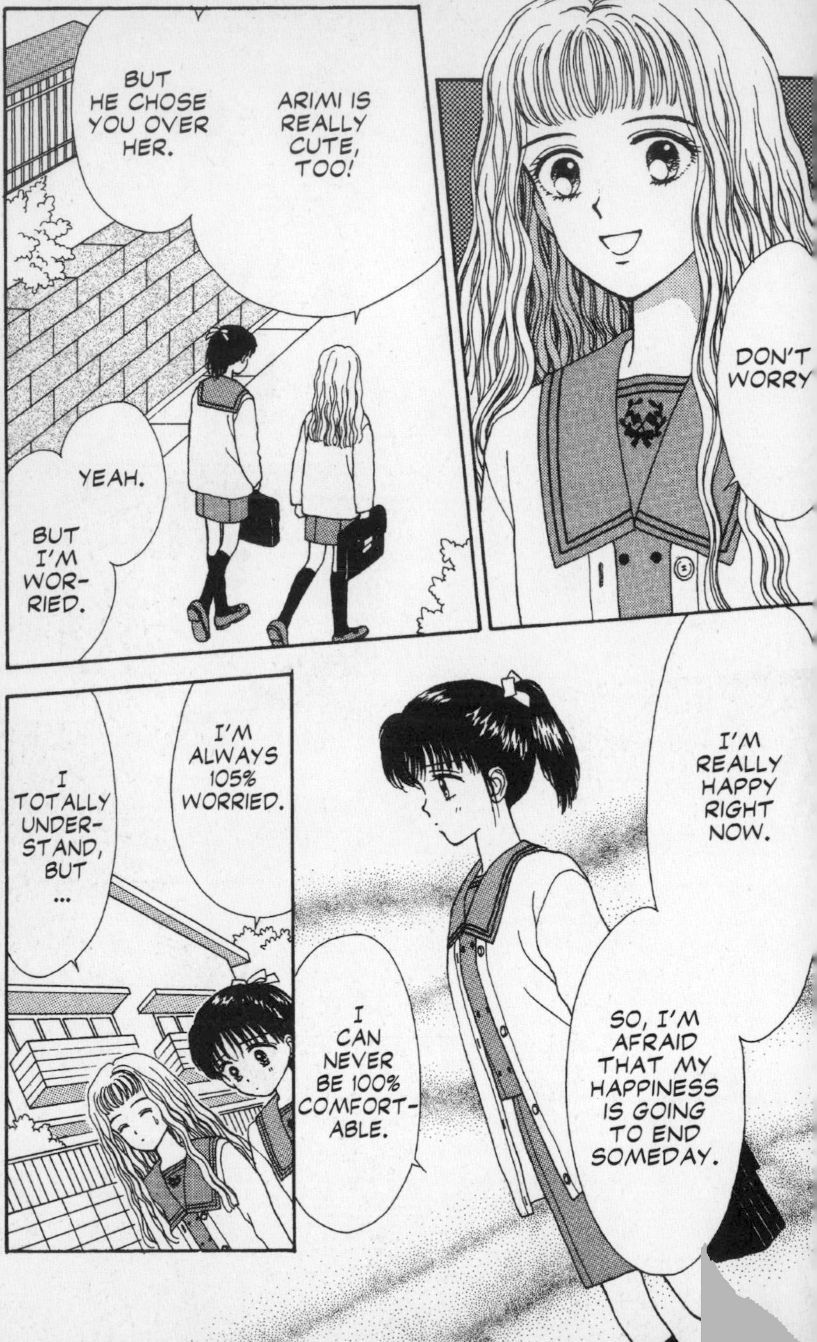
DON'T WORRY
ARIMI IS REALLY CUTE, TOO!
BUT HE CHOSE YOU OVER HER.
YEAH.
BUT I'M WOR-RIED.
I'M REALLY HAPPY RIGHT NOW.
SO, I'M AFRAID THAT MY HAPPINESS IS GOING TO END SOMEDAY.
I'M ALWAYS 105% WORRIED.
I TOTALLY UNDER-STAND, BUT ...
I CAN NEVER BE 100% COMFORT-ABLE.

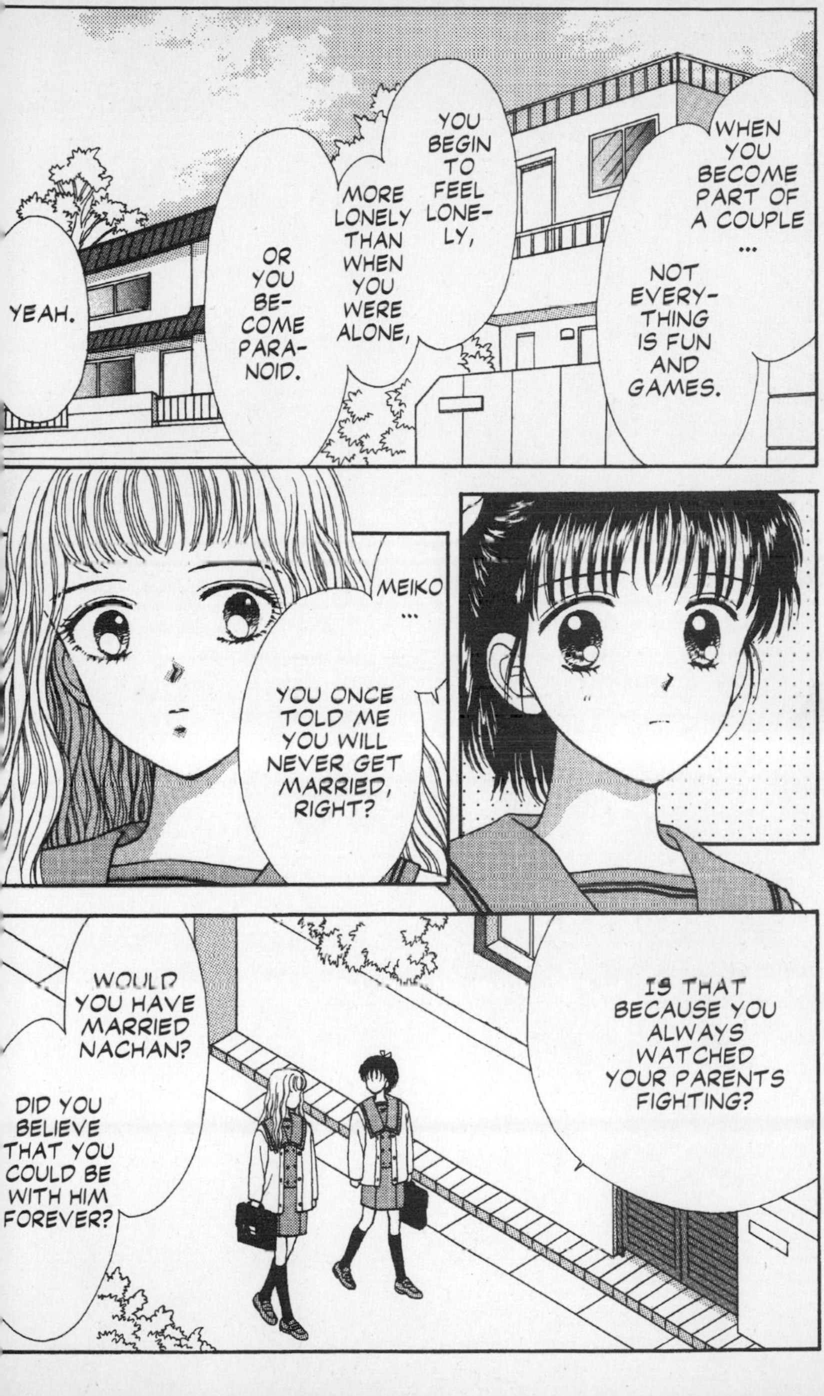
WHEN YOU BECOME PART OF A COUPLE...
NOT EVERYTHING IS FUN AND GAMES.
YOU BEGIN TO FEEL LONELY,
MORE LONELY THAN WHEN YOU WERE ALONE,
OR YOU BECOME PARANOID.
YEAH.
MEIKO...
YOU ONCE TOLD ME YOU WILL NEVER GET MARRIED, RIGHT?
IS THAT BECAUSE YOU ALWAYS WATCHED YOUR PARENTS FIGHTING?
WOULD YOU HAVE MARRIED NACHAN?
DID YOU BELIEVE THAT YOU COULD BE WITH HIM FOREVER?

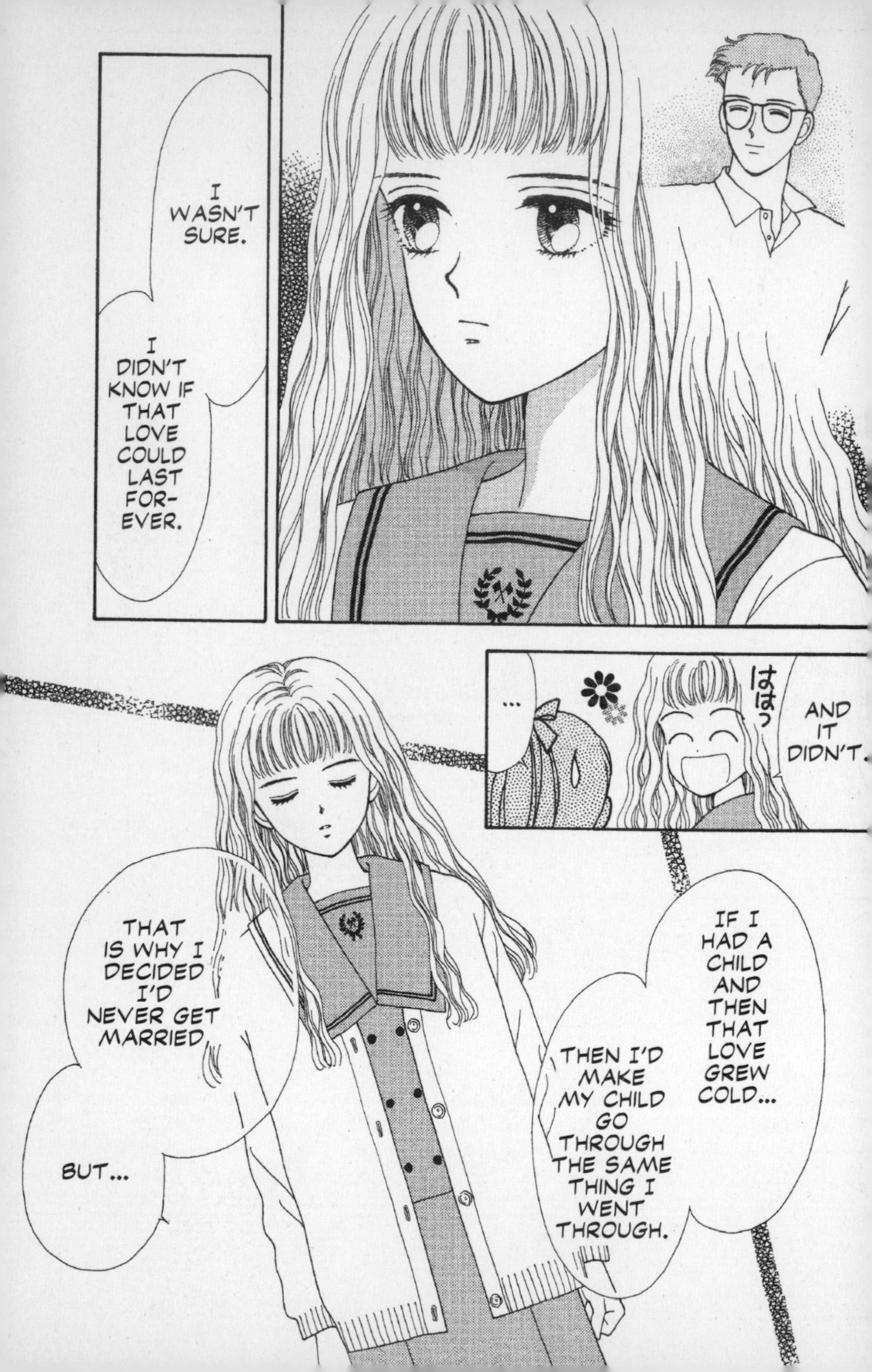
I WASN'T SURE.
I DIDN'T KNOW IF THAT LOVE COULD LAST FOR-EVER.
AND IT DIDN'T.
ははっ
...
IF I HAD A CHILD AND THEN THAT LOVE GREW COLD...
THEN I'D MAKE MY CHILD GO THROUGH THE SAME THING I WENT THROUGH.
THAT IS WHY I DECIDED I'D NEVER GET MARRIED
BUT...

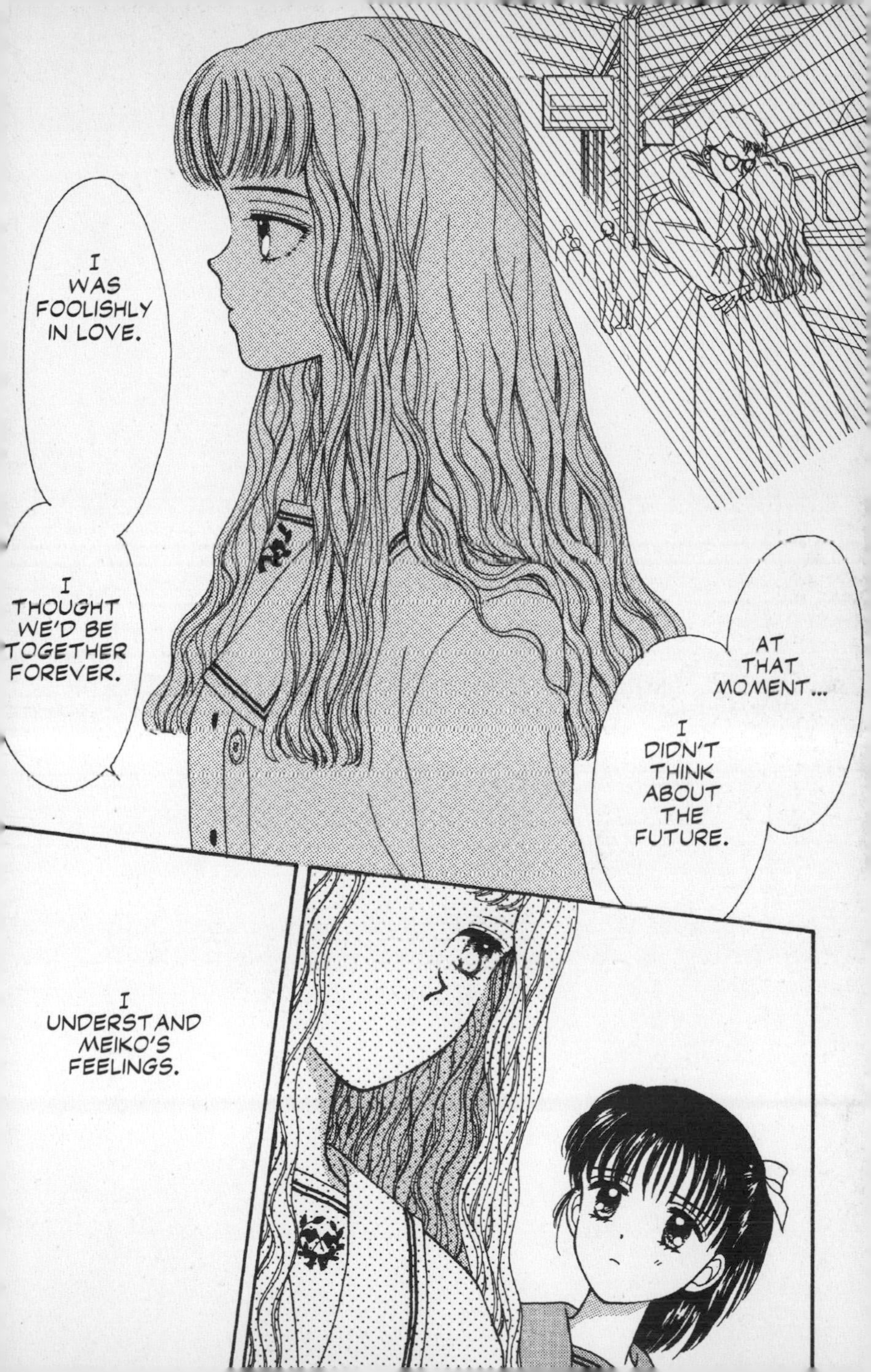
I WAS FOOLISHLY IN LOVE.
I THOUGHT WE'D BE TOGETHER FOREVER.
AT THAT MOMENT...
I DIDN'T THINK ABOUT THE FUTURE.
I UNDERSTAND MEIKO'S FEELINGS.

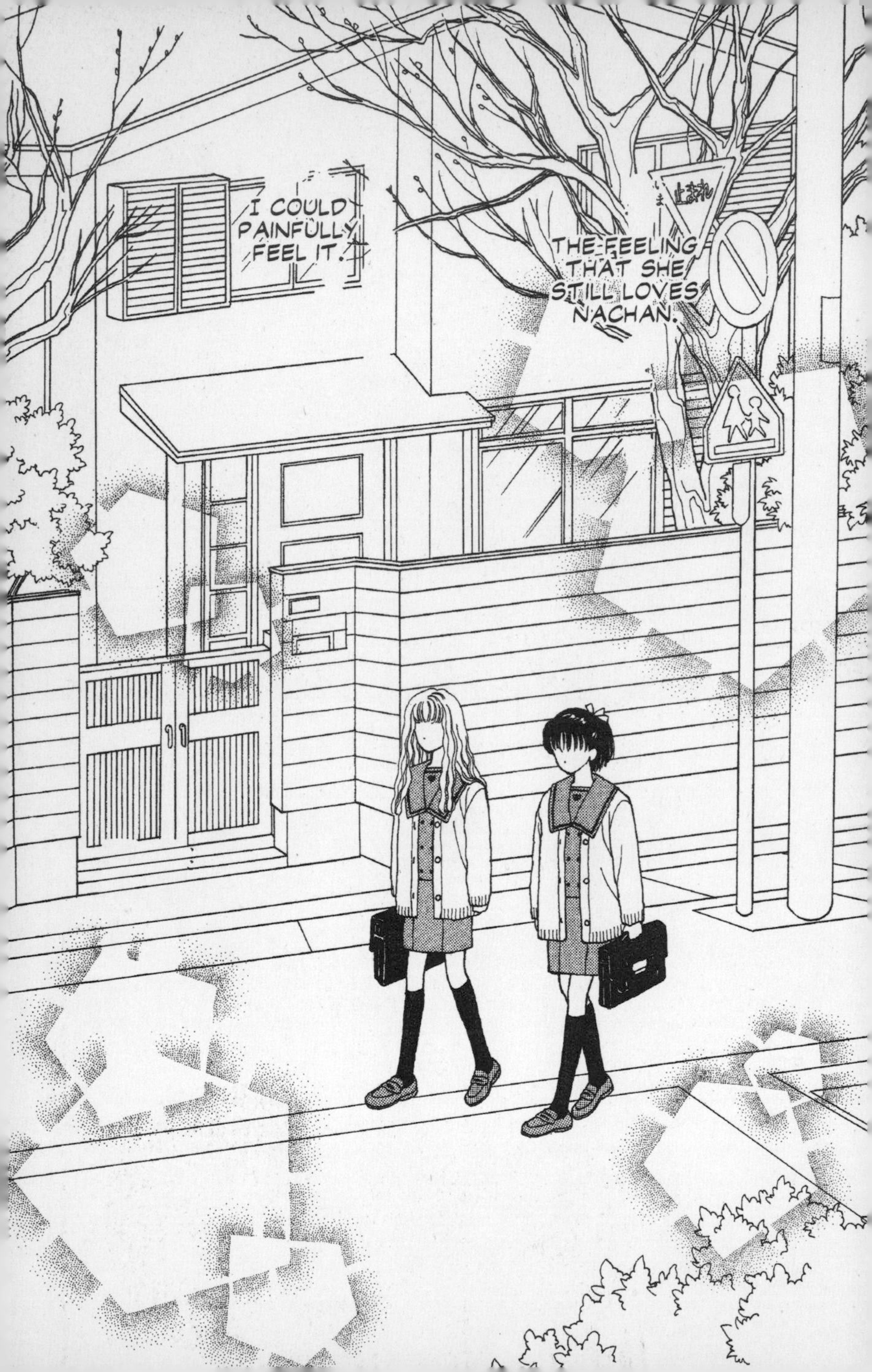
THE FEELING THAT SHE STILL LOVES NACHAN.
I COULD PAINFULLY FEEL IT.

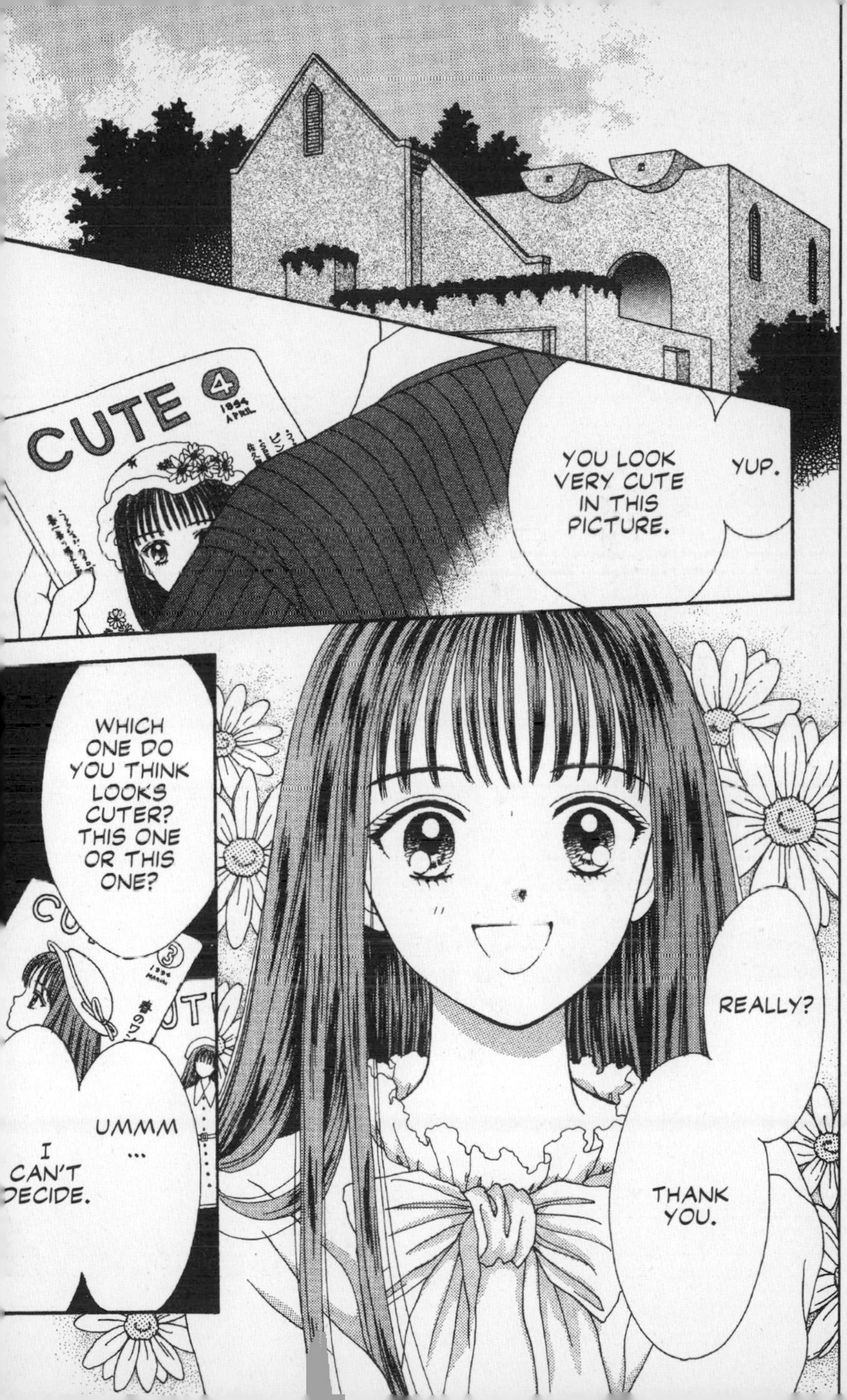
YUP.
YOU LOOK VERY CUTE IN THIS PICTURE.
CUTE
REALLY?
THANK YOU.
WHICH ONE DO YOU THINK LOOKS CUTER? THIS ONE OR THIS ONE?
UMMM ...
I CAN'T ECIDE.

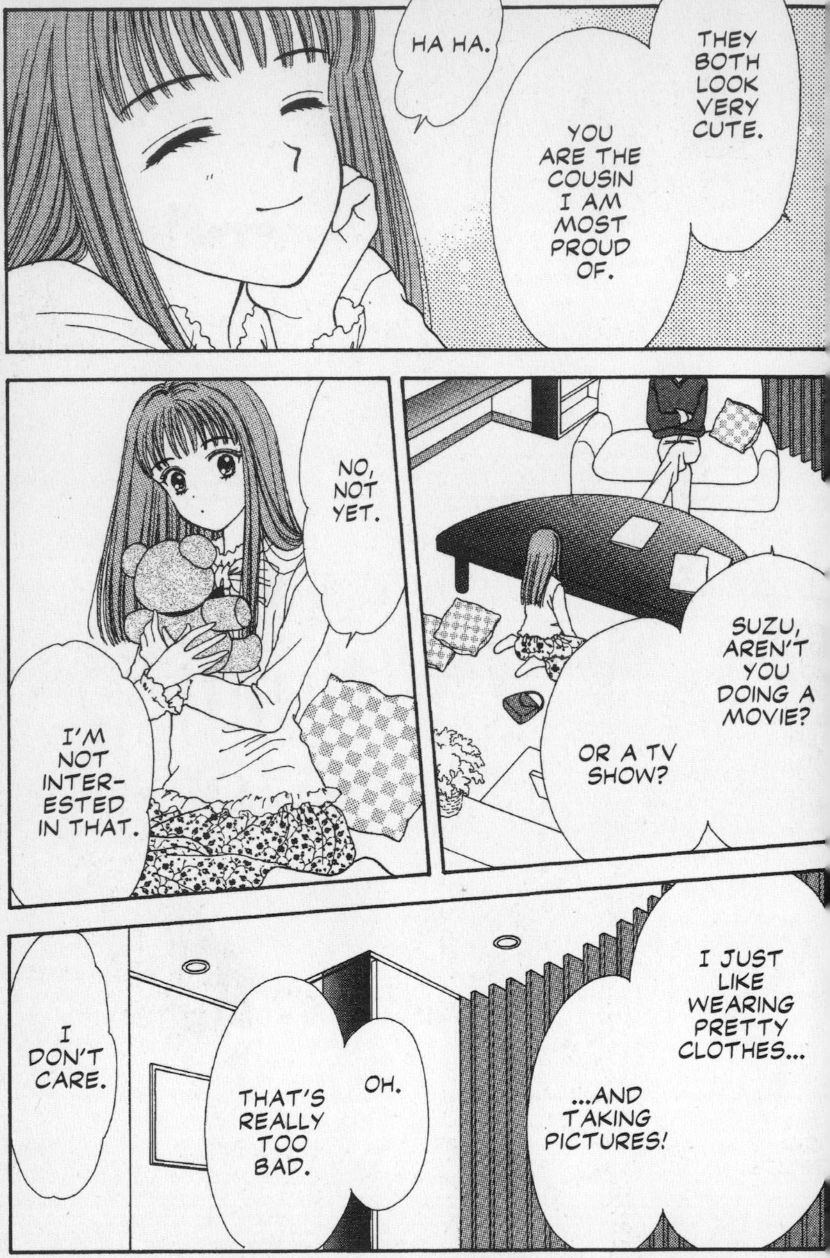
THEY BOTH LOOK VERY CUTE.
YOU ARE THE COUSIN I AM MOST PROUD OF.
HA HA.
SUZU, AREN'T YOU DOING A MOVIE?
OR A TV SHOW?
NO, NOT YET.
I'M NOT INTER-ESTED IN THAT.
I JUST LIKE WEARING PRETTY CLOTHES...
...AND TAKING PICTURES!
OH.
THAT'S REALLY TOO BAD.
I DON'T CARE.

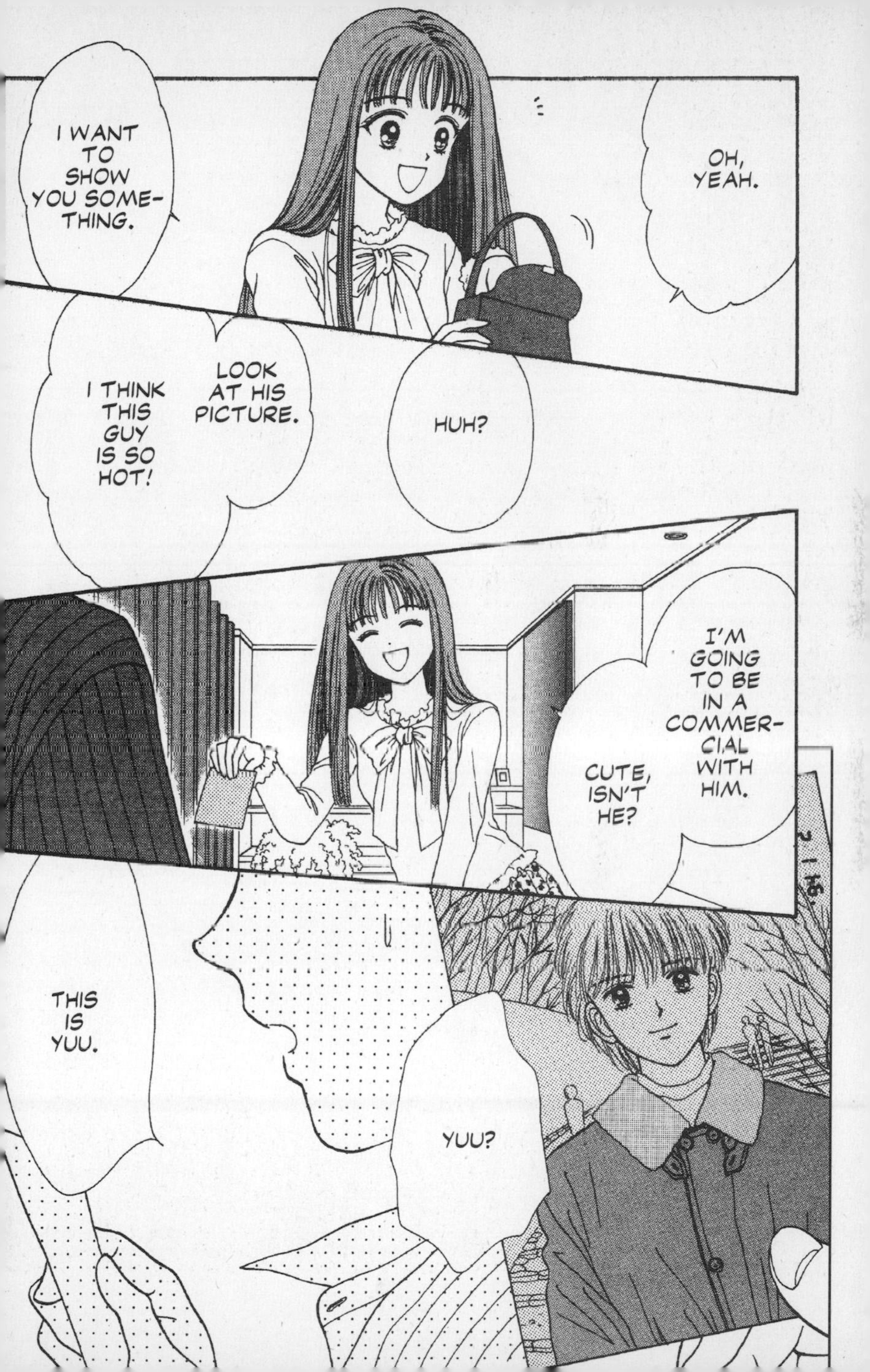
OH, YEAH.
I WANT TO SHOW YOU SOME-THING.
HUH?
LOOK AT HIS PICTURE.
I THINK THIS GUY IS SO HOT!
I'M GOING TO BE IN A COMMER-CIAL WITH HIM.
CUTE, ISN'T HE?
THIS IS YUU.
YUU?

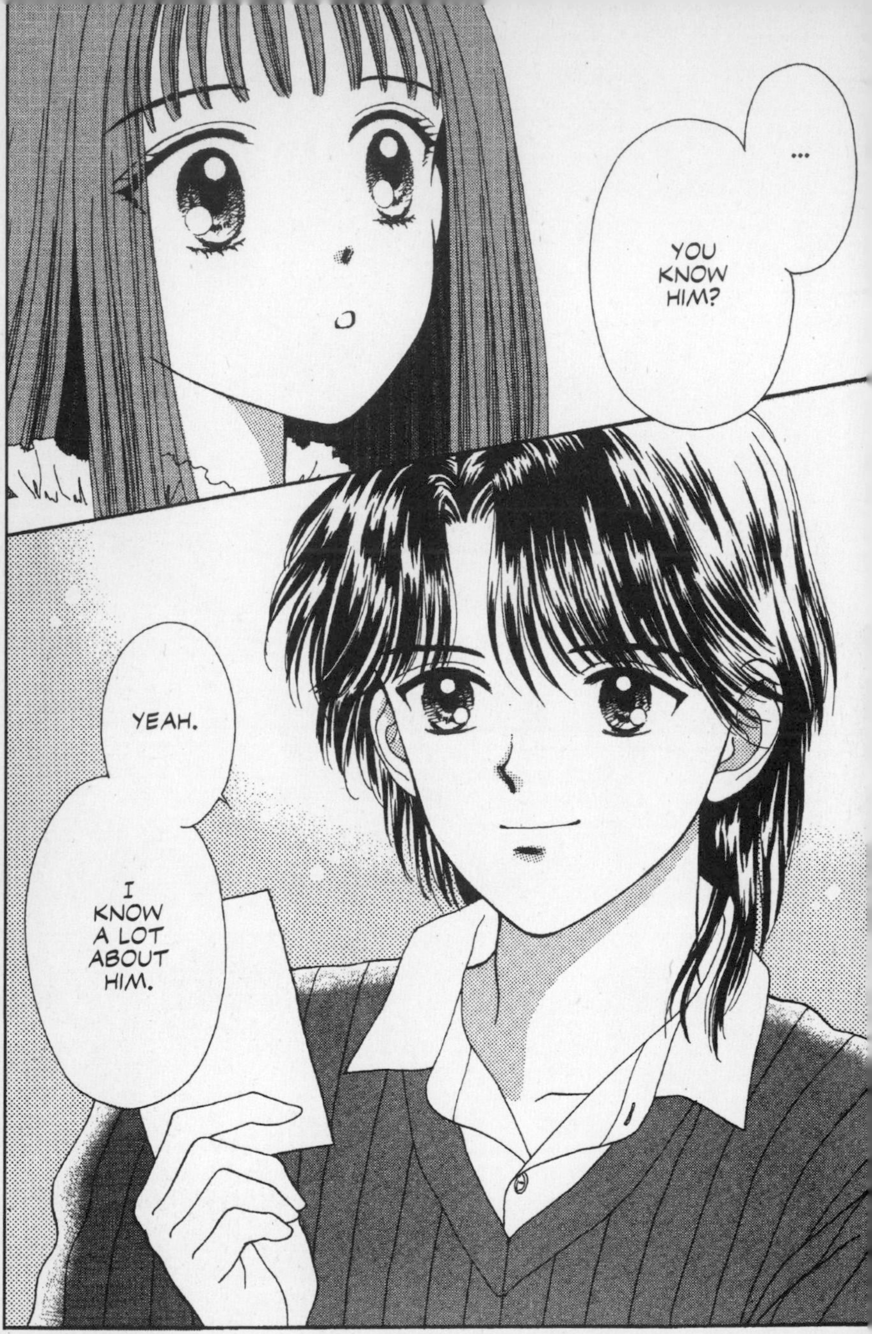
...
YOU KNOW HIM?
YEAH.
I KNOW A LOT ABOUT HIM.

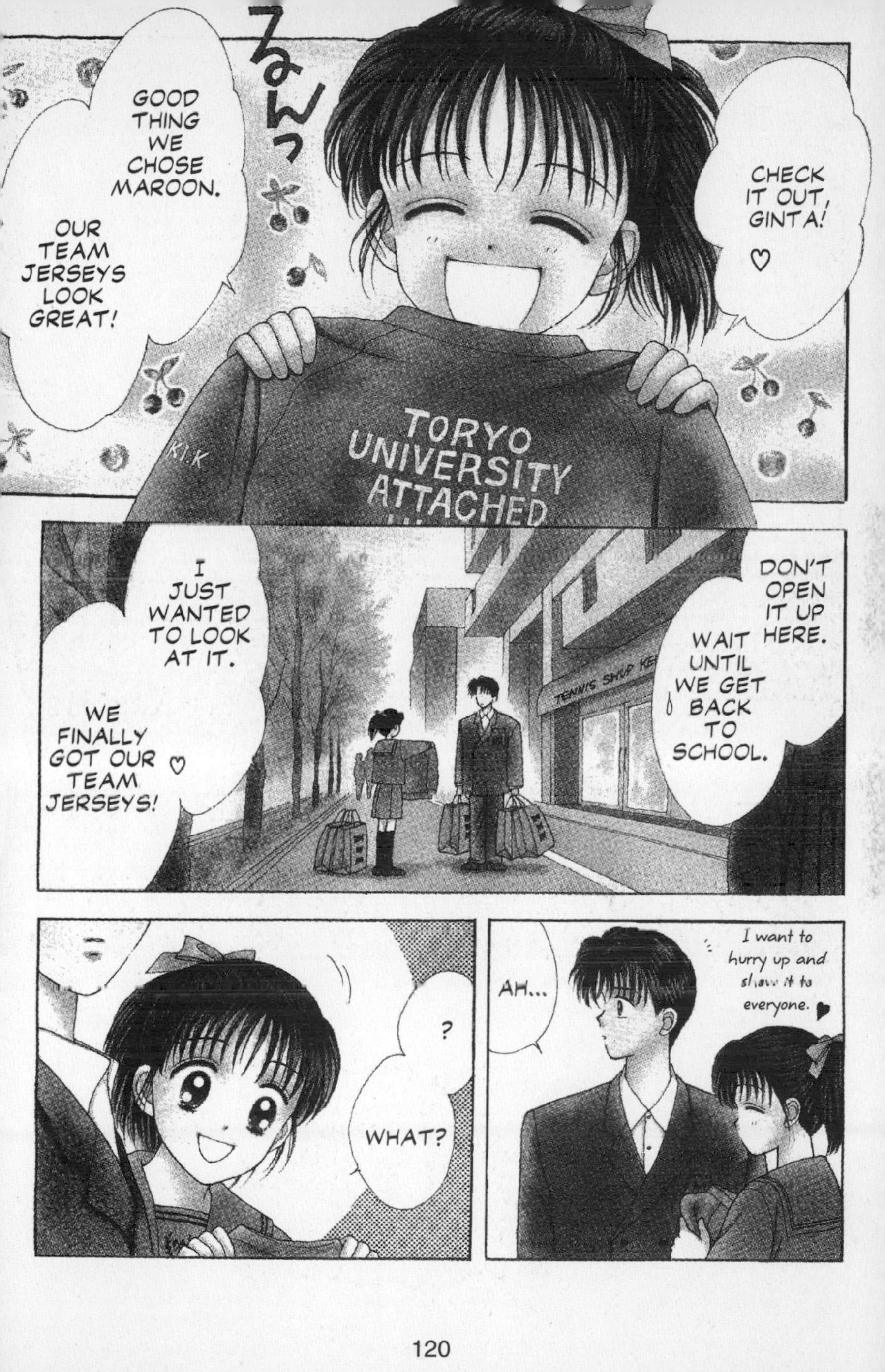
CHECK IT OUT, GINTA! ♡
るんっ
GOOD THING WE CHOSE MAROON.
OUR TEAM JERSEYS LOOK GREAT!
TORYO UNIVERSITY ATTACHED
K.I.K
DON'T OPEN IT UP HERE.
WAIT UNTIL WE GET BACK TO SCHOOL.
TENNIS SHOP
I JUST WANTED TO LOOK AT IT.
WE FINALLY GOT OUR TEAM JERSEYS! ♡
I want to hurry up and show it to everyone. ♥
AH...
?
WHAT?

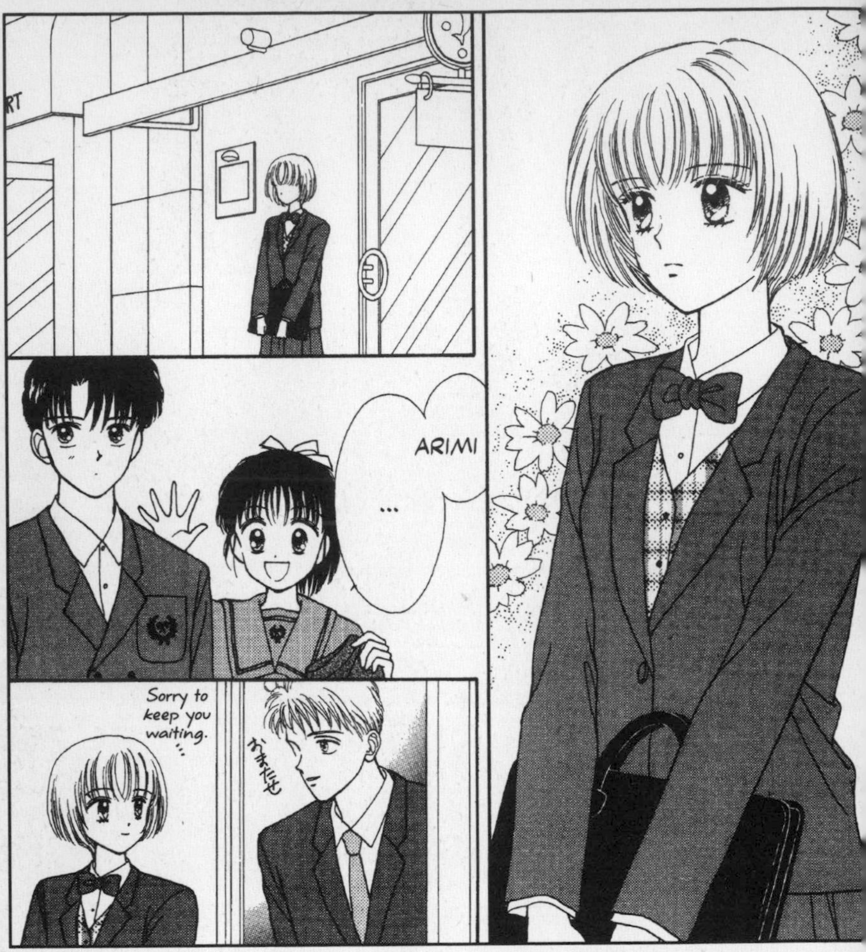
ARIMI
...
Sorry to keep you waiting. ...
おまたせ

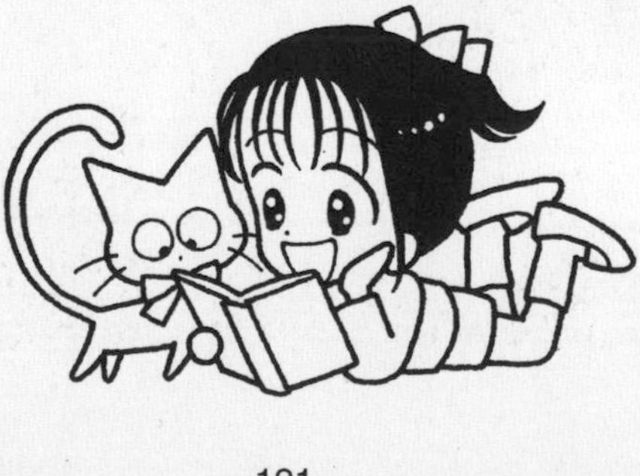

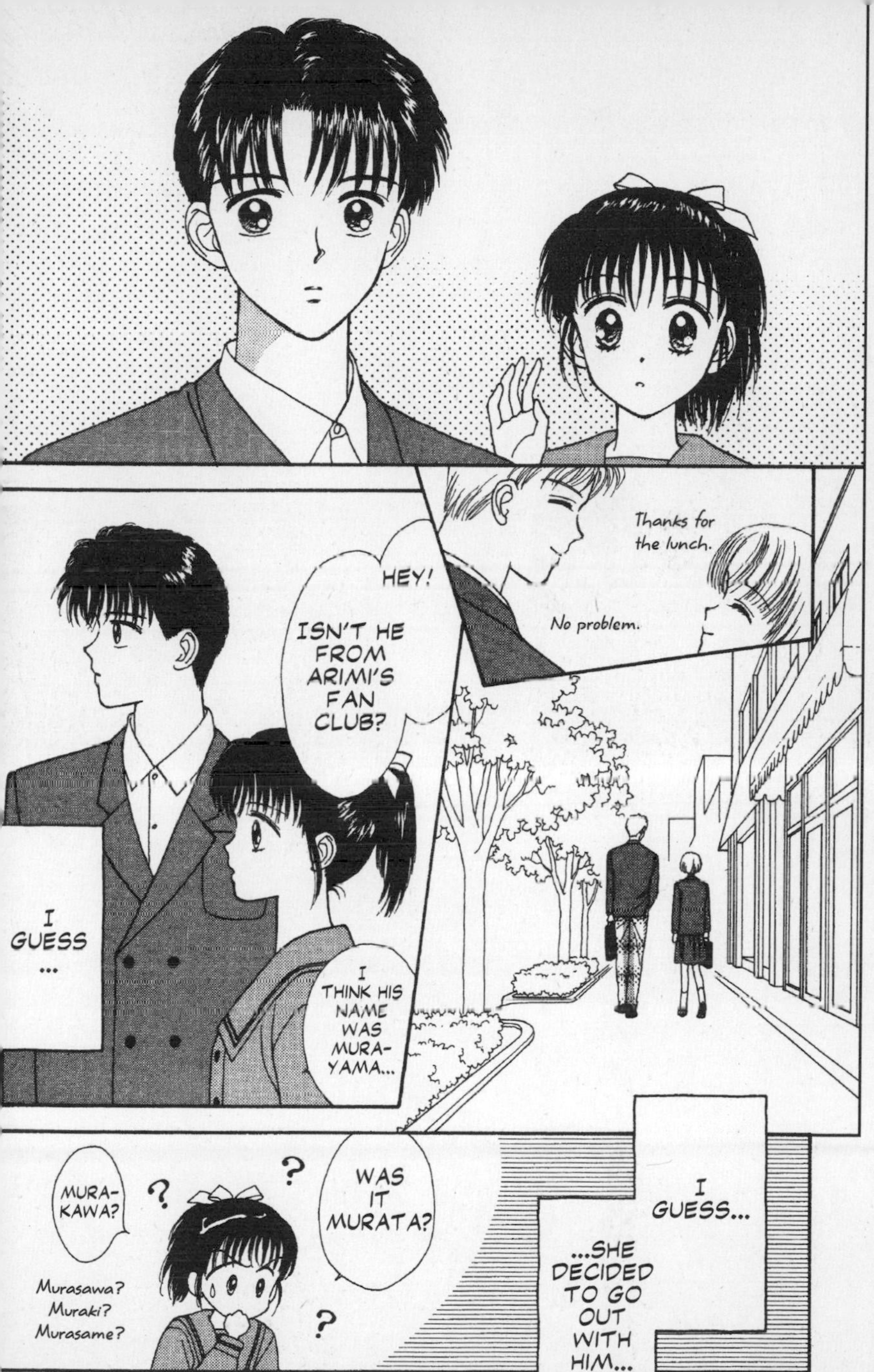
Thanks for the lunch.
No problem.
HEY! ISN'T HE FROM ARIMI'S FAN CLUB?
I GUESS...
I THINK HIS NAME WAS MURA-YAMA...
I GUESS...
...SHE DECIDED TO GO OUT WITH HIM...
WAS IT MURATA?
MURA-KAWA?
Murasawa? Muraki? Murasame?

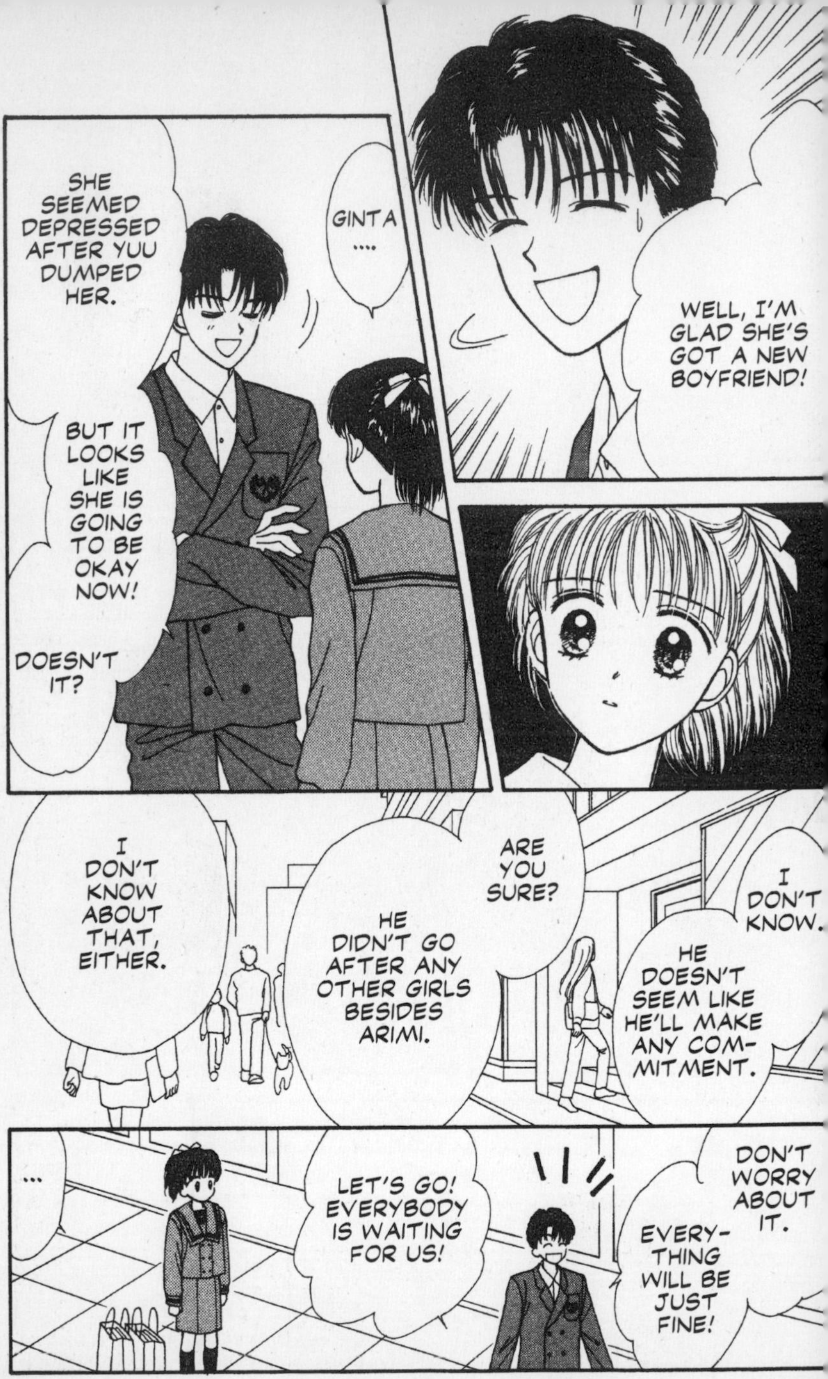
WELL, I'M GLAD SHE'S GOT A NEW BOYFRIEND!
GINTA ....
SHE SEEMED DEPRESSED AFTER YUU DUMPED HER.
BUT IT LOOKS LIKE SHE IS GOING TO BE OKAY NOW!
DOESN'T IT?
I DON'T KNOW.
HE DOESN'T SEEM LIKE HE'LL MAKE ANY COM-MITMENT.
ARE YOU SURE?
HE DIDN'T GO AFTER ANY OTHER GIRLS BESIDES ARIMI.
I DON'T KNOW ABOUT THAT, EITHER.
DON'T WORRY ABOUT IT.
EVERY-THING WILL BE JUST FINE!
LET'S GO! EVERYBODY IS WAITING FOR US!
...

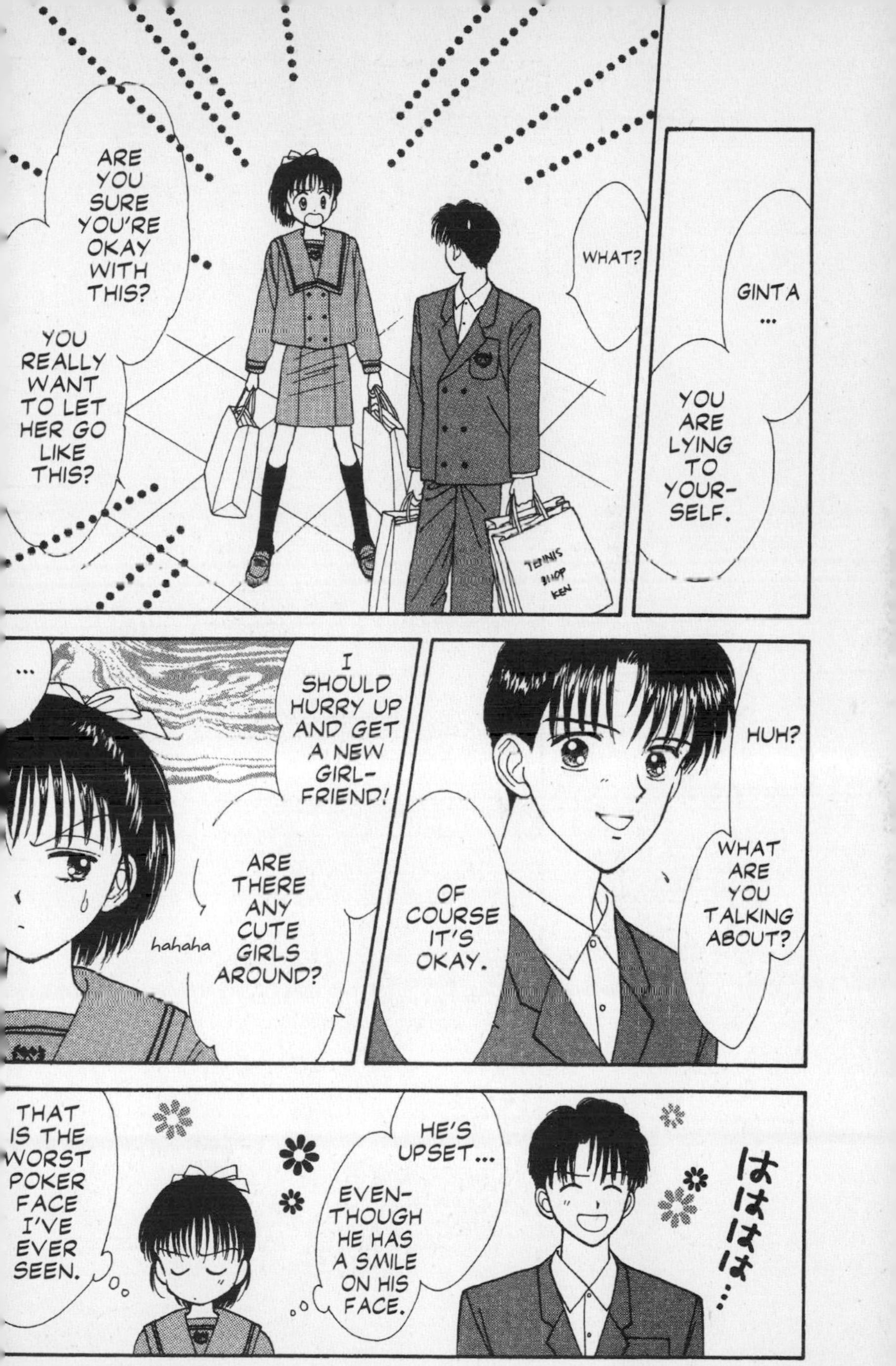
GINTA ...
YOU ARE LYING TO YOUR-SELF.
WHAT?
ARE YOU SURE YOU'RE OKAY WITH THIS?
YOU REALLY WANT TO LET HER GO LIKE THIS?
HUH?
WHAT ARE YOU TALKING ABOUT?
OF COURSE IT'S OKAY.
I SHOULD HURRY UP AND GET A NEW GIRL-FRIEND!
ARE THERE ANY CUTE GIRLS AROUND?
hahaha
...
ははは…
HE'S UPSET...
EVEN-THOUGH HE HAS A SMILE ON HIS FACE.
THAT IS THE WORST POKER FACE I'VE EVER SEEN.

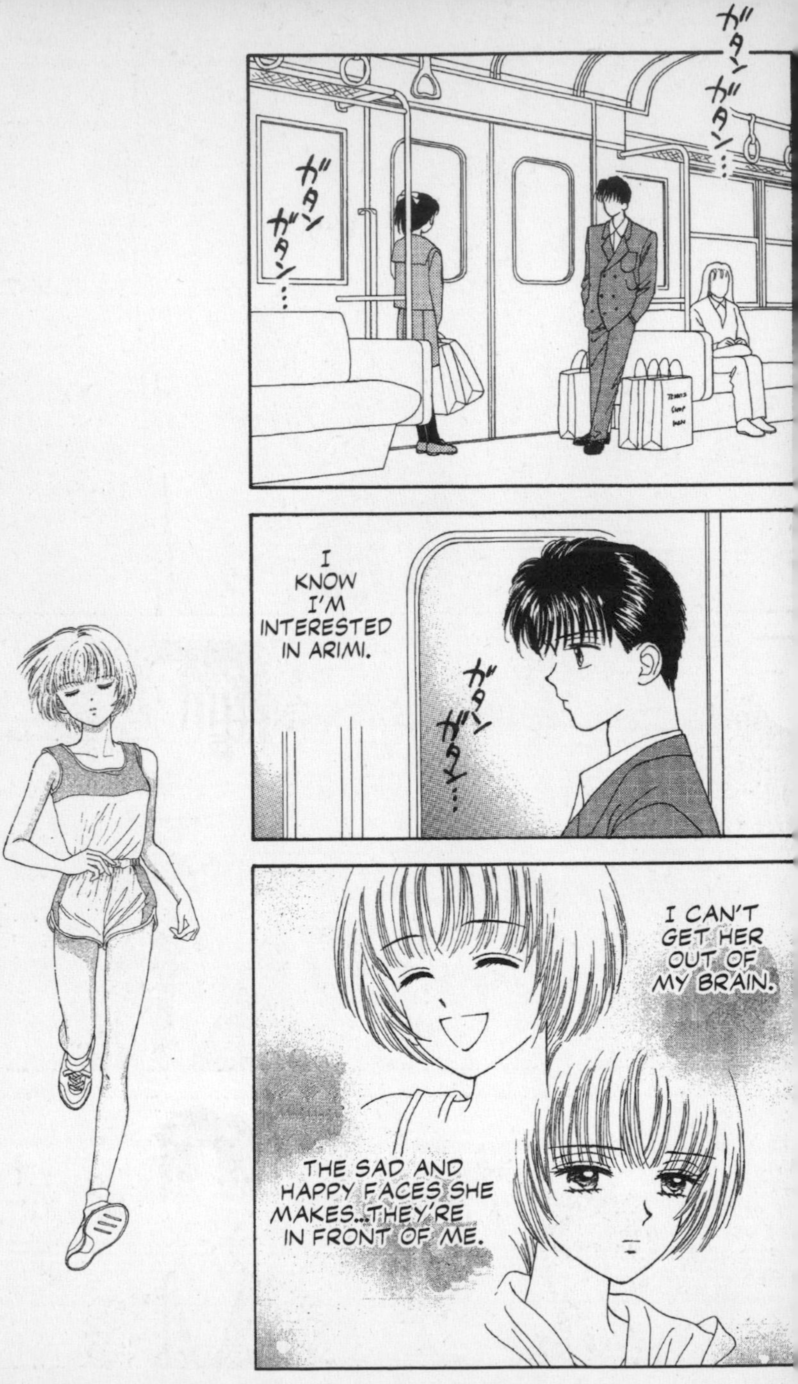
ガタンガタン…
ガタンガタン…
I KNOW I'M INTERESTED IN ARIMI.
ガタンガタン…
I CAN'T GET HER OUT OF MY BRAIN.
THE SAD AND HAPPY FACES SHE MAKES...THEY'RE IN FRONT OF ME.

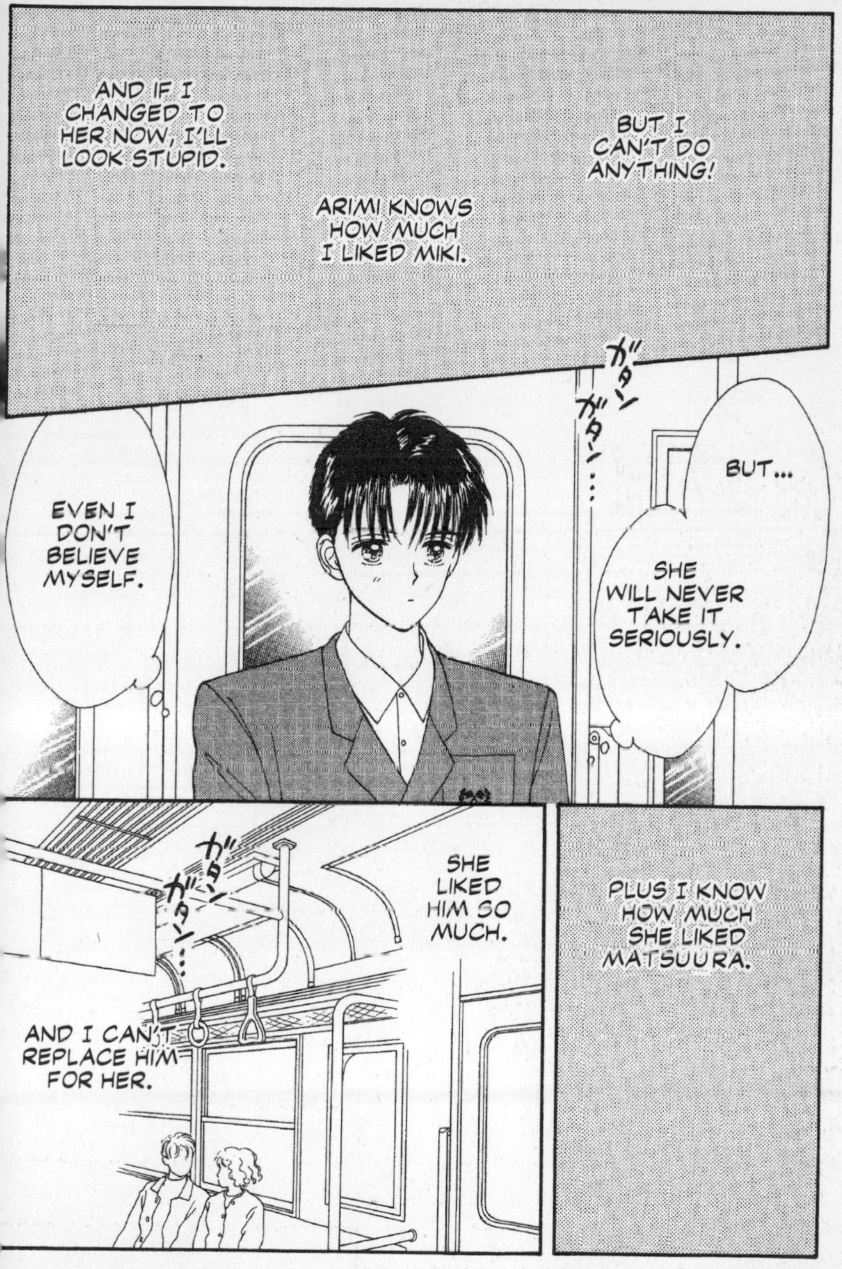
BUT I CAN'T DO ANYTHING!
ARIMI KNOWS HOW MUCH I LIKED MIKI.
AND IF I CHANGED TO HER NOW, I'LL LOOK STUPID.
ガタン ガタン…
BUT...
SHE WILL NEVER TAKE IT SERIOUSLY.
EVEN I DON'T BELIEVE MYSELF.
PLUS I KNOW HOW MUCH SHE LIKED MATSUURA.
SHE LIKED HIM SO MUCH.
ガタン ガタン…
AND I CAN'T REPLACE HIM FOR HER.

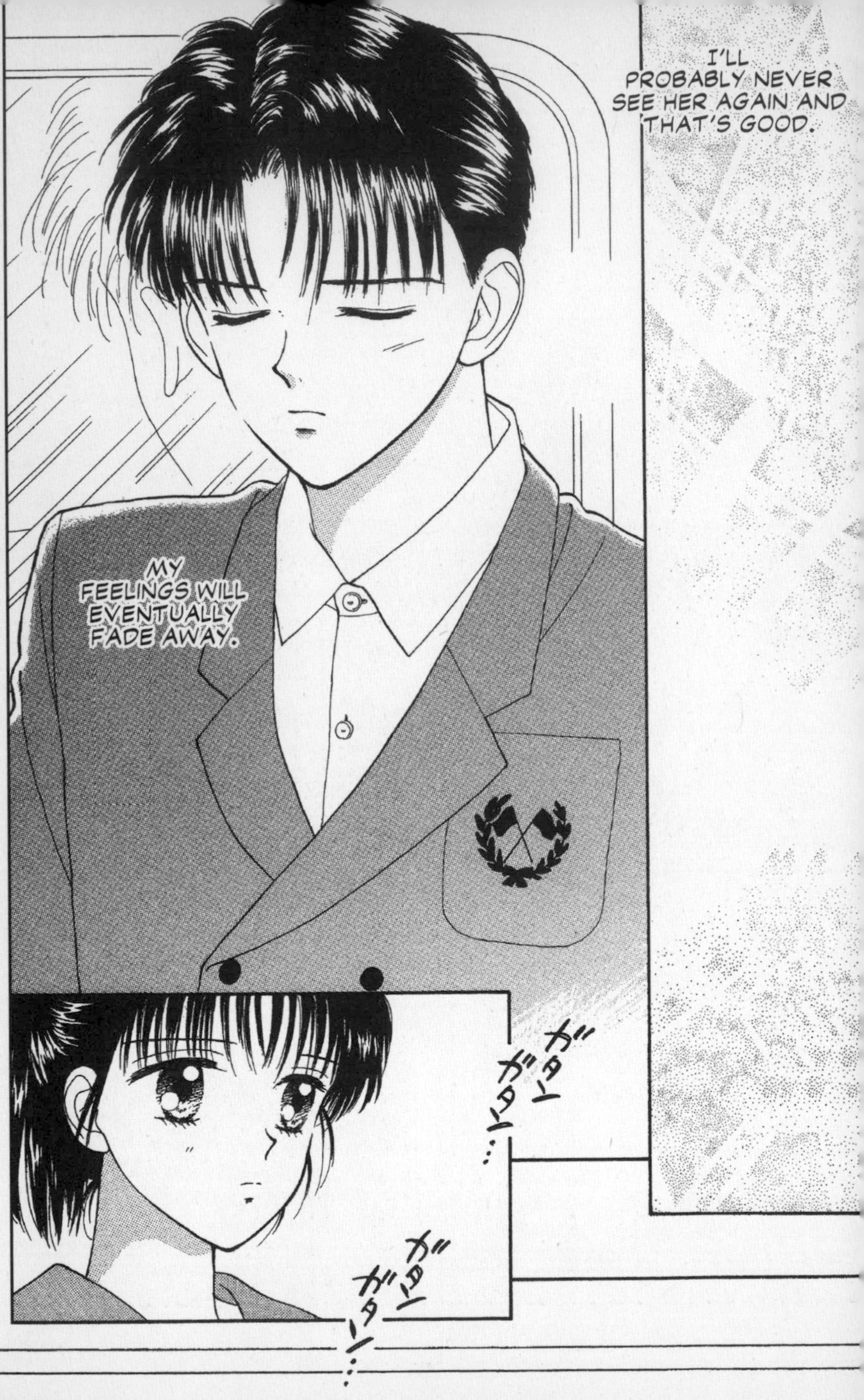
I'LL PROBABLY NEVER SEE HER AGAIN AND THAT'S GOOD.
MY FEELINGS WILL EVENTUALLY FADE AWAY.
ガタンガタン…
ガタンガタン…

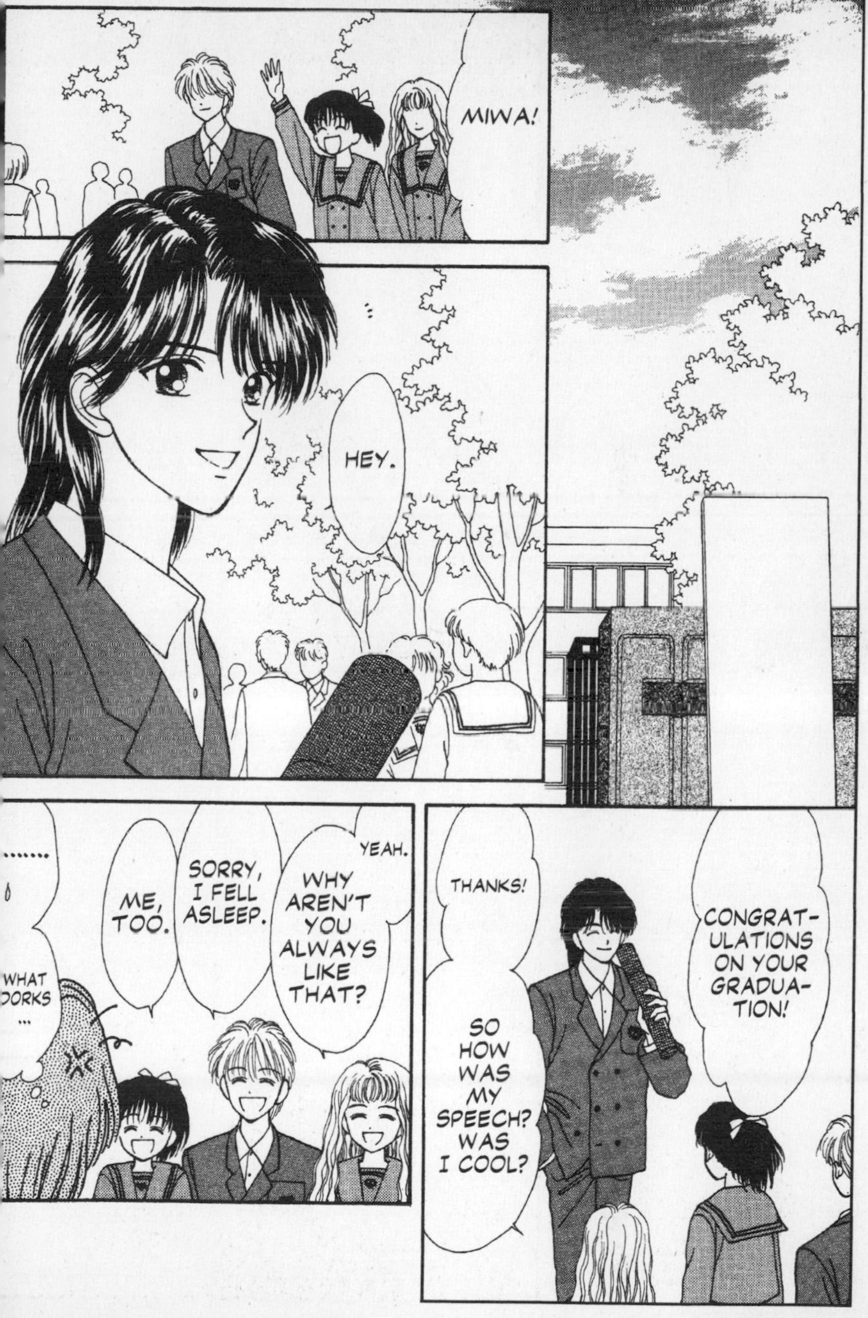
MIWA!
HEY.
CONGRAT-ULATIONS ON YOUR GRADUA-TION!
THANKS!
SO HOW WAS MY SPEECH? WAS I COOL?
YEAH.
WHY AREN'T YOU ALWAYS LIKE THAT?
SORRY, I FELL ASLEEP.
ME, TOO.
....
WHAT DORKS ...

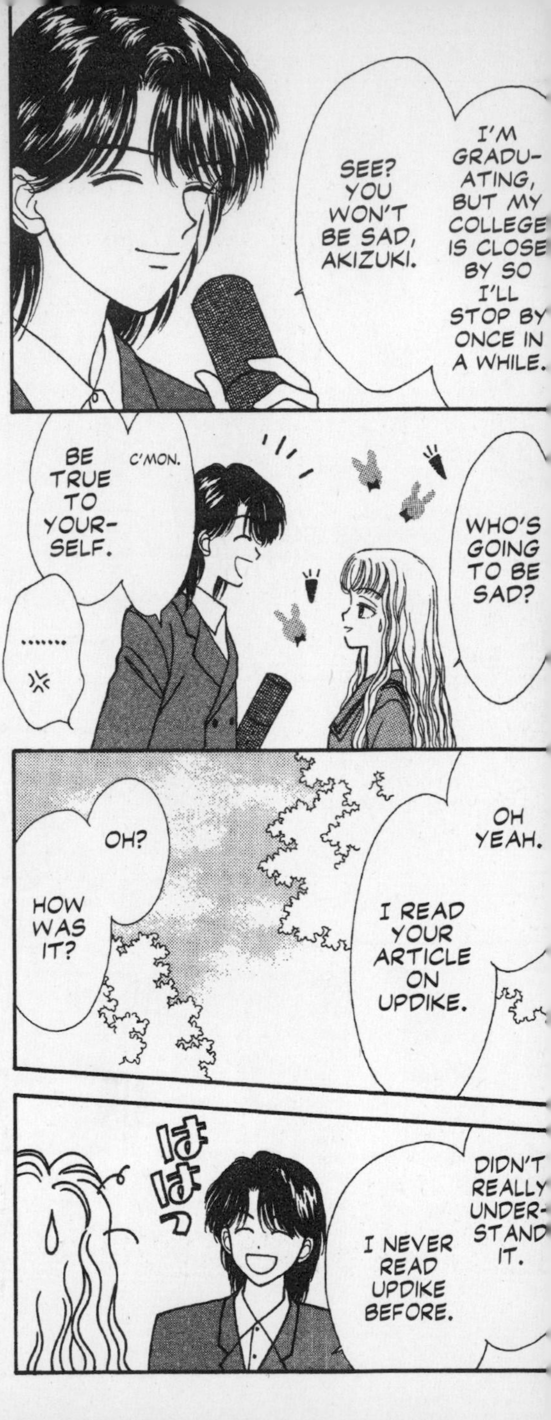
I'M GRADUATING, BUT MY COLLEGE IS CLOSE BY SO I'LL STOP BY ONCE IN A WHILE.
SEE? YOU WON'T BE SAD, AKIZUKI.
WHO'S GOING TO BE SAD?
C'MON.
BE TRUE TO YOURSELF.
....
OH YEAH.
I READ YOUR ARTICLE ON UPDIKE.
OH?
HOW WAS IT?
DIDN'T REALLY UNDERSTAND IT.
I NEVER READ UPDIKE BEFORE.
ははっ

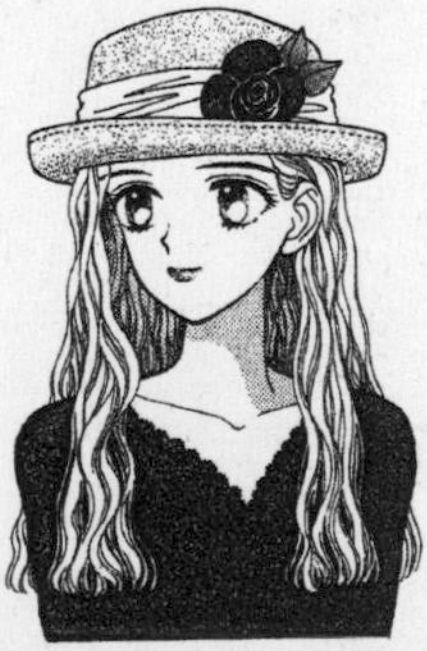

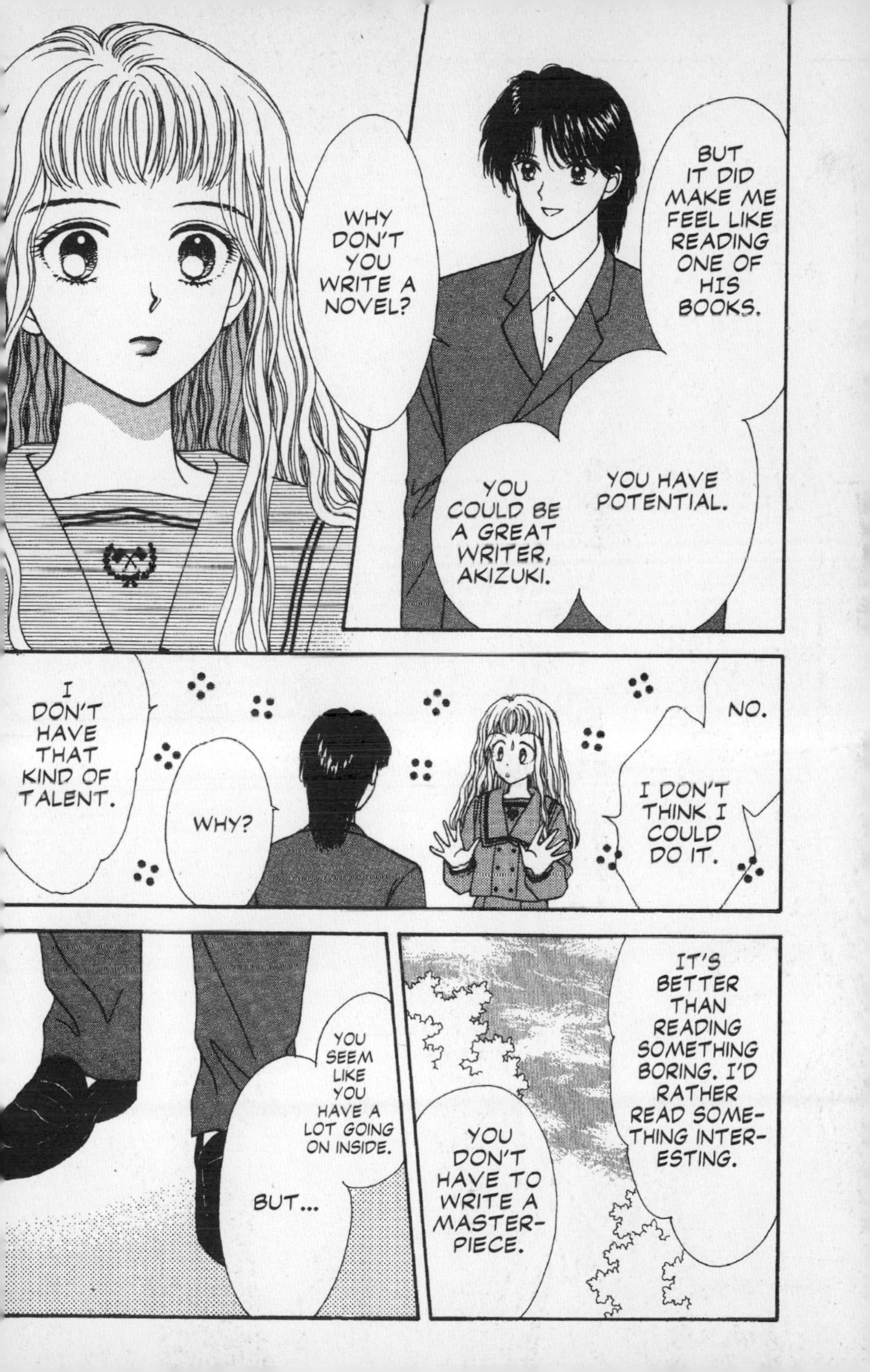
BUT IT DID MAKE ME FEEL LIKE READING ONE OF HIS BOOKS.
YOU HAVE POTENTIAL.
YOU COULD BE A GREAT WRITER, AKIZUKI.
WHY DON'T YOU WRITE A NOVEL?
NO.
I DON'T THINK I COULD DO IT.
WHY?
I DON'T HAVE THAT KIND OF TALENT.
IT'S BETTER THAN READING SOMETHING BORING. I'D RATHER READ SOME-THING INTER-ESTING.
YOU DON'T HAVE TO WRITE A MASTER-PIECE.
YOU SEEM LIKE YOU HAVE A LOT GOING ON INSIDE.
BUT...

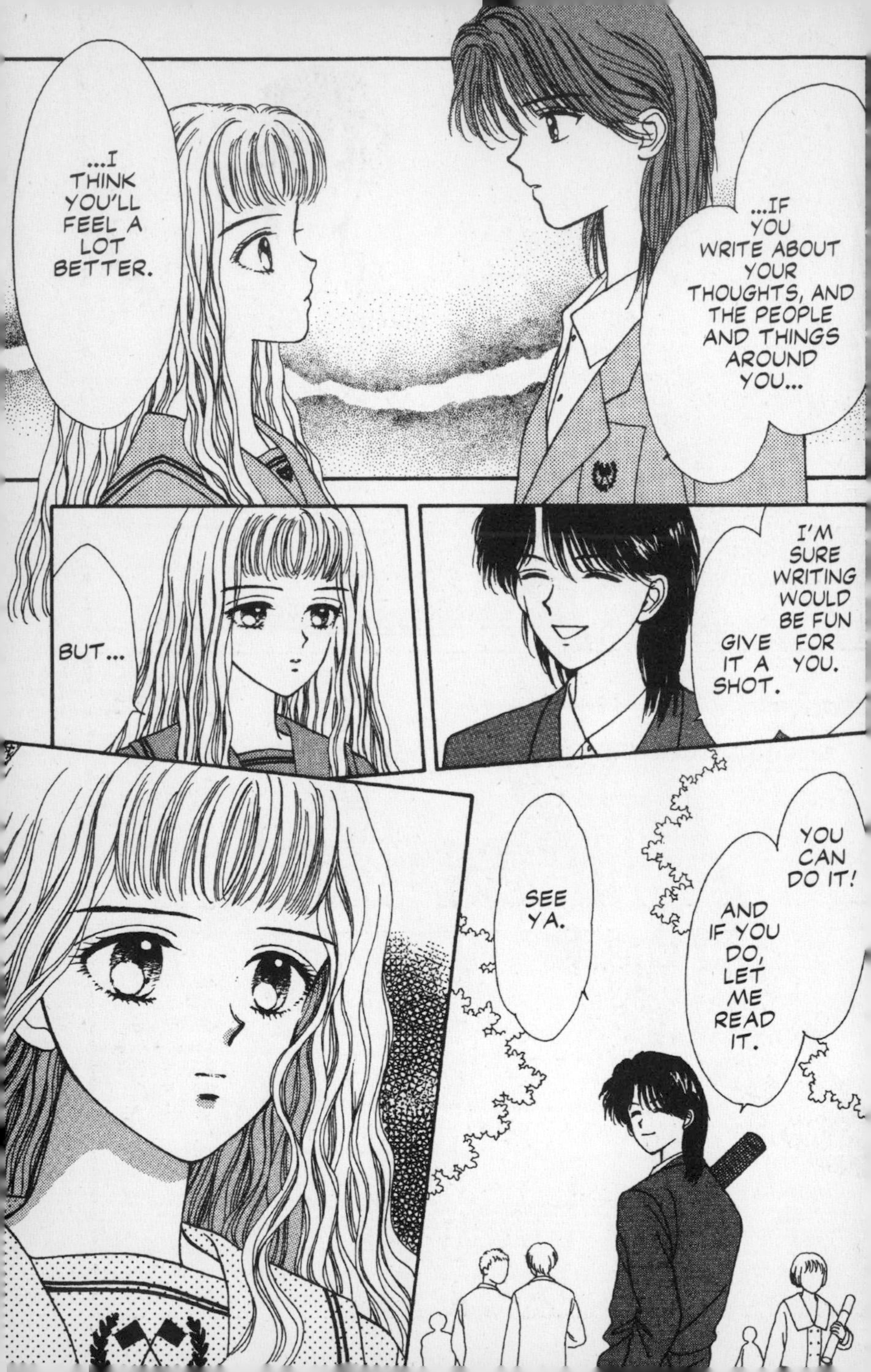
...IF YOU WRITE ABOUT YOUR THOUGHTS, AND THE PEOPLE AND THINGS AROUND YOU...
...I THINK YOU'LL FEEL A LOT BETTER.
I'M SURE WRITING WOULD BE FUN FOR YOU.
GIVE IT A SHOT.
BUT...
YOU CAN DO IT!
AND IF YOU DO, LET ME READ IT.
SEE YA.

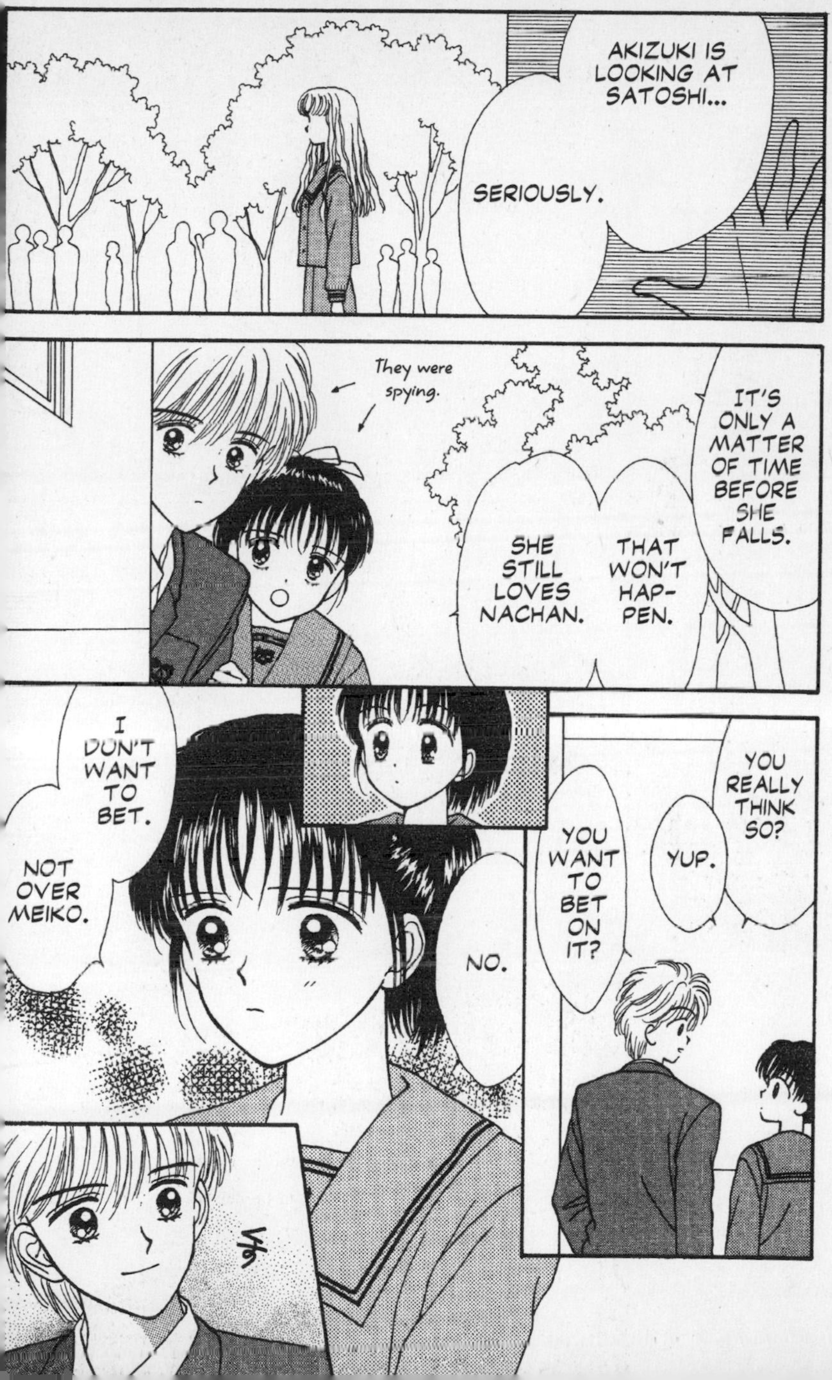
AKIZUKI IS LOOKING AT SATOSHI...
SERIOUSLY.
IT'S ONLY A MATTER OF TIME BEFORE SHE FALLS.
THAT WON'T HAP-PEN.
SHE STILL LOVES NACHAN.
They were spying.
YOU REALLY THINK SO?
YUP.
YOU WANT TO BET ON IT?
NO.
I DON'T WANT TO BET.
NOT OVER MEIKO.

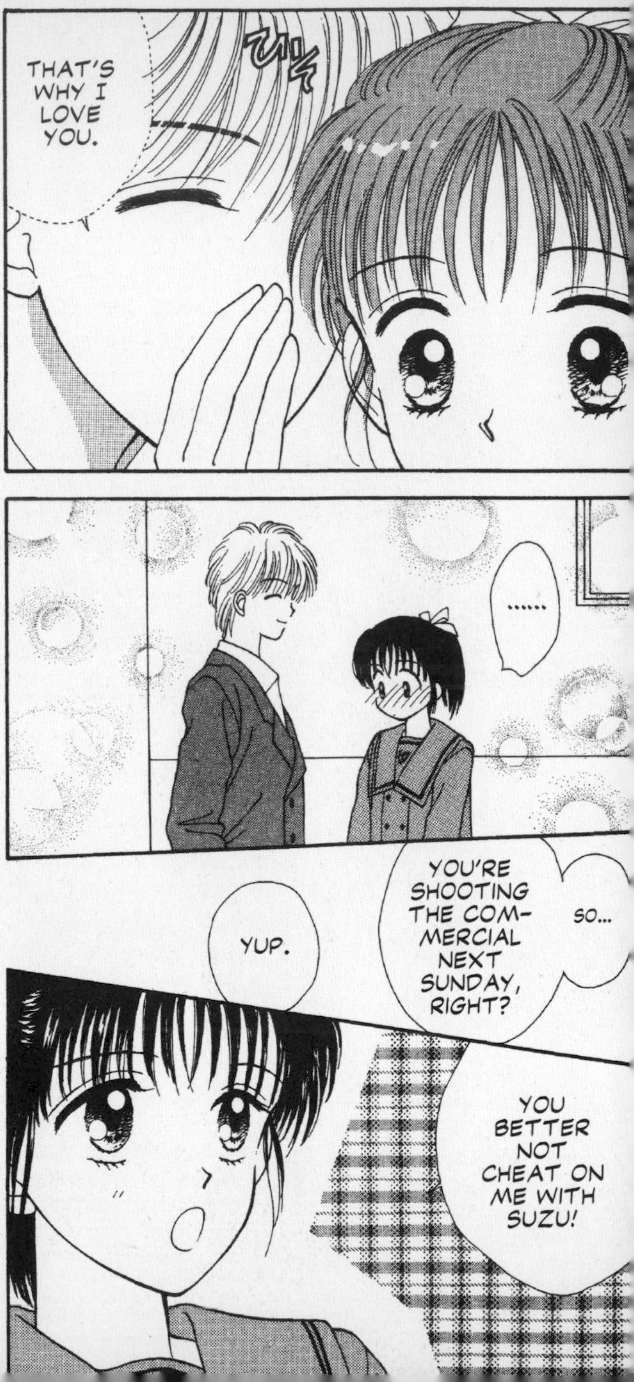
THAT'S WHY I LOVE YOU.
......
SO...
YOU'RE SHOOTING THE COM-MERCIAL NEXT SUNDAY, RIGHT?
YUP.
YOU BETTER NOT CHEAT ON ME WITH SUZU!

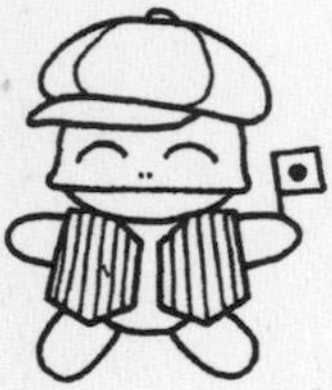

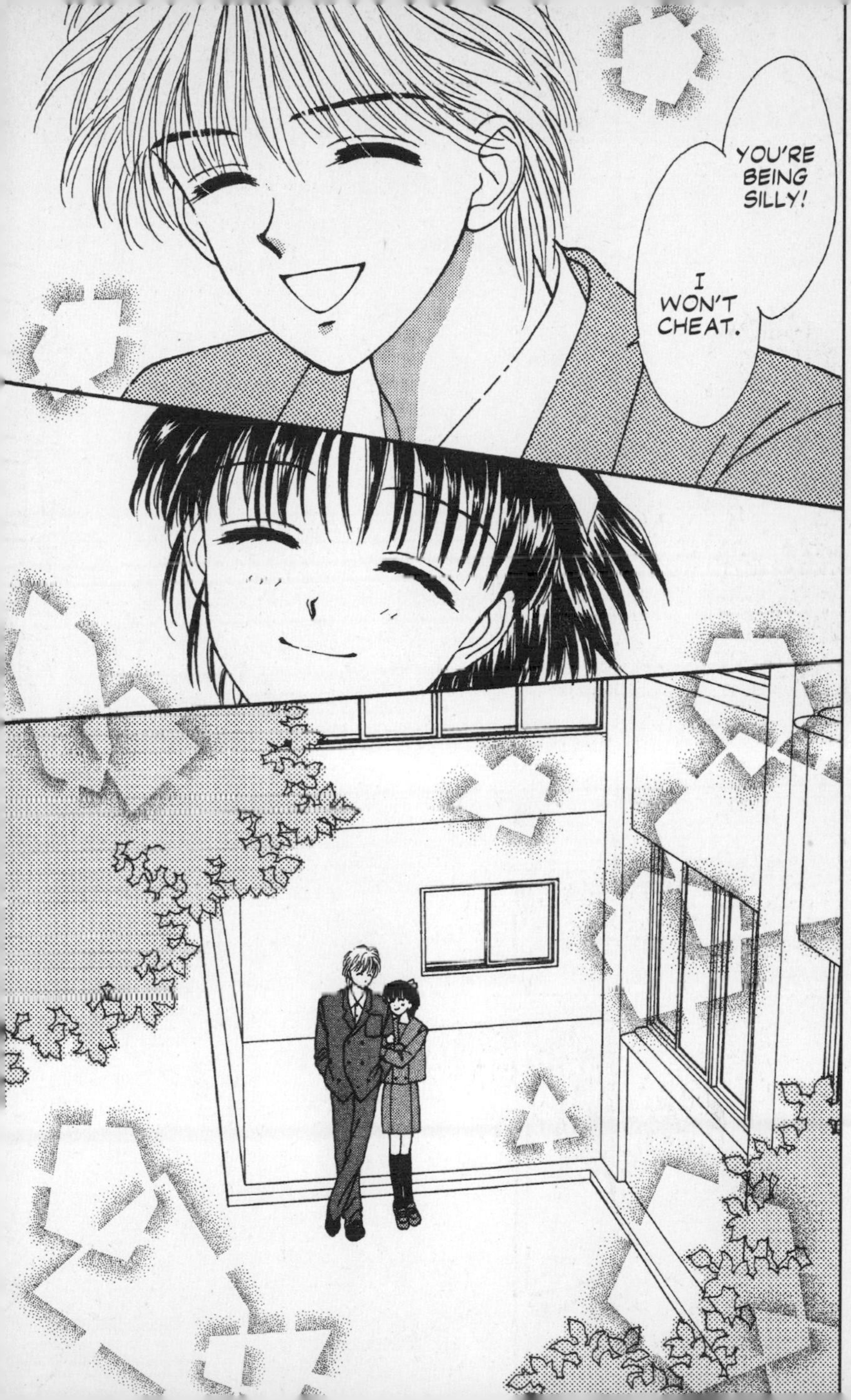
YOU'RE BEING SILLY! I WON'T CHEAT.

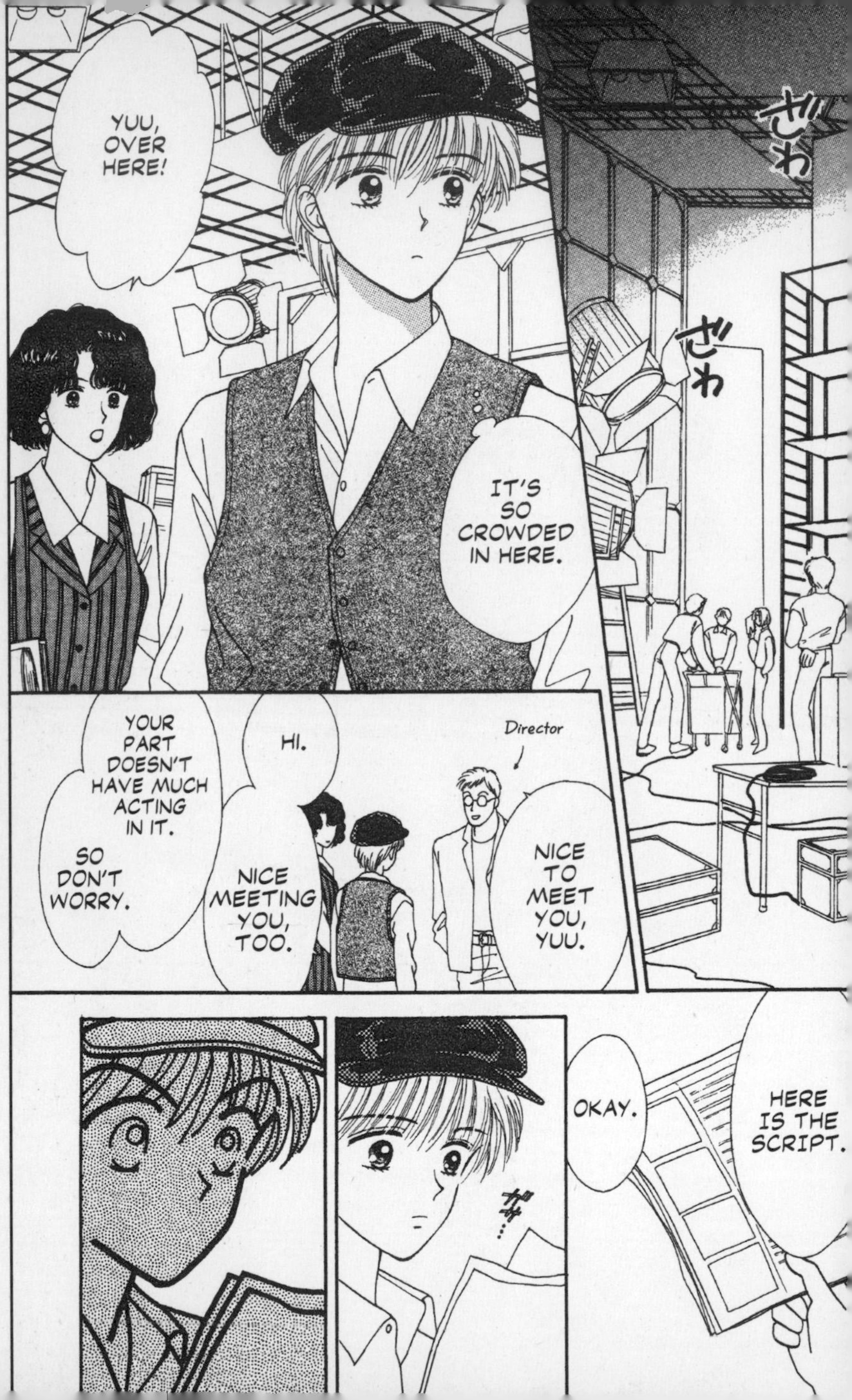
ざわ
ざわ
YUU, OVER HERE!
IT'S SO CROWDED IN HERE.
Director
NICE TO MEET YOU, YUU.
HI.
NICE MEETING YOU, TOO.
YOUR PART DOESN'T HAVE MUCH ACTING IN IT.
SO DON'T WORRY.
HERE IS THE SCRIPT.
OKAY.

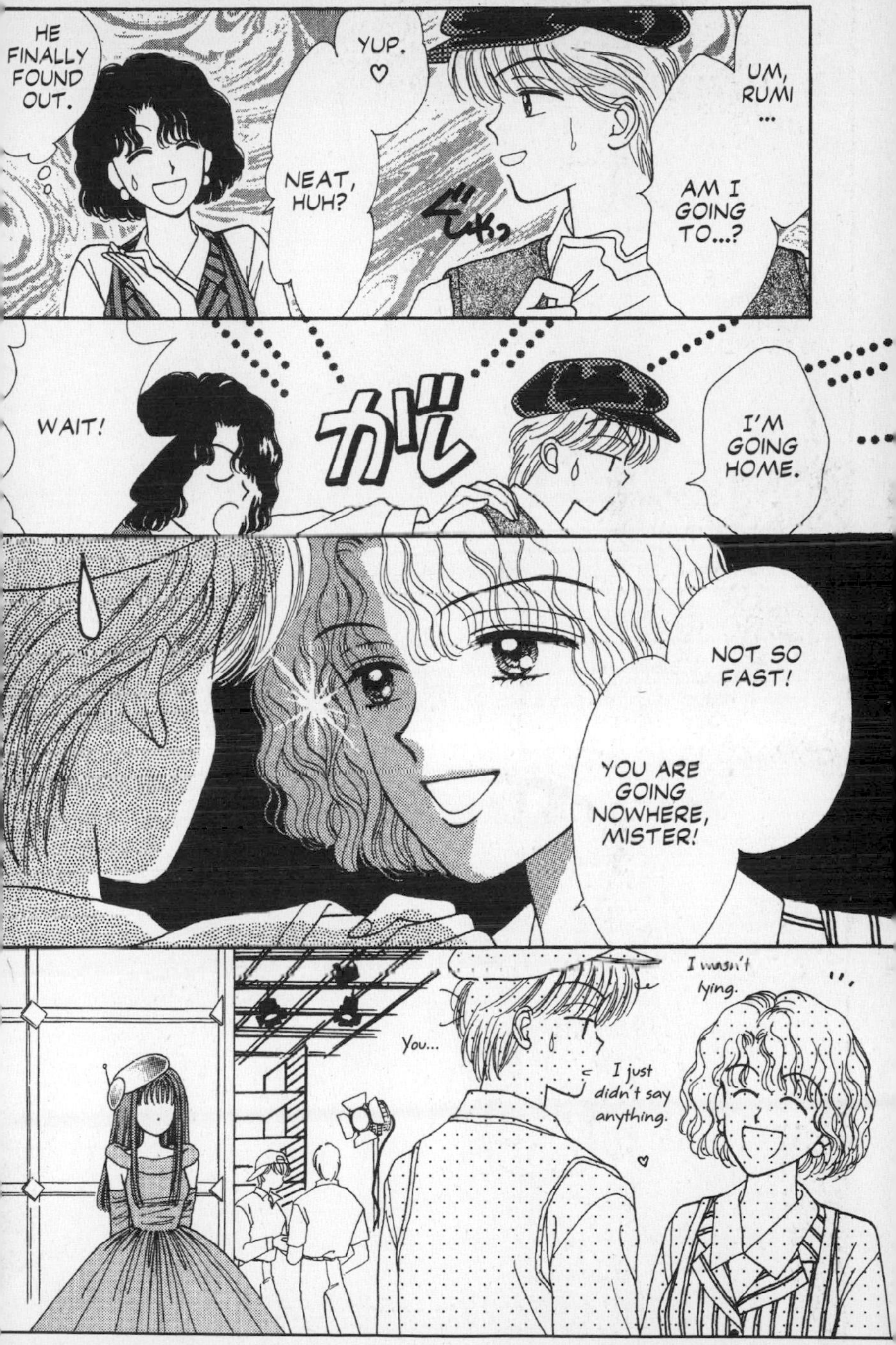
UM, RUMI ...
AM I GOING TO...?
YUP. ♡
NEAT, HUH?
ぐいっ
HE FINALLY FOUND OUT.
I'M GOING HOME.
がし
WAIT!
NOT SO FAST!
YOU ARE GOING NOWHERE, MISTER!
I wasn't lying.
I just didn't say anything.
You...

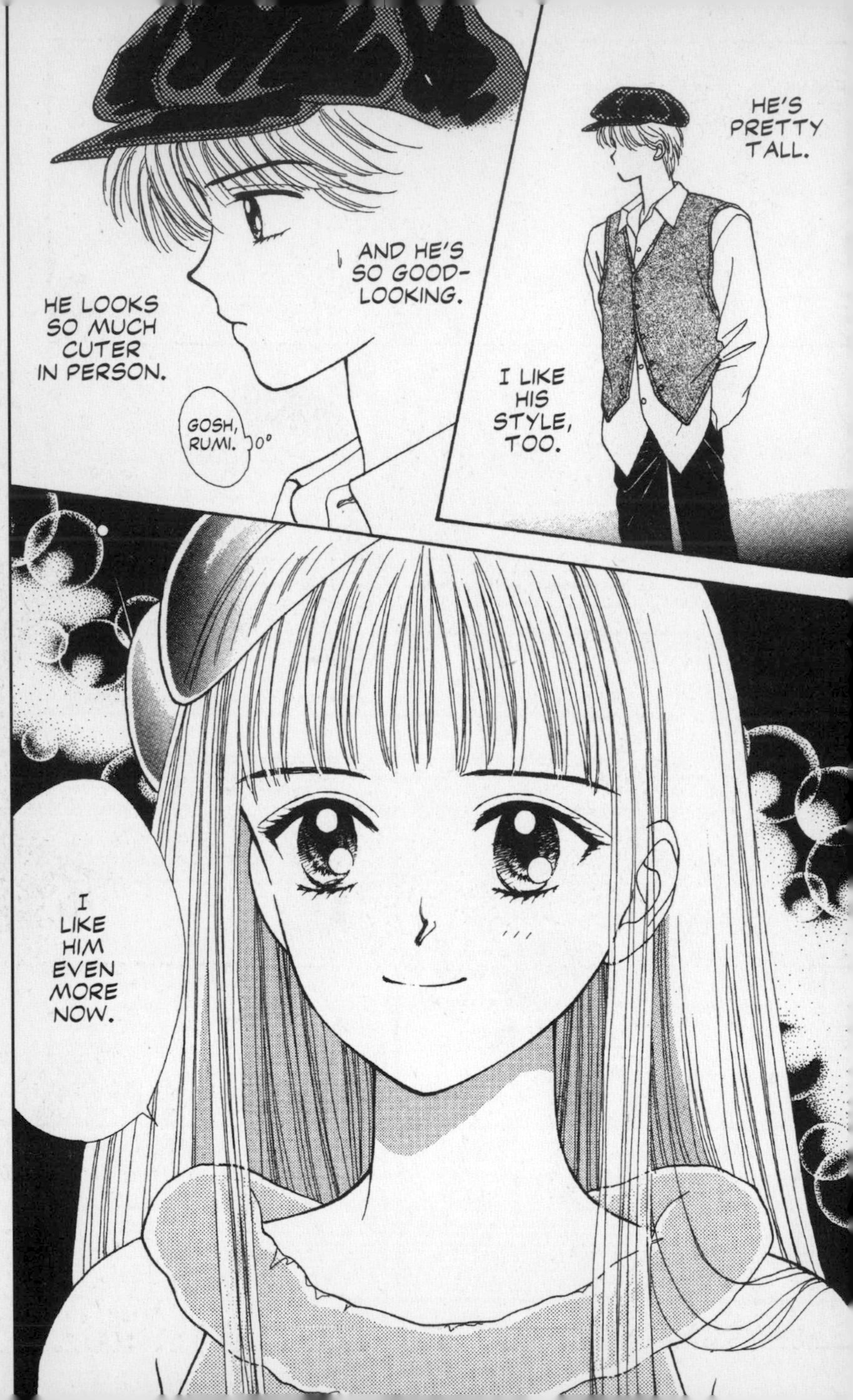
HE'S PRETTY TALL.
I LIKE HIS STYLE, TOO.
AND HE'S SO GOOD-LOOKING.
HE LOOKS SO MUCH CUTER IN PERSON.
GOSH, RUMI.
I LIKE HIM EVEN MORE NOW.

The sample Yuu brought back.

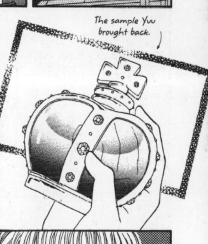

TELL US ABOUT THE COM-MERCIAL!

TALK TO US!

YUU...

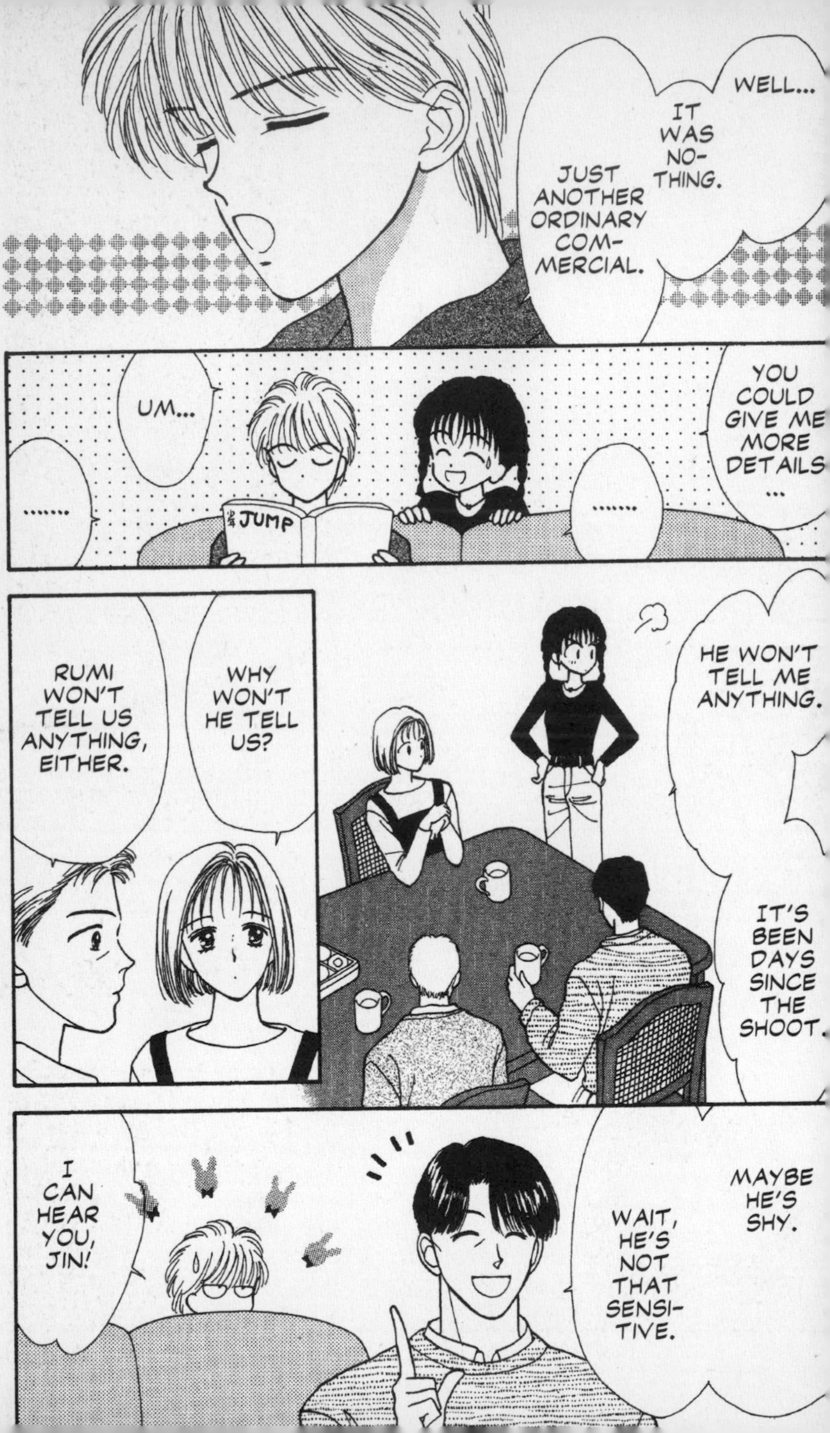
WELL... IT WAS NOTHING.
JUST ANOTHER ORDINARY COMMERCIAL.
YOU COULD GIVE ME MORE DETAILS...
....
UM...
JUMP
....
HE WON'T TELL ME ANYTHING.
IT'S BEEN DAYS SINCE THE SHOOT.
WHY WON'T HE TELL US?
RUMI WON'T TELL US ANYTHING, EITHER.
MAYBE HE'S SHY.
WAIT, HE'S NOT THAT SENSITIVE.
I CAN HEAR YOU, JIN!

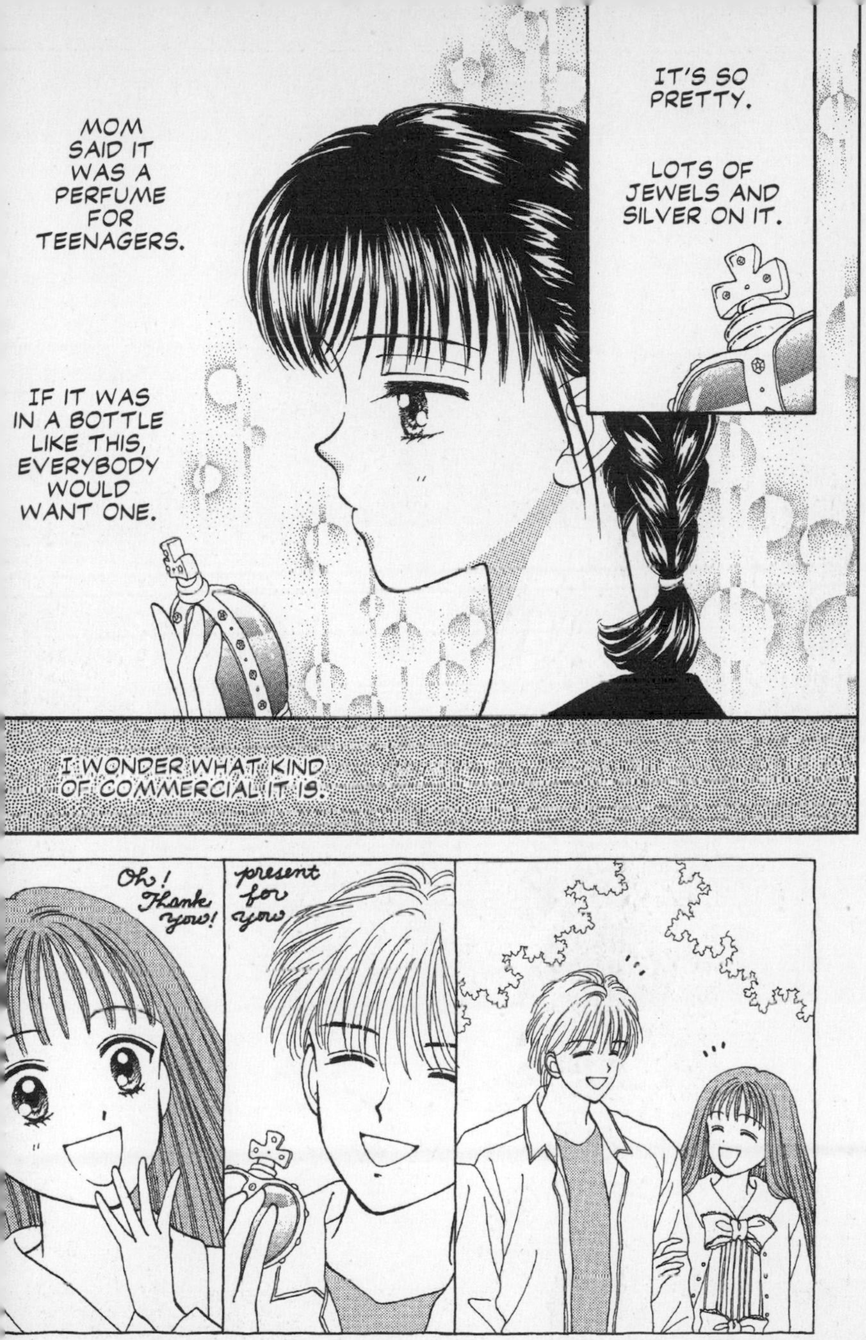
IT'S SO PRETTY.
LOTS OF JEWELS AND SILVER ON IT.
MOM SAID IT WAS A PERFUME FOR TEENAGERS.
IF IT WAS IN A BOTTLE LIKE THIS, EVERYBODY WOULD WANT ONE.
I WONDER WHAT KIND OF COMMERCIAL IT IS.
present for you
Oh! Thank you!

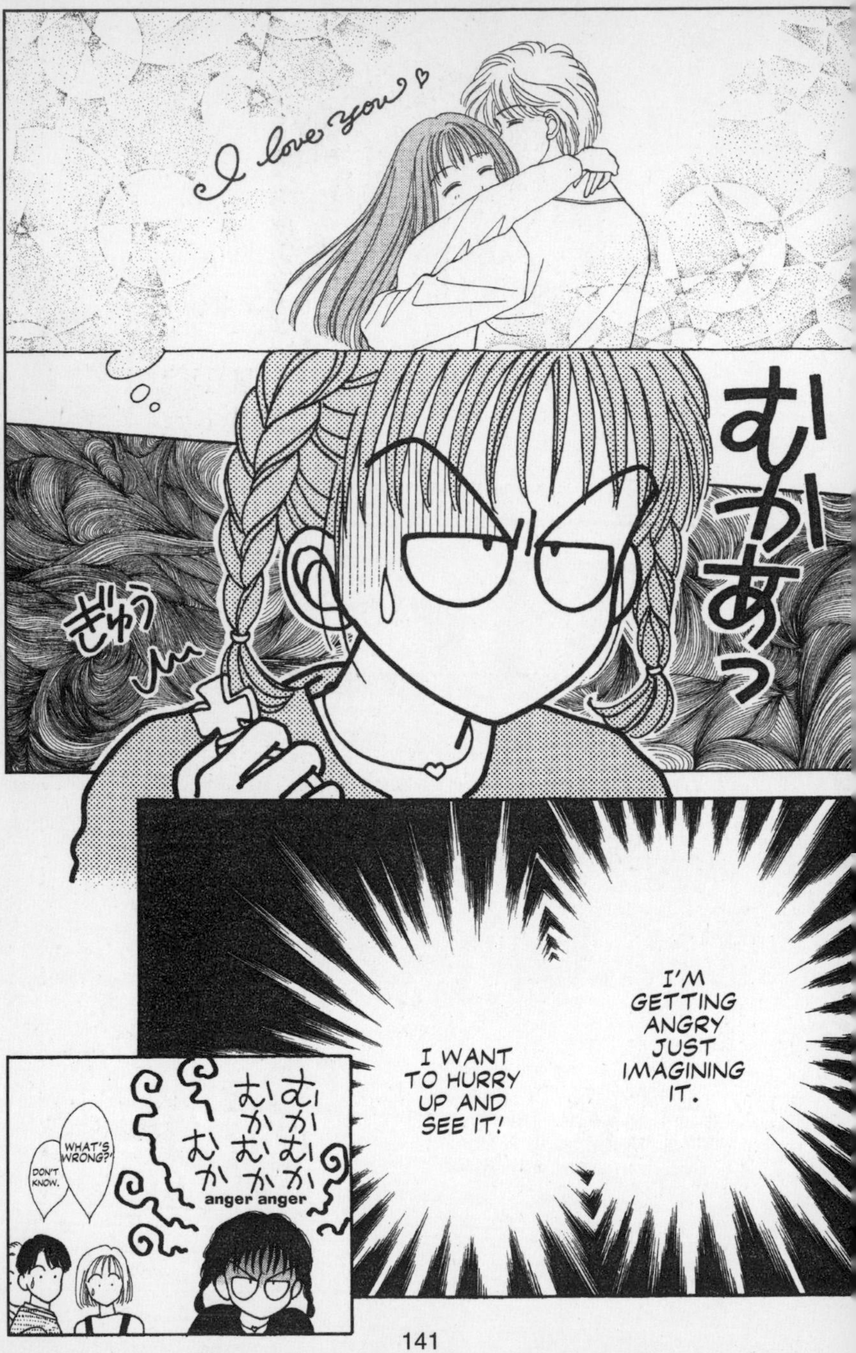

I love you
むかあっ
ぎゅうう
I'M GETTING ANGRY JUST IMAGINING IT.
I WANT TO HURRY UP AND SEE IT!
むかむか
むかむか
むかむか
anger anger
WHAT'S WRONG?
DON'T KNOW.

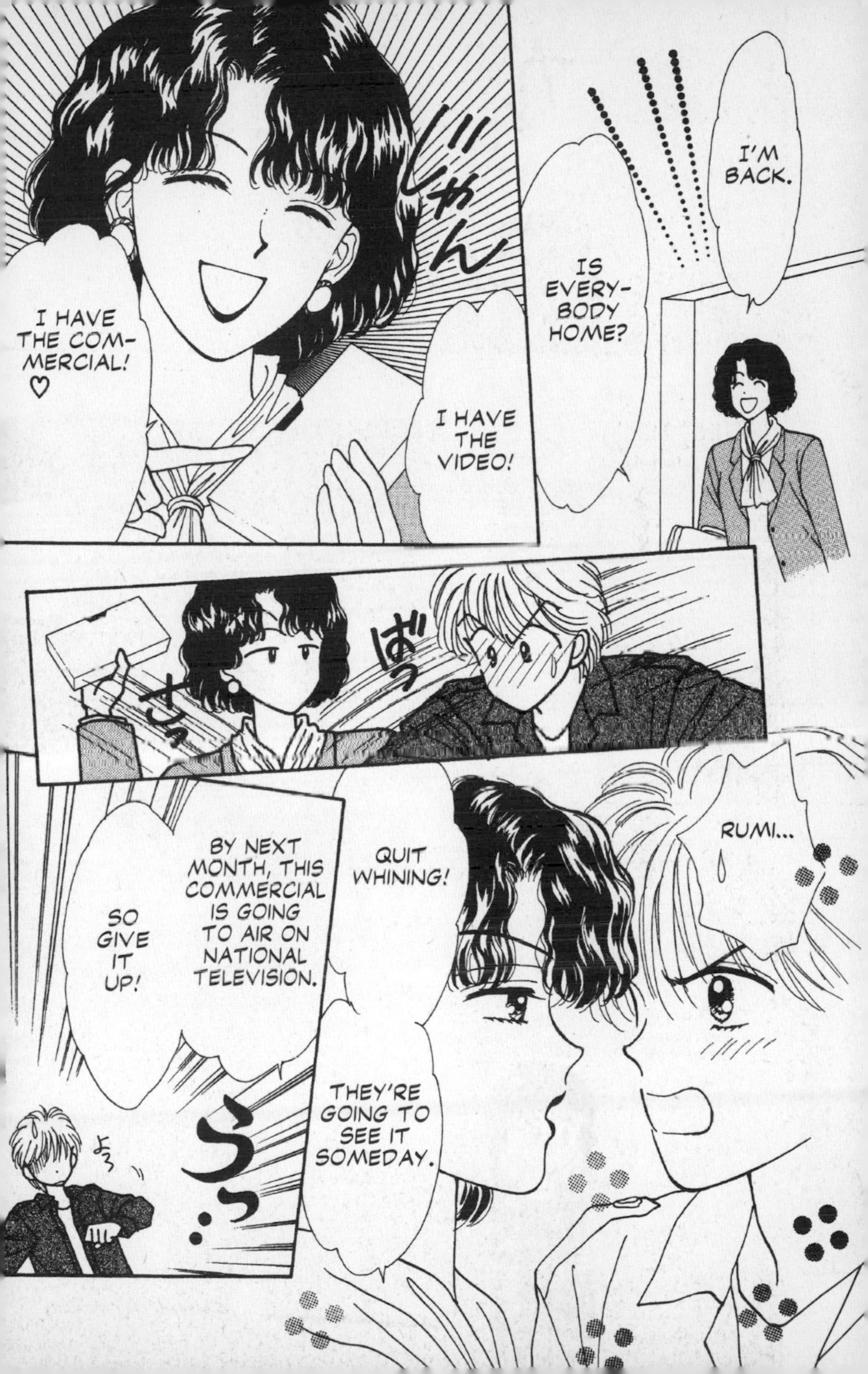
I'M BACK.
IS EVERY-BODY HOME?
I HAVE THE VIDEO!
I HAVE THE COM-MERCIAL! ♡
RUMI...
QUIT WHINING!
BY NEXT MONTH, THIS COMMERCIAL IS GOING TO AIR ON NATIONAL TELEVISION.
SO GIVE IT UP!
THEY'RE GOING TO SEE IT SOMEDAY.

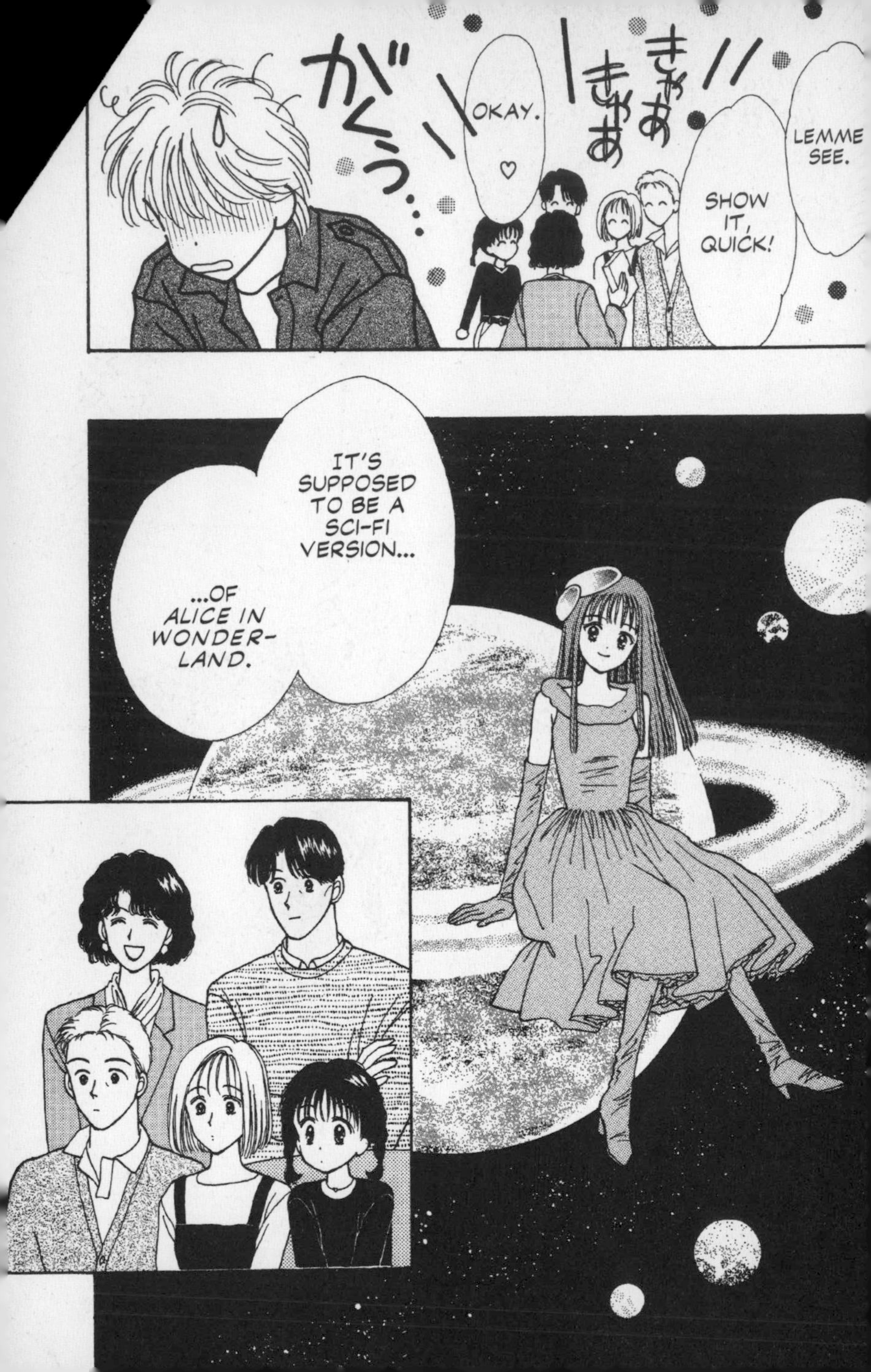
LEMME SEE.
SHOW IT, QUICK!
きゃあきゃあ
OKAY. ♡
がくう…
IT'S SUPPOSED TO BE A SCI-FI VERSION...
...OF ALICE IN WONDER-LAND.

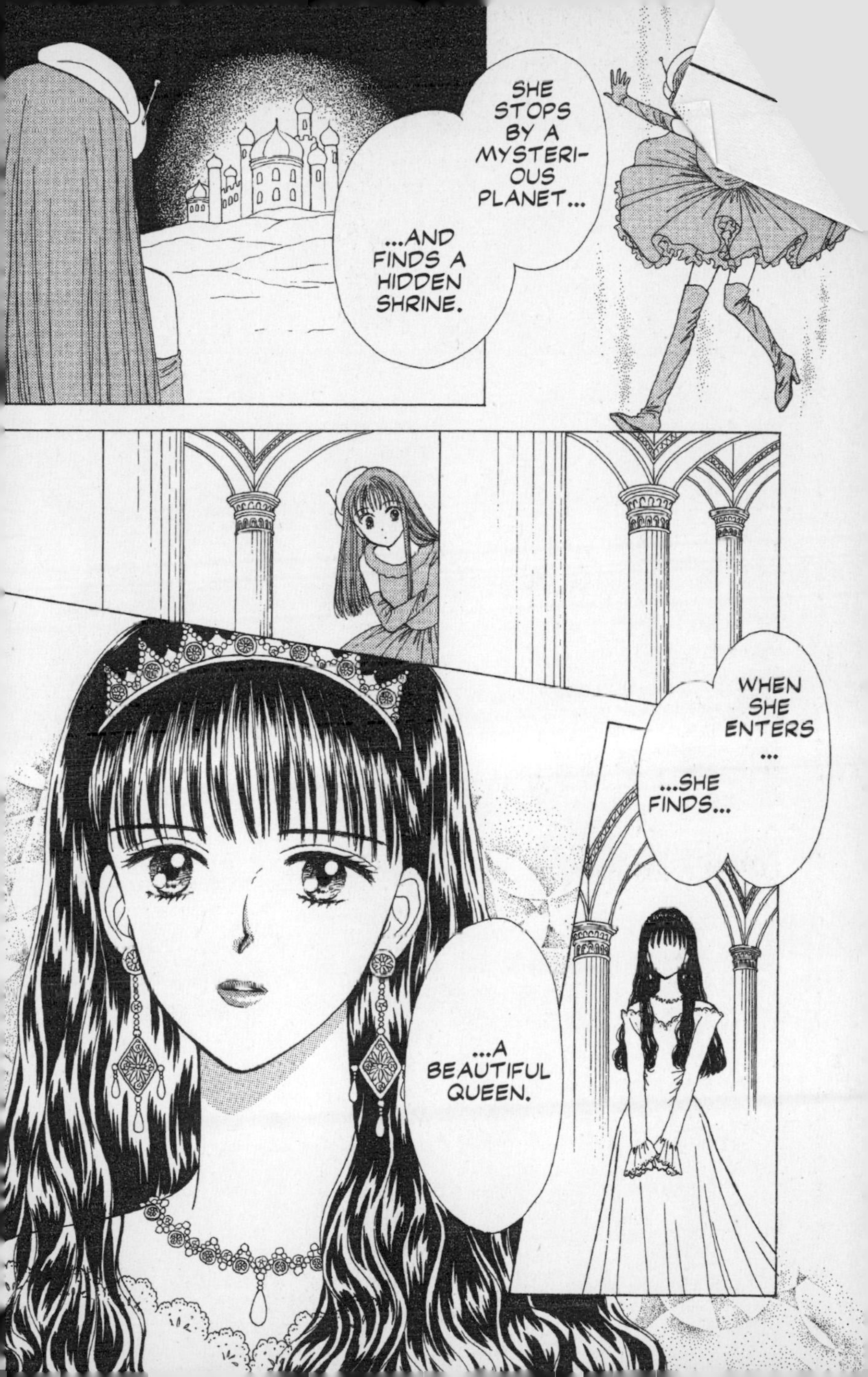
SHE STOPS BY A MYSTERIOUS PLANET...
...AND FINDS A HIDDEN SHRINE.
WHEN SHE ENTERS...
...SHE FINDS...
...A BEAUTIFUL QUEEN.

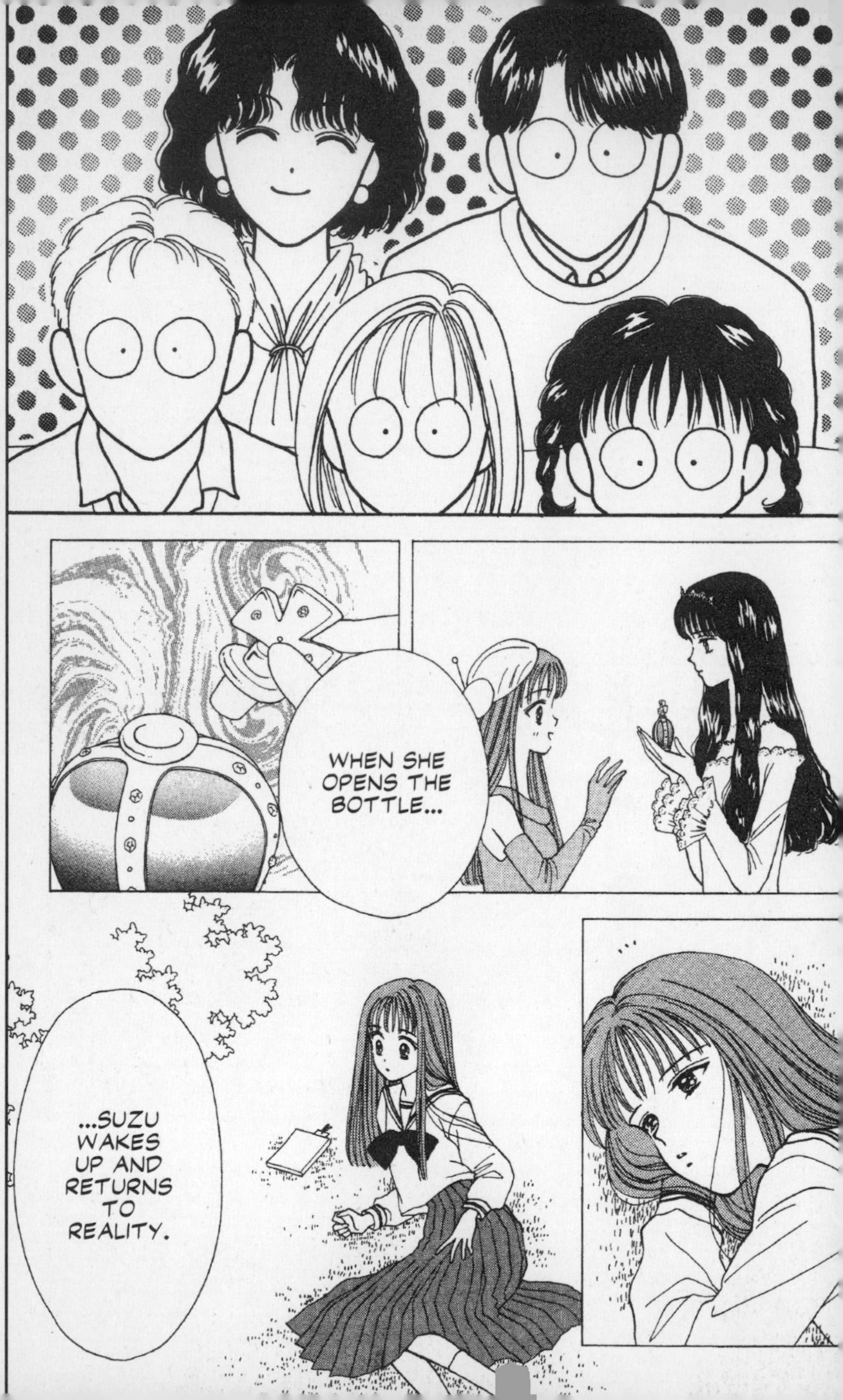
WHEN SHE OPENS THE BOTTLE...
...
...SUZU WAKES UP AND RETURNS TO REALITY.

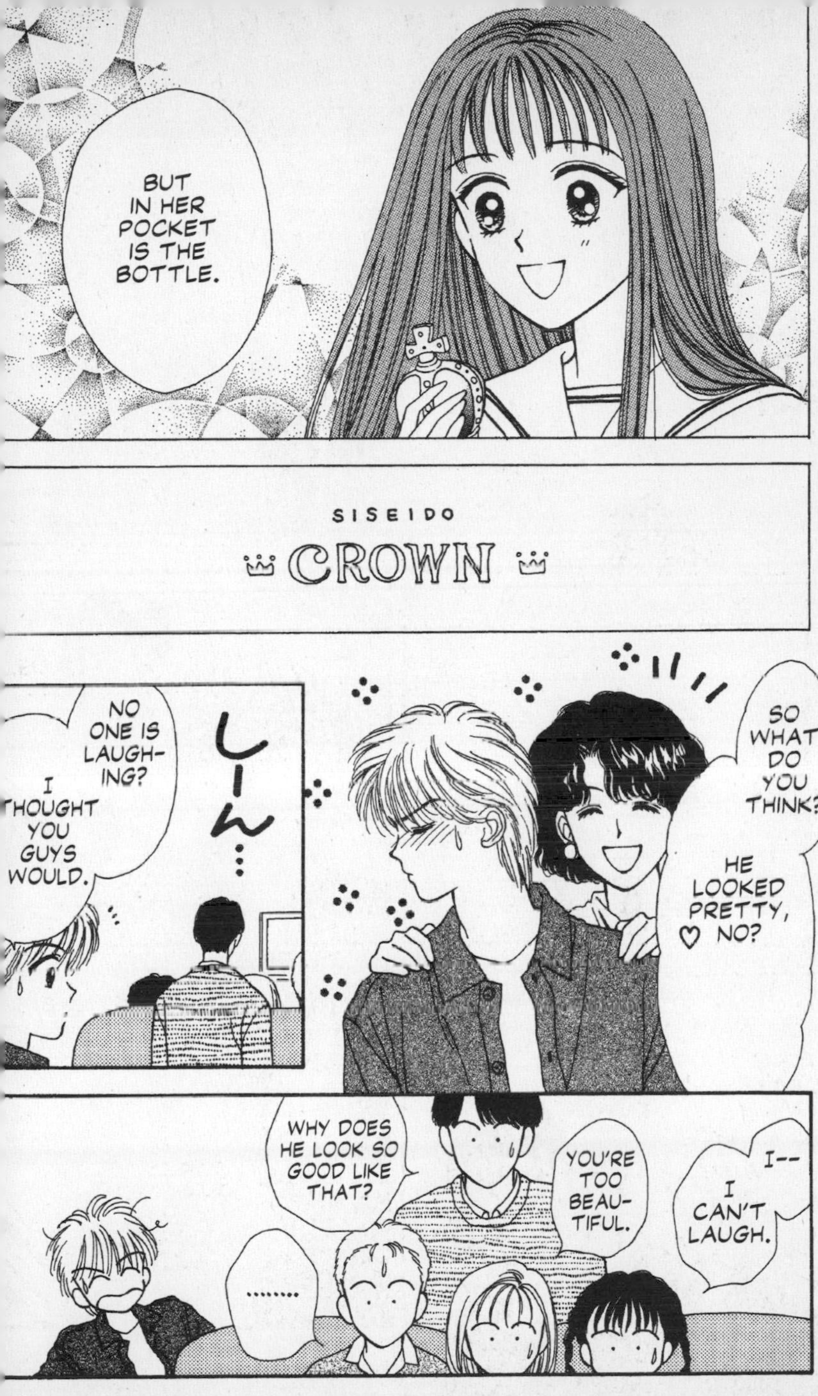
BUT IN HER POCKET IS THE BOTTLE.
SISEIDO
CROWN
SO WHAT DO YOU THINK?
HE LOOKED PRETTY, ♡ NO?
NO ONE IS LAUGHING?
I THOUGHT YOU GUYS WOULD.
しーん…
I-- I CAN'T LAUGH.
YOU'RE TOO BEAUTIFUL.
WHY DOES HE LOOK SO GOOD LIKE THAT?
....

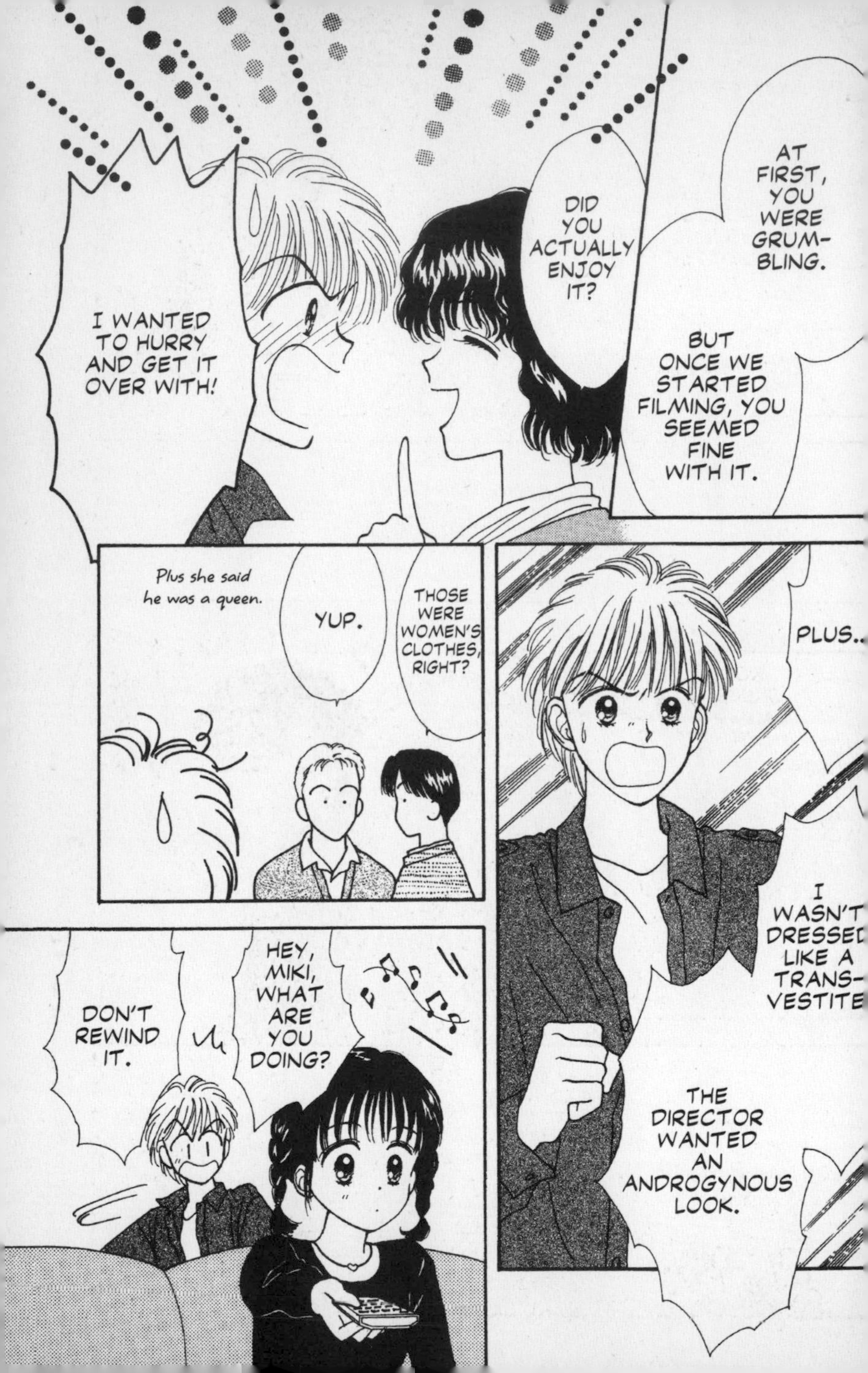
AT FIRST, YOU WERE GRUM-BLING.
BUT ONCE WE STARTED FILMING, YOU SEEMED FINE WITH IT.
DID YOU ACTUALLY ENJOY IT?
I WANTED TO HURRY AND GET IT OVER WITH!
PLUS...
I WASN'T DRESSED LIKE A TRANS-VESTITE.
THE DIRECTOR WANTED AN ANDROGYNOUS LOOK.
THOSE WERE WOMEN'S CLOTHES, RIGHT?
YUP.
Plus she said he was a queen.
HEY, MIKI, WHAT ARE YOU DOING?
DON'T REWIND IT.

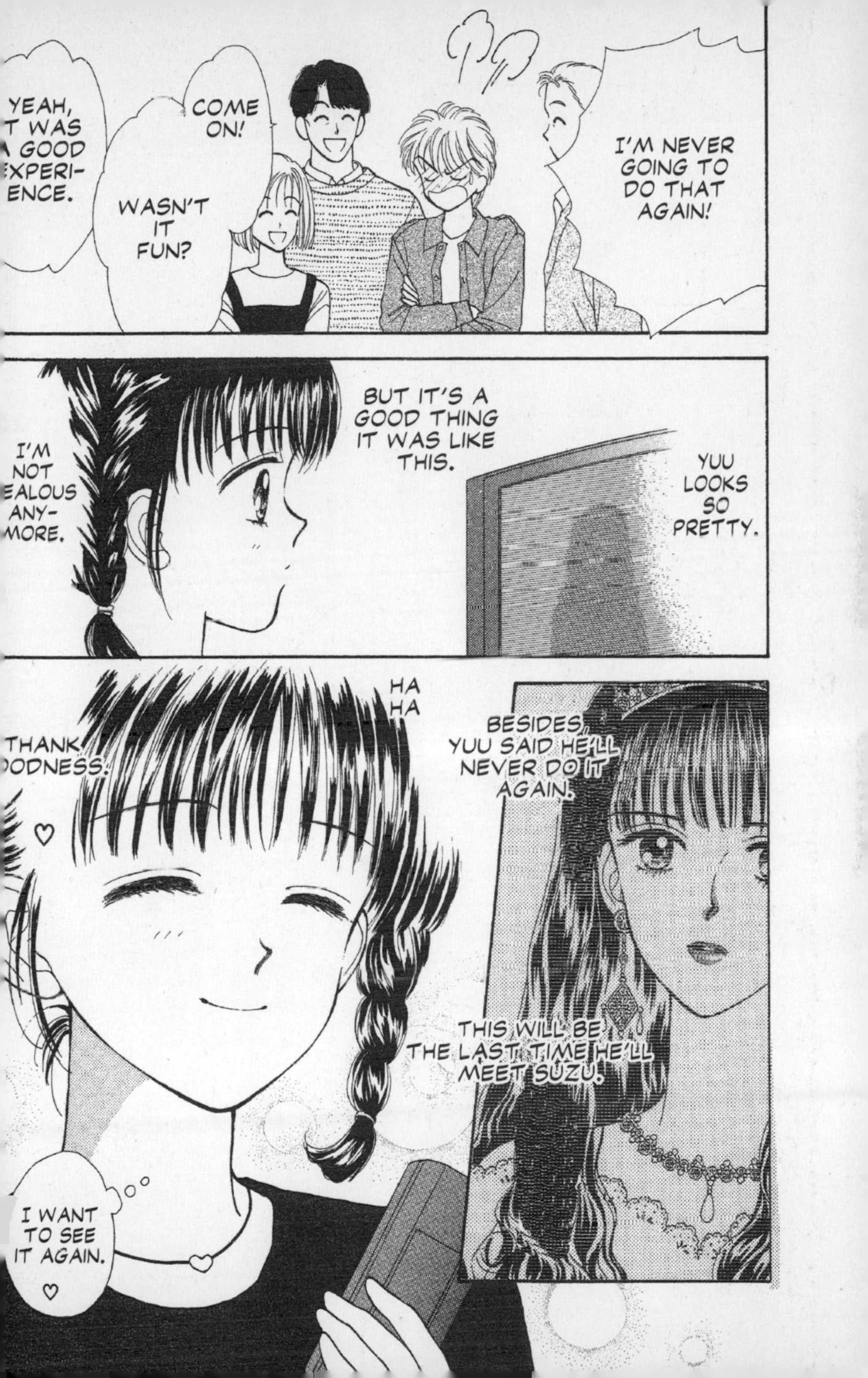
I'M NEVER GOING TO DO THAT AGAIN!
COME ON!
WASN'T IT FUN?
YEAH, T WAS GOOD XPERIENCE.
YUU LOOKS SO PRETTY.
BUT IT'S A GOOD THING IT WAS LIKE THIS.
I'M NOT EALOUS ANYMORE.
BESIDES, YUU SAID HE'LL NEVER DO IT AGAIN.
THIS WILL BE THE LAST TIME HE'LL MEET SUZU.
HA HA
THANK ODNESS.
♡
I WANT TO SEE IT AGAIN. ♡

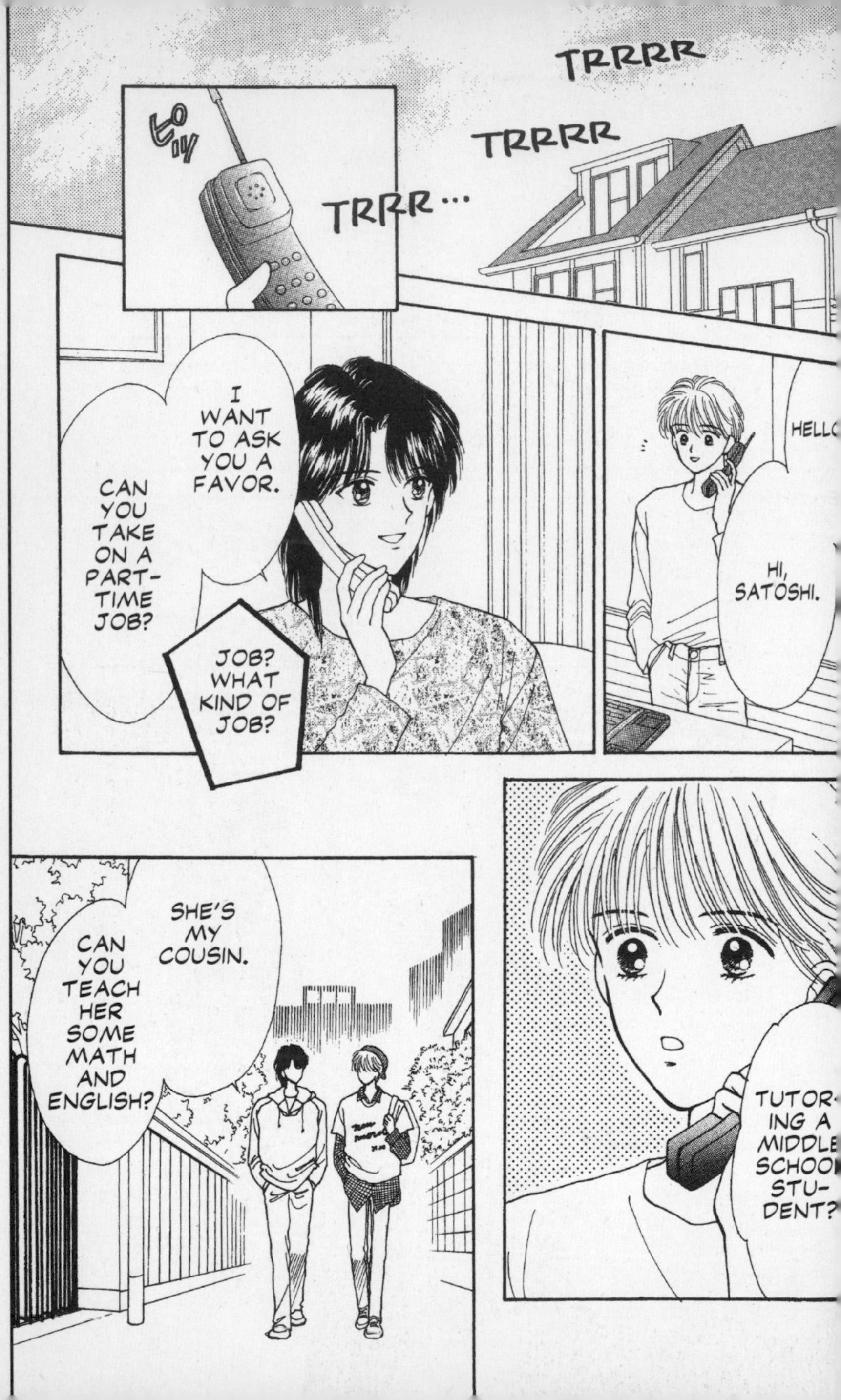
TRRRR
TRRRR
TRRR...
ピッ
HELLO
HI, SATOSHI.
I WANT TO ASK YOU A FAVOR.
CAN YOU TAKE ON A PART-TIME JOB?
JOB? WHAT KIND OF JOB?
TUTORING A MIDDLE SCHOOL STUDENT?
SHE'S MY COUSIN.
CAN YOU TEACH HER SOME MATH AND ENGLISH?

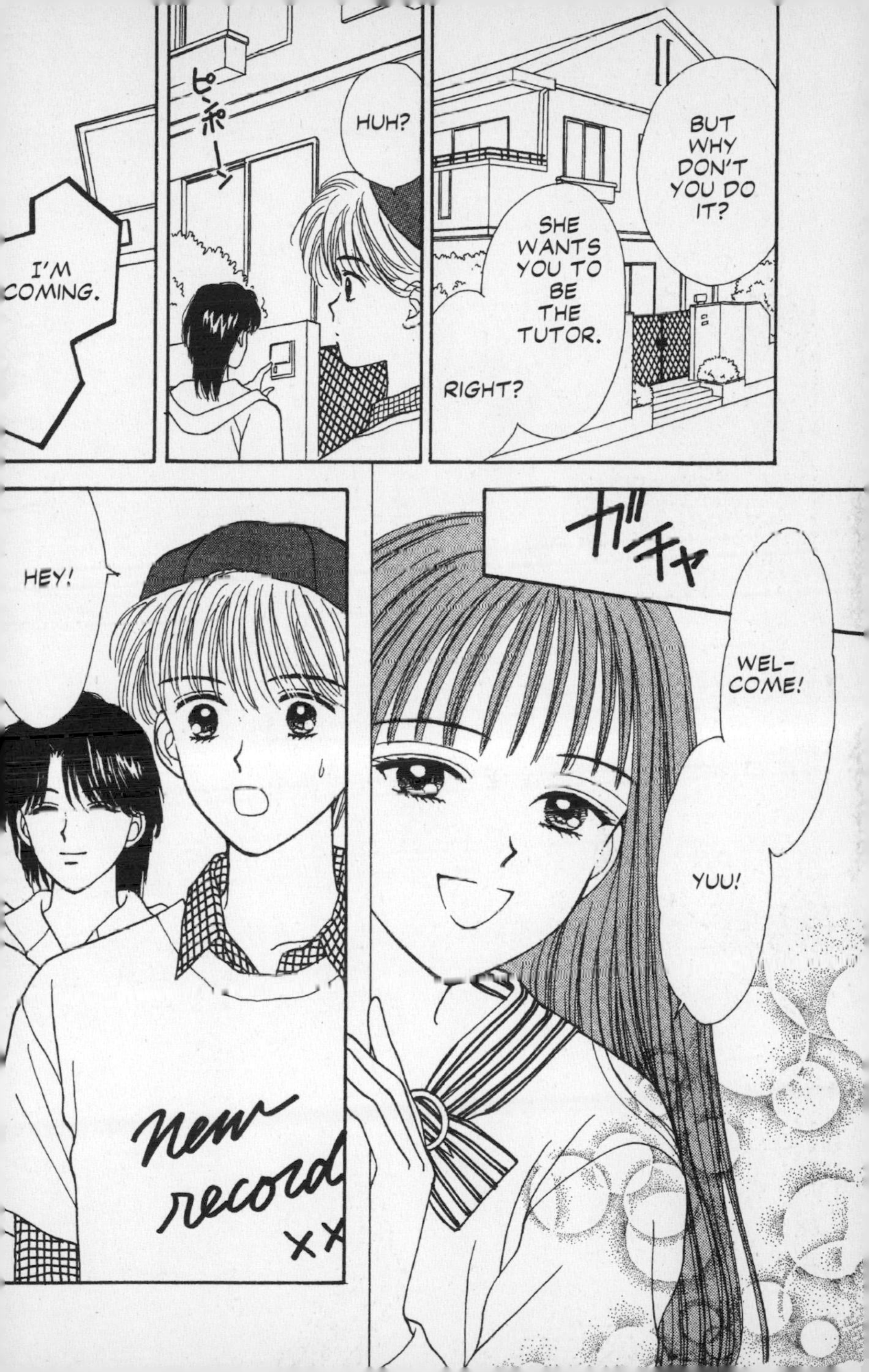
BUT WHY DON'T YOU DO IT?
SHE WANTS YOU TO BE THE TUTOR.
RIGHT?
ピンポーン
HUH?
I'M COMING.
ガチャ
WEL-COME!
YUU!
HEY!
New record ××

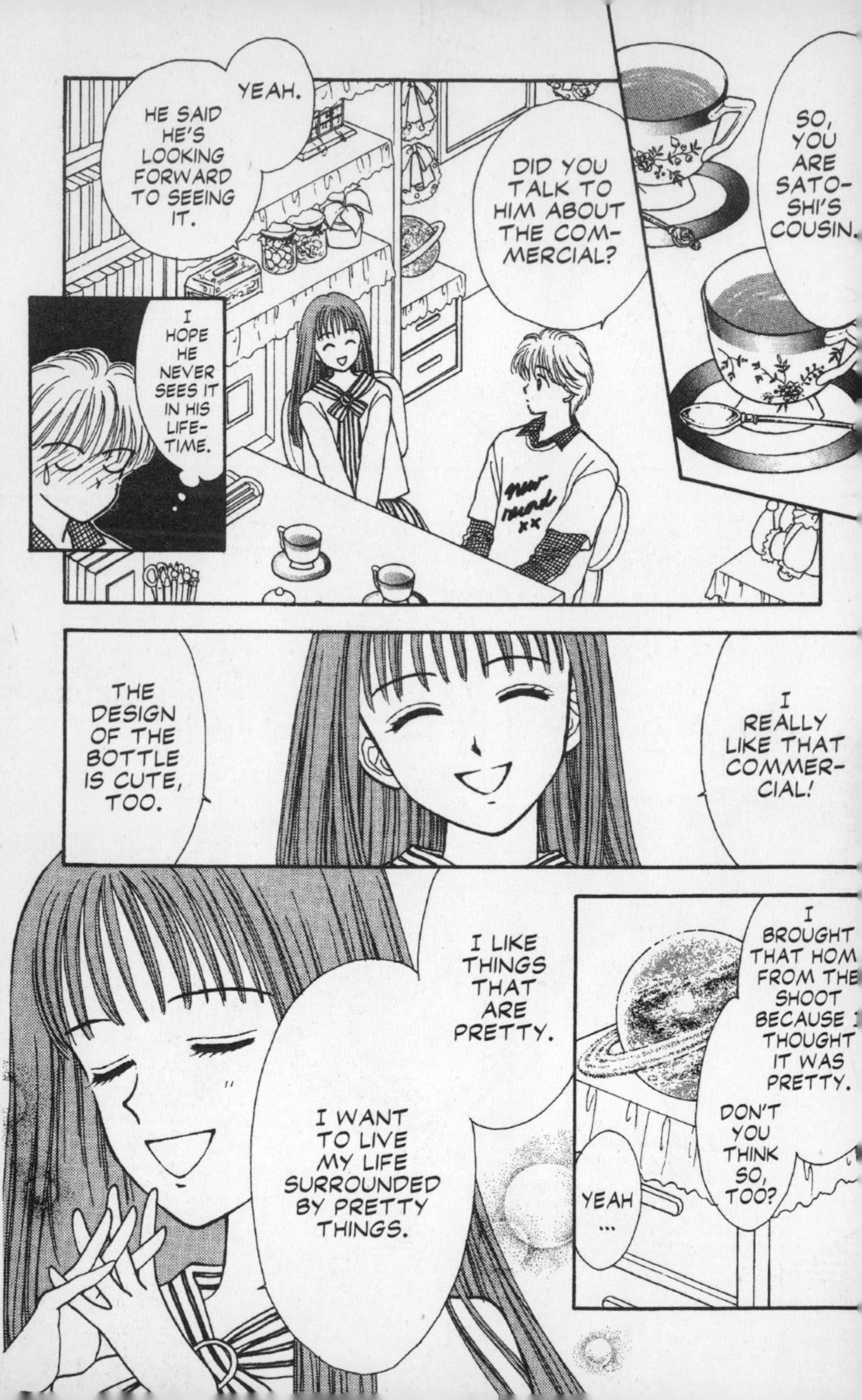
SO, YOU ARE SATOSHI'S COUSIN.
DID YOU TALK TO HIM ABOUT THE COMMERCIAL?
YEAH.
HE SAID HE'S LOOKING FORWARD TO SEEING IT.
I HOPE HE NEVER SEES IT IN HIS LIFETIME.
I REALLY LIKE THAT COMMERCIAL!
THE DESIGN OF THE BOTTLE IS CUTE, TOO.
I BROUGHT THAT HOM FROM THE SHOOT BECAUSE THOUGHT IT WAS PRETTY.
DON'T YOU THINK SO, TOO?
YEAH ...
I LIKE THINGS THAT ARE PRETTY.
I WANT TO LIVE MY LIFE SURROUNDED BY PRETTY THINGS.

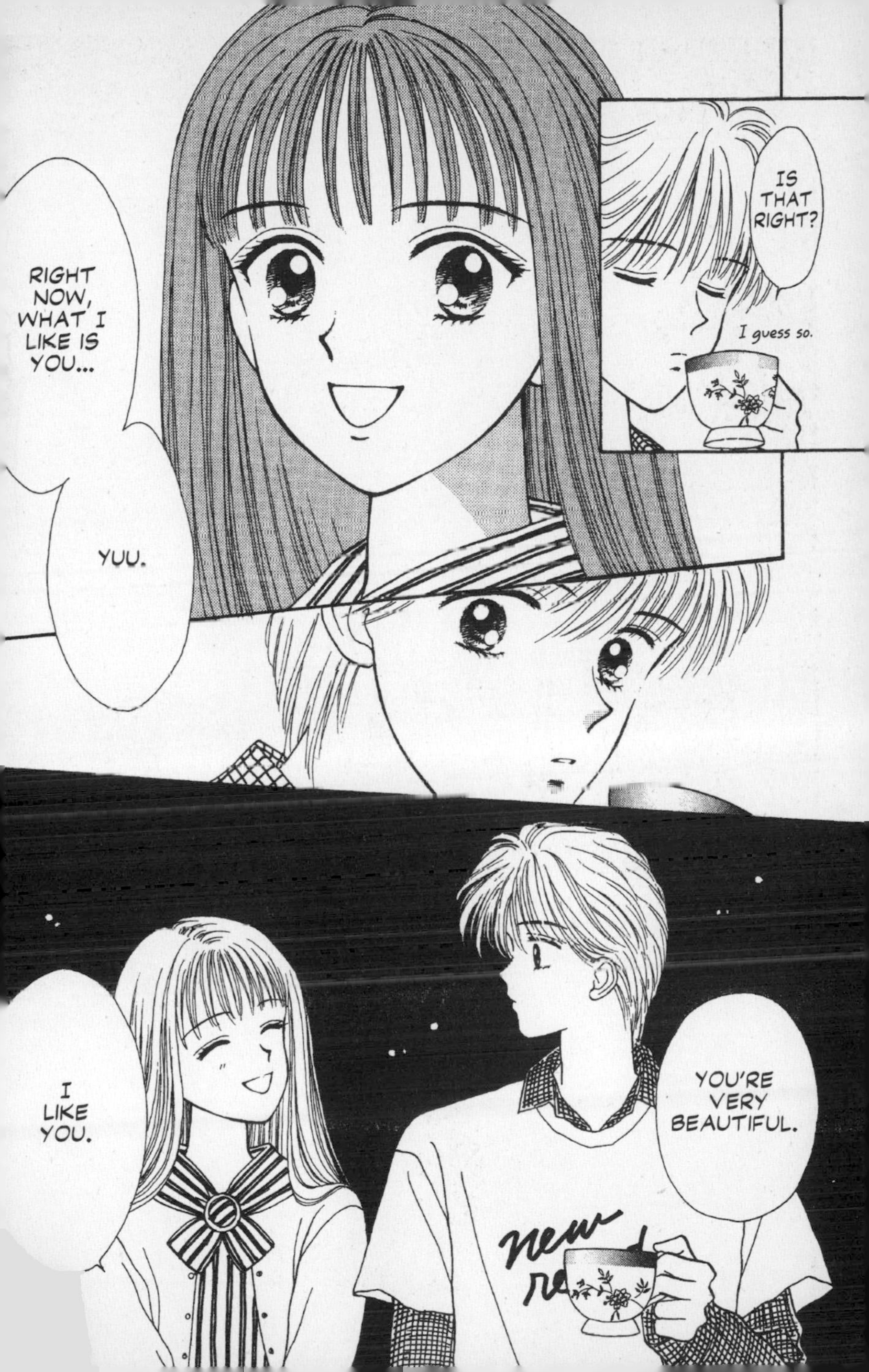
IS THAT RIGHT?
I guess so.
RIGHT NOW, WHAT I LIKE IS YOU...
YUU.
YOU'RE VERY BEAUTIFUL.
I LIKE YOU.

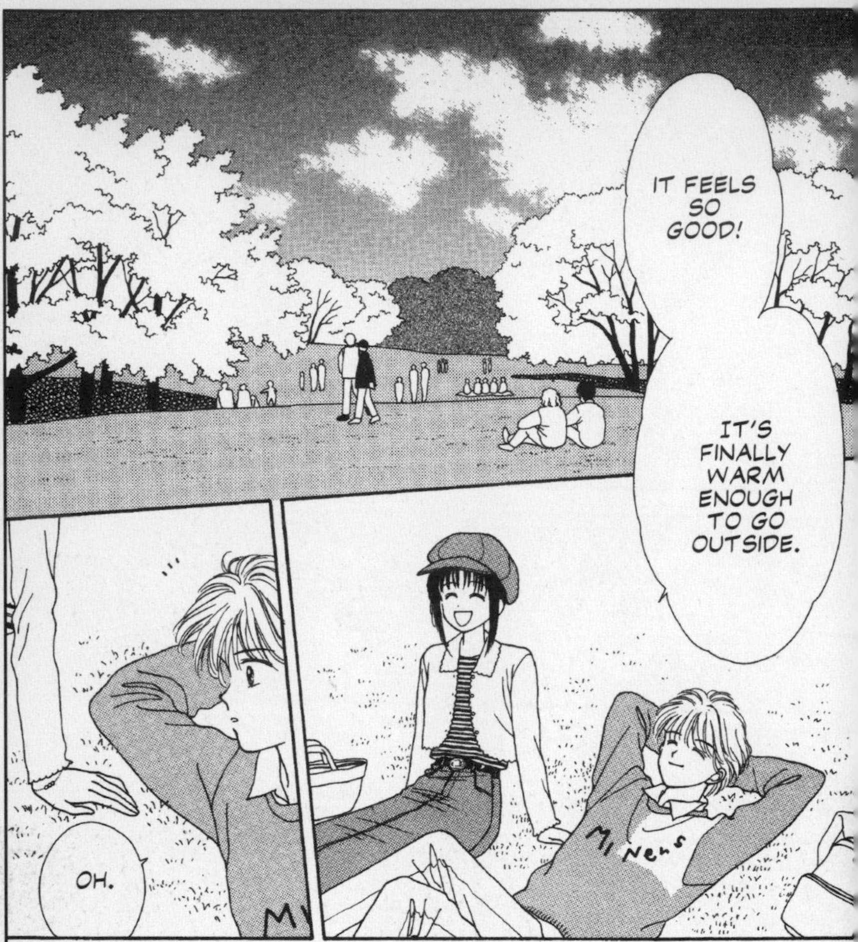
IT FEELS SO GOOD!
IT'S FINALLY WARM ENOUGH TO GO OUTSIDE.
OH.

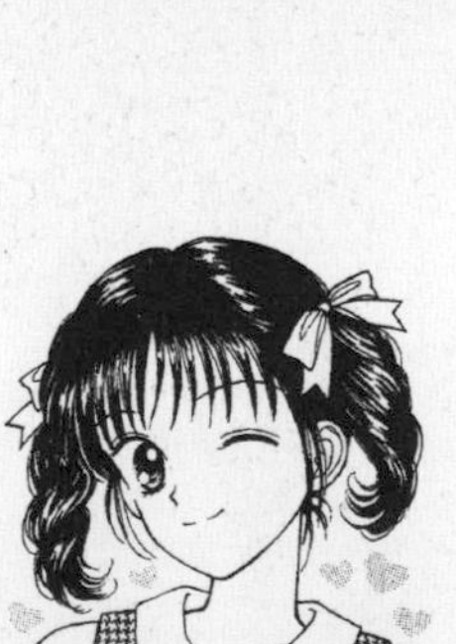

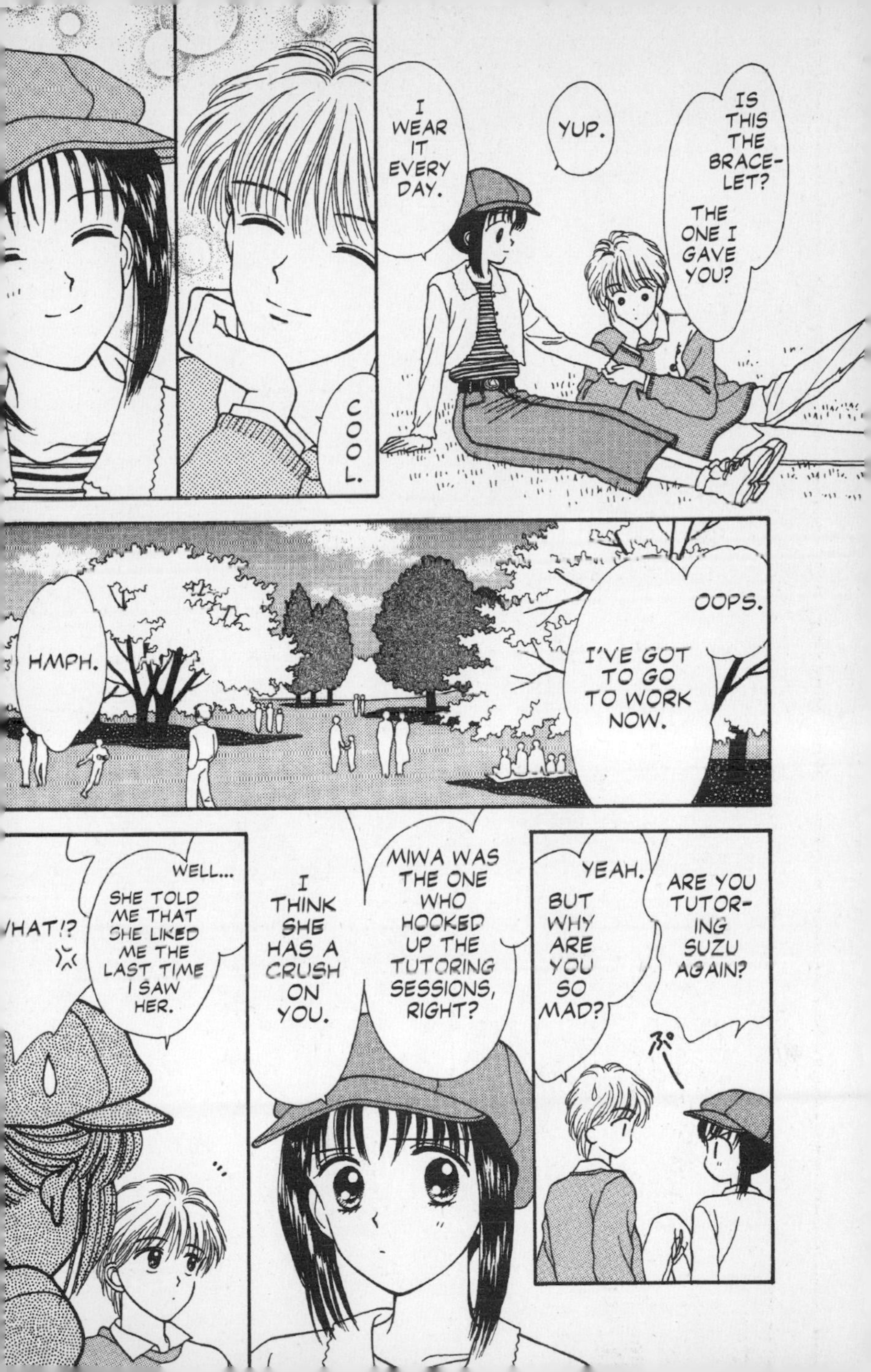
IS THIS THE BRACELET?
THE ONE I GAVE YOU?
YUP.
I WEAR IT EVERY DAY.
COOL.
OOPS.
I'VE GOT TO GO TO WORK NOW.
HMPH.
ARE YOU TUTORING SUZU AGAIN?
YEAH.
BUT WHY ARE YOU SO MAD?
ぷ
MIWA WAS THE ONE WHO HOOKED UP THE TUTORING SESSIONS, RIGHT?
I THINK SHE HAS A CRUSH ON YOU.
WELL...
SHE TOLD ME THAT SHE LIKED ME THE LAST TIME I SAW HER.
HAT!?

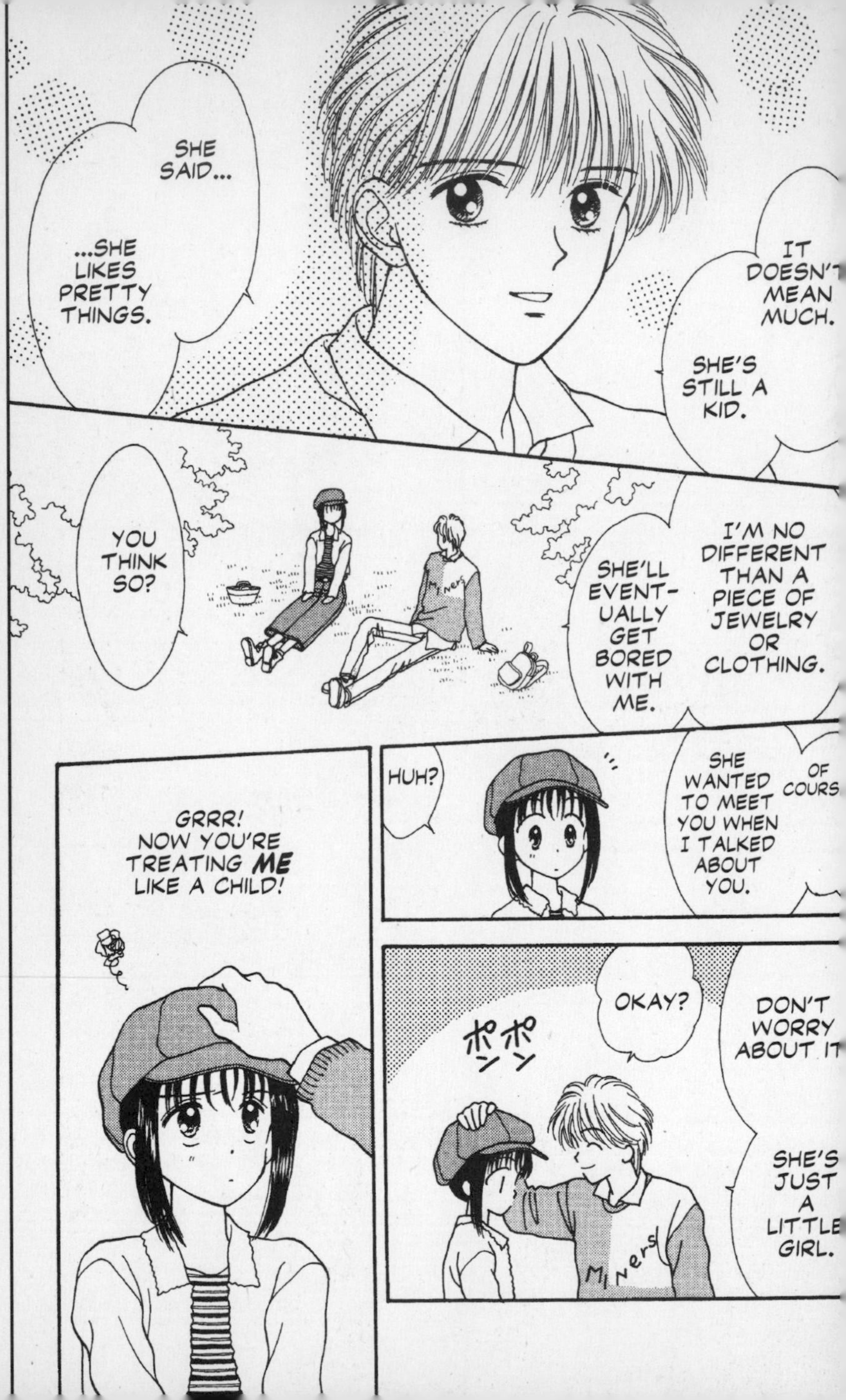
IT DOESN'T MEAN MUCH.
SHE'S STILL A KID.
SHE SAID...
...SHE LIKES PRETTY THINGS.
I'M NO DIFFERENT THAN A PIECE OF JEWELRY OR CLOTHING.
SHE'LL EVENT-UALLY GET BORED WITH ME.
YOU THINK SO?
OF COURS
SHE WANTED TO MEET YOU WHEN I TALKED ABOUT YOU.
HUH?
DON'T WORRY ABOUT IT
SHE'S JUST A LITTLE GIRL.
OKAY?
ポンポン
GRRR! NOW YOU'RE TREATING **ME** LIKE A CHILD!

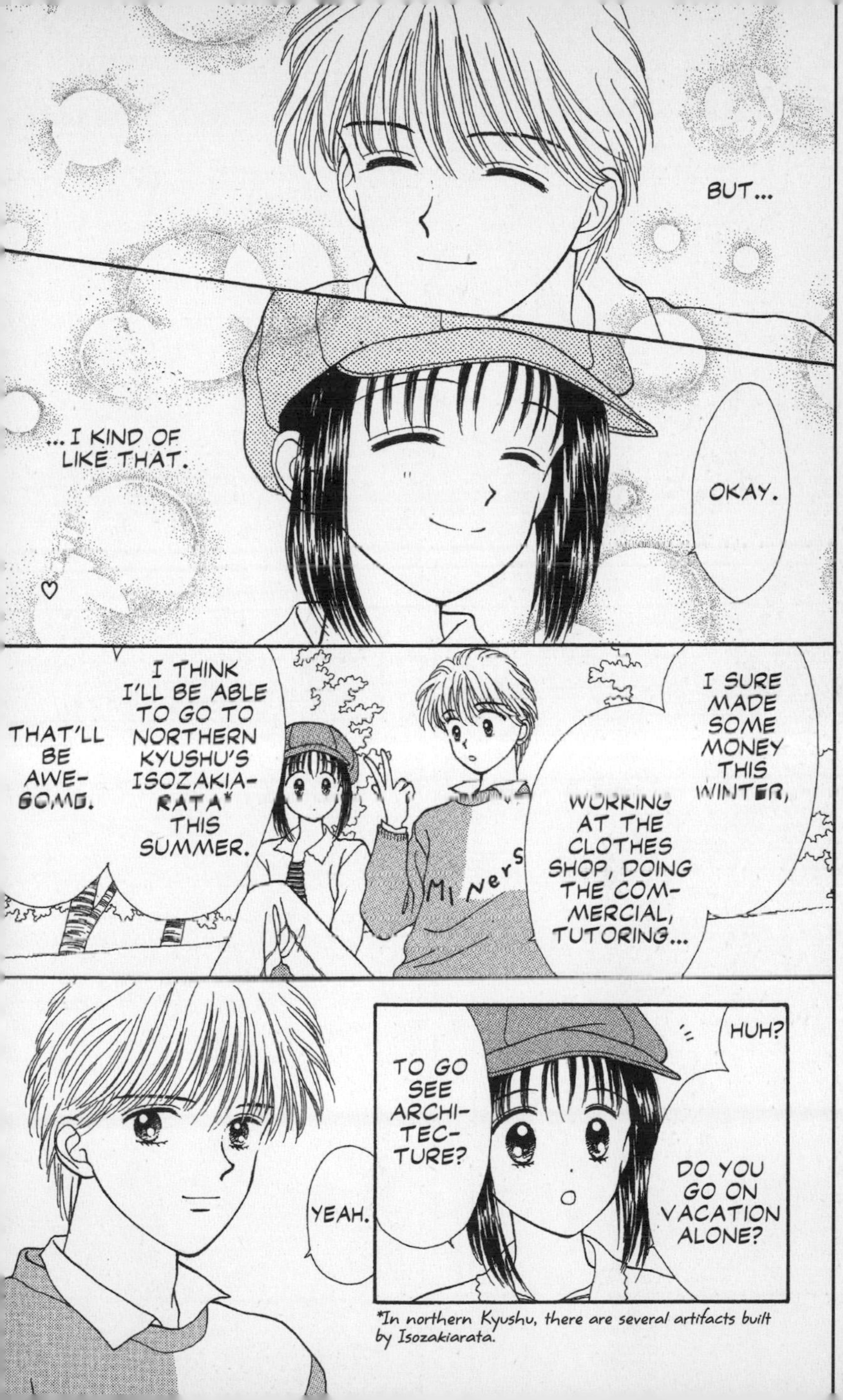
BUT...
OKAY.
...I KIND OF LIKE THAT.
I SURE MADE SOME MONEY THIS WINTER,
WORKING AT THE CLOTHES SHOP, DOING THE COMMERCIAL, TUTORING...
I THINK I'LL BE ABLE TO GO TO NORTHERN KYUSHU'S ISOZAKIARATA* THIS SUMMER.
THAT'LL BE AWESOME.
MINERS
HUH?
DO YOU GO ON VACATION ALONE?
TO GO SEE ARCHITECTURE?
YEAH.

*In northern Kyushu, there are several artifacts built by Isozakiarata.

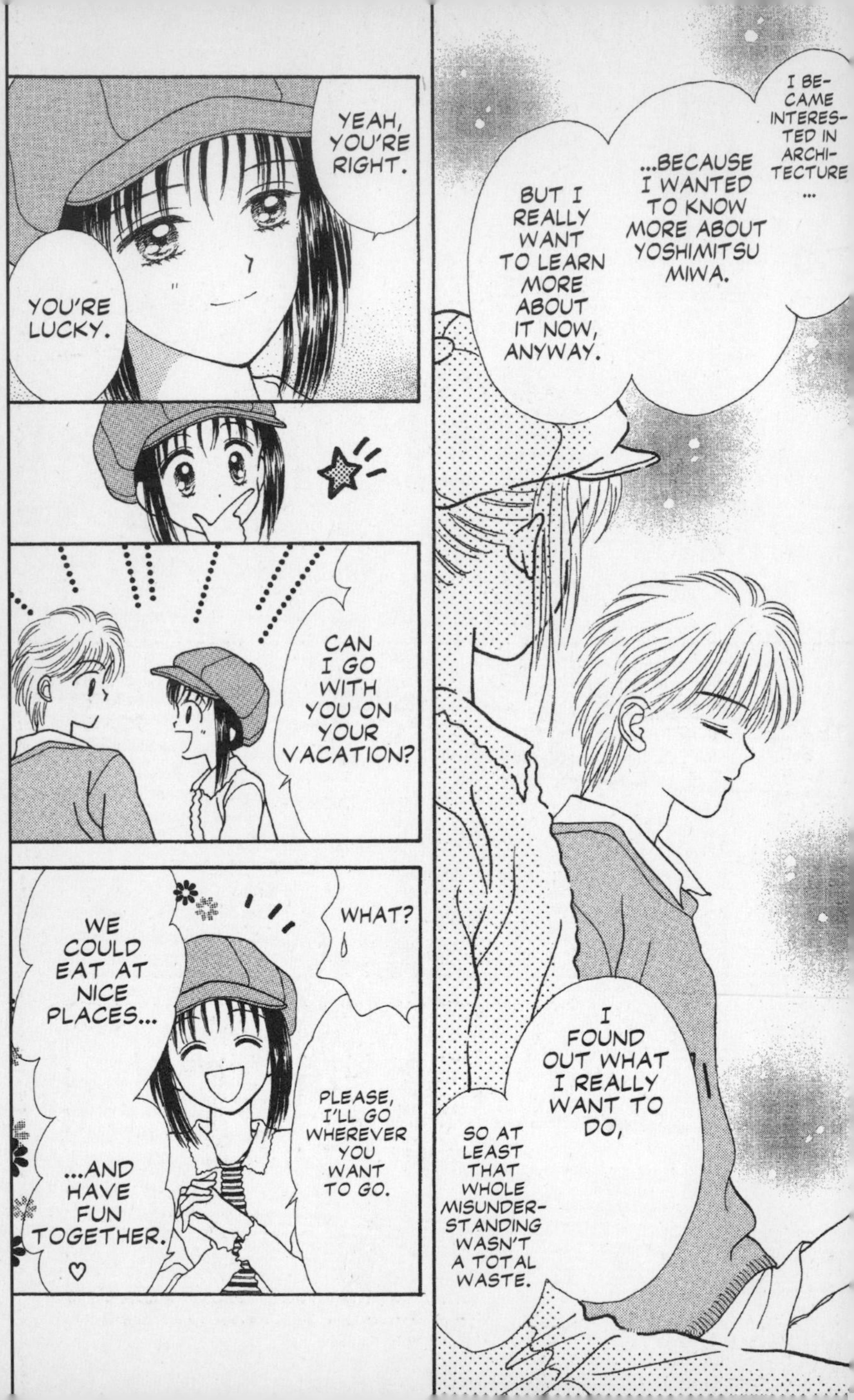
I BE-CAME INTERES-TED IN ARCHI-TECTURE...
...BECAUSE I WANTED TO KNOW MORE ABOUT YOSHIMITSU MIWA.
BUT I REALLY WANT TO LEARN MORE ABOUT IT NOW, ANYWAY.
I FOUND OUT WHAT I REALLY WANT TO DO,
SO AT LEAST THAT WHOLE MISUNDER-STANDING WASN'T A TOTAL WASTE.
YEAH, YOU'RE RIGHT.
YOU'RE LUCKY.
CAN I GO WITH YOU ON YOUR VACATION?
WHAT?
PLEASE, I'LL GO WHEREVER YOU WANT TO GO.
WE COULD EAT AT NICE PLACES...
...AND HAVE FUN TOGETHER. ♡

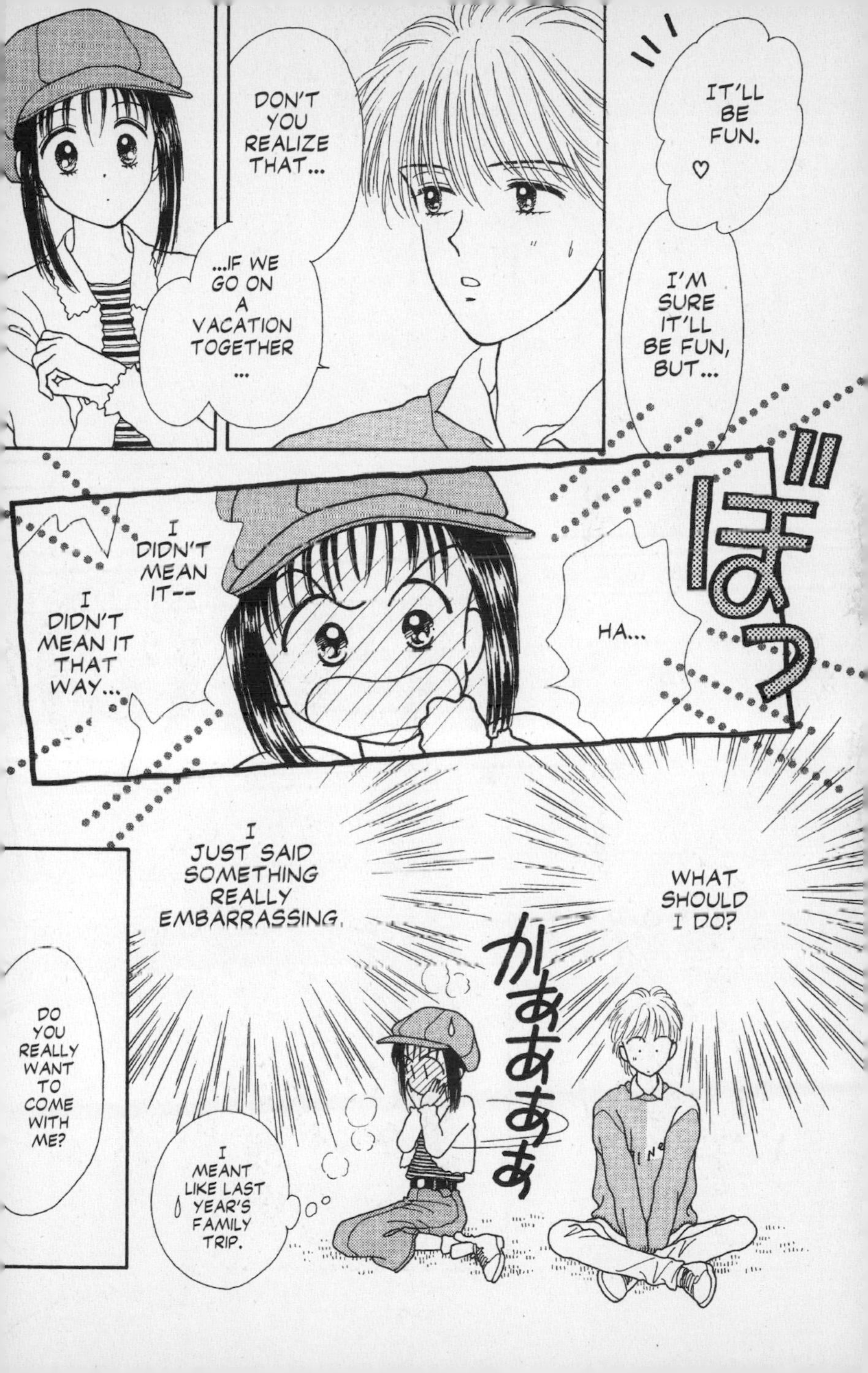
IT'LL BE FUN. ♡
I'M SURE IT'LL BE FUN, BUT...
DON'T YOU REALIZE THAT...
...IF WE GO ON A VACATION TOGETHER ...
ぼっ
HA...
I DIDN'T MEAN IT--
I DIDN'T MEAN IT THAT WAY...
WHAT SHOULD I DO?
I JUST SAID SOMETHING REALLY EMBARRASSING.
かあああ
I MEANT LIKE LAST YEAR'S FAMILY TRIP.
DO YOU REALLY WANT TO COME WITH ME?

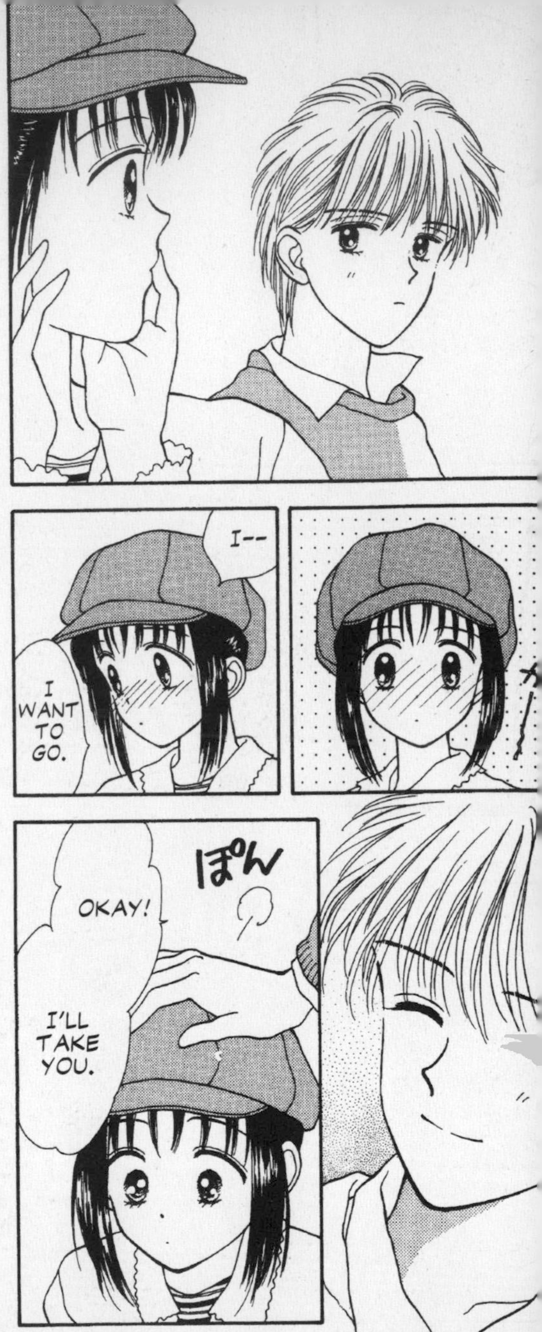
I--
I WANT TO GO.
ぽん
OKAY!
I'LL TAKE YOU.

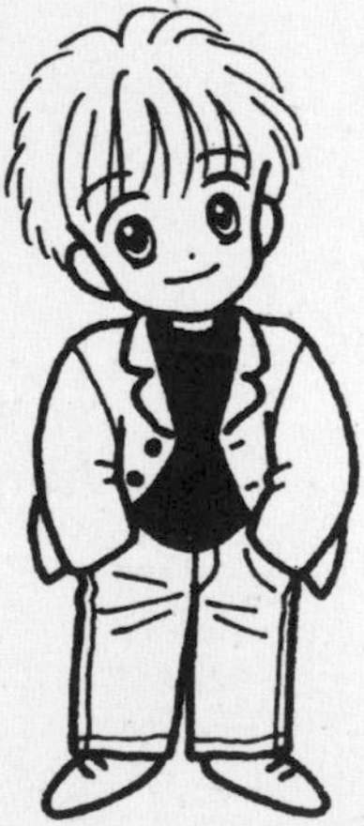

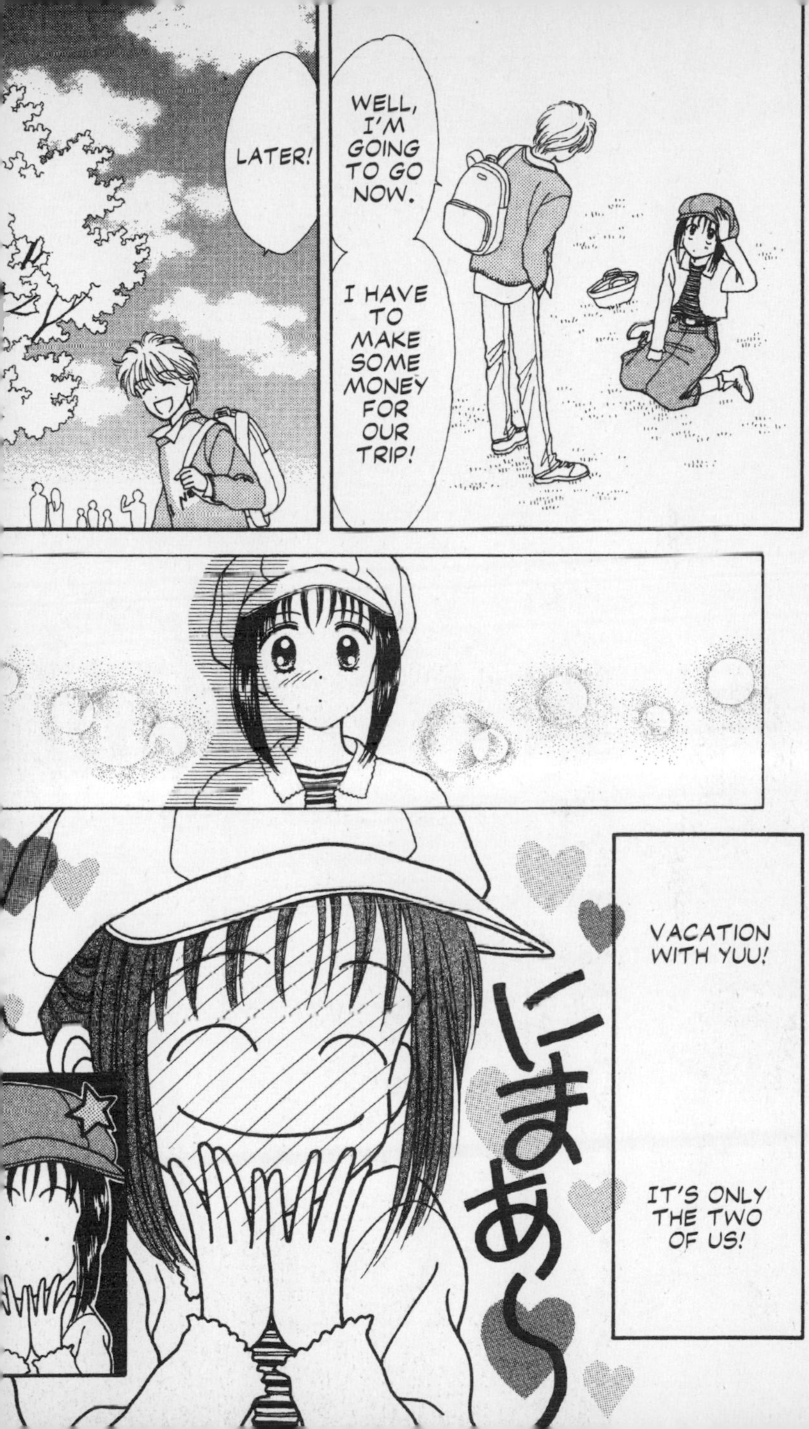
WELL, I'M GOING TO GO NOW.
I HAVE TO MAKE SOME MONEY FOR OUR TRIP!
LATER!
VACATION WITH YUU!
IT'S ONLY THE TWO OF US!
にまあ〜

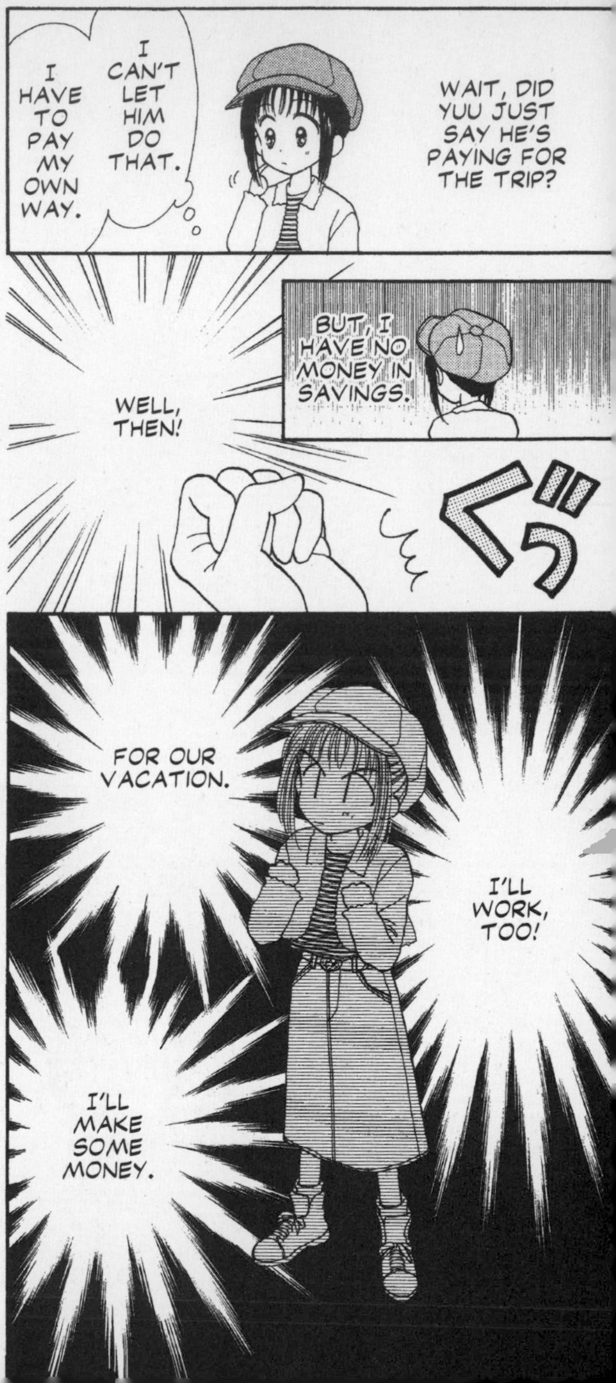
WAIT, DID YUU JUST SAY HE'S PAYING FOR THE TRIP?
I CAN'T LET HIM DO THAT.
I HAVE TO PAY MY OWN WAY.
BUT, I HAVE NO MONEY IN SAVINGS.
WELL, THEN!
ぐっ
I'LL WORK, TOO!
FOR OUR VACATION.
I'LL MAKE SOME MONEY.

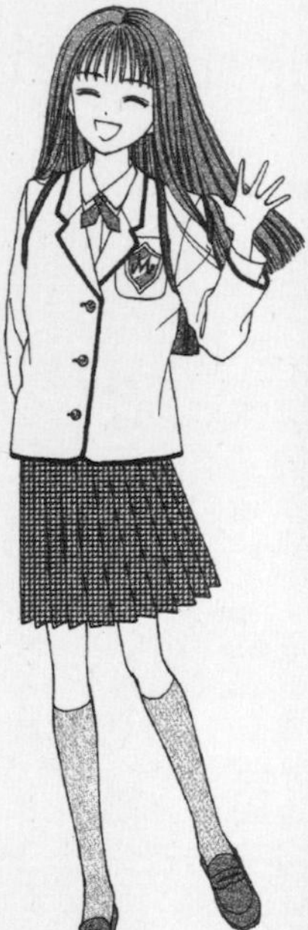

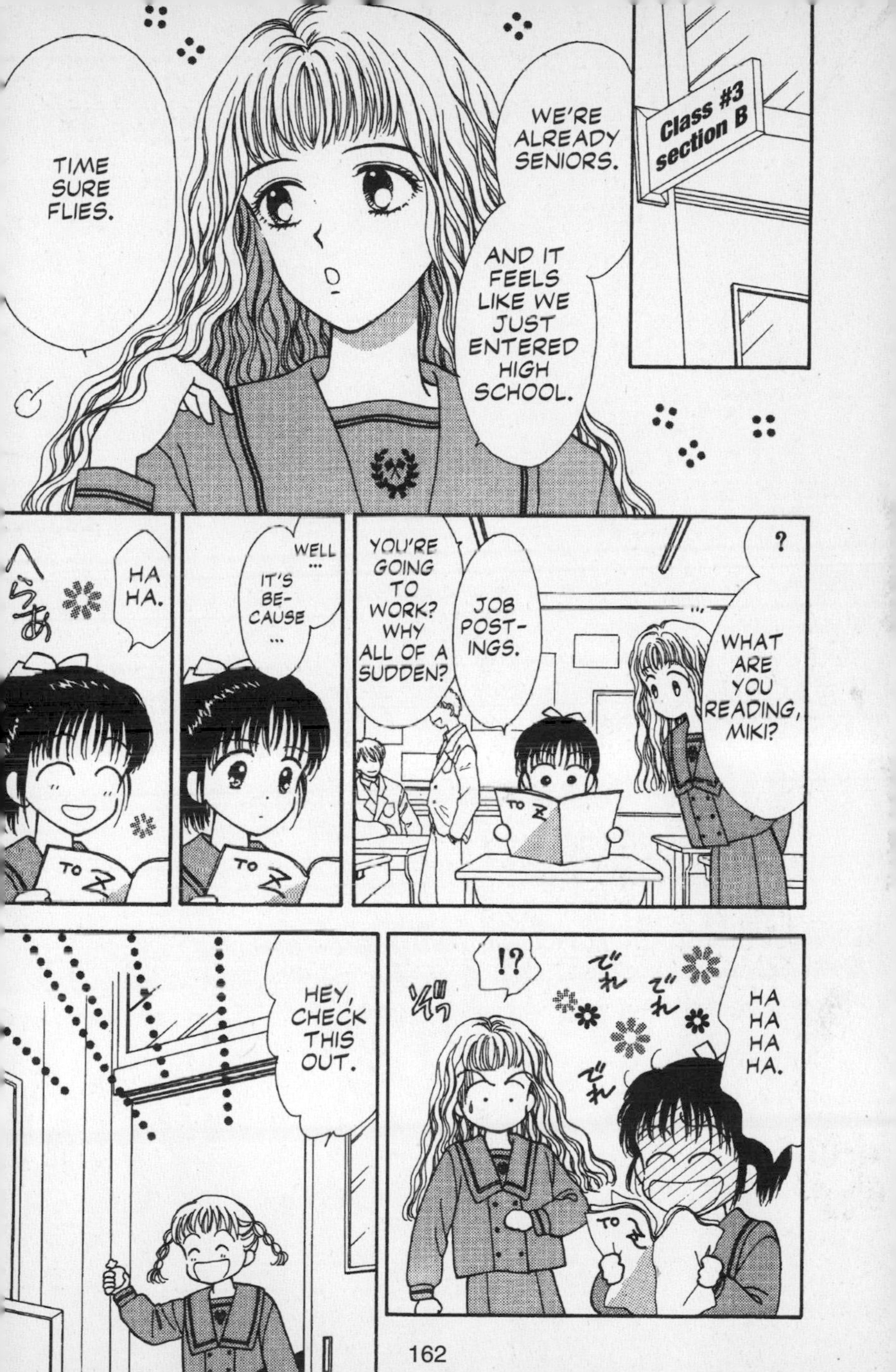
Class #3 section B
WE'RE ALREADY SENIORS.
AND IT FEELS LIKE WE JUST ENTERED HIGH SCHOOL.
TIME SURE FLIES.
?
WHAT ARE YOU READING, MIKI?
...
JOB POST-INGS.
YOU'RE GOING TO WORK? WHY ALL OF A SUDDEN?
WELL ...
IT'S BE-CAUSE ...
HA HA.
へらあ
HA HA HA HA.
でれ
でれ
でれ
!?
HEY, CHECK THIS OUT.

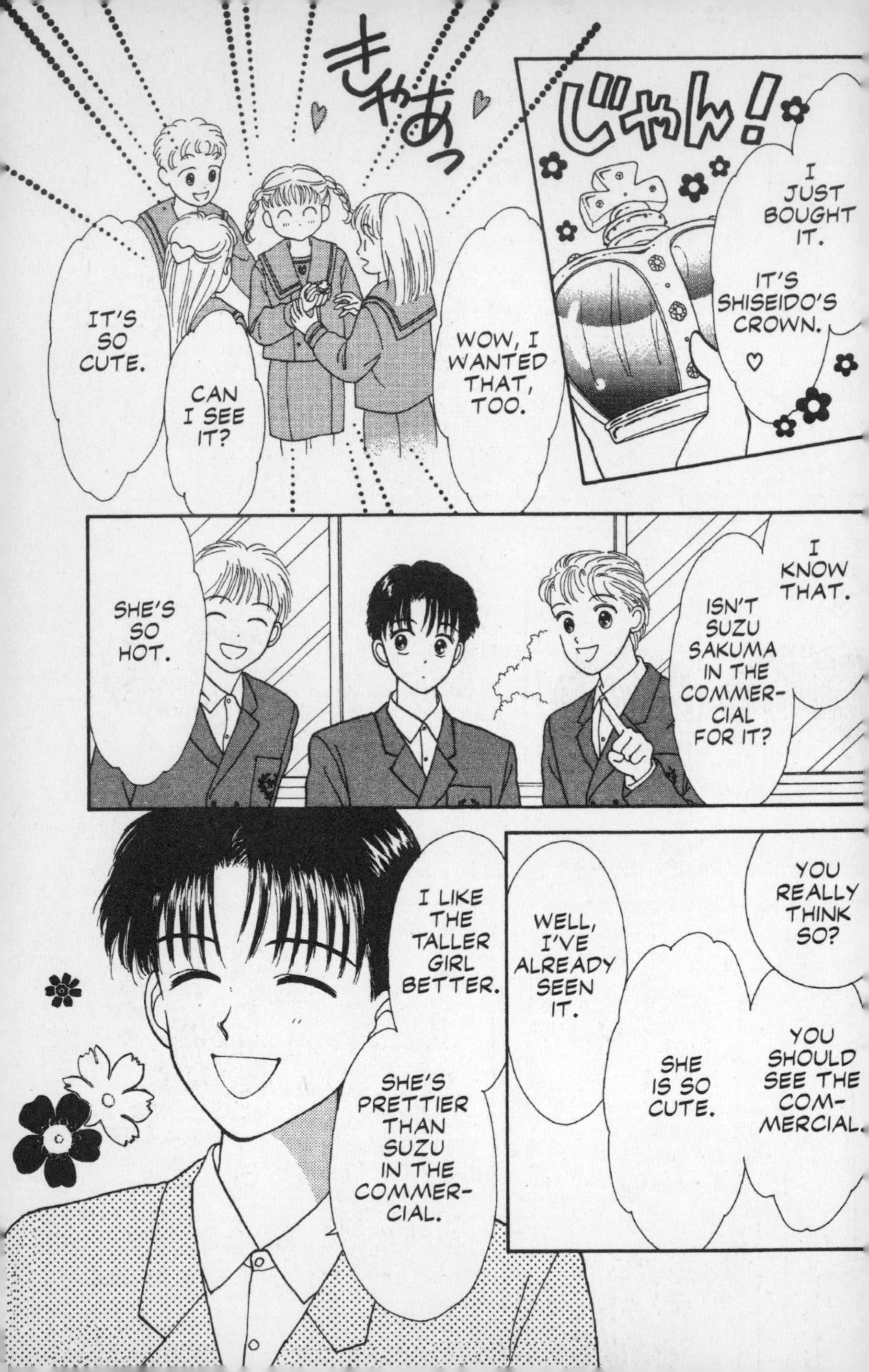
じゃん!
I JUST BOUGHT IT.
IT'S SHISEIDO'S CROWN. ♡
きゃあっ
WOW, I WANTED THAT, TOO.
CAN I SEE IT?
IT'S SO CUTE.
I KNOW THAT.
ISN'T SUZU SAKUMA IN THE COMMERCIAL FOR IT?
SHE'S SO HOT.
YOU REALLY THINK SO?
YOU SHOULD SEE THE COMMERCIAL.
SHE IS SO CUTE.
WELL, I'VE ALREADY SEEN IT.
I LIKE THE TALLER GIRL BETTER.
SHE'S PRETTIER THAN SUZU IN THE COMMERCIAL.

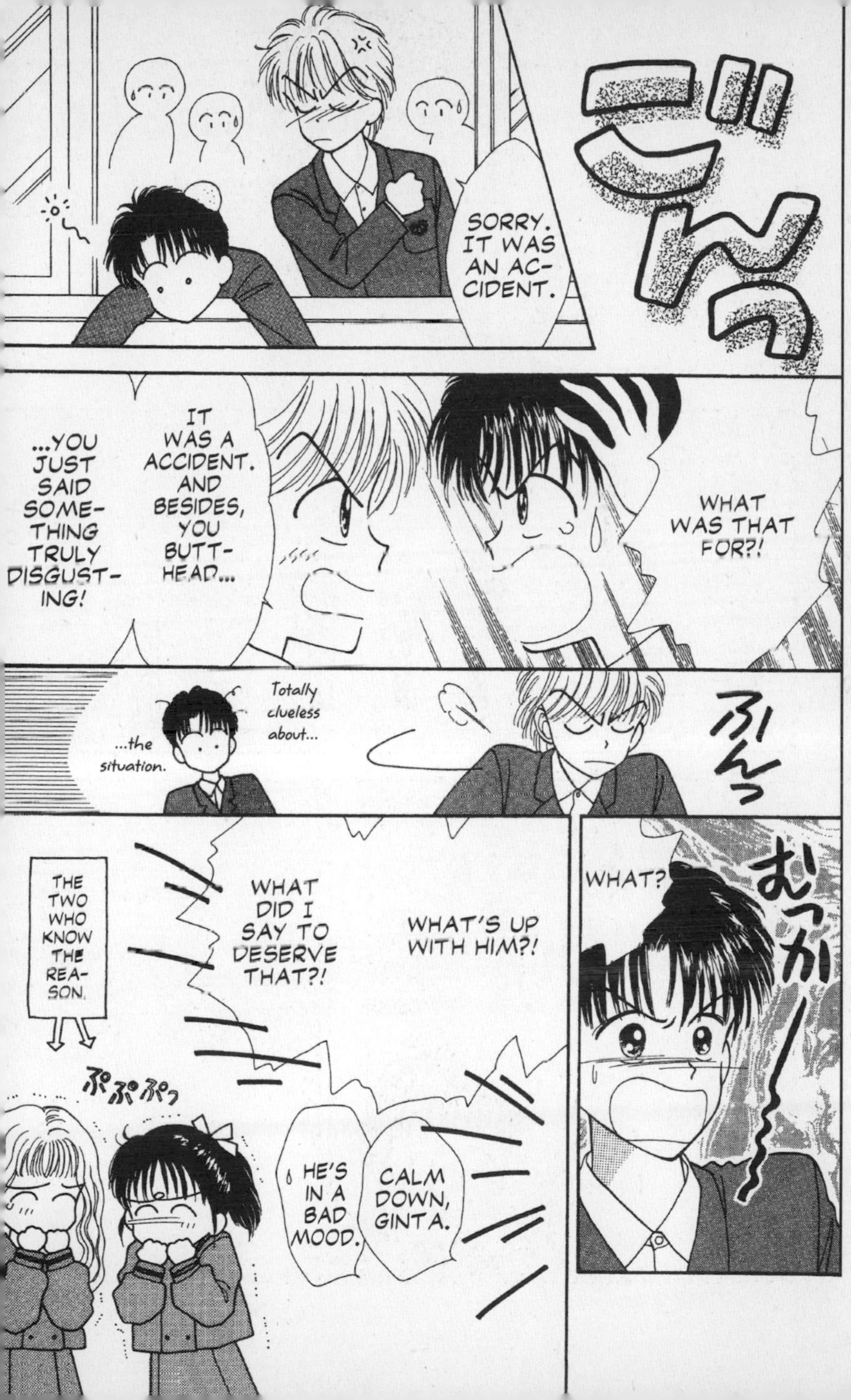
ごんっ
SORRY. IT WAS AN ACCIDENT.
WHAT WAS THAT FOR?!
IT WAS A ACCIDENT. AND BESIDES, YOU BUTT-HEAD...
...YOU JUST SAID SOMETHING TRULY DISGUSTING!
ぷんっ
Totally clueless about...
...the situation.
むっかー
WHAT?
WHAT'S UP WITH HIM?!
WHAT DID I SAY TO DESERVE THAT?!
THE TWO WHO KNOW THE REASON.
CALM DOWN, GINTA.
HE'S IN A BAD MOOD.
ぷぷぷっ

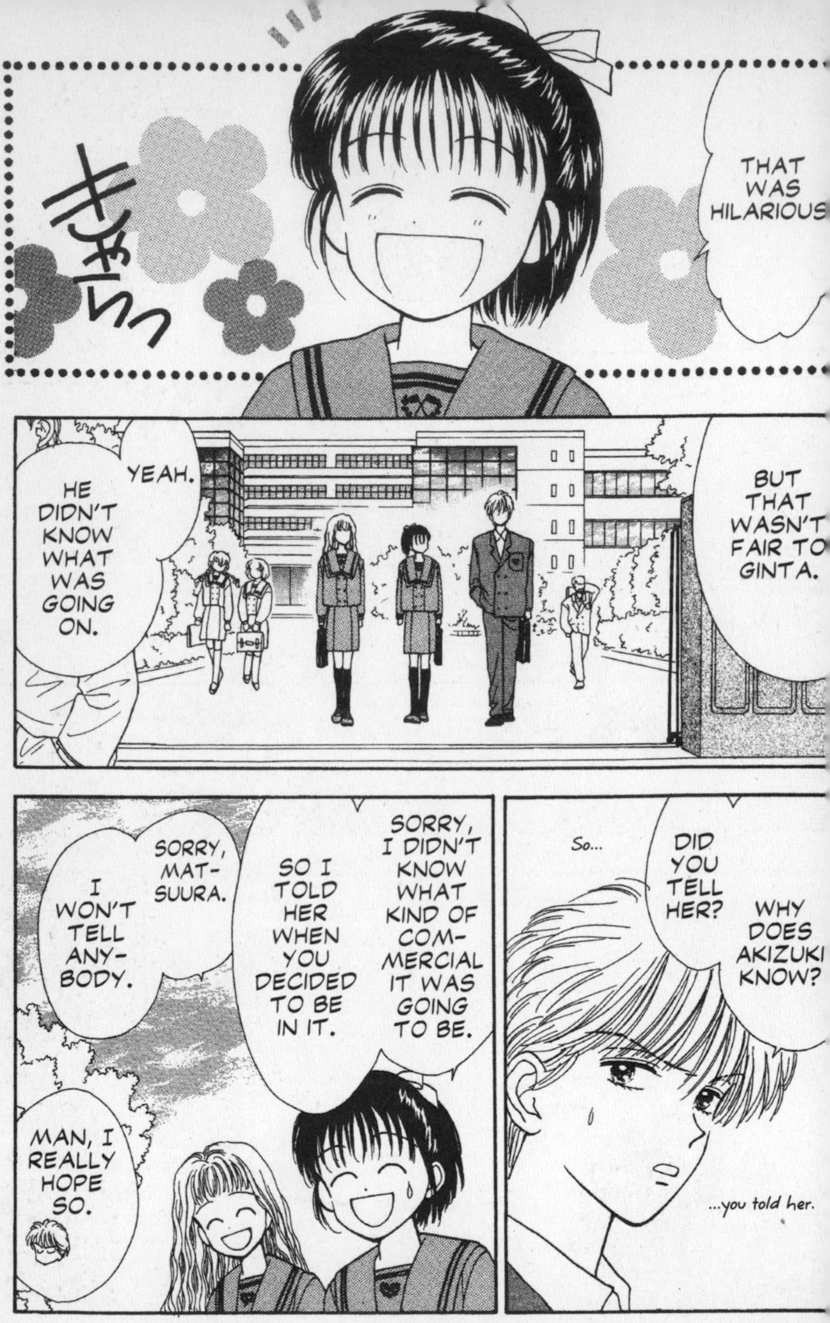
THAT WAS HILARIOUS
きゃらっ
BUT THAT WASN'T FAIR TO GINTA.
YEAH.
HE DIDN'T KNOW WHAT WAS GOING ON.
WHY DOES AKIZUKI KNOW?
DID YOU TELL HER?
So...
...you told her.
SORRY, I DIDN'T KNOW WHAT KIND OF COMMERCIAL IT WAS GOING TO BE.
SO I TOLD HER WHEN YOU DECIDED TO BE IN IT.
SORRY, MATSUURA.
I WON'T TELL ANYBODY.
MAN, I REALLY HOPE SO.

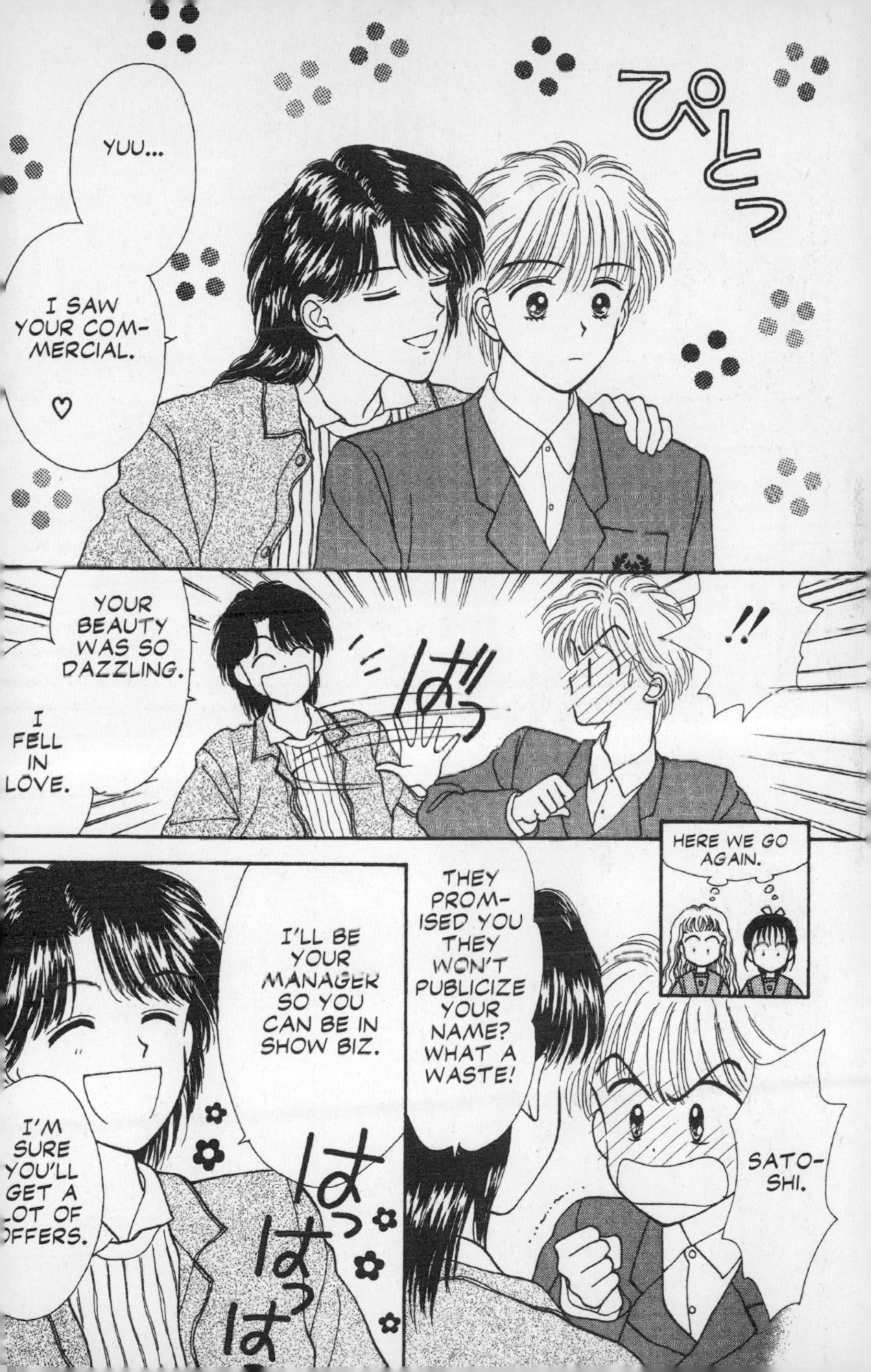
ぴとっ
YUU...
I SAW YOUR COMMERCIAL.
♡
!!
ばっ
YOUR BEAUTY WAS SO DAZZLING.
I FELL IN LOVE.
HERE WE GO AGAIN.
SATO-SHI.
THEY PROMISED YOU THEY WON'T PUBLICIZE YOUR NAME? WHAT A WASTE!
I'LL BE YOUR MANAGER SO YOU CAN BE IN SHOW BIZ.
はっはっは
I'M SURE YOU'LL GET A LOT OF OFFERS.

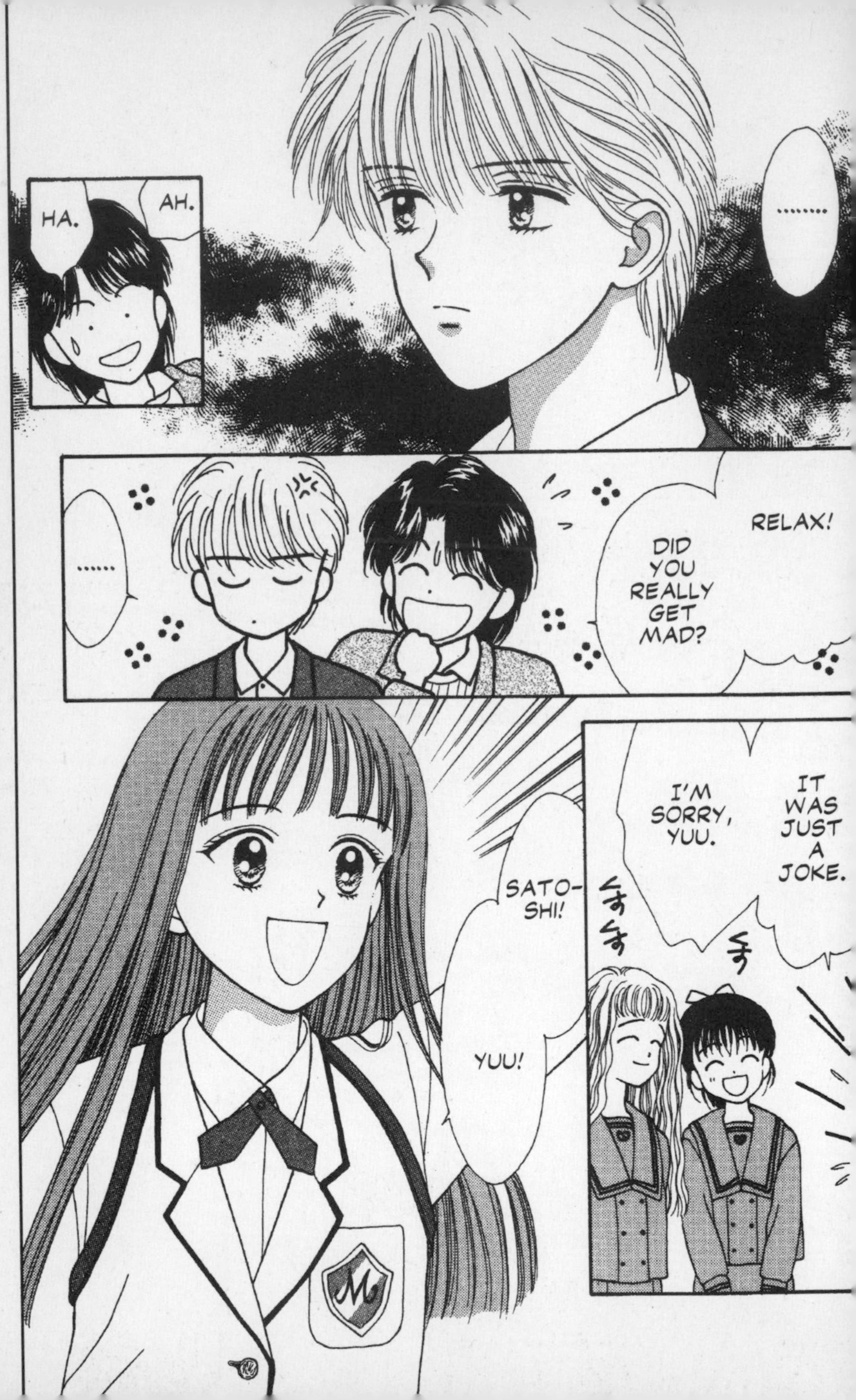
....
AH.
HA.
RELAX!
DID YOU REALLY GET MAD?
......
IT WAS JUST A JOKE.
I'M SORRY, YUU.
SATO-SHI!
YUU!

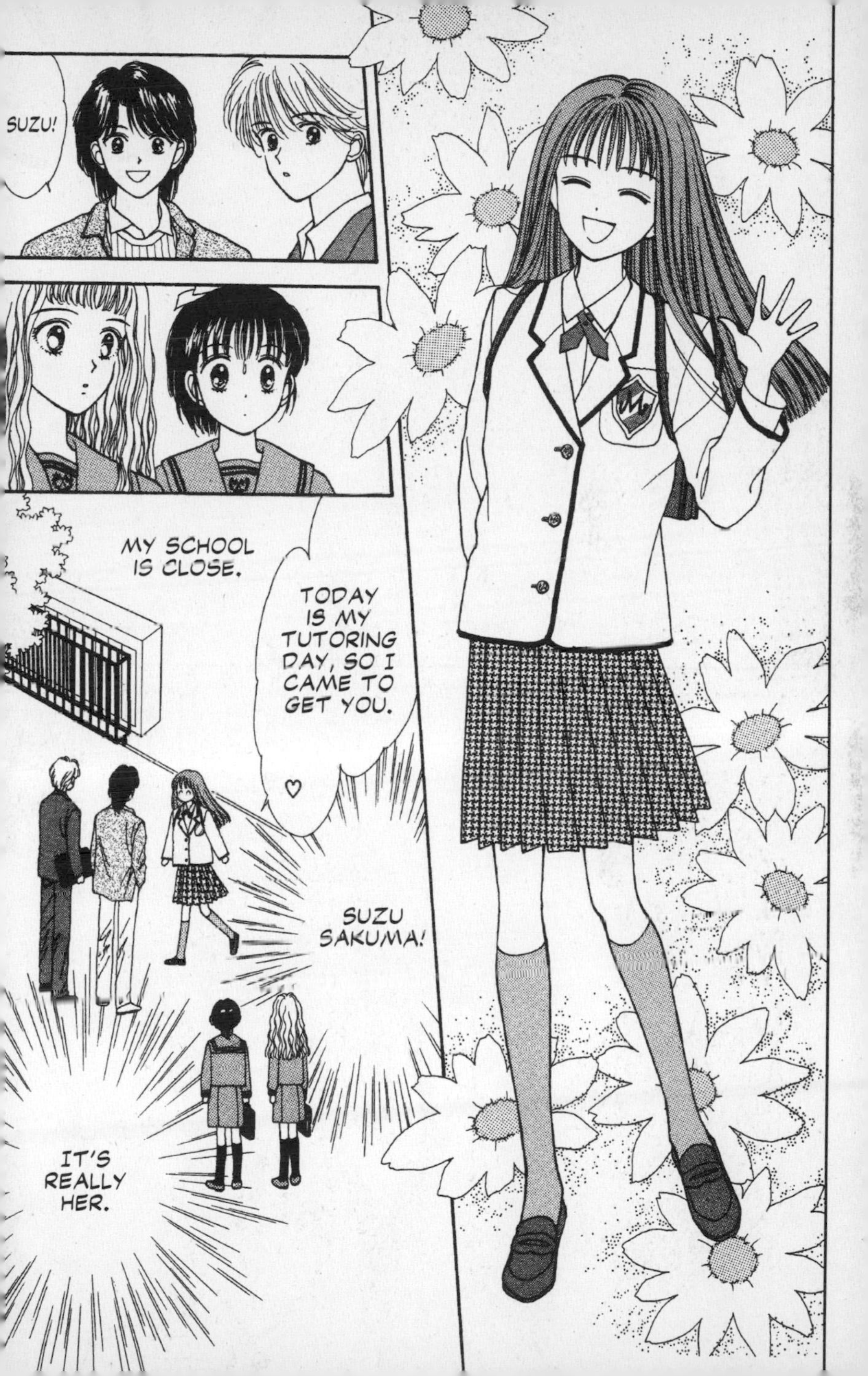
TODAY IS MY TUTORING DAY, SO I CAME TO GET YOU. ♡
SUZU!
MY SCHOOL IS CLOSE.
SUZU SAKUMA!
IT'S REALLY HER.

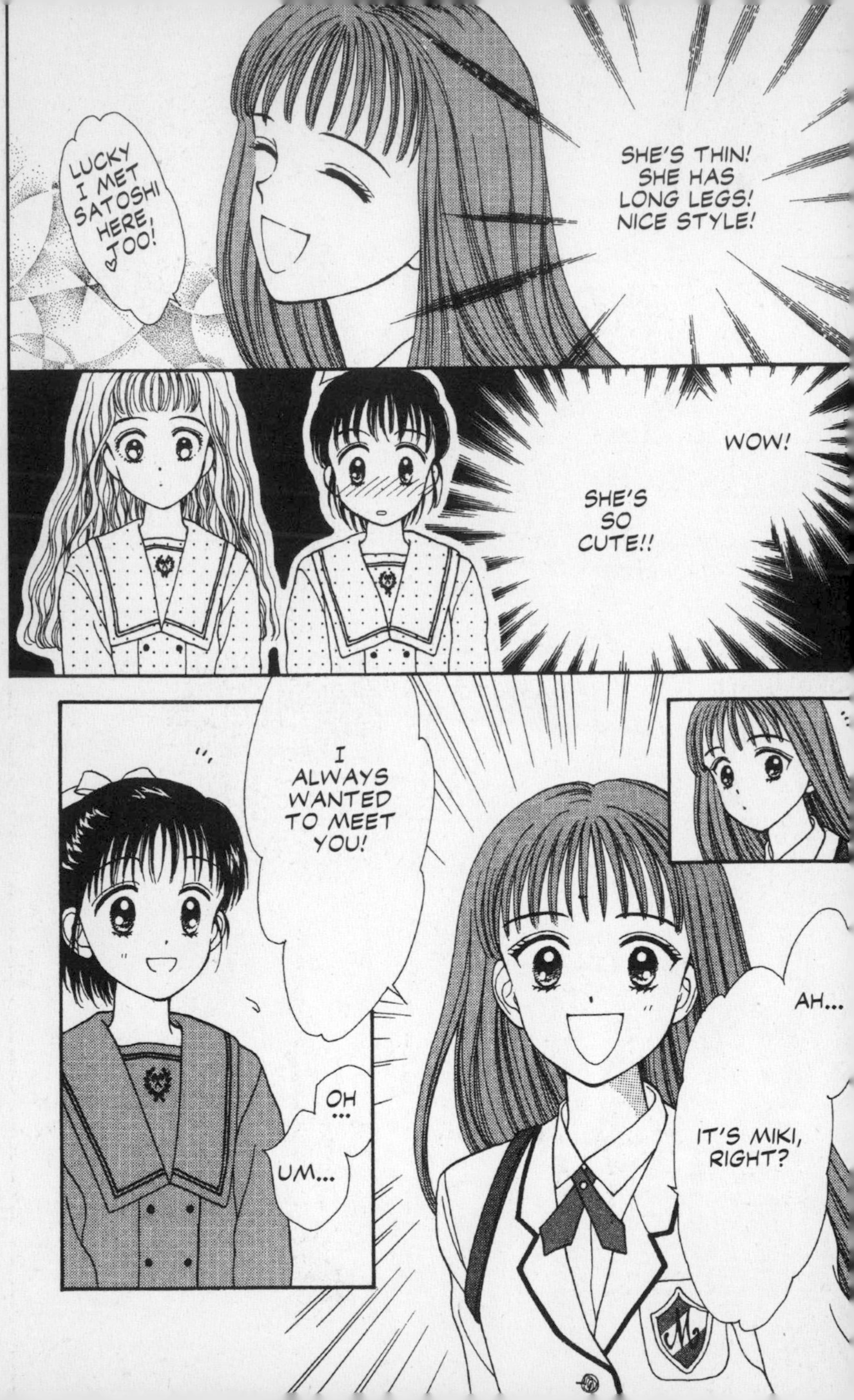
SHE'S THIN! SHE HAS LONG LEGS! NICE STYLE!
LUCKY I MET SATOSHI HERE, TOO! ♡
WOW!
SHE'S SO CUTE!!
AH...
IT'S MIKI, RIGHT?
I ALWAYS WANTED TO MEET YOU!
OH ...
UM...

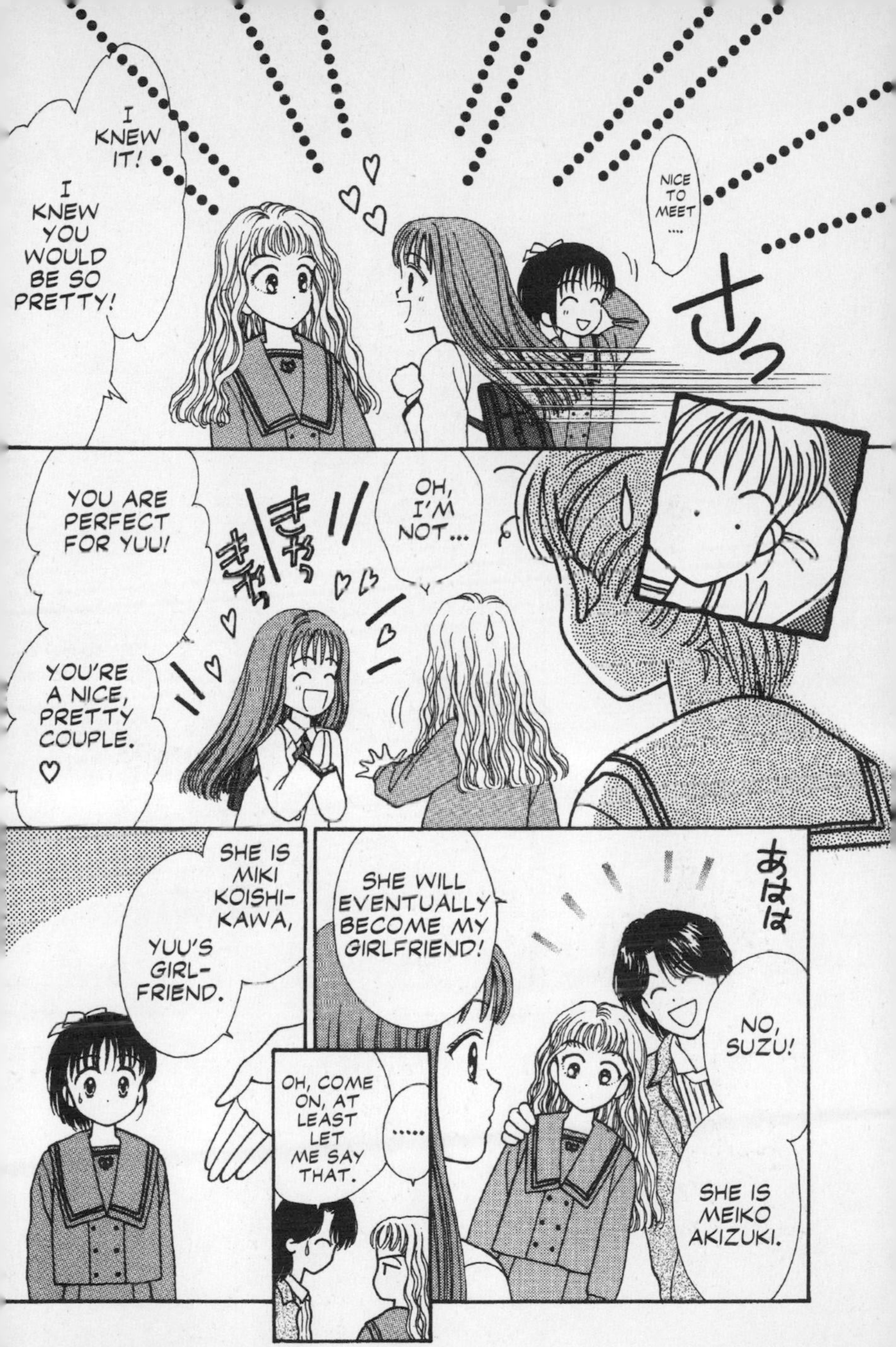
NICE TO MEET ....
さっ
I KNEW IT!
I KNEW YOU WOULD BE SO PRETTY!
OH, I'M NOT...
きゃっ
きゃっ
YOU ARE PERFECT FOR YUU!
YOU'RE A NICE, PRETTY COUPLE. ♡
あはは
NO, SUZU!
SHE IS MEIKO AKIZUKI.
SHE WILL EVENTUALLY BECOME MY GIRLFRIEND!
OH, COME ON, AT LEAST LET ME SAY THAT.
.....
SHE IS MIKI KOISHI-KAWA,
YUU'S GIRL-FRIEND.

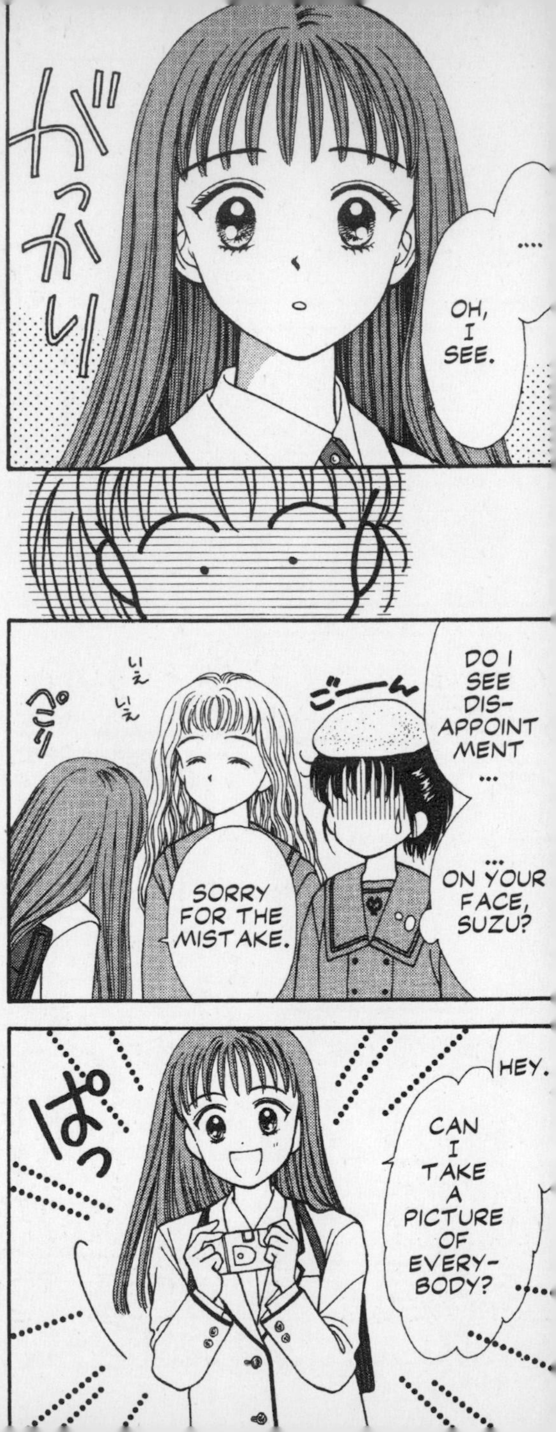
....
OH, I SEE.
がっかり
DO I SEE DIS-APPOINTMENT ...
... ON YOUR FACE, SUZU?
ごーん
いえ いえ
ぺこり
SORRY FOR THE MISTAKE.
HEY.
CAN I TAKE A PICTURE OF EVERY-BODY?
ぱっ

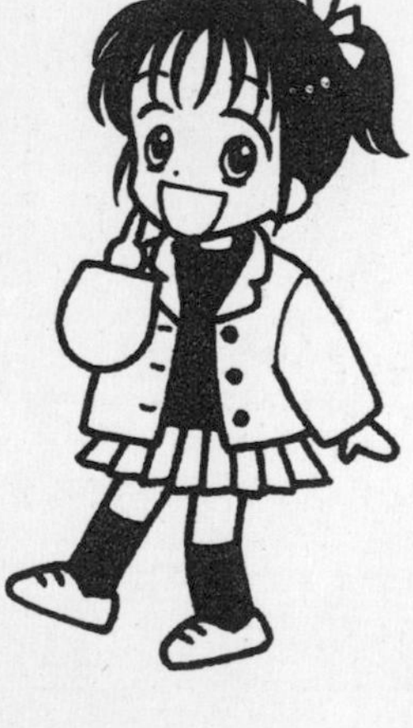

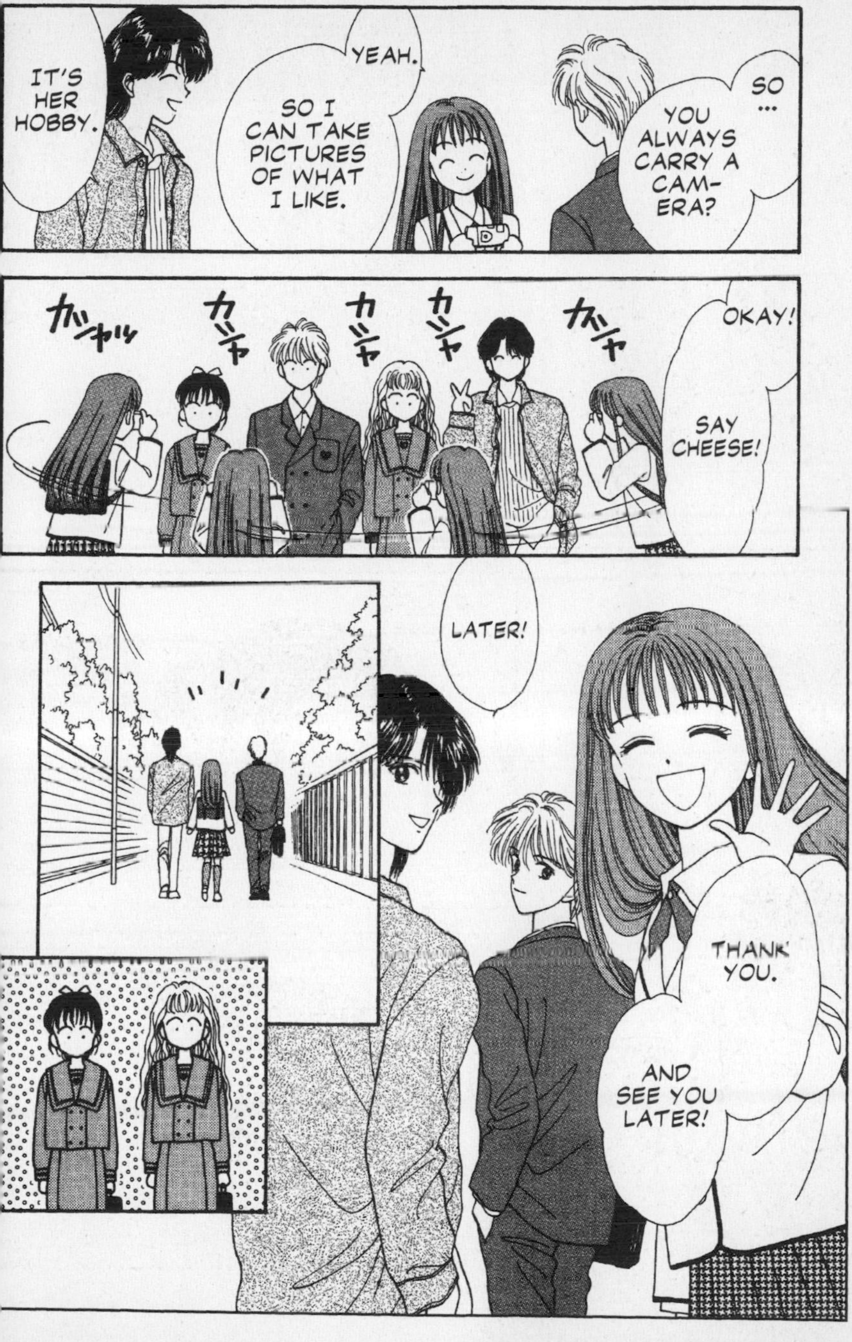
SO ... YOU ALWAYS CARRY A CAM-ERA?
YEAH.
SO I CAN TAKE PICTURES OF WHAT I LIKE.
IT'S HER HOBBY.
OKAY!
SAY CHEESE!
カシャ
カシャ
カシャ
カシャ
LATER!
THANK YOU.
AND SEE YOU LATER!

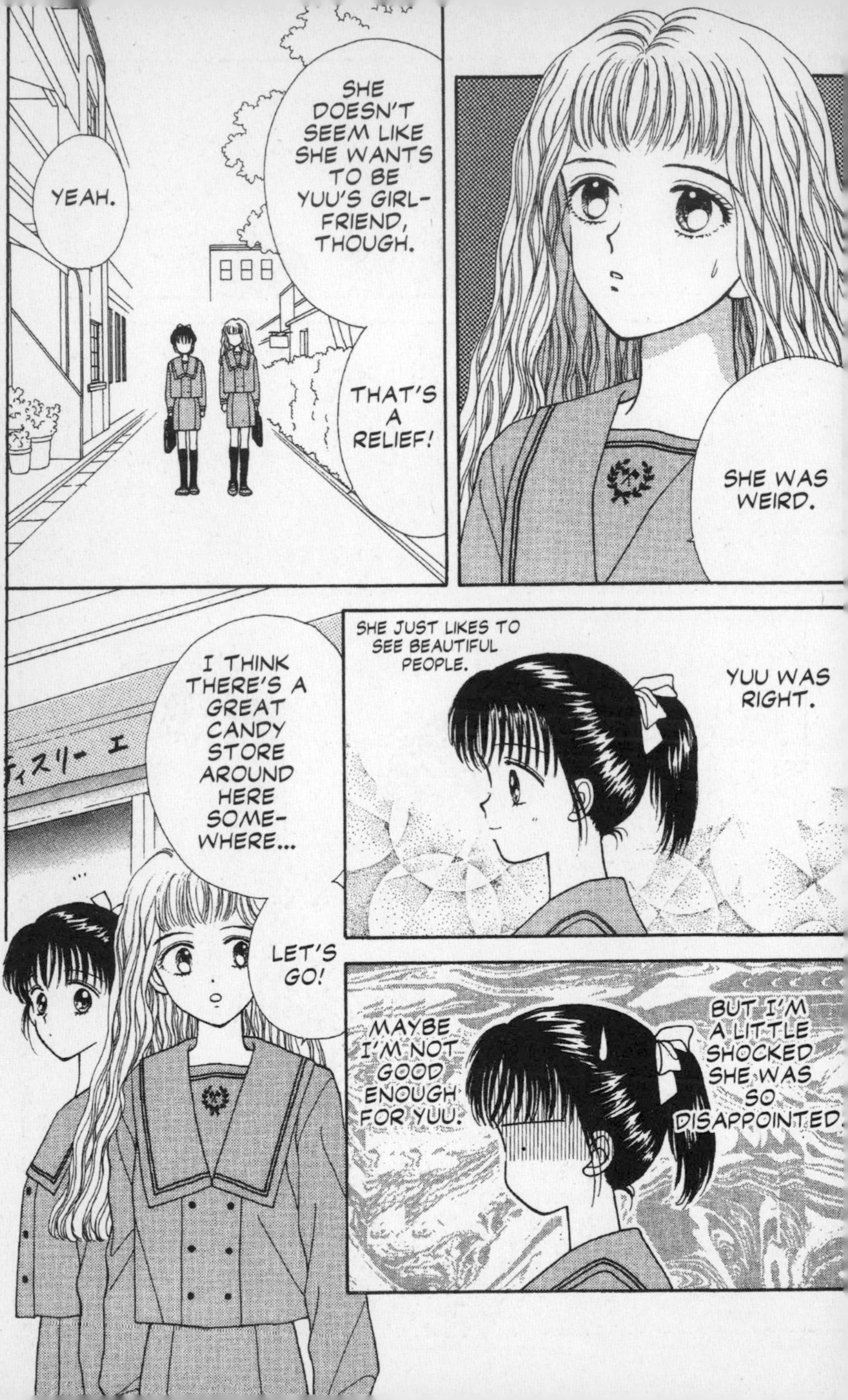
SHE WAS WEIRD.
SHE DOESN'T SEEM LIKE SHE WANTS TO BE YUU'S GIRL-FRIEND, THOUGH.
THAT'S A RELIEF!
YEAH.
YUU WAS RIGHT.
SHE JUST LIKES TO SEE BEAUTIFUL PEOPLE.
BUT I'M A LITTLE SHOCKED SHE WAS SO DISAPPOINTED.
MAYBE I'M NOT GOOD ENOUGH FOR YUU.
I THINK THERE'S A GREAT CANDY STORE AROUND HERE SOME-WHERE...
ティスリー エ
LET'S GO!
...

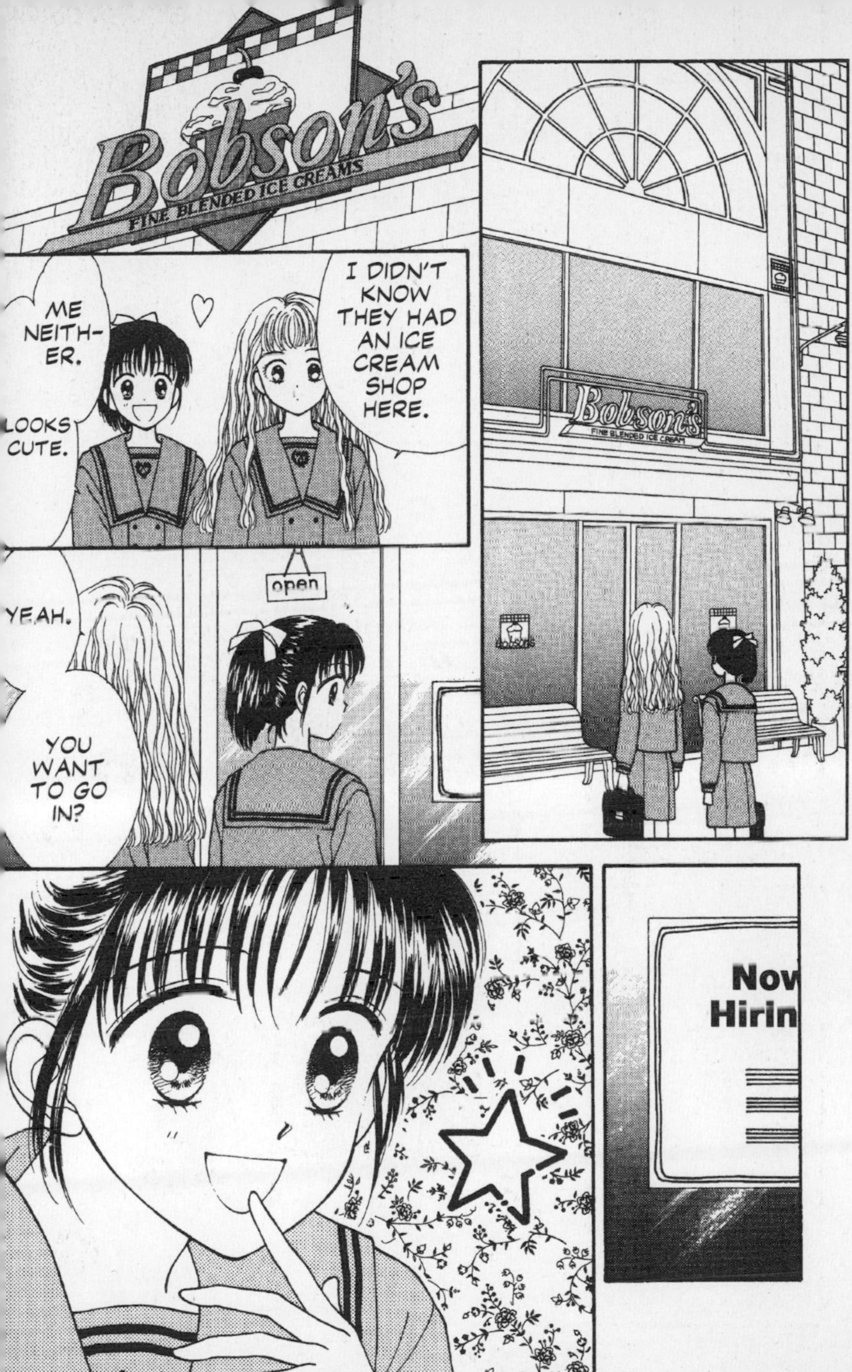
Bobson's
FINE BLENDED ICE CREAM
Bobson's
Bobson's
FINE BLENDED ICE CREAMS
I DIDN'T KNOW THEY HAD AN ICE CREAM SHOP HERE.
ME NEITHER.
LOOKS CUTE.
open
YEAH.
YOU WANT TO GO IN?
Now
Hirin

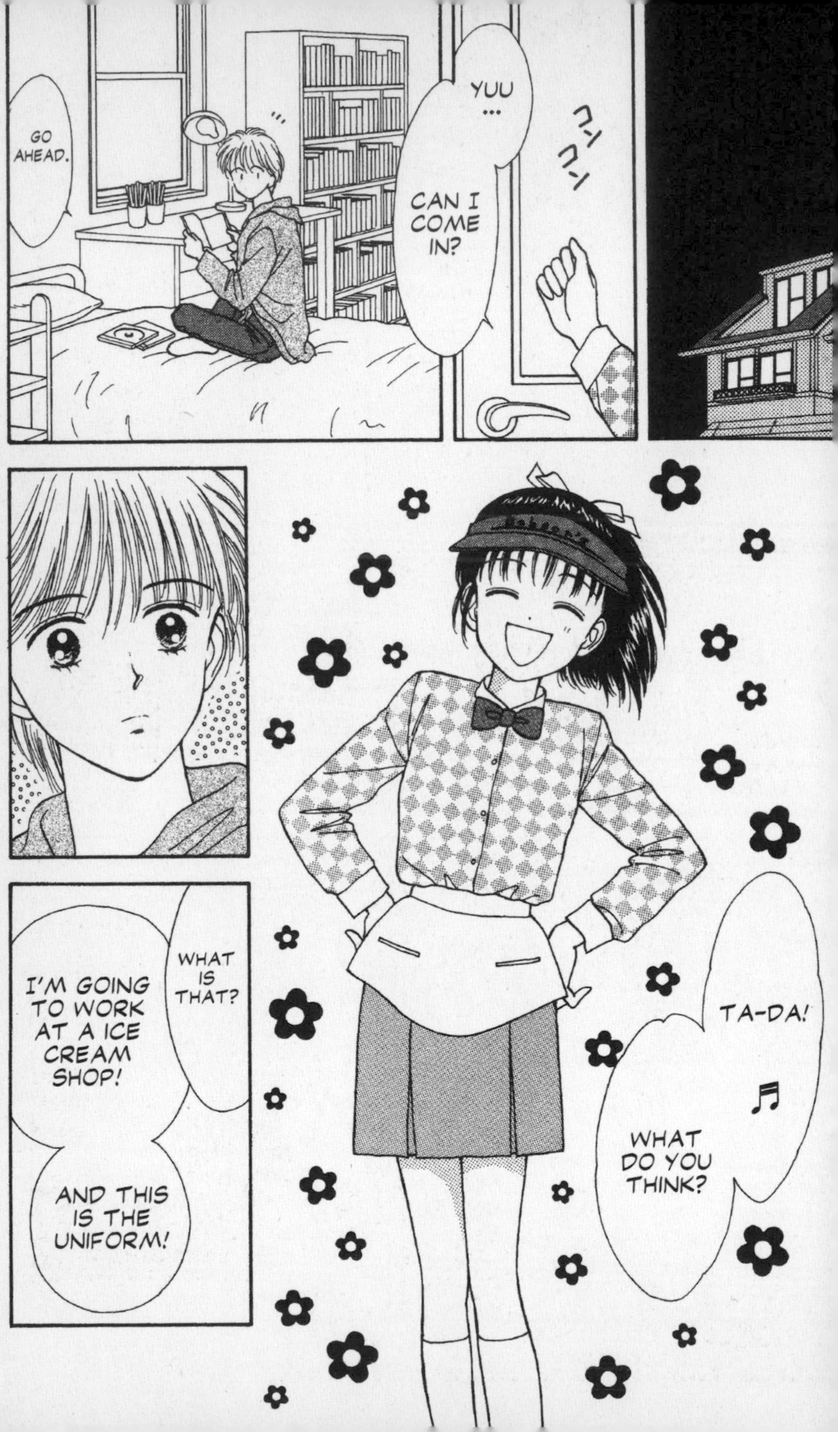
YUU ... CAN I COME IN?
コン コン
GO AHEAD.
TA-DA! ♬
WHAT DO YOU THINK?
WHAT IS THAT?
I'M GOING TO WORK AT A ICE CREAM SHOP!
AND THIS IS THE UNIFORM!

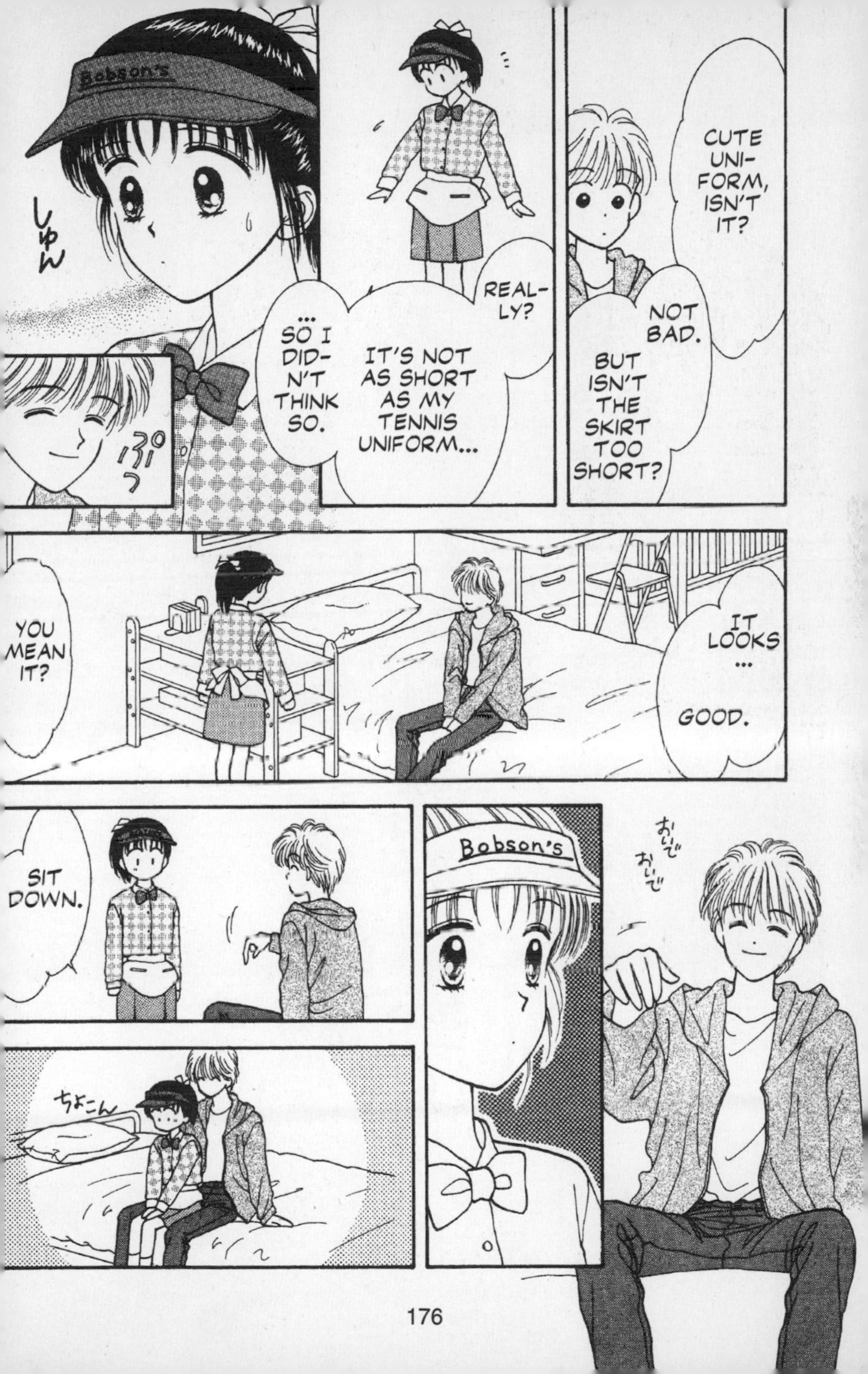
CUTE UNI-FORM, ISN'T IT?
NOT BAD.
BUT ISN'T THE SKIRT TOO SHORT?
REAL-LY?
IT'S NOT AS SHORT AS MY TENNIS UNIFORM...
... SO I DID-N'T THINK SO.
しゅん
ぷっ
IT LOOKS ...
GOOD.
YOU MEAN IT?
Bobson's
おいで おいで
SIT DOWN.
ちょこん

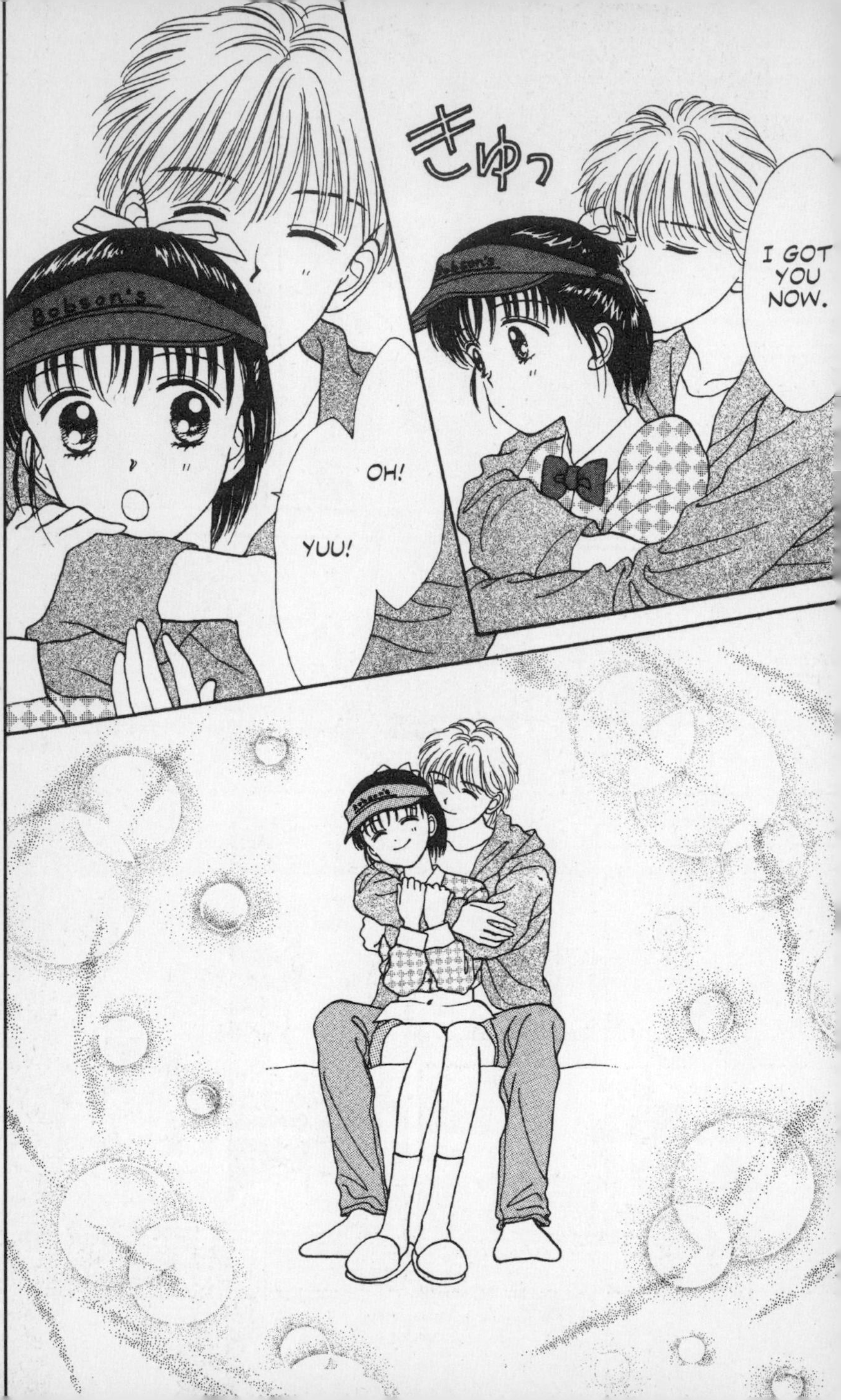
きゅっ
I GOT YOU NOW.
OH!
YUU!

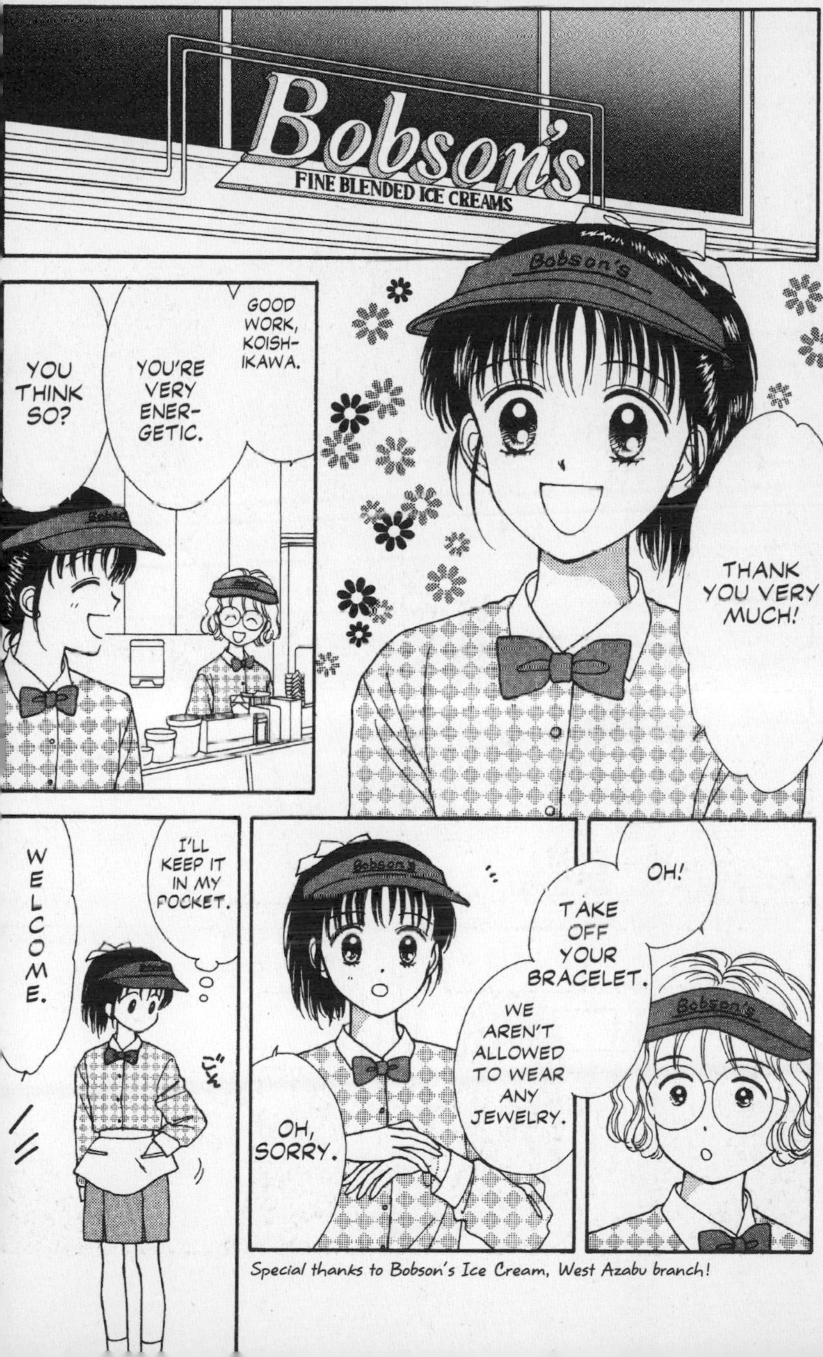
Bobson's
FINE BLENDED ICE CREAMS
Bobson's
THANK YOU VERY MUCH!
GOOD WORK, KOISHIKAWA.
YOU'RE VERY ENERGETIC.
YOU THINK SO?
OH!
TAKE OFF YOUR BRACELET.
WE AREN'T ALLOWED TO WEAR ANY JEWELRY.
OH, SORRY.
I'LL KEEP IT IN MY POCKET.
WELCOME.
Special thanks to Bobson's Ice Cream, West Azabu branch!

I SAW YOU FROM OUT-SIDE.

YOU WORK HERE?

YUP, I STARTED TODAY.

I COME HERE SOME-TIMES ON MY WAY HOME FROM SCHOOL.

Boosons

vors (フレーバー)
a (バニラ)
plate (チョコレート)
ie crumble (クッキークランブル)
mel cream (カラメルクリーム)
berry (ブルーベリー)
rawberry (ストロベリー)
rawberry daiquiri (ストロベリー ダイキリ)
pple pie (アップルパイ)
cappucino (カプチーノ)

OH, OKAY.

HEY!

HEY.

SUZU!

THANK YOU.

WHAT CAN I GET YOU? IT'S ON THE HOUSE.

YOU'RE WELCOME.

PLEASE, COME AGAIN.

179

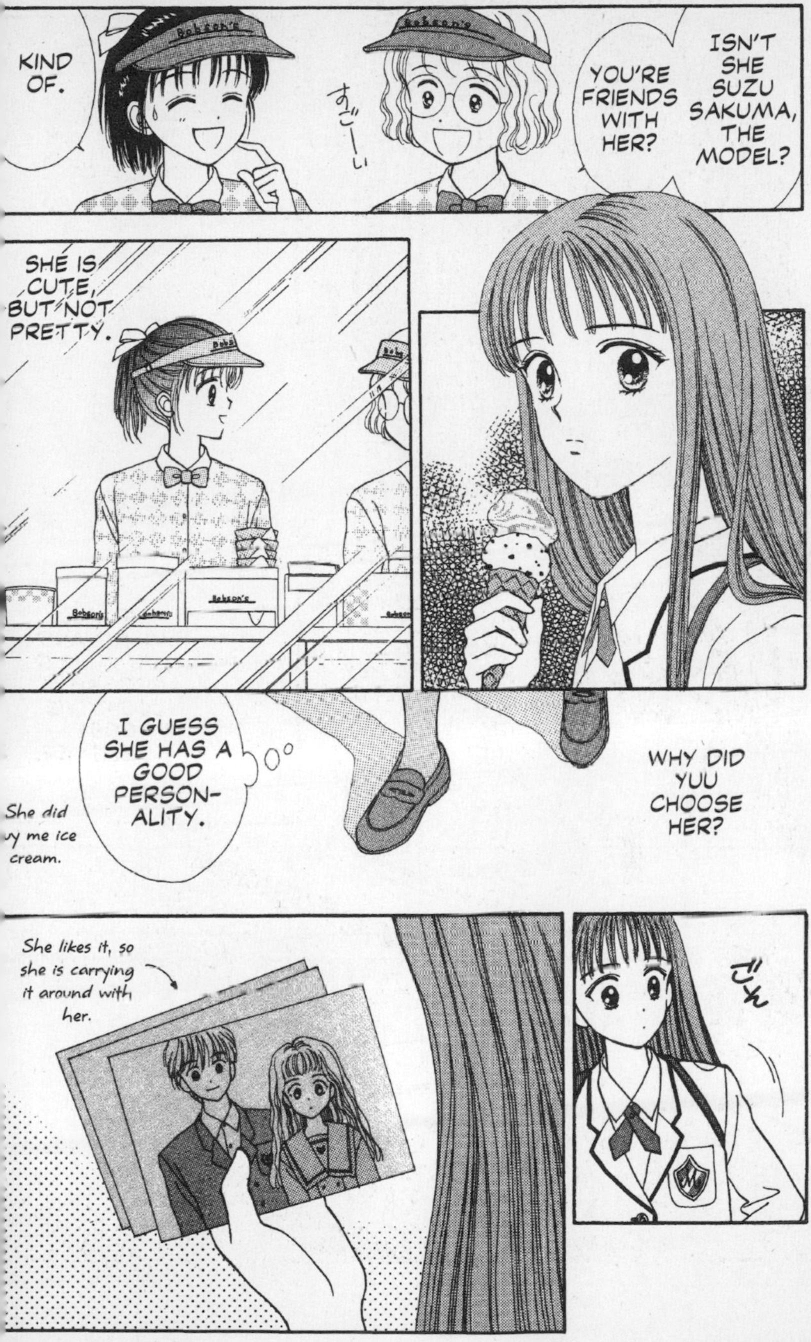
ISN'T SHE SUZU SAKUMA, THE MODEL?
YOU'RE FRIENDS WITH HER?
すごーい
KIND OF.
SHE IS CUTE, BUT NOT PRETTY.
WHY DID YUU CHOOSE HER?
I GUESS SHE HAS A GOOD PERSONALITY.
She did uy me ice cream.
ごん
She likes it, so she is carrying it around with her.

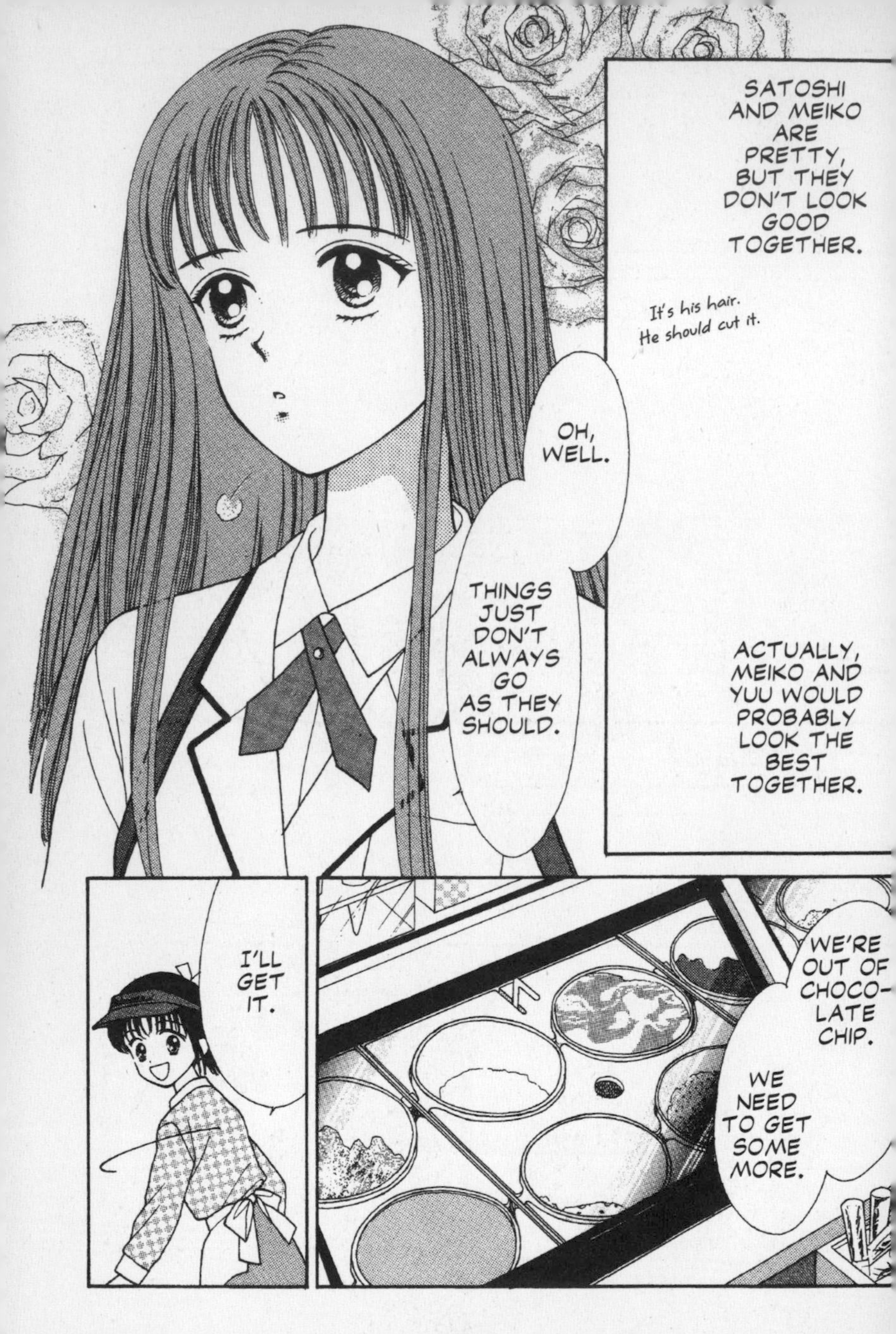
SATOSHI AND MEIKO ARE PRETTY, BUT THEY DON'T LOOK GOOD TOGETHER.
It's his hair. He should cut it.
ACTUALLY, MEIKO AND YUU WOULD PROBABLY LOOK THE BEST TOGETHER.
OH, WELL.
THINGS JUST DON'T ALWAYS GO AS THEY SHOULD.
WE'RE OUT OF CHOCO-LATE CHIP.
WE NEED TO GET SOME MORE.
I'LL GET IT.

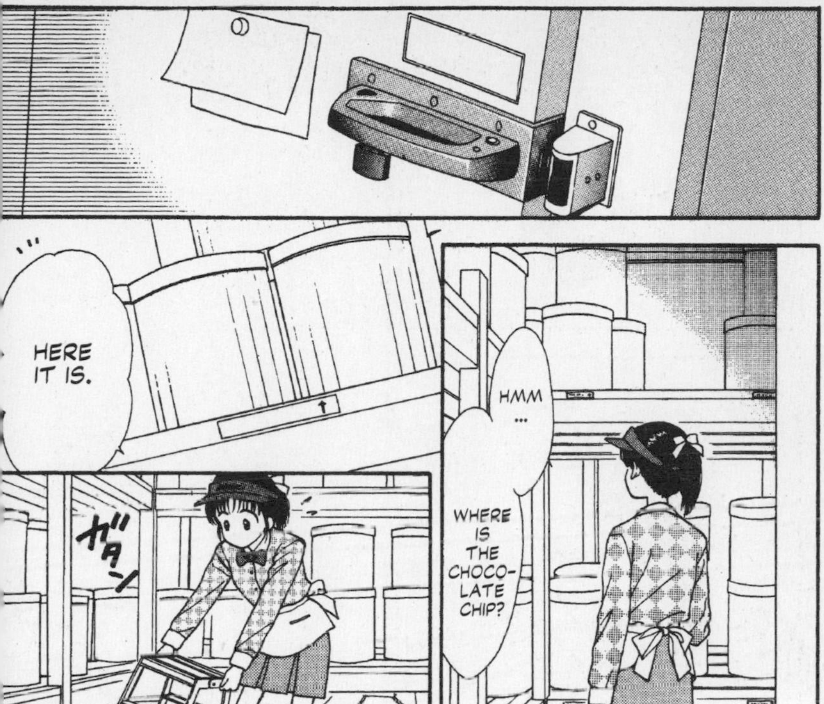
HMM ...
WHERE IS THE CHOCO-LATE CHIP?
HERE IT IS.
ISN'T THAT SKIRT TOO SHORT?

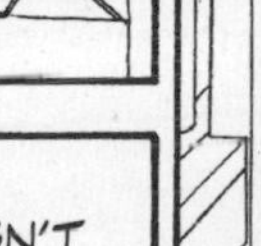

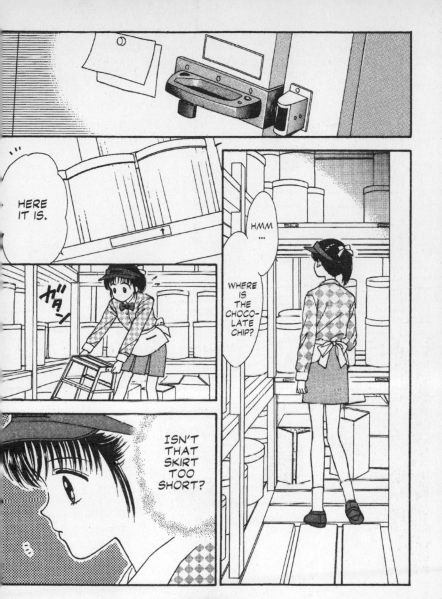

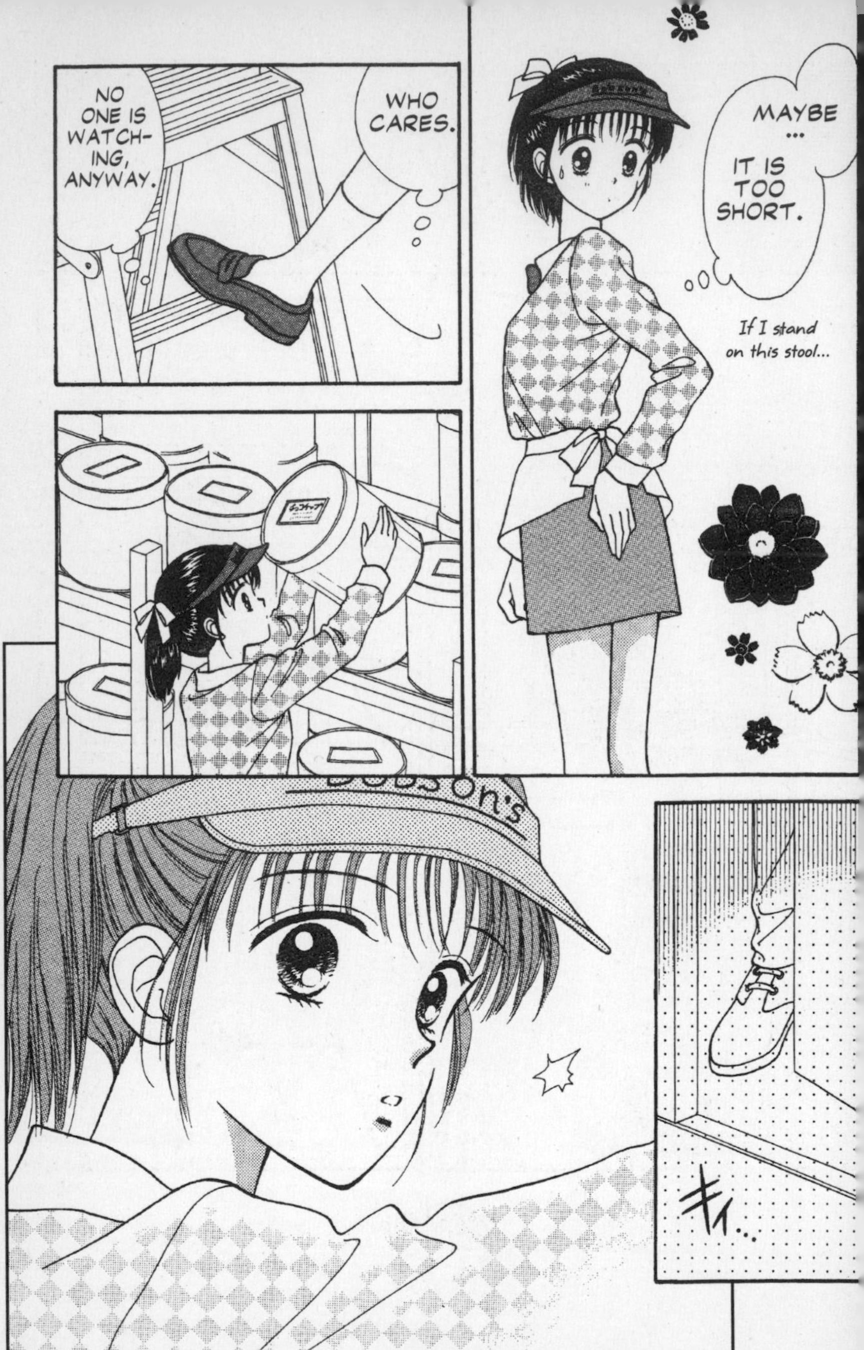
MAYBE ... IT IS TOO SHORT.
If I stand on this stool...
WHO CARES.
NO ONE IS WATCHING, ANYWAY.
キィ...

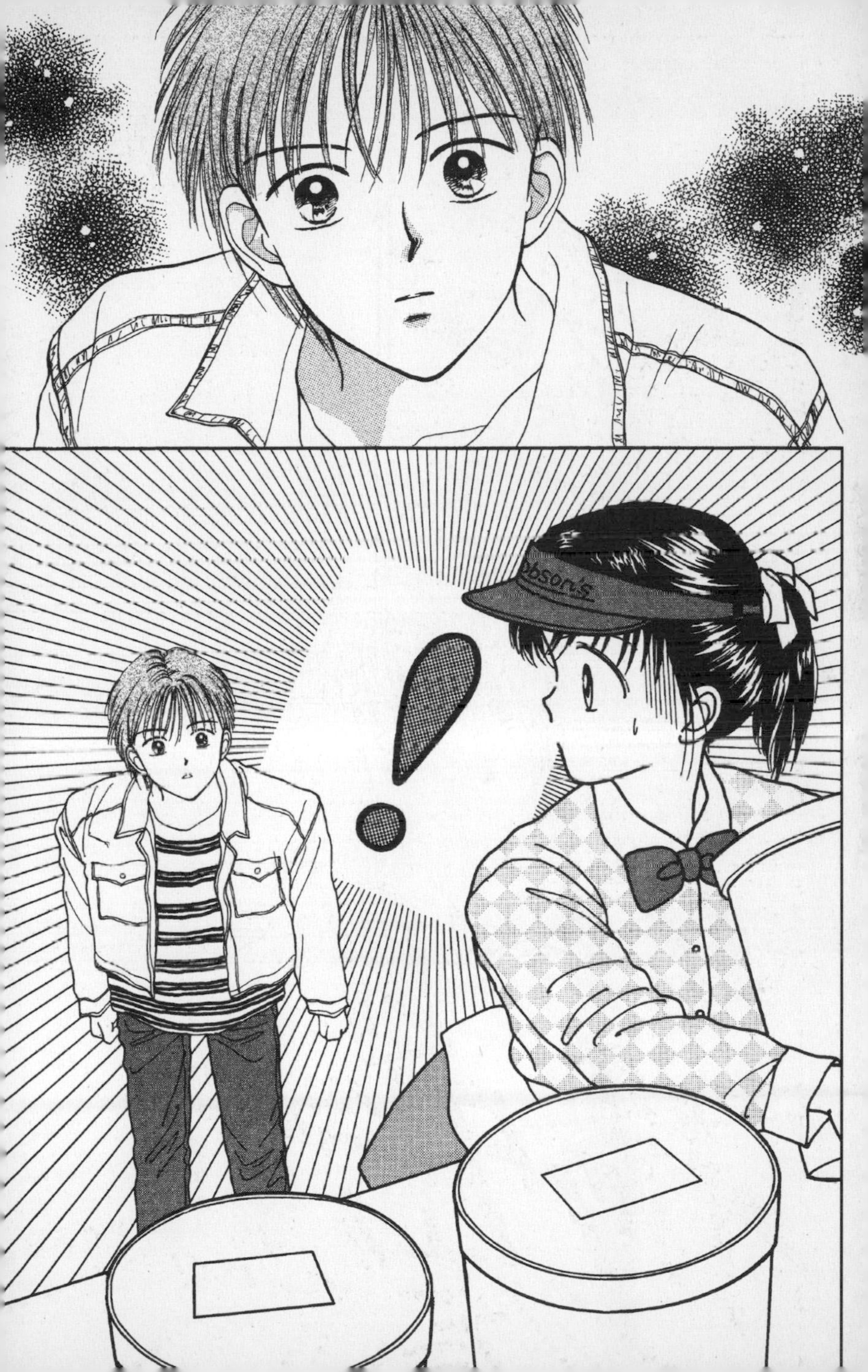
!

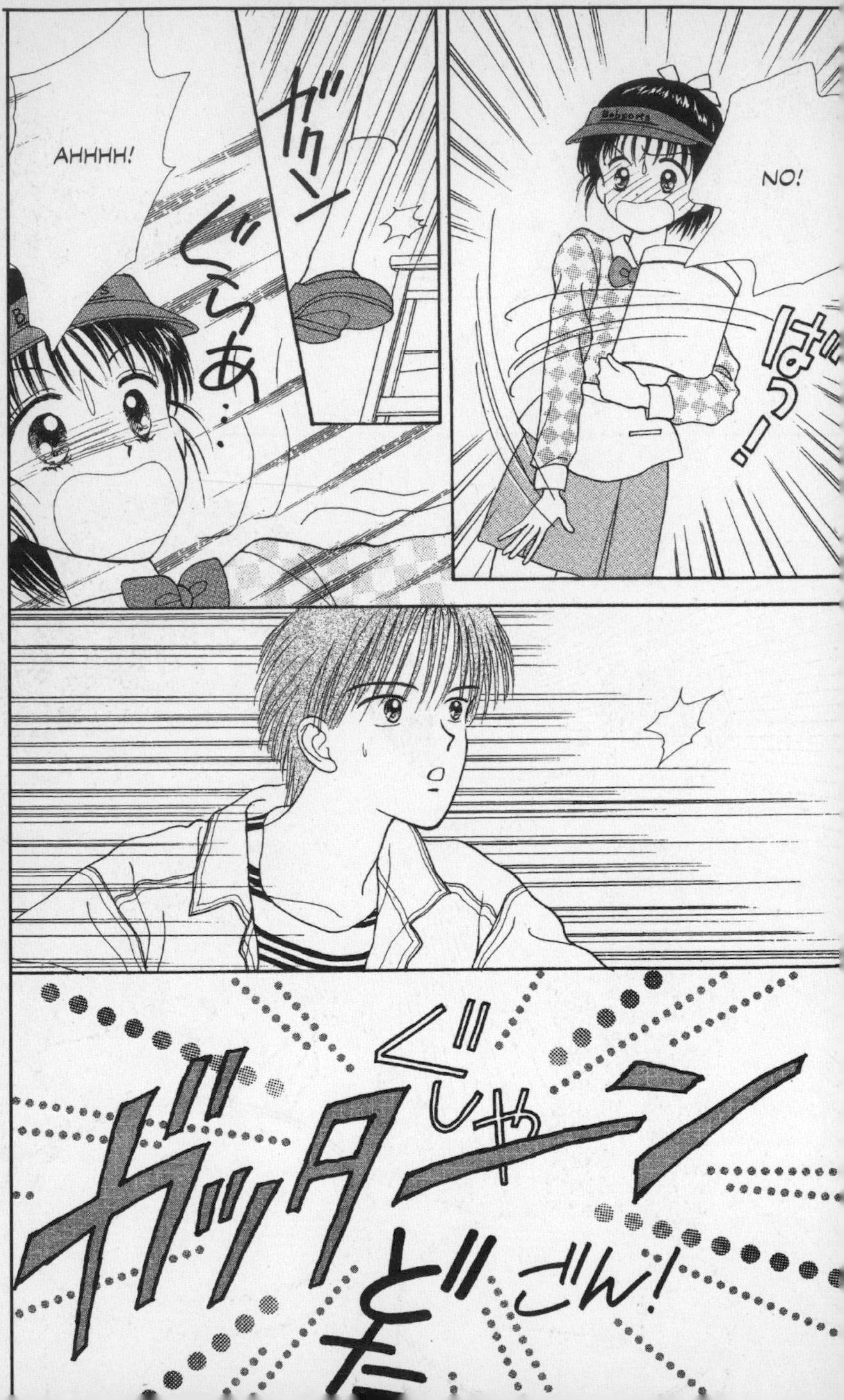
NO!
はっ!
ガクン
ぐらあ…
AHHHH!
ガッターン
ぐしゃ
どた
ごん!

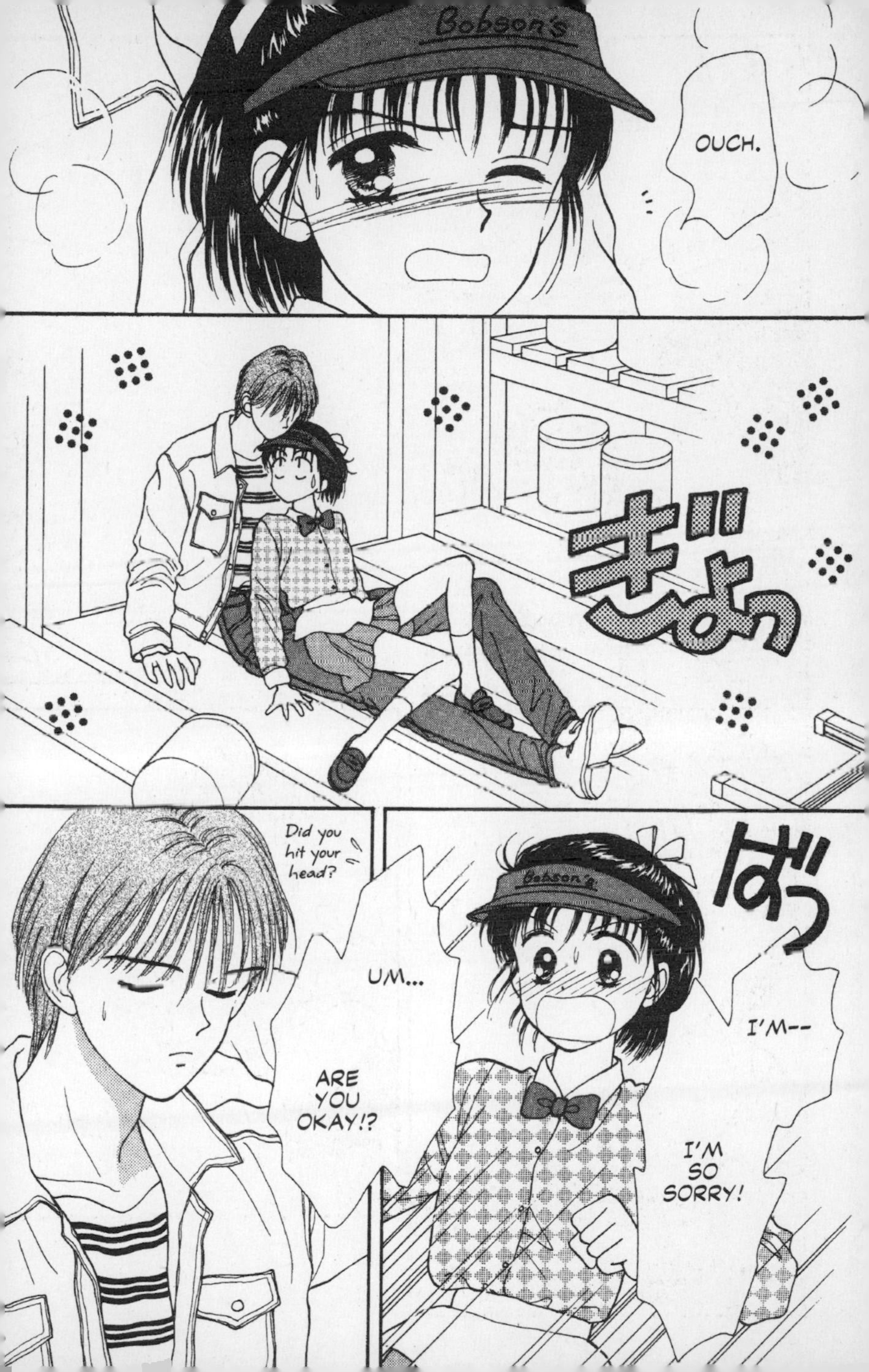

OUCH.
ぎゅっ
ぱっ
I'M--
I'M SO SORRY!
UM...
ARE YOU OKAY!?
Did you hit your head?

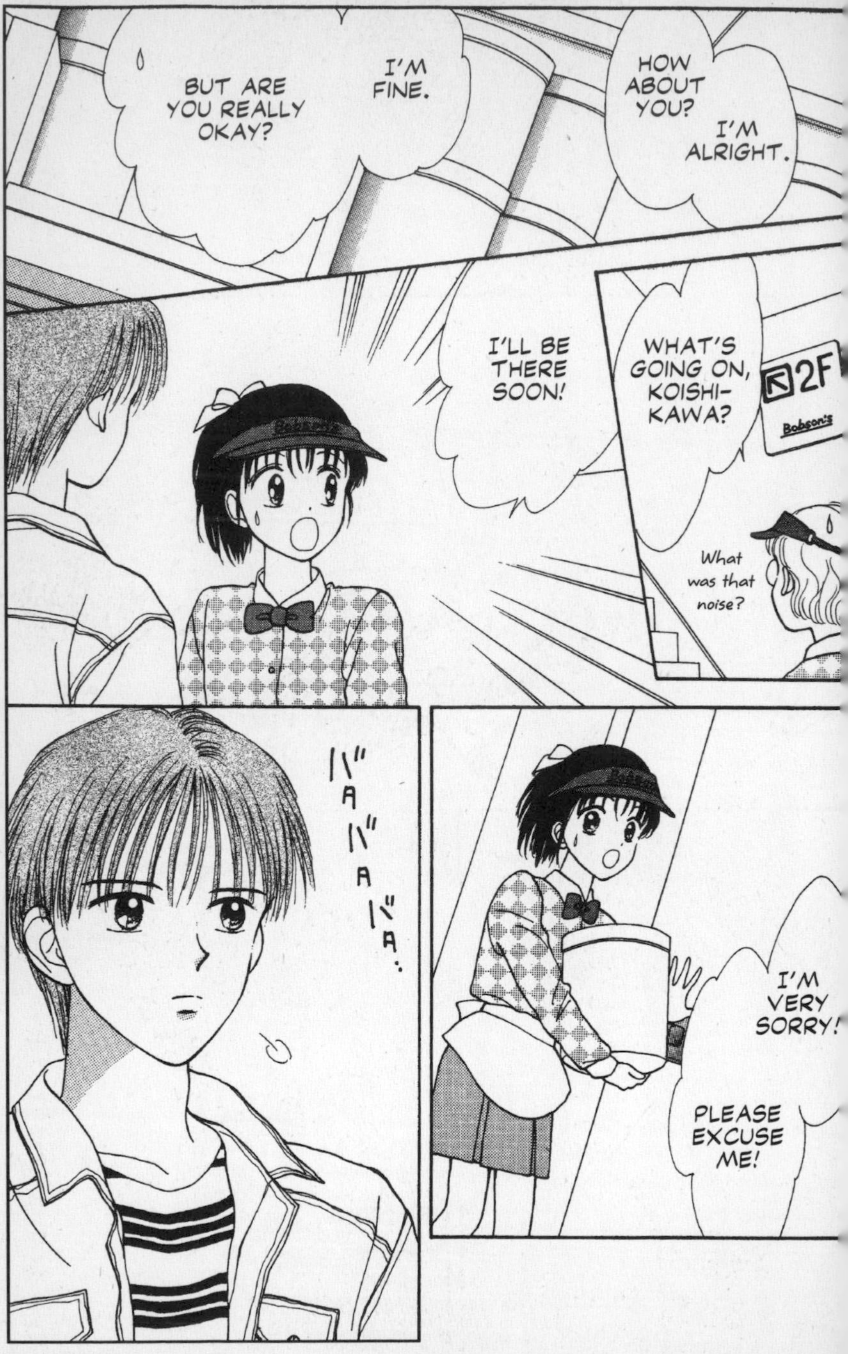
HOW ABOUT YOU?
I'M ALRIGHT.
I'M FINE.
BUT ARE YOU REALLY OKAY?
2F
Bobson's
WHAT'S GOING ON, KOISHI-KAWA?
What was that noise?
I'LL BE THERE SOON!
I'M VERY SORRY!
PLEASE EXCUSE ME!
バA バA バA..

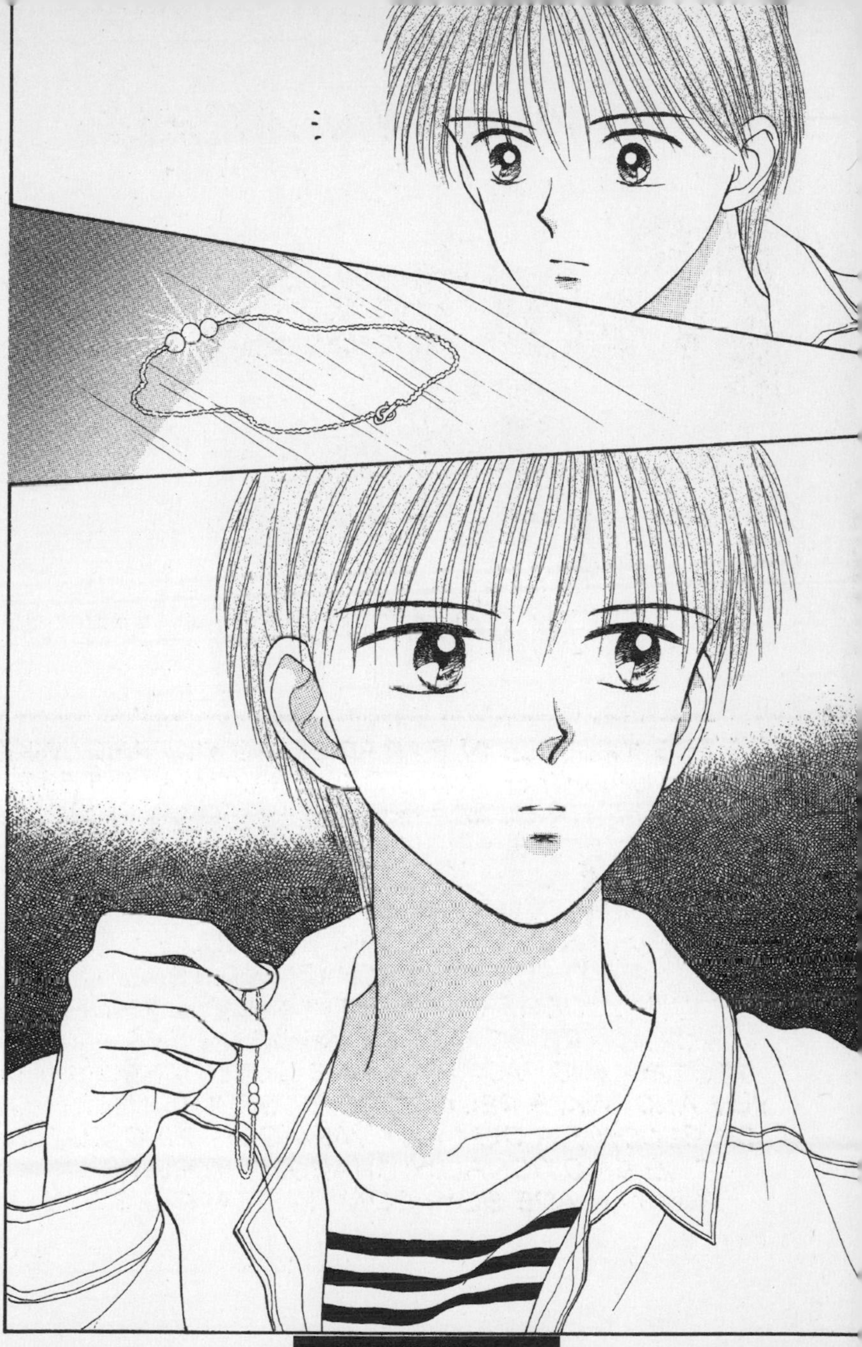

TO BE CONTINUED

COMING IN APRIL

Marmalade Boy

VOLUME 6

THERE'S TROUBLE IN PARADISE AS YUU AND MIKI'S
RELATIONSHIP IS PUT TO THE ULTIMATE TEST.
MIKI (IN HER ULTRA-SHORT UNIFORM SKIRT)
ATTRACTS THE AFFECTIONS OF A CO-WORKER
AND IGNITES YUU'S JEALOUSY. EVEN THOUGH IT'S
ALMOST UNTHINKABLE, THERE SEEMS TO BE
SOLID EVIDENCE THAT MIKI AND YUU HAVE BEEN
UNFAITHFUL TO EACH OTHER. (GASP!)
THEIR RELATIONSHIP AND THEIR IDEAL VACATION
PLANS ARE AT STAKE AS LOYALTIES ARE
TESTED AND MOTIVES ARE QUESTIONED. WILL
YUU AND MIKI'S RELATIONSHIP GO THE DISTANCE
OR BECOME A DISTANT MEMORY? FIND OUT IN
THIS EMOTIONALLY CHARGED VOLUME OF
MARMALADE BOY, COMING IN APRIL, 2003!

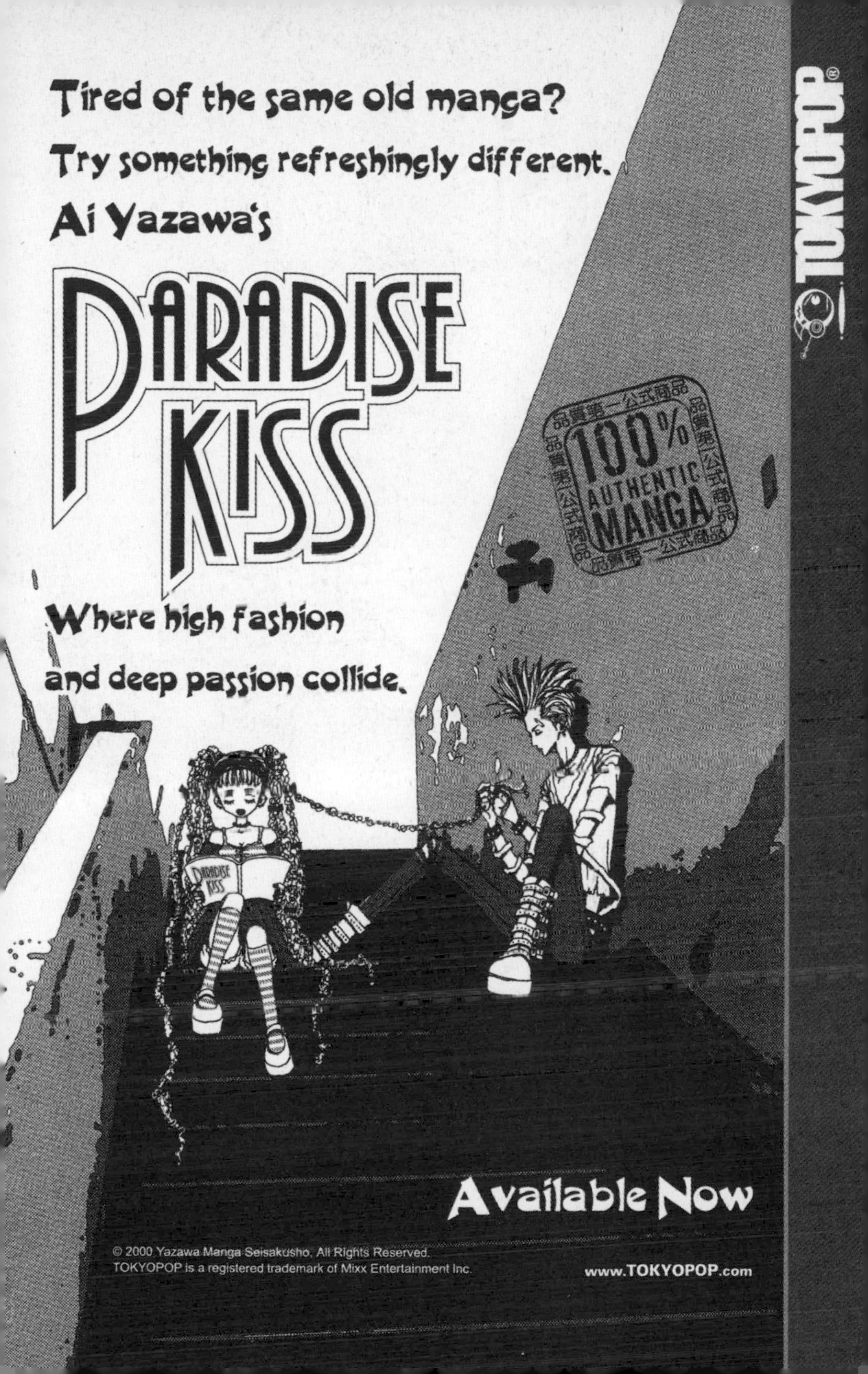
Tired of the same old manga?
Try something refreshingly different.
Ai Yazawa's
PARADISE KISS
100% AUTHENTIC MANGA
Where high fashion
and deep passion collide.
Available Now
© 2000 Yazawa Manga Seisakusho. All Rights Reserved.
TOKYOPOP is a registered trademark of Mixx Entertainment Inc.
www.TOKYOPOP.com
TOKYOPOP

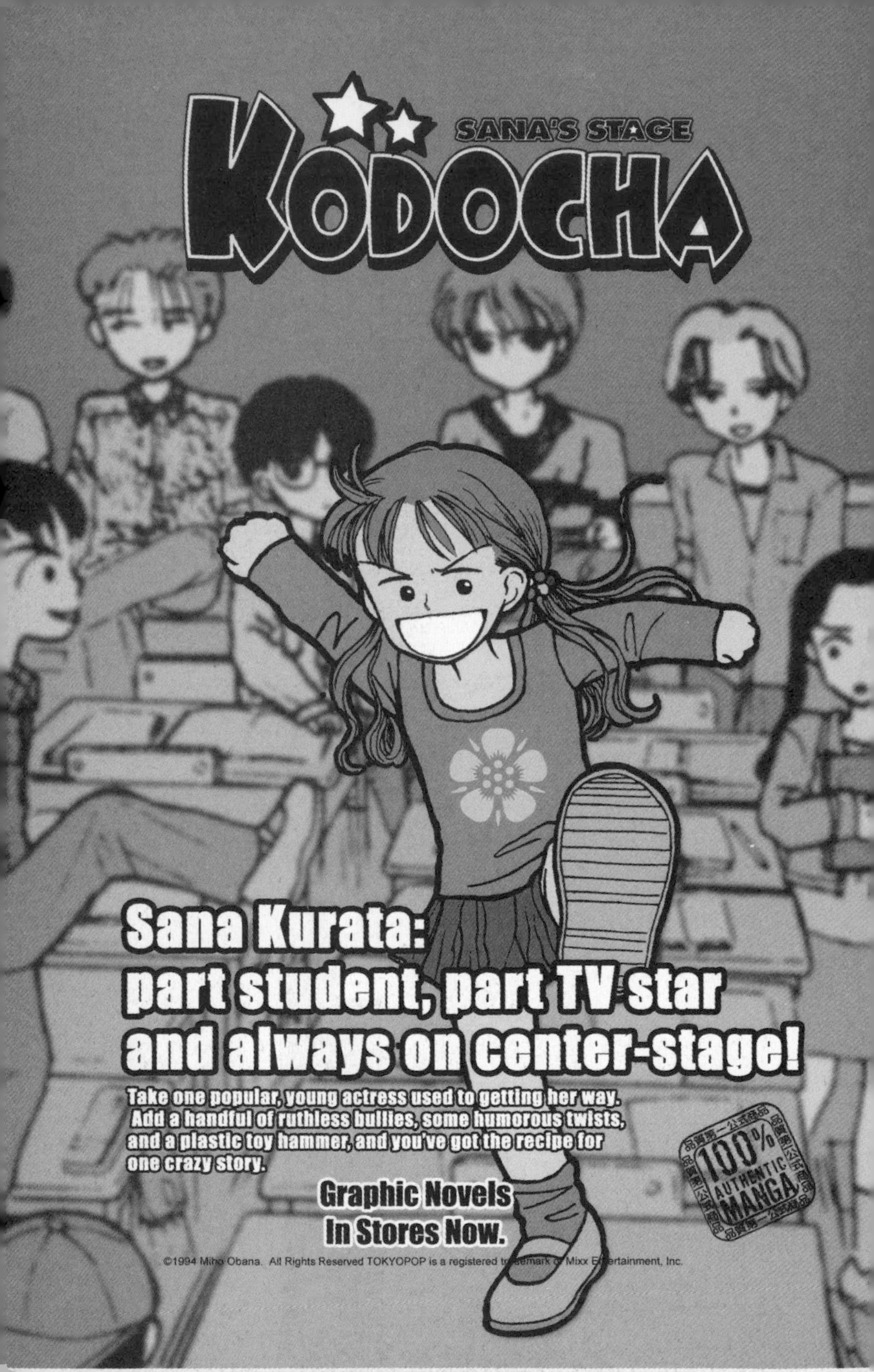
KODOCHA
SANA'S STAGE
Sana Kurata:
part student, part TV star
and always on center-stage!
Take one popular, young actress used to getting her way. Add a handful of ruthless bullies, some humorous twists, and a plastic toy hammer, and you've got the recipe for one crazy story.
Graphic Novels
In Stores Now.
100% AUTHENTIC MANGA
©1994 Miho Obana. All Rights Reserved TOKYOPOP is a registered trademark of Mixx Entertainment, Inc.

STOP!

This is the back of the book.
You wouldn't want to spoil a great ending!

This book is printed "manga-style," in the authentic Japanese right-to-left format. Since none of the artwork has been flipped or altered, readers get to experience the story just as the creator intended. You've been asking for it, so TOKYOPOP® delivered: authentic, hot-off-the-press, and far more fun!

...IT'S A MOCKERY OF LOVE. MOM AND DAD ARE BOTH HAVING AFFAIRS, BUT THEY REFUSE TO GET DIVORCED.
MOM THINKS ABOUT HER FINANCES. AND DAD'S JUST CONCERNED WITH APPEARANCES.
WHAT ABOUT ME?!
DON'T THEY UNDERSTAND HOW DAMAGING IT IS TO WATCH YOUR PARENTS IN SUCH A HOLLOW, SPITEFUL MARRIAGE?
I'M...
I'M NEVER GETTING MARRIED
MEIKO...
IS THAT WHY YOU NEVER GO OUT ON DATES?
OH, NO! DON'T GET ME WRONG. I JUST HAVEN'T MET ANYONE WHO'S MY TYPE.
I STILL LIKE BOYS. I JUST DON'T WANT TO MARRY THEM.
UH-OH.
I'VE GOTTA GO.
WHAT'S GOING ON?
MY FAMILY'S HAVING DINNER WITH THE MATSUURAS.
I HAVE TO TALK THE FOUR OF THEM OUT OF THIS NONSENSE, NO MATTER WHAT!

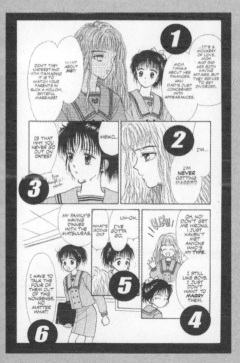

DIRECTIONS:

If this is your first time reading manga-style, here's a quick guide to help you understand how it works.

It's easy...just start in the top right panel and follow the numbers. Have fun, and look for more 100% authentic manga from TOKYOPOP®!

100% AUTHENTIC MANGA
品質第一公式商品

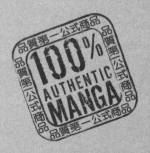